AF540689

POLITICAL, LEGAL AND MILITARY HISTORY OF INDIA

(Ancient, Medieval, Modern)

VOLUME 3

SOCIETY, LAW AND ADMINISTRATION IN ANCIENT INDIA

NEW 3RD EDITION

BY THE SAME AUTHOR

- Encyclopaedic History of the Sikhs and Sikhism (6 Vols.)
- European Women in India—Their Life and Adventures
- History of the Conquest of China
- International Law and Practice in Ancient India
- Legal & Political System in China
- Martial Law—Theory and Practice
- Military Dictionary and Encyclopaedia
- Military History of British India
- Origin & Development of Legal & Political System in India (3 Volumes)
- Political, Legal and Military History of India (10 Vols.)
- Portrait of a Political Murder—Trial and Execution of Z.A. Bhutto
- Rare Documents on Sikhs and Their Rule in the Punjab
- Studies in Islamic Law, Religion and Society
- Unity and Discipline through Law

POLITICAL, LEGAL AND MILITARY HISTORY OF INDIA

(Ancient, Medieval, Modern)

VOLUME 3

SOCIETY, LAW AND ADMINISTRATION IN ANCIENT INDIA

Edited by

H.S. BHATIA

Founder Editor

Civil & Military Law Journal, New Delhi

Distinguished Scholar and Author

NEW 3RD EDITION

DEEP & DEEP PUBLICATIONS PVT. LTD.

F-159, Rajouri Garden, New Delhi - 110027

SOCIETY, LAW AND ADMINISTRATION
IN ANCIENT INDIA

(POLITICAL, LEGAL AND MILITARY HISTORY OF INDIA)

ISBN 978-81-8450-334-0 (Vol. 3)
ISBN 978-81-8450-342-5 (Set)

First Published: 1984/86
Second Edition: 1992
Reprint Edition: 2001
Third Edition: 2012

© 2012 THE PUBLISHERS

All rights reserved with the Publisher, including the right to translate or to reproduce this book or parts thereof except for brief quotations in critical articles or reviews.

Typeset by THE LASER PRINTERS, 8/15, 3rd Floor, Subhash Nagar, New Delhi-110027.

Printed in India at MAYUR ENTERPRISES, WZ Plot No. 3, Gujjar Market, Tihar Village, New Delhi-110 018

Published by DEEP & DEEP PUBLICATIONS PVT. LTD., F-159, Rajouri Garden, New Delhi-110027. Phones: 25435369, 25440916.
E-mail: ddpubs@yahoo.com • ddpubs@gmail.com
Sales Showroom: 2/13, Ansari Road, Daryaganj, New Delhi-110002
Phone/Fax: 23245122

Contents

Preface xiii
Key to Important Terms xvii

1. **Celebrated Ancient Countries in Eastern India** 1
Magadha 2
Videha 2
The Kingdom of Vaicali 5
The Second Group of Five Nations 6
Anga 10
Vanga 14
Kalinga 14
Pundra and Paundra 16
Suhma and Tama-lipta 19
Udra or Odra 20
Prag-jyotisa 21
The Kiratas 26
Utkala 27
Character of the Four Groups 28
American Example 29
Prag-jyotisas Descended from Mongolian Tablelands 29
Last Came the Aryas 30

2. **The Law of Nations in Ancient India** 31
The Family of Nations in India 32
Kautilya's Arthasastra and Manu's Dharmasastra 33
Impact of Buddhism 35
Peace and War 36
Concept of Chakravartin 37
Just and Unjust Wars 38
Temperamenta Belli 38
Status of Prisoners of War 39
No-war Doctrine 39
Treaties of Peace and Hostages 40

Foreign Invasions 40
Exchange of Embassies 41
Foreigners in India 42
Foreign Trade 42
Maritime Jurisdiction 42
Conclusion 43

3. **The Village Headman in Ancient India** **48**
Functions of Headman 48
Under Royal Control 49
Status in Maurya Period 50
Office Becomes Hereditary 50
Village Headman under the System of Manu 51
In Gupta Period 52
Enormous Power and Position Acquired 53

4. **Jails and Jail Administration in Kautilya** **56**
Arthasastra. The Earliest Codification of Laws in India 56
Interesting Jail Regulations 57
Prisoners Set Free on Auspicious Occasions 58

5. **Buddhist India and Rest of the World** **60**
I. Buddhism as an International Link 60
Afghanistan and N.W. Frontier 61
Central Asia 61
China 63
Master of Law 66
Chinese Visits to India 66
Tibet 68
Nepal 69
Sri Lanka 70
Burma 73
Siam 74
Takua-pa Inscriptions 75
Cambodia 76
Champa 77
Indonesia 78
Nagapatam (S. India) 79
II. The Hierarchy of the Dalai Lama (1398-1745) 80

6. **Foreigners in Ajanta Paintings** **94**
Admirable True to Life Paintings 96
Unsurpassed in the History of Art 97
No Better Examples for Art Education 97
First to Note Foreigners in Ajanta Paintings 98

Persian Embassy in Indian Court 101
Man of Central Asiatic Race 101
Negro Looking Servants 102
Bactrian Greeks—The Authors of Ajanta Caves? 103
Two Thousand Years Old Ajanta Paintings 105

7. Foreign Influences in Ancient India 110
Prehistoric Trade Ties 110
Indus Valley—A Mine of Gold 111
Intercourse Between India and Soloman's Judaea 112
Overland Route Between India and the West 113
Buddhism at Variance with Hinduism 114
Buddhism among the Products of Early Foreign Influence 115
When Darius Occupied Panjab 115
Marriage Market 116
Greek Influence 117
Period of Renaissance 117
Irrigation Schemes and GT Road Built by a Bactrian 119
Panjab—Meeting Place of Nations 119
Bactrian Conquest and Influence 120
Indo-Greek Culture 121
Saka's Arrival and Influence 123
Greek Artists from Asia Minor 125
Revival of Brahmanism and Hindu Art 127
Indian and Greek Dramas 128
East and West Interaction 129

8. Sailors of Sixty Centuries 135
When Indians went to America 136
Migration in Third Century 136
Evidence from Sanskrit Literature 137
Three Classes of Ships 138
Carried 1000 Passengers 139
Early History 139
Literary Evidence 140
In Ramayana 140
In Mahabharata 141
Evidence from Sculpture 142
Temples give Proof 142
Sculptures at Boro-Budur 143
What Historians Say 143
India's Extensive Sea-Borne Trade 144
Indo-Roman Trade 144
Archaeologist's Testimony 145
In Old Paintings 147
When India Ruled Waves 149

9. **Ancient Hindu Geography** 150

Two Kinds of Hindu Geography 151
Regarding the Earth 151
Knowledge of Asia 152
Asia—Jambu Dvipa 152
Nine Principal Divisions of Asia 153
Countries of India as per Astronomical Work 154
Arab Countries 156

10. **Guilds in Ancient India** 157

Composition of the Guilds 157
Origin of the Guilds 158
Functions of the Guilds 160
Constitution of the Guilds 161
Comparison 161

11. **Medical Sciences and Industries in Vedic India** 162

12. **Woman in the Ayurvedic Literature** 171

General Treatment 172
Physiological Peculiarities 172
Ethics 172
Woman and the Bhisaj 173
Relationship of a Patient with a Woman 173
Woman as Mother 174
Diseases of Woman and Remedies 174
Woman as a Wife 175
Woman's Role as Dhatri 175
King and Women 176

13. **Modern Light on Ancient Law** 178

14. **The Hindu Conception of Moral Judgment** 184

Necessity of Judgment (Udyoga Parvan) 184
- Characteristics of Moral Judgment 184
- Postulates of Moral Judgment 184
- The Object of Moral Judgment 185
- Necessity of Moral Judgment 185
- Characteristics of Moral Judgment 186
- Moral Judgment—Regulative 186
- Moral Judgment Refers to the Highest Good 188
- Moral Judgment Implies Freedom 189
- Postulates of Moral Judgment 189
- Self-determination 189
- Discrimination 189

Moral Standard 190
Virtue 190
Wealth 190
Pleasure 191
Virtue, Wealth and Pleasure 191
Various other Goods 192
Personality 192
The Object of Moral Judgment 194
Consequence, the Object of Moral Judgment 194
Motive—The Object of Moral Judgment 195
The End Justifies the Means 196
Intention—The Object of Moral Judgment 200
Overt Act is the Object of Moral Judgment 201
Agent—The Object of Moral Judgment 201
Faith and Action 202

15. The Concept of 'Samrambhayoga' in Hindu Thought 204
Peculiar to Hinduism 204
Salient Features 204
More Light on the Concept 206
Essentials of 'Samrambhayoga' 206
Path of Concentrated Hostility 207
Passion in Spiritual Life 207
Glorious End and Liberation 208

16. Some Mathematical Achievements of Ancient India 209
Eminent Mathematicians 210
Arithmetic: Mathematical Notations 211
Zero 211
Additions, Substractions, etc. 212
Fractions 213
Negative Sign 213
Plus Sign 213
Square Root 213
Tallying 213
Rule of Three, etc. 213
Dust Abacas 214
Algebra 214
Geometry 216
Trigonometry 217

17. Disposal of the Dead and Funeral Ceremonies in Ancient India 219
I. Disposal of the Dead in Ancient India 219
Various Modes of Disposal of the Dead 220

Raising a Mound Over the Grave 221
Embalming the Dead Body 221
Burning—The Most Accepted Mode 222
Practice in the Jain Period 222
Two Modes in the Buddhist Literature 223
Cremation of Buddha 223
Kautilya Refers to Cremation 224
Chinese Travellers' Accounts 224

II. Funeral Ceremonies of the Ancient Hindus 227
Rites Immediately After Death 227
A New Suit of Unbleached, Uncut Cloth 228
Three Stages of Corpse Journey 229
An Animal Sacrificed at the Funeral 229
Corpse Placed on Pyre along with the Wife 230
Ceremonial Vessels Placed on the Dead Body 232
Pile Lighted with Prayer 233
Mourners Purify themselves by Bathing 233
Ceremony of Burial 234
Double Ceremonial of Burning and Burial 236
Rites for the Well-being of the Living 236
The Sati Controversy 238

18. Widow in Ancient India 246
Meaning of the Word Vidhava 246
Hard Life 247
Second Husband 247
Chaotic State of Society 248
Niyoga and Marriage of Widows during Vedic Period 248
Son of Widow Entitled to Inheritance 249
Unwidowed Wives could take Second Husbands 250
Women—Field, Man—Giver of the Seed 251
Later Scholars Forbid Widow Marriage 252
Kautilya's Rules for Re-marriage 252
Customary Marriages 253
Manu's Laws Regarding Widows 255
Suttee not Mentioned in Vedic Literature 256
Two Interpretations 257
Kings' and Generals' Families Performed Suttee 258
The First Sanction of Suttee to Preserve Widow Chastity 259
Custom of Suttee Criticised 259
Widows Regarded as Inauspicious Sights on Auspicious Occasions 260

19. Wine Drinking in Ancient India 262
Wine, A Forbidden Drink 262
An Item of Sumptuous Meals 263

Drinking very Common Among Royalties 263
Wine and Women 264
Drinking, a Grave Sin 264
Wine and Courtesans 265
Banqueting Hall 265
Types of Wine in the Kathasaritsagara 266

20. Proceedings and Judgment of a Hindu Court in Sanskrit 268
Translation of the Judgment in Sanskrit given by Sachala Misra
Chief Judge 272
Pleadings 272
Onus of Proof 272
Settlement of Issues 272
Adjournments 273
Default and Retrial 273
Objection to Evidence 273
Proof by Ordeal Claimed, Objected to, and Disallowed 274

21. The Royal Court in Hindu Period (600 to 1200 A.D.) 279
Separate Court of Justice 281
Court Etiquettes 283

22. The Angel and Devil in Indian Scriptures 286
Introduction 286
The Angels in Indian Scriptures 286
The Nature of the Angels 288
The Function of the Angels—Rulers and Administrators 290
Equality of Nature between Angels and Demons 291
A Period of Trial for All the Angels 291
The Rebellion of the Angels 293
The Fight between the Good and the Evil Angels 294
The Corruption of the Original Tradition 298
Final Punishment of the Asuras 299
The Reward of the Devas 300
The Fight Between the Devas and the Asuras in Myth and Iconography 303
The Intervention of the Demon in the Original Fall of Man 306
The Devil in Man's Daily Life 307
Conclusion 311

23. Ancient Military India 319
I. King and His Army 319
Duties of Kings 319
Council Deliberations 320
National Prosperity—Causes 320

Subsistence to Government Servants 320
Control of Departments 321
Security 322
Fire Prevention 323
Weapons and Armour 324
Weapons 325
(a) Static Weapons 325
(b) Mobile Weapons 325
(c) Edged Weapons 326
(d) Razor Sharp Weapons 326
(e) Rock Missiles 326
(f) Archery (Bow and Arrows) 326
(g) Swords 327
(h) Armour 327
(i) Battle Dress 327
(j) Personnel Defence Gear 327
Miscellaneous Weapons 327
Conclusion 327
II. Fire-Arms in Ancient India 328
High Achievements of Ancient India 328
Pros and Cons of the Question 328
Mostly Puranic Evidence 329
Oppert's Arguments 330
The other Side 330
Meaning of Fire-arms 330
Missiles Discharged Accompanied by 'Mantras' 331
Sataghni—A Hundred-killer 332
Nalika—The Gun 332
Fire-arms Unknown in Vedic Age 333
No Mention of Fire-arms in the Smrtis 334

24. Strategy of Alexander the Great and his Campaign Against Porus 336
Introduction 336
Discussion 337
Definition of 'Strategy' 337
Field Strategy 337
Grand Strategy 338
Interaction 339
Factors of Comparison 339
Highlights 346
Conclusion 348

Select Bibliography 349

Index 350

Preface

In the last two volumes, we examined the origin and growth of India's civilization *vis-a-vis* polity, law, social manners, religious practices, culture, military organisation and several connected matters. It appears that people in ancient India had developed distinct characteristics of their own civilization with art and literature flourishing in their midst and their culture, civilization and religion making a great headway in the neighbouring countries.

When the Aryans had established themselves in Northern India, the South still remained free to develop its own culture, manners and traditions, e.g., the Dravidian civilization prevailed. The life and customs of the people living in the northern plain and the southern plateau became different from each other. It was the Mauryas (later the Mughals) who brought the two portions of the Indian sub-continent together under one regime. Otherwise the two parts had very rarely joined their lot to face foreign attacks which the Northerns and the Panjabis particularly braved. Nevertheless, there was an underspirit of unity which bound the Indians inspite of geographical, political, cultural and religious diversity.

We turn now to some pioneer achievements of Ancient Hindu India and a detailed study of important subjects either left out or briefly metioned in the previous two volumes. Magadha, Vaicali, Kalinga and Utkala had been prominent and advanced centres of art, culture and learning in ancient India. F.E. Pargiter in his article "Celebrated Ancient Countries in Eastern India" makes a historical purview of these states "to determine their position as exactly as possible". M.K. Nawaz in "The Law of Nations in Ancient India" disputes the theory of Wheaton and Oppenheim that modern international law originated from the usages and practices of the Greek city states, the Roman Empire and the Jews points out that "Both the internal and external evidence points to the existence of a Family of Nations in ancient India," and "besides the Vedas, Kautilya's Arthasastra and Manu's Dharmasastra supplied the body of inter-state rules in ancient India". "The Village Headman in Ancient India", according to D.K. Ganguli was a fairly popular institution, as old as the Rgveda, as the village administration was carried out through a headman and with the passage of time the post became hereditary and the incumbent acquired vast powers. B.K. Majumdar writes on "Jails and Jail Administration in Kautilya" indicating that "The administration machinery described in Kautilya is considered to be that of a highly organised State" and "the Arthasastra contains greater details about jails and jail regulations". T.N. Ramachandran brings out the value of Buddhism being an international link in the past. "What looms large", he says "in the formation of Indian civilization and international image in the dark centuries before Alexander's invasion of India is the advent of the Buddha". The teachings of the Buddha were spread by Buddhist envoys "not only in Afghanistan, Central Asia, China, Tibet and Nepal, but also in Ceylon, Burma, Siam and Indonesia" thus creating goodwill, understanding and cultural affinity between India and rest of the world. "Foreigners in Ajanta Paintings" by Rajendra Lal Mitra confirms the international links which the people of Western India had with the foreigners two thousand years ago. Rawlinson on "Foreign Influences in Ancient India" points out that "Trade between India and the West, both by land and sea, stretches, no doubt, beyond the dawn of history". He then writes about the intercourse between India and Solomon's Judaea, Persian Gulf, Babylon, Greece, China and several other countries and influence of their cultures on ancient India. He suggests that irrigation schemes in Kathiawar and the Grand Trunk Road was built by a Persian official. Similarly, Chaman Lal in his article "Sailors of Sixty Centuries" asserts that Indians in ancient India were expert sailors and their ships went all the way, besides other countries, to Mexico and Peru centuries before Columbus.

The "Ancient Hindu Geography" according to Akshoy Kumar Mazumdar is of two kinds, i.e., Mathematical/Astronomical Geography and Political Geography. The ancient Indians knew much about the Earth, Asia and Arab countries. V. Natesan claims the existence of "Guilds in Ancient India" and describes their origin, functions, and constitution. Chapters 11, 12 and 13 deal with Ayurveda—the ancient Indian science of medicine (Jyotir Mitra), the position of "Woman in the Ayurvedic Literature" (H.G. Ranade) and Manu's injunctions on the mode of taking meals in "Modern Light on Ancient Law" (Prof. B.M. Ghosh). Prof. Charu Chandra Sinha analyses "The Hindu Conception of Moral Judgment" as compared to legal judgment and its object, necessity, characteristics, postulates, consequence *vis-a-vis* the enigma 'the end justifies the means'. Dr. K. Raghavan Pillai deals with a unique concept of "Samrambhayoga" or 'Vairayoga' that is 'the choice of the path of hostility to God to reach him' which is peculiar to Hinduism. H.S. Ursekar in his article narrates "Some Mathematical Achievements of Ancient India". "Disposal of the Dead and Funeral Ceremonies in Ancient India" by K. Krishnamurthy and Rajendra Lal Mitra indicate the prevalence of both burial and burning among the Vedic Aryans. According to Sutrakaras, an animal should be sacrificed at the funeral and the corpse was placed on the pyre along with wife. "A younger brother should then proceed to the pyre, hold the left hand of the woman, and ask her to come away". Position of "Widow in Ancient India" is given by N.K. Dutt in Chapter 18. Her hard life, second marriage, inheritance, customary marriage, ancient laws regarding widows and the subject of Suttee are discussed elaborately. 'Wine Drinking in Ancient India" by A. Chattopadhyay provides an interesting reading.

"Proceedings and Judgment of a Hindu Court in Sanskrit" by K.P. Jayaswal reveals the similarity of form and content between modern and ancient Indian jurisprudence and M.K. Dhar's "The Royal Court in Hindu Period" vividly portrays the Royal Court in olden times. "The Angel and Devil in Indian Scriptures" by Rev. H. Heras tabulates the *devas* and the *asuras*, their functions, fight, punishment of the asuras and the reward of the devas and concludes: The faith of the Indian nation in the nature, sin and punishment of the devils, as well as in their intervention in the fall of mankind is preserved in Indian ***Sruti*** for the enlightenment of the people of India on the high tenets of the true religion.

While describing ancient military India, C.S. Sangameswaran in "King and His Army" throws vivid light on the Indian society and military prowess of a king, namely, military department and its staff, security, fire prevention, weapons and armour. And the last article by Sham S. Rangnekar on "Strategy of Alexander the Great and His Campaign Against Porus" studies the strategy of Alexander in the main encounters of his career—the campaigns against Tyre, Darius, Spitamenes and in particular against Porus.

New Delhi

H.S. BHATIA

Key to Important Terms

Abaddha. Prisoner.
Abhibhartsana. Intimidation.
Adesa. Orders.
Adhikara. Authority.
Adhipati. Paramount.
Adhipatya, Maharajya, Samrajya, Svarajya, Vairajya. Grades of Kingship.
Adhirat, Ekarat, Samrat, Svarat, Virat. Grades of Kings.
Adroha. Armistice.
Adrshtapurusha Sandhi. Peace on condition that the king and the army should be detained.
Adhiraja. Overlord.
Adishta. Peace secured on cession of territory.
Agnichurana. Gun powder.
Ahimsa. The Hindu doctrine of non-violence.
Ais varyam. Sovereignty.
Agnijvalita. Incendiary.
Ajna. Writ of Command Ordinance; Order.
Akrtachikirsha. Arrangement previous to alliance.
Amitrabala. Forces drawn from enemy.
Amitra Vishaya. Enemy territory.
Anka. Seal.
Annapanarakshin. Commissariat.
Anugraha. Ransom.
Aparadha. Offence.
Aparapaksa. Opposition.
Aparipanita. Indefinite alliance.
Aparuddha. King in exile.
Arajaka. Anarchy.
Ari. Enemy.

Arthashastra. A Hindu text on political administration, especially that traditionally attributed to Kautilya, a famous minister of Emperor Chandragupta Maurya.

Arya. The name of the fair-skinned tribes which invaded north India in the second millennium B.C.

Asamhata—(Detached), Bhoga— Snake), Chakra—(Wheel), Danda —(Staff), Makara—(Crocodile), Man'dala—(Circle), S'akata—(Cart), Sarvatobahdra— (Many-sided), Suchi—(Needle), S'yena —(Hawk), Vajra—(Diamond), Vyala—(Dragon). Battle arrays with innumerable sub-divisions.

Asana. Withdrawal from hostility; State of neutrality.

Asandi. Throne.

Asanaprajnapaka. Seating officer in assembly of states.

As'raya. Alliance.

Ashram. Hermitage.

Atavibala. Forces trained for forest warfare.

Atmamisha. Peace on surrender with the flower of troops.

Avaghurna. Whipping.

Avakraya Sandhi. Peace secured on cession.

Avamaidana—(Assualt & battle), Paryupasana—(Blockade), Upasarpa—(Espionage), Upajapa—(Intrigue), Vamana—(Winning over the enemy). Methods employed to capture a fort.

Avatar. The descent or incarnation of a deity.

Avas'irshakriya. Loosening of the bonds.

Ayudna-jivin. The Military.

Ayudha-sthana. Armoury.

Bala. Armed force; Forces.

Bandhikrtah. Prisoner of war.

Bhaga. Land tax; In ancient India the king's share of the produce of land.

Bhaga-graha. Share of spoils (war).

Bharatavarsha. India.

Bhumipa. Emperor.

Bhrta. Mercenaries.

Bhrti. Booty in war.

Buddhism. A religion originating in India in the 6th century B.C. and founded by Gautama Buddha who is believed to have lived from 560 to 480 B.C. The other dates are 557-477 B.C. (F. Maxmuller); 563 to 483 B.C. (Fachu); 718 to 638 B.C. (Pegu and Chinese Tradition); 733 to 653 B.C. (Tibetan Tradition).

Caste. Subdivisions of Hindu society according to professions.

Chakravarti. The title assumed by the most exalted ancient Hindu sovereigns; a universal emperor.

Chala Sandhi. Unstable and shaky peace.

Chara. Spy.

Charitra. Customary Law.

Chikitsakah. Army Medical Corps.

Danda. Punishment; Amercement; Fine.

Danda-nayakya. Military Commander.

Dandopanata-Sandhi. Treaty offering the army.

Dasa. Slave.

Dauvarika. Sentinel.

Des'opanata Sandhi. Treaty offering the territory.

Dharma. The Hindu Sacred Law; Virtue; Legal and moral duty; Universal rule of law applicable to individual as well as nations.

Dharmashastra. An ancient authoritative writing on Hindu law and institutions. The Hindu code.

Dharma Yuddha. Fighting in accordance with rules.

Dharamasana. Court; Hall of Justice.

Dhvaja. Flag.

Digdha. Poisoned.

Digvijaya. Conquest of quarters.

Divya. An oath, especially on ordeal, various kinds of which were admitted by the Hindu laws.

Durga. Fortress.

Duta. Diplomatic Minister; Envoy.

Dutadharma. Duties of envoys; Rules governing envoys.

Dwaidhibhava. Double Policy; Making peace with one and waging war with another.

Eka-raja. Supreme king.

Ekaisvaryam. Absolute Sovereignty.

Gana. A military division.

Ganarajya. Republic.

Gudha-lekhya. Cipher writing.

Gudha-purusha. Secret emissary.

Gulma. A military division.

Hinasandhi. Alliance on unequal terms.

Hinduism. A way of life, rather than a creed, followed by the Hindus.

Hindustan. 'The country of the Hindus'; India.

Jainism. A religion founded in the 6th century B.C. by Vardhamana Mahavira, differing from Hinduism.

Jatidbarma. Caste Laws.

Kaleh. Cold war.

Kapala. Huge indemnity.

Karma. Act, action, work; an act of piety; fate as the consequence of acts.

Karmaklesa. Torture.

Karraanta. Manufactory.

Karnayudha. Barbed weapons.

Karya-karta. Agent.

Kautilya. Also known as Chanakya and Vishnugupta, the Chancellor of Chandragupta Maurya; author of 'Arthasastra'.

Kos'oponata Sandhi. Treaty offering treasure.

Krtas'leshana. Maintenance of terms.

Krtavidushana. Attempt to dissolve the alliance.

Kuladharma. Family Law.

Kupya. Seized enemy property.

Kuta Yuddha. Unfair fighting.

Madhyama. Neutral; Mediator.

Maba. Great.

Mahabharara. A great Indian epic concerning Great Indian War fought as early as 575 B.C. (Bentley); 950 B.C. (Pargiter); 1370 B.C. (H.H. Wilson); 2448 B.C. (Kalhana); 3137 B.C. (Trivedi).

Mahamatra. Prime Minister; Censor of the law.

Maharaja. A sovereign prince; applied in courtesy to all rajas.

Mahasabha. Governing body in a village.

Mahisi. Crowned Queen.

Mandala. Circle of states. Besides the king in point, twelve in number.

Mandalika, Maharaja, Raja Samanta, Sarvahauma. Other terms for king.

If a king's income is:	*He is styled as a:*
1 to 3 Lakhs of Karsha (5/6 Rs.)	Samanta.
3 to 10 Lakhs of Karsha	Mandalika.
10 to 20 Lakhs of Karsha	Raja.
20 to 50 Lakhs of Karsha	Maharaja.
50 to 100 Lakhs of Karsha	Svarat.
1 to 10 crores	Samrat.
10 to 50 crores	Virat.
50 crores and above	Sarvabhauma.

Mantra. Policy.
Mantra Parishad Cabinet.
Manu. In Hindu mythology, the first man, traditional author of *Manusmriti* or *Manavadharmashastra*, the most important of the dharmasaṣtras.
Maulibala. Standing army.
Mitra. Friend.
Mitrabaia. Forces drawn from allied territory.
Mudra. Printing; Seal, Insignia; Passport.
Nagara. City.
Nalika. Gun.
Nalika naracha. Cannon.
Namaskạr. Salutation.
Nissohtarrha. Ambassador with full rights.
Nisrstartba. An ambassador endowed with full powers.
Niti or Naya. Science of Polity.
Nitis'astra. Law; Code; Jurisprudence.
Niyamana. Election.
Nyaya. Justice.
Nyayadhis'a. Judge.
Nyayavadin. Vakil; Advocate; Writ conveying remission.
Pada. Legal procedure.
Panchayat. A native court of arbitration (properly of five persons) chosen by the parties themselves or by the officers of the government for the determination of petty disputes.
Pandit. Learned Hindu.
Parakara. Writ conveying information.
Parihara. Atonement.
Parokta. Perjury. **Paribhushana Sandhi.** Peace secured on cession of more than the yield.
Paribbashana. Censure.
Parihara. Atonement.
Parikraya Sandhi. Peace secured by offer of all wealth.
Parkrti. Sovereign independent state.
Parimitartha. Ambassador with defined duties.
Paripanita. Definite alliance.
Partapa. Ultimatum.
Paiipricha. Judicial enquiry.
Parishad. Tribunal of arbitration; Prize court.
Parivara. Non-combatants.

Pathi. Foot soldier.
Patra. Document.
Patti. Infantry.
Prahita. One sent on mission.
Prakas'a. Open and fair.
Pataka. Flag.
Pramana. Authority.
Pratapa. Ultimatum.
Prati. Writ conveying reply.
Pratibhu. Security for observance of treaty terms; Voluntary alliance.
Pratibhavya. Surety.
Pratigraha. Hostage for enforcing treaty terms; Purchased alliance.
Pratigraha. Purchased alliance.
Pratishiddba. Contraband of war.
Prativedaka. News reporter.
Prawasana. Exile.
Pravasya. Deportation.
Pravrajana. Banishment.
Praves'yam. Imports.
Purushantara. Peace on surrender by commander-in-chief and Crown Prince.
Pravritti. Writ conveying guidance.
Rajuka. Officers of the Central Government.
Rajas'abdopajivin. Republican bodies.
Rajas'asana. Ordinance, Royal order.
Rajdhani. Capital.
Rajatva. Royalty.
Rajapratinidhi. Viceroy; Consul General.
Rajya. A kingdom; A rule; Sovereignty; State.
Rajyavibhrama. Civil war.
Ramayana. A great Indian epic, which recounts the adventures of Rama about 300 B.C.
Rashtra. A province; Kingdom; Territory.
Rashtrapati (Rashtra-mukhya). Governor of a state or province.
Rigveda. The oldest sacred book of the Hindus, containing over a thousand hymns in classical Sanskrit.
Sabha. An assembly of the elect.
Sachivottama. Prime Minister.
Saka, Shaka. An era reckoned, according to popular tradition, from the reign of a Shaka prince of South India, Shalivahana.

Sama, Samadhi, Sandhi. Terms denoting treaty.

Sama, Dana, Bbeda, Danda. Four expedients to be successively employed in dealing with the enemy.

Samiti. Assembly; Committee.

Sams'raya, Samas'raya. Firm alliance.

Samvatsara (Samvat) A year, particularly applied to the years of the era of Vikrama beginning with the year 58 B.C.

Sandhi. Peace.

Sandhivigrahika. Minister for foreign affairs.

Sandhaya Asana. Truce (agreed neutral status).

Sanghattan. Unity.

Sangrama Samili. Council of War.

Shastra. A scripture, a work of authority.

Sanskrit. The sacred language of the Hindus.

Sati (Suttee). (Literally, 'good woman'). The site of widow burning practised especially among the Rajputs; A Hindu wife who consummated a life of duty by burning herself on the funeral pile of her husband.

Sena. Army; **Senapati.** In ancient India, the commander-in-chief.

Sishtachara. Conventions.

S'renibala. Supply by local guilds.

Suvarna Sandhi. Treaty on amicable terms.

Udasina. Neutral: Neutralised State.

Utthana. Preparation for hostilities.

Vyavahara. Secular Law.

Vadhaki. Homicide.

Vabana. Conveyance: Vehicle.

Vari. Cess.

Varta. Trade.

Veda. The name of the chief scriptual authorities of the Hindus.

Vyadhitah. Sick and wounded in war.

Vishiv Nagrikta. World citizenship.

Yana. Invasion.

Yuddha. Warfare.

Yuddha Asura. Where machines of destructions were used.

Yuddha Manusha. Where arrays of the army were used.

Yuddha Tushni. Where the enemy is won over by superior diplomacy.

1

Celebrated Ancient Countries in Eastern India

F.E. PARGITER

The countries into which Eastern India was divided in ancient times consisted of four groups, (1) Magadha, Videha and the small kingdom of Vaicali; (2) Anga, Vanga, Kalinga, Pundra and Suhma, with Odra and Tama-lipta; (3) Prag-jyotisa and the Kiratas; and (4) Utkala. The last three groups are always recognized in Sanskrit writings, and were without doubt based on real ethnological differences; but Magadha and Videha denoted territory rather than races, for these countries in their conditions resembled those to their west in Madhyadeca, viz., Kosala and Kaci, and their inhabitants appear, especially in Magadha, to have been a mixture of the Aryas with earlier races, as in Madhyadeca, the chief difference being that the earlier races do not seem to have been so completely subjugated and incorporated by the Aryas as in Madhyadeca.

I propose in this paper to collect and examine all the passages of any importance, that I have been able to find, bearing on these countries, and to determine their position as exactly as possible. Most of the passages cited here are taken from that vast storehouse of information, the Maha-Bharata, and therefore in giving the references I have dropped the name of the book for the sake of convenience and specified the Parvans only. For passages cited from other books the references have been given in full, and the Ramayana is quoted according to Gorresio's Edition.

Magadha

Magadha is too well known to call for much notice here. It comprised the modern districts of Patna, Gaya and Shahabad. Its ancient capital was Giri-vraja (Sabha-p., xx. 798-800; Hari-V., cxvii. 6598; and Ramayana, Adi-k., xxxv. 1-9), which Cunningham has identified with the modern Giryek on the Pancana river about 36 miles north-east of Gaya (Arch. Surv. Repts., I. 16 and plate iii). Raja-grha appears to have been another name of the capital (Adi, p., cxiii. 4451-2, and Acvamedh.-p., lxxxii. 2435-63), but Cunningham identifies it with the modern Raj-gir about six miles west of Giryek (Arch. Surv. Repts., I. 20 and plate iii). The people were called Magadhas.

Magadha appears to have been the arena of many early conflicts. Its oldest name is said to have been Kikata, which occurs in Rg. V., iii. 53.14 (Muir's Sansk. Texts, II. 362-3). In the Ramayana, Vicvamitra gives the youthful Rama an account of Magadha and the countries near it. He says its old name was Vasu; Kuca, a great king who was sprung from Brahma, had four sons who established four kingdoms, (1) Kucacva at Kaucacvi (or, Kucamba at Kaucambi according to another reading), (2) Kucanabha at Mahodaya or Kanyakubja, (3) Amurtarajas in Prag-jyotisa, and (4) Vasu at Giri-vraja (Adi-k., xxxv. 1-10 and 35). This story professes to hand down what occurred several generations before Rama's time, but presents many difficulties, and clashes in some of its details with the next event that I now cite. According to the Maha-Bharata, at a later time about half way between Rama's age and that of the Pandavas, Vasu Upari-cara, king of Cedi, conquered Magadha and established his son Vrhad-ratha as king over it (see paper on "Ancient Cedi, Matsya and Karusa" mentioned above).

The later history of Magadha is well-known, and it played the leading part in Buddhism.

Videha

Videha derived its name from Mathava the Videgha who colonized it according to the Cata-P. Brahmana (I. iv. 1). The passage runs thus, briefly, according to Dr. Eggeling's translation. "Mathava, the (king of) Videgha, carried Agni Vaicvanara in his mouth. The Rsi

Gotama Rahugana was his family priest. When addressed (by the latter) he made no answer to him, fearing lest Agni might fall from his mouth. [The priest continued to invoke Agni, and at length Agni Vaicvanara flashed forth from the king's mouth and fell down on the earth.] Mathava the Videgha was at that time on the river Sarasvati. He (Agni) thence went burning along this earth towards the east; and Gotama Rahugana and the Videgha Mathava followed after him as he was burning along. He burnt over (dried up) all these rivers. Now that (river) which is called Sada-nira flows from the northern (Himalaya) mountain; that one he did not burn over. That one the brahmans did not cross in former times, thinking it has not been burnt over by Agni Vaicvanara. Now-a-days, however, there are many brahmans to the east of it. At that time it (the land east of the Sada-nira) was very uncultivated, very marshy, because it had not been tasted by Agni Vaicvanara. Now-a-days, however, it is very cultivated, for the brahmans have caused (Agni) to taste it through sacrifices. Even in late summer that (river), as it were, rages along; so cold is it, not having been burnt over by Agni Vaicvanara. Mathava the Videgha then said (to Agni), 'Where am I to abide?' 'To the east of this river be thy abode !' said he. Even now this river forms the boundary of the Kosalas and Videhas; for these are the Mathavas."

Sada-nira means "the river that is always full of water." Sayana says it is the river Karatoya, the modern Kurattee which flows through the Bogra district; and Dr. Muir (Sansk. Texts, II. 419-422) and Dr. Eggeling (see note in his edition) prefer to identify it with the Gandaki, the modern Gandak. Sayana's explanation must be mistaken, because there can be no doubt Videha could never have been east of the Kurattee. Nor can the river be well identified with the Gandaki, because they are mentioned as distinct rivers in Sabha-p., xix. 794. This passage is noticed by Dr. Muir. Though it is hardly intelligible in its description of the route taken by Krsna, Arjuna and Bhima in going from the Kurus to Magadha, unless they took a zigzag course eastward, south-westward and again eastward, in order to avert suspicion before finally making for Magadha; still it indicates plainly that the Gandaki and Sada-nira were different rivers. Moreover the Gandaki flows *through* the country which has always been considered to be Videha, and could not therefore have been its western boundary.

It seems then that the Sada-nira must lie further to the west, and it should probably be identified with the Rapti. I have not been able to find any Sanskrit name for the Rapti. Lassen calls it the Ajita-vati

(Ind. Alt., Map), but this name is not in the dictionary, nor have I met with it anywhere. This identification then fills up a blank and agrees with the well-known situation of Videha. It offers also an explanation of the marshy nature of ancient Videha, viz., the Gandak flows through the middle of the country, it has always been liable to shift its course greatly, its numerous channels intersect the country, and its floods would have rendered the soil extremely marshy.

A further consideration of the facts will, I think, throw some light on this passage from the Cata-P. Brahmana. Videha in ancient times must, like most other parts of India, have been more or less covered by forest, the remains of which survive at the present day along the foot of the Himalayas in the tract called the Terai, and was no doubt inhabited by aboriginal tribes such as inhabit the Terai now. The deadly malaria of such a forest is well-known, and only such tribes have been able to live in its climate. To this must be added the effect, which periodic floods from the Gandak during the rainy season must have produced in the rank vegetation of such a region. Very swampy and uncultivable would be moderate expressions to apply to it. No Arya could have ventured within it, and the only way in which Aryas could have colonized it was by felling and burning the forest down wholesale, and opening out the soil to the purifying rays of the sun. That is what (it seems to be implied) Mathava must have done.

Prof. Weber considers Agni Vaicvanara to be a personification of the sacrificial worship of the brahmans, and Dr. Muir and Dr. Eggeling appear to acquiesce in this interpretation *(loc. cit.)*; but I venture to submit that the wide import of the epithet Agni *Vaicvanara*, "the fire that burns for all men," hardly expresses the narrow view that the brahmans would have of their own peculiar sacrificial fire. May it not rather mean 'fire which is the common property of all men," that is not sacrificial fire, but fire in its ordinary every-day uses as applied to human wants? It seems to me a distinction is implied between the Agni Vaicvanara that Mathava himself had and the sacrificial fire of the brahmans.

The explanation suggested here, regarding Agni Vaicvanara's going burning along the ground and his tasting and improving the soil, pourtrays with poetical force, how the fire seized on the forests and raged along devouring them with its flames, and how it licked and scorched the pestilential soil, and so laid the marshy ground bare to the sun's parching heat.[1] The races who preceded the Aryas appear to have been forest tribes, Agni must have cleared away the primeval forests from fhe Sarasvati to the Sada-nira, and there the course of the colonizing Aryas stopped, until (as seems implied) Mathava carried Agni on to the east of the latter river. It seems highly probable the forest tribes were not acquainted with fire. They shun the bright life of the open country, and would have retreated terrified and silent into the depths of the forest; and it is noteworthy that no mention is made of any fighting before Mathava established himself there.

It has pleased the brahmans in this passage to ascribe the improvement in the land to their sacrifices, but the passage implies, as Prof. Weber observes, that they did not venture across the Sada-nira till Mathava with his devouring fire had cleansed the ground before them. I would therefore suggest that we have here described how Mathava, with no doubt his comrades, burnt the forest down and began cultivating the land, and how the brahmans, finding the new tract developing into a good land, followed afterwards and soon appropriated the merit to themselves and their sacrifices. I venture to commend this explanation to those who know the country.

Videha then comprised the country from Gorakhpur on the Rapti to Darbhanga, with Kosala on the west and Anga on the east. On the north it approached the hills, and on the south it was bounded by the small kingdom of Vaicali. Its capital was called Mithila (Canti-p., cccxxvii. 12233-8; and Ramay., Adi-k., xlix. 9-16); and this name often designated the country itself, especially in the Ramayana. The people were called Videhas, Vaidehakas and also Mithilas (Vana-p., ccliii. 15243). Its kings traced their descent from Nimi (Ramay., Adi-k., lxxiii. 2-12) and were generally called Janaka, which seems to have been the ordinary royal title (Vana-p., cxxxiii. 10637). They were often highly educated (Canti-p., cccxxvii. 12215-25; Kausitaki Up., iv. 1; Brhad-Aran. Up., II. i. I, and IV. i. and ii.). Cunningham says the capital was Janakpur, which is now a small town just within the Nepal border, north of where the Muzaffarpur and Darbhanga districts meet (Arch. Surv. Repts., XVI. 34, and map), but I have not met this name in Sanskrit works, and it is not in the dictionary.

The Kingdom of Vaicali

Between Magadha and Videha lay a small kingdom of the north side of the Ganges, with its capital at Vaicali, for Vicvamitra, when taking the youthful Rama from the slaughter of Tadaka in the Shahakid district to Mithila, stopped at Vaicali on the way. Their route appears from the Ramayana to have been as follows: crossing the R. Cona or Sone from the Shahabad district and travelling north-east they reached the Ganges near the site of the present city Patna (Adi-k., xxxvii. 1-7); and then crossing the Ganges by boat, and travelling northwards towards Mithila the whole of one day, they reached Vaicali at evening *(id.*, xlvi. 5-11; xlviii. 21-25; and xlix. 1-8). This agrees with the situation of the modern town Besarh, 27 miles north and a little east of Patna, which Cunningham has identified with Vaicali (Arch. Surv. Repts., I. 55, and XVI. 6 and 34).

No name appears to be given to this country and it plays a very small part in Sanskrit writings. Its kings claimed descent from Iksvakus, the founder of the Solar dynasty of Ayodhya, and called themselves all Iksvakus (Ramay., Adi-k., xlviii. 13-20). In the Buddhist writings the country is called Vrji (Mahavamsa, early chapters; and Arch. Surv. Repts. XVI. 34), but this name is not in the Sanskrit dictionary nor have I met with it in any Sanskrit work. It played however an important part in early Buddhist history, for Buddha is said to have announced his approaching Nirvana at Vaicali, and the second Buddhist Synod was held there.

The Second Group of Five Nations

The Angas, Vangas, Kalingas, Pundras and Suhmas were habitually classed together, and the first two, with the third often added, are generally found linked together, partly no doubt because they were neighbouring nations, but chiefly it seems because the names made a jingle. They are stated in the legends and genealogies to have been the descendants of five brothers of the same names, Anga, Vanga, Kalinga, Pundra and Suhma, who were the sons of king Bali's queen Sudesna by the rsi Dirgha-tamas or Dirgha-tapas. The accounts vary somewhat, but agree in this—that the rsi (who had been blind from his birth in consequence of a curse) was abandoned on a raft in the Ganges, was carried down the stream and was rescued by king Bali, and that Bali who wanted children commissioned his queen and the rsi to raise up offspring for him. The story is told with much circumstantial detail, as if it was a well known event, and it is said these five sons were called "Baleya-ksetra" and even "Baleya brahmans," though Bali himself is called a Danava (Adi-p, civ. 4179-4221; Hari-V., xxxi. 1682-97; Matsya Pur., xlviii. 23-78; and Visnu Pur., iv 18). Bali is styled "king of the East," and is shown in the igenealogies as a descendant of Titiksu, king of the East; but Titiksu's descent is uncertain for the Hari-Vamca traces it from Puru king of Madhya or the Middle region (xxxi.), and the Visnu and Matsya Puranas from Anu, king of the East (e.g., Matsya Pur, xlviii).

Statements, like this one regarding these five brothers, that a certain person was the progenitor of a certain people, occur frequently in Sanskrit genealogies and legends. They do not invite ready belief, and their meaning is a matter of uncertainty and difficulty, but looked at in the light of history they may admit of one probable interpretation. It is a trite saying that history repeats itself, and certainly one feature that appears in all ages of Indian history is the course of conquest. A handful of strangers have invaded a part of the country, conquered the old inhabitants and established themselves in it, their leader as king and themselves as the aristocratic class; and the contest has rarely been an internecine one, unless religion or patriotism has been involved in it. The earliest struggles, in which the Aryas fought their way into India, seem to have been rendered fiercer by the strong religious and social differences between them and the aboriginal races; but after the time when the Aryas established themselves in Madhya-deca, and universal respect was accorded to them because of their chivalry and prestige, it is hard to find traces of a fierce struggle between them and the aborigines except in the story of Rama and Ravana. The Aryas, being the dominant race, considered themselves, and were esteemed by the other nations, as the elite of India. Those nations gradually imitated them and adopted their customs. What happened then between the Aryas and aborigines may no doubt be compared to what is happening now between the English and the natives in South Africa.

Rsis and ascetics exerted a strong influence towards extending the Aryan supremacy. They wandered through every country in ancient India, and established themselves in every spot, where the bracing air of the hills or the cool temperature of a well-watered shady wood attracted them and induced them to linger. In this way they became pioneers of the religion and civilization of the Aryas, and afford a strange parallel to the part which Christian missionaries have played in extending British influence over barbarous countries. Where the ascetics were received with favour and reverence, they soon brought the people of their new country more or less effectually within the pale of Aryanism, as in the case of the rsi Dirgha-tamas; but where they were harassed or cut off, their sufferings and complaints brought retribution on the offending nation, as in Rama's slaughter of the so-called Raksasas in Jana-sthana on the Godavari, which is commemorated in simple and grateful terms in Drona-p., lix. 2226-7; and no doubt to somewhat similar incidents must be assigned the frequent yet vague mention of wars in which kings aided the goods against the demons.

In the same direction tended ancient sentiments regarding marriage. In early time the rules restricting inter-marriage between different classes were very easy, if indeed it can be said there were any definite prohibitions of that kind. The Maha-Bharata is full of instances of mixed unions, which were manifestly regarded at the time as involving no slur or siain, and the rsi Dirgha-tamas is said to have bestowed his favours freely and indiscriminately, and to have left a numerous progeny of various ranks in Anga and Magadha, not only without incurring any reprobation but even with emphatic approval and blessing from Surabhi (Matsya Pur., xlviii. 60-63 and 79-84; and also Sabha-p., xx. 802 with Adi-p. civ. 4193-4216). The result of such practices must have been an infusion of Aryan blood into the populace and the growth of classes, which (like the Eurasians of the present day) would have sought to connect themselves more with the Aryan aristocracy than with their aboriginal kindred; and it would not be an altogether unreasonable and extravagant assertion to say that, in countries where an extensive blending of that sort occurred, the people were descended from the invading leader who founded a new dynasty or territorial sovereignty.

Looked at in this way the story may therefore possibly be true that five brothers Anga, Vanga, Kalinga, Pundra and Suhma, may have conquered five countries, established five kingdoms, and given their names to their countries and the inhabitants; but it cannot be pushed beyond this, nor can they have been the progenitors of the bulk of the people, because the genealogies make king Loma-pada, who was the contemporary of Daca-ratha and Rama, only the fifth or sixth descendant of Anga; and because it is impossible that the country of Anga could have been uninhabited before Anga's time, or that his descendants could have extirpated the previous inhabitants or filled the country themselves in so short a time.

There is, however, one serious objection to this explanation, viz., there is no mention that these countries had any other names prior to the age of these five brothers, and they bear the same names in the earliest allusions. The two most prominent of these countries in the most ancient times were Anga and Kalinga, and the earliest references to them occur, I believe, in the marriages of kings of the Lunar dynasty with princesses of these countries (e.g., Adi-p., xcv. 3772-80). From the general tenor of the old stories, and according to the genealogies if they are traced downward from Puru or Anu, it appears incontestable that those kinds belonged to a prior time (e.g, sec the two lines of Rceyu and Kakseyu in Hari-V., xxxi. and xxxii.); but if the genealogies are reckoned upwards from the Pandavas' time, this inference is much weakened, so that it does not seem absolutely impossible the founding of Anga and Kalinga may have been earlier than those kings, and thus the difficulty might disappear. Otherwise it may be, supposing there is truth in this story of the five brothers, that, if Anga was really the later name it superseded the ancient name so completely that it was substituted for the ancient name in the genealogies; for it seems a reasonable supposition that (apart from the deliberate fabrication of genealogies for the purpose of gratifying vanity, ambition or religious arrogance) all ancient genealogies and legends would be gradually modified by the substitution of current words in lieu of obsolete words, in order to render them intelligible to new generations and without any intention to falsify them.

The estimation in which these five nations were held by the brahmans of Madhya-deca varied remarkably. The curious harangue in which Kama abused Calya, king of Madra, and Calya's retort (Karna-p., xl.-xlv.) disclose some strange and inconsistent remarks on the composition and character of various races in India, which no doubt represent the handiwork of different authors and ages.

Calya asserts that it was the custom in Anga to abandon the sick and sell one's wife and children (xlv. 2112); and in one passage it is said that the Kalingas should be shunned as unrighteous, together with certain other people picked here and there out of Southern and Western India (xliv. 2066-7). Yet in other passage it is said—the Angakas (Angas) and Magadhas when old live according to the rules of righteousness which they have learnt (xlv. 2101); and Paundras, Kalingas and Magadhas are held up to honour along with the people of Madhya-deca as being conversant with eternal righteousness (xlv. 2084-5).

Originally these nations did not belong to the Aryan stock; they appear to have been mlecchas. The story of the five brothers no doubt indicates that these nations were brought within the Aryan pale, yet they did not rank high, for even at the time of the Great War the Anga prince is styled a mleccha (Karna-p., xxii. 877 and 880), and if such a term could he applied to him, when Anga was the foremost of these nations, it is certain the others must have been in a lower plight. The elevation of the Angas, Kalingas and Paundras to the same degree of esteem, which the nations of Madhya-deca enjoyed, must be a later development, and be the sign of some marked change which passed over Northern India. The alteration is most marked in the estimation of the Kalingas. Does it represent the opinion of the age when Brahmanism hard-pushed by Buddhism found a refuge in Orissa?

The Aitareya Brahmana says the Paundras, the Andhras and certain rude tribes in Central India are most degraded; they were Vicvamitra's descendants and were reduced to that state by his curse (vii. 3.18). Manu says, the Paundrakas, Odras and Dravidas and various well-known nations on the northern and northwestern confines of India were Ksattriyas and sank gradually to the rank of Sudras by reason of the neglect of sacred rites and the absence of brahmans (x. 43-4). These statements seem to represent an intermediate opinion of doctrinaire speculation, or the dogmatism of a late and ignorant period.

We may now consider the position of these five countries and their extent.

Anga

The position of Anga is well-known and requires only a few remarks. It was at all times closely connected with Magadha. The kings of Anga and Vanga used to frequent Dirgha-tamas' or Gautama's dwelling at Giri-vraja (Sabha-p., xx. 802-4; and the passages cited above regarding Dirgha-tamas; and Canti-p., cccxliii. 13183-5). The famous king Anga Vrhad-ratha sacrificed on Mt. Visnupada, which appears to be a hill at Gaya (Canti-p., xxix. 924-31). Jarasandha king of Magadha bestowed the city Malini, the capital of the Angas, on Kama as a fief (*id.*, v). It adjoined Magadha on the east as appears from the description of Bhima's conquests in the Eastern region, which is quoted here as it will serve to elucidate the position of the other eastern nations considered in this paper.

Marching from Magadha, Bhima conquered Kama (king of Anga) in battle and brought him into subjection. Then he vanquished the kings who dwelt in the hills. Next he slew a very powerful king in battle at Modagiri. Then he conquered Vasudeva, the mighty king of Pundra, and the valiant king who dwelt in Kauciki-kaccha, both powerful heroes, both fierce in prowess. He attacked the king of Vanga. Conquering Samudra-sena and king Candra-sena (who appear to have been kings of Vanga), and the Tamralipta king and the lord of Karvata, he vanquished also the lord of the Suhmas, and those who dwell beside the sea, and all the tribes *(gana)* of Mlecchas. Then he went to Lauhitya. He made all the kings, who dwell in the marshy tracts near the sea *(sagaranupa)*, pay tribute (Sabha-p., xxix. 1094-1100).

This description appears unusually clear and natural. Marching from the Patna and Gaya districts Bhima met and defeated Kama on the western limits of Anga, that is, in the west of the Monghyr or Mungir district; then turning aside and subduing the petty kings in the northern part of Chutia Nagpur, he marched on eastward to Modagiri. Lassen has identified Modagiri with the modern town of Monghyr or Mungir; this is extremely probable both from the resemblance of the names and from the situation and natural features of the town. Modagiri or (nasalized, as so frequently happens in Indian vernaculars) Modagiri might easily be corrupted into Mungir. The king of this place would then have been one of Kama's vassals.

The capital was called Malini or Malina at first, and this name was superseded by that of Campa bestowed on the city in honour (it is said) of Loma-pada's great grandson, king Campa (Canti-p., v. 134-5; Hari-V., xxxi. 1699-1700; and Matsya Pur., xlviii. 97); but the latter name is often used indiscriminately in regard to time, and the city is called Campa in an account of Loma-pada's reign (Ramay., Adi-k., xvii. 23). It was situated on the Ganges (Vana-p., lxxxv. 8156; and cccvii. 17150-51), and is identified with the modern town of Bhagalpur.

Cunnigham says Mudgala-puri, Mudgalacrama and Mudga-giri were the old names of Mungir; and an earlier name was Kasta-harana parvata (Arch. Surv. Repts., XV. 15 and 18). Madgurakas are mentioned as a people in Eastern India (Matsya Pur., cxiii. 44), and Mudakaras (Markand. Pur., lvii. 42); probably the correct reading should be Mudagiras. The Mudgalas are cursorily mentioned in Drona-p., xi. 397. None of these names, however, can well be older than Modagiri in the Maba-Bharata.

Anga therefore comprised the modern districts of Bhagalpur and Monghyr, and also extended northwards up the river Kauciki, the modern Kosi, and included the western portion of the district of Purnia. For it was on that river that Kacyapa Vibhandaka had his hermitage, there his son Rsyacrnga was brought up in the strictest seclusion, and from there the young rsi was beguiled by a courtesan of. Malini into a boat and brought down the river to the capital (Vana-p., ex. 9990-10080; and Ramay., Adi-k., viii. and ix.). The forest in which Rsyacrnga lived is said to have bordered on Anga (Adi-k., ix. 55-61), and the whole of this quaint story implies that he was living within the territory of Anga, for no embassage was sent to any other king for permission to bring him away, as when Daca-ratha paid a special visit to Loma-pada to invite the rsi's attendance at Ayodhya to perform the sacrifice which was to bless the king with a son (*id.*, 14-23).

The tract near Campa was called Suta-visaya, "the land of bards or charioteers". It was there that Kama, Kunti's illegitimate son, was adopted and brought up by the Suta Adhi-ratha (Adhi-p., Ixvii. 2764-83, and cxi.; and Vana-p., cccvii. 17150-51, and cccviii).

Anga was a kingdom from very early times, for it is said that Ariha, the eighth descendant from Puru, married Angi or Aangi, and his fifth descendant who bore the same name married Angeyi, both presumably Anga princesses (Adi-p., xcv. 3772 and 3777). And Vasuhoma is mentioned as king of Anga contemporary with the great Mandhatr, one of the early kings of the Solar race, and is eulogized in high terms (Canti-p., exxii). Passages such as these present difficulties as noticed above, and are also open to distrust as being fabrications of a later age, but there are these considerations in favour of their genuineness and authenticity, namely, that in all countries and especially in ancient times genealogies have been esteemed matters of very great importance and kept up with jealous pride, and that Anga lay at first outside the Aryan pale, so that no honour could be gained by alleging false alliances with its princes who were prior to the time of Anga. In Jarasandha's time, Anga appears to have been an appanage of Magadha, and it was through his favour that Kama gained it as his kingdom (Sabha-p., xxix. 1090-93; Vana-p., ccxlv. 15052; and Canti-p., v. 134-5).

The ancient history of Anga appears to consist of two periods, first, the age before the eponymous king Anga, and secondly that which he inaugurated. In the former age the country must have belonged to a pre-Aryan race and dynasty, and their rule must have ended with king Bali. Although his lineage is traced up to Anu or Puru, sons of Yayati, so as to connect it with the royal Aryan lines of North India, yet he is called a Danava (Matsya Pur., xlviii. 60), and it was no doubt a remembrance of its old non-Aryan stock that led to the application of the opprobrious term Mleccha to the Anga prince who joined in the Great war (Karna-p., xxii. 877 and 880).

The second period no doubt represents the change when the country passed under the influence of the Aryas, as they extended their dominion eastward. It has been mentioned already that Daca-ratha's contemporary Loma-pada was fifth or sixth in descent from Anga, hence the beginning of this period may be placed some six generations prior to Rama's time. There was a close friendship between Loma-pada and Daca-ratha, so genuine that the latter is said to have given his daughter Canta in adoption to the former (Ramay., Adi-k., x. 1-10, and 23-27). The connexion between Ayodhya and Anga at that time is shewn in such detail and referred to so often, that it appears to be a real historical fact; and it is corroborated incidentally in a remarkable manner in the enumeration of the kings and princes who were invited to attend Daca-ratha's sacrifice *(id.*, xii. 18-24). That list differs surprisingly from similar lists in the Maha-Bharata, which describe all the kings and princes through the length and breadth of India, who assembled at Drupadi's svayam-vara (Adi-p., clxxxvi. and clxxxvii), at the opening of the Pandavas' Court (Sabha-p., iv.), and at the Raja-suya sacrifice *(id.*, xxxiii.). The Ramayana list is short and is noteworthy as much for its omissions as for its contents; it mentions the kings of Mithila (North Behar), Kaci (Benares), Kekaya (North Panjab) and Anga, and then in general terms those of the East (Pracya), of Sindhu (North Sindh) and Sauvira (West Panjab), of Su-rastra (Gujarat) and of the Dekhan, and "whatever other kings were particularly friendly" (Adi-k., xii. 18-24). Madhya-deca is ignored with the exception of Kaci; and the connexions of Kosala and Ayodhya were closest with Kaci, Mithila and Anga, and after them with the distant kingdoms of the Panjab and Western India.

The Aitaieya Brahmana says that Anga was inaugurated with the Mahabhiseka ceremony by Udamaya, son of Atri, and in consequence conquered the whole earth; and that Anga gave him a thousand elephants in the country Avacatnuka (viii. 4, 22). This passage probably refers to Anga Vrhad-ratha, one of the sixteen famous kings (Canti-p., xxix. 924-31) who seems to be the same as Dharma-ratha, the great grandson of Anga, from the special allusion to Mt. Visnu-pada (Hari-V., xxxi. 1693-5); but I have not met the name Avacatnuka elsewhere, nor is it in the dictionary.

Vanga

Vanga or Banga is often mentioned and its people were called Vangas and Vangeyas; but the allusions seldom yield any clear information. As shewn in the description of Bhima's conquests in the eastern region quoted above, it lay beyond Anga, to the south-east, and was the original of the modern Bengal.

The only definite information occurs in a passage in the Raghu-Vamca which of course belongs to a comparatively late date (iv. 36 and 37). The Vangas are described there as essentially a boating people, using boats for all purposes of life *(nau-sadhana)*, and as growing rice for their staple crop, which they uprooted when seedlings and transplanted into their fields, as they do to this day. Raghu planted his columns of victory in the islands of the Ganges delta, *ganga-srotontaresu*. It is difficult to say at what rate land has been forming in the delta, yet it is clear from this description that, apart from its extent sea-ward, the delta must have different greatly from its present condition 1200 or 1500 years ago. The rivers which traverse it now are partially silted up, but at that time they must have been wide and free-flowing streams, dividing the lands into numerous distinct islands; in fact, the condition of the whole delta then must have been very much like what the extreme south-eastern portion is now.

Vanga must have comprised, the modern districts of Murshidabad, Nadia, Jessor, and parts of Rajshahi, Pabna and Faridpur.

Vanga occupied a much lower position than Anga or Kalinga; I have found no mention of any marriages between its princes or princesses and the royal families of North India. Its kings are spoken of in general terms and names are seldom mentioned. A prince Candra-sena, son of Samudra-sena, attended Draupadi's svayam-vara (Adi-p., clxxxvi. 6991), and it appears probable on comparing this passage with the description of Bhima's conquests quoted above, that these two persons were princes of Vanga. It seems likely that this Samudra-sena is the king of the same name who was famed as far as the confines of the sea (*id.*, lxvii. 2690). No capital appears to be even alluded to.

Kalinga

Kalinga is generally ranked third in this five-fold group of countries, but resembled Anga in being a settled kingdom with a capital, and in having a longer history than the rest.

The fullest and clearest information is given in a passage of the

Raghu-Vamca (iv. 38-43) describing Raghu's conquests. After conquering the Vangas, Raghu crossed the Kapica (or Karabha, according to another reading) by bridging it with his elephants, and took the road pointed out by the Utkala kings towards Kalinga. He planted his own splendour on the summit of Mount Mahendra as a mahaut strikes his iron hook into the head of an unruly elephant. The Kalinga king with an array of elephants attacked him, but Raghu withstanding the storm of arrows defeated his foes there (at Mt. Mahendra). His soldiers made open spaces for revelry and quaffed fermented cocoa-nut juice out of betel-leaves. Observing the rules of fair warfare, he took from the lord of Mahendra his glory but not his territory.

Lassen has identified the R. Kapica with the modern Subarnarekha on the confines of the Midnapur and Balasore districts (Ind. Alt. Map), but I venture to suggest that the Kapica is the modern Cossye or Kansai, which flows a little further north through Midnapur. The name Kansai is said to be modified from Kamsavati, but I do not know on what authority, nor have I met with this name anywhere, nor is it in the dictionary. Kansai or Kamsai may easily be a corruption of Kapica-vati; names of this form are not uncommon, e.g., Amaravati, Utpala-vati.

This passage shows that Kalinga lay southward of Vanga beyond the R. Kapica. and stretched southward so as to include Mount Mahendra. The Mahendra Mountains were one of the seven chief ranges of India, and are the northern portion of the Eastern Ghats above the R. Godavari, and the hills near Ganjam are still called Mahindra. It is not stated that the Kapica was the northern limit of Kalinga; rather the above passage suggests that Utkala jutted in between this river and Kalinga, and that Raghu secured the help and guidance of the Utkala kings in order to reach Kalinga. The northern limit of Kalinga was approximately the river Vaitarani, the modern Bytarni; for the Maha-Bharata, describing the Pandava's pilgrimage to all the *tirthas*, says—After bathing at the junction of the Ganges and the sea, they travelled along the sea-coast towards the Kalingas, and reached that people and the R. Vaitarani about the same time; its northern bank is spoken of as greatly frequented by rsis (Vana-p., cxiv. 10096-10107). On its bank was Viraja-tirtha, the later Birajaksetra, the modern Jaipur (*id.*, lxxxv. 8148).

Kalinga therefore comprised modern Orissa about as far north as the modern town Bhadrak in the Balasore district, and the sea-coast southward as far as Vizagapatam; it does not appear to have reached as far as the Godavari, because this river is never connected with Kalinga in any passage as far as I am aware. Its limits inland are not clear. Kalinga as a settled country appears to have consisted properly of the plain between the Eastern Ghats and the sea, yet its monarchs seem to have exercised a kind of suzerainty over the aboriginal tribes which inhabited the hilly tracts far inland, for the Amara-kantaka hills, in which the Narmada rises, are said to be in the western part of Kalinga (Kurma Pur, II. xxxix. 9) Lassen places Kalinga along the inner side of the Eastern Ghats from the Vizagápatam district south-westward as far as the Karnul district.

The capital is called Raja-pura, which however simply means "capital" (Canti-p., iv). In the Raghu-Vaṁca it is placed on the sea-coast, and the palace is described as being so near the sea, that the windows looked out on the sea, and the deep roar of the waves drowned the bray of trumpets (vi. 56). This description can only apply to Kalingapatam, and that town was no doubt the capital in Kalidasa's time. Kalinga-patam and Chicacole (said to be corrupted from Cri-kakola) are reputed to be the two ancient capitals, and the latter is said to be the more ancient (Arch. Surv. of S. India, by R. Sewell, I. 2 and 7), but I have not met the name Cri-kakola anywhere, nor is it in the dictionary.

The people were called Kalinga, and Kalingaka; and "all the Kalingas" are spoken of as if they were a numerous people (Bhisma-p., xvii. 668; and lxxi. 3132). Their kingdom dates back to very early times. Three famous kings are named, Ksema, Agra-tirtha and Kuhara (Adi-p., lxvii. 2701), and their princesses married two of the early kings of the Lunar dynasty *(id.*, xcv. 3775 and 3780). Duryodhana moreover attended a svayam-vara held by a Kalinga princess, and carried her off with Kama's help (Canti-p., iv). Krsna is said to have crushed the Kalingas in a pitched battle at a place called Dantakura (Udyoga-p., xlvii. 1883); it is not clear where that place was, but it may be noticed that Rama Jamadagnya slew the ksattriyas and the haters of the brahmans and Dantakrura (Drona-p., lxx. 2430-31).

Pundra and Paundra

The Pundras dwelt in the Eastern region as stated in the description of Bhima's Eastern conquests quoted above, though they are also assigned sometimes to the Southern region (e.g., Markand. Pur., lvii. 45). The name occurs in various other forms, Pundraka

(Sabha-p., iv. 119), Paundra (Adi-p., clxxxvii. 7020), Paundraka *(id.,* clxxxvi. t992; and Sabha-p., xxxiii. 1270) and Paundrika (Sabha-p., li. 1872). These names are used sometimes as if equivalent, thus, "Famous in the world is the mighty king among the Vangas, Pundras and Kiratas, named the Paundraka Vasudeva" *(id.,* xiii, 584). and yet a distinction is made between Paundras and Pundras, for they are mentioned separately in the list of peoples in India (Bhisma-p., ix. 358 and 365), and Pundras, Pundrakas and Paundrikas are all mentionad in one passage (Sabha-p., li. 1872-4).

This distinction appears also in the list of kings who attended the opening of the Pandavas' Court. Among them are mentioned "Anga and Vanga with Pundraka, the two kings of Panda and Udra *(Pandodrarajau)* with Andhraka" *(id,* iv. 119). The reading *Panda* here seems to be a mistake for *Paundra,* because there is no passage, that I know of which alludes to any country or people called Panda in Eastern India, and because the reading Paundra occurs in the same combination in the list of kings who attended Yudhisthira's raja-suya sacrifice, viz, *sa-paundrodrjn,* "with Paundras and Udras" (Vana-p., li. 1988). It seems clear then that there was a distinction between Pundras and Pundrakas on the one hand, and Paundras, Paundrakas and Paundrikas on the other; and yet the two people appear to have been but two branches of the same nation, for the Paundraka Vasudeva was king of the Pundras as stated in the quotation from Sabha-p., xiii, 584 above. This inference is corroborated in the further passages which are now cited to elucidate their position.

Lassen places Pundra in the northern half of the modern Chutia Nagpur, and does not show P^undra as separate. The passages that I have found which give indications of the position of Pundra and Paundra are these. I will consider Paundra first.

In the two passages last quoted the Paundras are linked with the Udras and the second runs thus—"With Bangas and Angas *(sa-bangangari),* with Paundras and Udras *(sa-paundrodran),* with Colas, Dravidas and Andhrakas *(sa-cola-dravidandhrakan).*" These three groups denote real territorial proximity. The Colas, Dravidas and Andhrakas occupied the whole of the east coast of the Dekhan; the Angas and Vangas were near each other; hence it seems certain, the Paundras and Udras were neighbours also. The Paundras and Audras are placed together in the Bhisma-p. list (ix. 365). Udra, as will be seen further on, was in the extreme west of West Bengal. Again the Paundras are grouped along with the Utkalas, Mekalas, Kalingas and

Andhras (Drona-p., iv. 122). The Utkalas were in Chutia Nagpur and the Orissa Tributary States. The Mekalas were the inhabitants of the Mekala hills, the modern Mekal hills, which bound Chattisgarh on the west and north. Kalinga has been already defined. Andhra, which is an old name of the Telingas and Telugus, comprised the eastern portion of the Nizam's Dominions and the southern portion of the Central Provinces. The Paundras therefore were connected with the races situated west and south-west of Bengal proper.

The grouping of the Pundras was markedly different. In the first passage cited (Sabha-p., xiii. 584), they are linked with Vangas and Kiratas. Kirata was the general name of all the tribes of Mongolian affinity which inhabited the hilly regions from the Panjab to Assam and Chittagong, as will be shewn further on. The Pundras are grouped with the Angas and Vangas in Sabha-p., iv. 119 cited above. There are other passages which yield no definite information, such as Adi-p., cxiii. 4453: Sabha-p., li. 1872-4, and Acvamedh-p., lxxxii. 2435-65; but the inference appears to be that the Pundras occupied some intermediate position between the Angas and Vangas and the Himalayas.

From these conclusions we may proceed to consider the description of Bhima's Eastern expedition (Sabha-p., xxix. 1094-1100) which has been quoted above in relation to Anga. As already remarked, it appears unusally clear and natural. Beyond the Monghyr and Bhagalpur districts reigned two kings who are spoken of together in the dual number as if closely connected. One is called Vasudeva the mighty king of Pundra, but Vasudeva is generally spoken of as the king of Paundra, see for instance, besides the passages cited already, Sabha-p, xxxiii. 1270, and Hari-V., cxvii. 6580-84, and 6606-8. The other king is not named, but Kauciki-kaccha where he reigned means the land bordering on the R. Kauciki, that is on the east side, because Anga lay on the west side; and stretching east of that river is a high tract of stiff red clay known as the Barind. This agrees with the position which has been already indicated for Pundra. Hence it seems unmistakable that the joint kings of Pundra and Paundra are meant. Vasudeva was properly king of Paundra, but being the chief is spoken of as lord both of Pundra and Paundra, and the other would have been king of Pundra proper. Beyond these kings lay Vanga, says the passage.

From all these results it follows that Paundra must have lain on the south side of the Ganges, and Pundra on the north side, between

Anga and Vanga. Paundra must have comprised the modern districts of the Santal Parganas and Birbhum and the north portion of the Hazaribagh district; and Pundra the district of Maldah, the portion of Purnia east of the R. Kosi, and part of Dinajpur and Rajshahi.

From their name, the Paundras were presumably an offshoot of the Pundras; hence it would seem probable that, after the Pundras established themselves in the above-mentioned region north of the Ganges, a branch of them must have crossed that river, pushed their way into the hilly tract of the Santa! Parganas and its outskirts, and formed a sister kingdom under the name of Paundras.

Suhma and Tama-lipta

The last of the five kindred nations was Suhma. It is mentioned last, but was well-known and was grouped oftenest with Pundra. The evidence to fix its position is clear.

In the account of Bhima's Eastern conquests (Sabha-p., xxix) which has been often cited above, the Suhmas and Pra-suhmas are mentioned between Videha and Magadha (1089-91), and again Tamra-lipta, Karvata, Suhma and the sea-coast are named in close succession after Vanga (1097-99). In the account of Raghu's conquests it is said—"marching east and subduing various countries, Raghu reached the neighbourhood of the sea which was dark with forests of tallier palms *(tali-vana)*, and the Suhmas submitted to him" (Raghu-V., iv. 34-35). Lastly, it is stated plainly in the Daca-kumara-carita that Damalipta is a city among the Suhmas (Story of Mitra-gupta).

Damalipta is the same as Tamalipta. The Tamaliptas were a well-known people and are often mentioned. This name is written in various ways, viz., Tamra-lipta, Tamra-liptaka, Tamo-lipti, Tamalika, and Tamalini. Prof. Sir M. Monier-Williams treats Tama-lipta (q. v.) as the proper form of the name, and the others as variations, which seemingly sought to read meanings into it. Tamra-lipta is, I belive, the form most commonly met with in Sanskrit writings. Their capital was called Tamra-lipta, Tamra-lipti or Tamra-liptika, and this name has been corrupted into the modern Tamluk, which is a well-known town near the mouth of the R. Rupnarayan in Midnapur.

From these data it appears that Suhma must have comprised the modern districts of Hooghly, Howrah, Bankura and Bardhwan, and the eastern portion of Midnapur. The first of the above allusions to the Suhmas and Pra-suhmas seems to be an error, for there do not appear to be any other references to such people close to Videha and

Magadha. Perhaps the reading should be Conas and Pra-conas, which would mean people living near the river Cona, the modern Sone; and this suggestion may be compared with the name Canavatyas which occurs along with Angas, Vangas, Pundras and Gayas (Sabha-p., li. 1872), and which seems to be a mistake for Conavatyas, as it is not in the dictionary and I have not met with it elsewhere.

According to the passage cited from the Daca-kumara-carita, Tama-lipta or Tamra-lipta was part of the Suhma territory, but Tamra-lipta is frequently alluded to as if it were a country by itself, e.g., Adi-p., clxxxvi. 6993; Sabha-p., li. 1874; Bhisma-p., ix. 364; Drona-p., lxx. 2436 and Karna-p., xxii. 863. It would have comprised the modern district of Howrah and the eastern part of Midnapur. In fact Tamra-lipta appears to occur oftener than Suhma, and this is perhaps because the town Tamra-lipta was a famous sea-port, especially during the centuries of Buddhist activity.

Another name, which was equivalent to or was included within Tamalipta, is Vela-kula, "the stream-bank," or better perhaps, "the sea-shore". It is said to be the same as the modern town Birkul, which is on the coast in the extreme south of the Midnapur district.

Udra or Odra

The Udras have been mentioned above in conjunction with the Paundras; otherwise they are, I believe, rarely alluded to in Sanskrit writings. They are also called Odras (Sabha-p., 1. 1843), and Audras (Bhisma-p., ix. 365), and they are also persumably the Udhras of Bhisma-p., 1. 2084, and the Audras of Acvamedh.-p., lxxxiii. 2476-7. They have given their name to modern Orissa, i.e., Odra-deca, and Lassen places them in his map more or less conterminous with Orissa, but this cannot have been their position because it has been shewn that Kalinga comprised all Orissa except the narrow northern part of the Balasore district, and because the Udras play a very insignificant part in the early accounts of Eastern India, quite incompatible with the supposition that they inhabited the fine extensive plain of Orissa; and also because Orissa has not always meant what it denotes now.

The Uriya or Odiya language is spoken throughout Orissa and the Ganjam district, in the northern part of the Vizagapatam district and along the south-eastern limits of Chattisgarh (Maltby's Uriya Grammar, Preface)—a peculiarly curved area. A territory of such size and such a shape could hardly have been the ancient home of any tribe, much less of so small a tribe as the Udras appear to have been. The allusions to Kalinga leave no doubt about its position, and it will be seen that the Utkalas, who were more important in old times than the Udras, probably occupied the northern part of the Balasore district; hence it seems impossible that the Udras can have inhabited any part of Orissa. In the last century Orissa included the tract of country between the rivers Rupnarayan and Subarna-rekha, which flow through the Midnapur district (see Bengal Administration Report 1872-73, p. 40); that tract is now part of the Midnapur district and is considered part of Bengal proper.

These considerations give, I think, an indication where the Udra territory was in ancient time. The eastern part of Midnapur belonged to Tamalipta and Suhma, hence there remains only the western part of that district which no other nation appears to have occupied; and if to this be added the modern district of Manbhum, the eastern part of Singhbhum, and perhaps the southern portion of Bankura, a well-defined tract is obtained, which no other tribe appears to have owned and which bordered on Paundra. I would suggest that this must have been Udra in ancient times.

If this be a reasonable inference, it discloses how an insignificant early tribe developed and spread during the confusion which prevailed in the dark times of medieval Indian history. I would suggest that the Udras must have pushed southward, overrun the whole of Orissa and Ganjam, and driven the Kalingas downward into the Vizagapatam district, till there further course was checked by the Dravidian powers on the south; then they must have turned westward and forced their way round into the southern portion of Chattisgarh.

Prag-jyotisa

Prag-jyotisa was a famous kingdom in ancient times and is often mentioned in the Maha-Bharata. The references to it are however rather perplexing, for in some passages it is styled a Mleccha kingdom, in others a Danava or Asura kingdom, and to others again the allusions seem mixed: These passages may be taken in order.

Prag-jyotisa is placed in the North region (Vana-p., ccliii. 15240-42), but was also considered to be in the Eastern region (Markand. Pur., lvii. 44). In the account of Arjuna's conquests it is placed in North India and his course is described thus. After conquering all the kings who dwelt in Cakala-dvipa and in the seven dvipas, Arjuna advanced to Prag-jyotisa. Bhaga-datta was the great king there, and

Arjuna had a great conflict with him. The Prag-jyotisa king was surrounded with Kiratas and Cinas and many other soldiers who dwelt in the marshy regions near the sea, and after a battle lasting eight days submitted amicably to Arjuna. From there Arjuna marched to the North region governed by Kuvera and conquered Antar-giri and Vahirgiri and Upa-giri (Sabha-p., xxv. 999-1012). Similarly, in the description of Kama's conquests it is said he conquered Bhaga-datta and ascended Himavat (Vana-p., ccliii. 15241).

The three names Upa-giri, Antar-giri and Vahir-giri in this place can only denote different tracts in the Himalayas, viz., the southern slopes, the middle valleys and the further region on the north respectively. Bhaga-datta is called Cailalaya, "dwelling among the mountains" (Stri-p., xxiii. 644). It is stated in the foregoing passage and again in Udyoga-p., xviii. 584-5, that his army was composed of Kiratas and Cinas. The Kiratas, as will be explained, were the Himalayan tribes of Mongolian affinity, and the Cinas were the Chinese: as they formed his army, they were his close neighbours. Hence it is clear that Prag-jyotisa lay in the north-east of India and touched the Himalayas.

But as stated in the above passage from Sabha-p., Bhaga-datta drew part of his troops also from the people who dwelt in the marshy regions near the sea, *sagaranupa* (see also Karna-p., v. 104-5); and when he attended Yudhisthira's raja-suya sacrifice, he was accompanied by all the Mlecchas who lived in the marshy regions near the sea (Sabha-p., xxxiii. 1268-9). This word can only mean the low alluvial tracts and islands east of Vanga, around the mouth of the R. Brahma-putra. That tract was peopled by Mlecchas as mentioned in the description of Bhima's Eastern conquests quoted above. It is also stated definitely that Bhaga-datta dwelt at the Eastern Ocean (Udyoga-p., iii. 74). The Brahma-putra till last two century flowed round the south side of the Garo hills, and then southward through the districts of Maimansingh and Dacca (Major Rennell's Atlas, 1781). Presumably therefore Prag-jyotisa stretched southward along both sides of that river as far as the delta, or even perhaps as far as the sea itself.

Lassen places Prag-jyctisa north of the R. Lohita or Brahmaputra in Bhutan, but this position does not satisfy the conditions already mentioned. It is implied in the Raghu-Vamca that Prag-jyotisa lay east of that river, for, when Raghu returning from Himavat crossed the river, the Prag-jyotisa king trembled (iv. 81); but I venture to think that Kalidasa cannot have been entirely right in this allusion to distant geography, because if he is right the whole of North Bengal must be assigned to Pundra, there being no other people of note mentioned who could have occupied all that territory. Pundra, however, hardly plays as important a part in the ancient stories as the possession of so rich and extensive a kingdom would have warranted, and Prag-jyotisa on the other hand would be relegated to hilly tracts of small fertility east of the old course of the Brahma-putra, whereas the allusions indicate that Bhaga-datta was a wealthy and powerful monarch. But see page 47.

Bhaga-datta is called a "warrior-king" and "the mighty king of the Mlecchas" (Sabha-p., 1. 1834), and is seldom mentioned without some complimentary epithet. He alone of the northern kings is allowed to have maintained a long and equal contest with Arjuna (Udyoga-p., clxvi. 5805-6). He is dignified with the title "Civa's friend," and esteemed "not inferior to Cakra in battle" (Sabha-p., xxv. 1005 and see Karna-p., v. 104). He is also called specially "the friend of Pandu" *(ibid.,* 1008), and is referred to in terms of respect and kindliness by Krsna when addressing Yudhisthira—"Bhaga-datta is thy father's aged friend; he was noted for his deference to thy father in word and deed, and he is mentally bound by affection and devoted to thee like a father" (id., xiii. 579-80). His Cina and Kirata troops glittered as with gold—*tasya cinaih kirataic ca kancanair iva samvrtam babhau balam*—unless the allusion be to their yellow complexions (Udyoga-p., xviii. 584-5).

For these reasons it seems that Prag-jyotisa must have comprised the country along both sides of the Brahma-putra from the Himalayas down to Tippera, that is the modern districts of Jalpaigori, Cooch Behar, Goalpara, Rangprur, Bogra, Maimansingh, Dacca, Tippera, and part of Pabna and also probably part of the east of Nepal. Strictly speaking, the southern portion of Prag-jyotisa as thus defined would have fallen within the Eastern region and would have included Lauhitya mentioned in the description of Bhima's conquests there quoted above, that is, the country beside the R. Lohita or Brahma-putra; but if Lauhitya was only a portion of the Prag-jyotisa realm, and the strength of that realm lay, as it appears it did, in the north, it was natural to treat Prag-jyotisa as situated in the Northern region.

The region assigned to Prag-jyotisa bordered on forests and hills where elephants still abound, and where a hardy race of ponies still exists; and the allusions to it notice this. Thus Bhaga-datta is described as "the best wielder of the elephant-hook" among the kings assembled on the Pauravas, side in the Great War, and as "skilful with the chariot" (Udyoga-p., clxvi. 5804); and it would seem from this that in ancient days kings did not consider it unbecoming to excel in the manege of elephants. He gave as presents to Yudhisthira "horses of noble breed, swift as the wind, an iron vessel, and swords with fine ivory hilts" (Sabha-p., 1. 1835-6). The description of the horses is, of course, exaggerated according to our ideas, for the best horses in ancient India could not well have exceeded what we should call galloways, and the majority of them could not have been more than ponies.

No name is given to the capital in this class of passages but it is called Prag-jyotisa in the other classes. The people were Mlecchas as indicated in some of the foregoing quotations; and this word, no doubt means here people of Mongolian affinity.

The second and third classes of passages occur, 1 believe, only in connexion with Krsna and relate to an attack which he is said to have made on Prag-jyotisa. In the second class may be quoted first a part of Krsna's denunciation of Cicu-pala—"Cicu-pala, knowing that we had gone to the Prag-jyotisa city, set fire to Dvaraka" (Sabha-p., xlvii. 1567). This almost belongs to the first class, but the idea is developed in a speech by Arjuna in praise of Krsna—"Thou didst destroy Muru's fetters *(maurava paca)* and slay Nisunda and Naraka; thou didst render the path to the Prag-jyotisa city safe again" (Vana-p., xii. 488). Here we see the country Prag-jyotisa described in the first class of passages disappears and becomes a city, Krsna becomes a hero and conqueror, and the suggestion comes in that the people were demons.

This suggestion is fully developed in the third class of passages, and the laudation of Krsna grows fulsome and hyperbolical as addressed to a divine personage. Thus Arjuna praising him says—There was a very strong fortress-city called Prag-jyotisa belonging to the Asuras; and Bhauma Naraka carried-off Aditi's two jewelled ear-rings there; the gods could not cope with him, and therefore invoked Krsna's help to slay the Dasyus; Krsna severed six thousand fetters *(paca)*. slew Bhauma Naraka and Mura, and recovered the ear-rings (Udyoga-p., xlvii. 1887-92). Visnu prophesying about his incarnations says—While dwelling at Dvaraka as Krsna, I shall slay Naraka Bhauma, who did wrong to Aditi, and also Maru and Pitha the Danava, and destroy the charming Prag-jyotisa city filled with all kinds of wealth (Canti-p., cccxli. 12954-6). Vidura says—Naraka and the

Danavas tried to seize Krsna, when he went to Prag-jyotisa, and failed (Udyoga-p., cxxix. 4408-9).

This class of allusions occurs especially in the Hari-Vamca. It is said there—Krsna went to the Prag-jyotisa city and killed the Danava Naraka in the sea, *samudra-madhye* (clxxiv. 9790). Narada speaking of Krsna's exploits says—The two Danavas Maya and Tara delighted in Bhauma Naraka's city Prag-jyotisa (lv. 3116-7). It is said Naraka Bhauma, king of the Danavas, seized Tvastr's daughter Kaceru; he was king of Prag-jyotisa; he made a fine city Maniparvata for the Gandharva maidens and Apsaras, whom he carried-off, upon the Alaka towards his own country of Muru—*Alakayam muroh sva-visayam prati* (cxxi. 6791-6801). The Alaka seems to be the river Alaka-nanda, one of the eastern sources of the Ganges, but Muru seems to be generally the name of a Danava prince. The climax of marvel is perhaps reached in the continuation of that story in Hari-V., cxxi to cxxiii, where Kisna's exploits are described at great length—how at Indra's request he rode on Garuda from Dvaraka to the Prag-jyotisa city, how he fought in a superhuman battle with Naraka's four wardens *(dvara-pala)*, with the hosts of Daityas, Danavas and Raksasas and finally with Naraka, and slew them all, how he captured the city with its fabulous riches, and how the Earth gave up Aditi's ear-rings which Naraka had carried-off. It was through this great victory that Krsna gained his wonderful bow Carnga (Udyoga-p., clvii. 5353-8).

To the same class of passages belongs the allusion in a doubtful verse of the Ramayana, where Prag-jyotisa is mistakenly placed in the *Western* region—"A city made of gold called Prag-jyotisa is there; in it dwells the evil-souled Danava called Naraka" (Gorressio's Edition, Annotations to Kisk-k., xliii).

The difference which has taken place in the aspect of Prag-jyotisa from the first to the last of these passages is most striking. We have no longer a prosperous Mleccha kingdom of barbaric splendour, but a nation of Asuras and Danavas; no longer the noble and imposing figure of the warrior-king Bhaga-datta, the ally and friend of the Kurus, and the friend of Civa, but malignant demon-kings Naraka and Muru, who were the foes of the gods and with whom the divine hero Krsna could have nothing but internecine war. There can be, no doubt, that this change marks very clearly the development of the Krsna legend, from his rise as a new chieftain of great vigour and capacity to his deification as an incarnation of Visnu.

There is only one other passage of importance that I am aware of viz., Ramay., Adi-k., xxxv. 1-9, which has been quoted above in connexion with Magadha. It says Prag-jyotisa was founded by Amurtarajas, a son of a great king Kuca, who was apparently an Arya king in Madhya-deca. It does not agree with any allusion that I have found, and can hardly be reconciled with any of the passages already discussed.

A few words may be added about Kama-rupa, which is the modern district of Kamrup or Gauhati in Assam. The Kama-rupas were not an ancient nation, for their name does not occur as far as I am aware, in the Maha-Bharata or Ramayana or any early Sanskrit work; in fact they are rarely mentioned. They seems therefore to have sprung up only in medieval times, and to have developed as Prag-jyotisa had dwindled into a small state. Thus they are mentioned in the Raghu-Vamca (iv. 83-84), where it is said Raghu conquered them after the Prag-jyotisas, so that they were distinct from the latter. In ancient times their territory was probably included within Prag-jyotisa.

The Kiratas

The word Kirata is, no doubt, the same as the modern names Kirati and Kiranti, which mean "a native of the Kirant-des or mountainous country lying between the Dud-Kosi and the Karki rivers in Nepal. The term includes the Khambu, Limbu and Yakha tribes; and the Danuar, Hayu and Thami also claim to be Kiranti"; but their claim is disputed by the first three tribes which are superior (Risley's Castes and Tribes of Bengal, I, 490). But formerly they had a much larger range, or their name was used in a comprehensive way, for it was applied to tribes inhabiting the Himalaya range and its southern slopes from the Panjab to Assam and Chittagong.

Arjuna in the course of his conquests in the Northern region encountered Kiratas in the army of Bhaga-datta king of Prag-jyotisa (Sabha-p., xxv. 1002; and see other passages cited below). Bhima, after vanquishing Videha in his Eastern expedition, proceeded from there against the Kiratas *(id.*, xxix, 1089); and they were even further to the east *{id.*, xiii. 584). They are spoken of as dwelling in the marshy regions near the sea *(sagaranupa-vasiri*) under Bhaga-datta's rule (Karna-p., v. 104-5), that is, as explained in discussing Prag-jyotisa, in the low lands around the mouth of the Brahma-putra, so that they occupied all the eastern bounds of Bengal. Moreover, Nakula in his Western expedition is said in general terms to have encountered Kiratas along with Pahlavas (Persians), Barbaras, Yavanas (Greeks), and

Cakas (Scythians), (Sabha-p., xxxi. 1199); and they are classed with those and other north-western nations (Canti-p., lxv. 2429, and ccvii. 7560; and Vana-p., li. 1990).

The Kiratas formed a series of allied yet distinct tribes or clans, for the Kiratas are mentioned twice in the Bhisma-p. list (ix. 358 and 364), and again "all the Kiratas" are mentioned *(ibid.,* 376); and it is almost impossible that tribes so wide-spread could have been homogeneous. They were also intermixed with similar hill tribes called Tanganas and Pulindas, and all appear to have lived together amicably (Vama-p., cxl. 10863-6). They dwelt in the fastnesses of Himavat (Drona-p., iv. 121; and Raghu-Vamca, iv. 76), and their chief territory was among the ranges of Kailasa, Mandara and Haima, that is, the region around lake Manasa, the modern Manasarowar lakes (Anucas-p., xix. 1434; Vana-p., exxxix. and cxl). It was there that the great king Su-bahu resided, who is called king of the Pulindas *(ibid.)* and also king of the Kiratas (Vana-p., clxxvii. 12349).

In that region they formed a settled kingdom and had a city (*ibid.* 12350). Eastwards they were also organized into chieftainships, for Bhima conquered seven kings of the Kiratas on the confines of Videha (Sabha-p., xxix. 1089). But the various tribes differed much in material condition, for some were civilized and open to friendly intercourse (Vana-p., cxl. 10865-6; and Udyoga-p., lxiii. 2470), and others were clad in skins, lived on fruit and roots and were cruel (Sabha-p., li. 1865). Their women were used as slaves, for large numbers of Kirata slave-girls are said to have been presented to Yudhisthira *(ibid.,* 1867). The Ramayana describes the Kiratas as wearing thick top-knots (Kisk-k., xl. 30). They were looked upon with comprehensive disapproval, for they are called wicked and are said to have followed evil customs (Canti-p., ccvii. 7560-61). Manu declares they were ksattriyas and became degraded because of the extinction of sacred rites and the absence of brahmans (x. 43 and 44); but this appears to be the opinion of a rather late age, for there does not seem to be any indication that the Kiratas ever set much store by those privileges. Considering their position and their affinities, it seems clear the Kiratas were tribes of the Mongolian family.

Utkala

The Utkalas were well-known, though not mentioned often in the Maha-Bharata. They are linked with the Mekalas (Bhisma-p., ix. 348; Drona-p., iv. 122; and Ramay., Kisk-k., xli. 14), and with the

Mekalas and Kalingas (Karna-p., xxii. 882). The position of Kalinga has been explained. The Mekalas inhabited the Mekal hills in the west and north of Chattisgarh. The Utkalas must therefore have occupied an intermediate position. From the passage quoted from the Raghu-Vamca with reference to Kalinga, it appears the Utkala territory stretched nearly as far as the R. Kapica or Cossye in Midnapur; that passage does not mean it reached that river, for it was only after he crossed that river that Raghu had occasion to accept the guidance of the Utkala kings. From these data and the positions assigned to Paundra and Odra; it may be inferred that Utkala comprised the hilly tracts from Balasore to Lohardaga and Sarguja.

The Utkalas were a hill tribe of rude habits. They stood by themselves and were not considered to have any close affinities with the races around them, except probably the Mekalas, because their origin was thrown back to the fabulous times of Ila (Hari-V., x. 631-2); hence they seem to have been an aboriginal race. According to the Raghu-Vamca which speaks of the Utkala *kings (loc cit.)*, they must have consisted of a number of clans, each governed by its own chieftain.

Various derivations have been suggested of the name Utkala, but it is worthy of note that Utkala and Mekala are linked together as if the two words possessed some element in common. These two tribes must apparently from their situation have been Kolarian tribes. Can it be that the termination in both names is to be identified with the word *Kol?*

Character of the Four Groups

In conclusion some conjectures may be put forward which the foregoing results tend to suggest.

The character of the four groups of nations may be summed up thus. Magadha, Videha and Vaicali seem to have been the outposts of Aryan conquest and colonization. Anga, Vanga, Kalinga, Pundra and Suhma with Tamalipta and Odra were kindered nations, which were not of Aryan stock and were not subjugated by the Aryas, but passed under Aryan influences and became Aryanized. Prag-jyotisa was a nation of Mongolian extraction. Utkala was a congeries of Kolarian tribes occupying the hilly tracts where they are still found.

I venture to suggest that we have here the results of the immigration of four different races.

The Utkalas, being so-called aboriginal tribes, must of course have come into this region first; and their position among hills also suggests the same inference. They must have been driven into the hills by later invaders.

American Example

Next probably came the Angas and their kindered nations. It seems most probable that they entered India from the Bay of Bengal, for their condition does not agree with the theory, that they were in the Ganges plain before and were driven eastward by the advancing Aryas. What happened in North America illustrates what we should expect to find, when one race invades and conquers others and takes possession of their territory on a large scale. As the pale-faces multiplied and forced their way westward, each tribe of Red Indians was broken and flung on the tribes behind it, and the tribes became involved in seething confusion. But nothing of that kind is to be perceived in the accounts of Anga and its kindered nations. On the other hand their possession of all the Ganges delta, their extension up the Ganges basin narrowing at their furthest limit, their spread along the Orissa sea-board, their occupation of the plains and their slight penetration into the hills—all these facts that these nations came from the sea, settled on the sea-coast and gradually carved out kingdoms inland. And if their names are not really derived from the alleged eponymous brothers but perpetuate original appellations, no doubt the termination of the names Anga, Vanga and Kalinga contains some common meaning.

Prag-jyotisas Descended from Mongolian Tablelands

Third came the invasion of the Prag-jyotisas. This seems the most probable order, because they did not push their way so far into India as the Angas, etc., and because all the accounts make them out to have been a powerful nation from the earliest times, which would hardly have been their condition, if they had preceded the Angas, etc., and been driven back towards the hills by them. They must have descended from the Mongolian tablelands through the passes along the north-east. They had a strong position in ancient times, but gradually disappeared so completely that no trace of their name, which is a singular one, seems to be discoverable. If, however, Kalidasa is right in the passage quoted in page 40. it indicates how Prag-jyotisa was dwindling away in his time. Pressed by the Pundras on the west, by the Vangas on the south, by the new Kama-rupas on the north-east, and probably by fresh Mongolian tribes on the north, the Prag-jyotisas were forced to retreat to the east side of the Brahmaputra, into the Garo and Khasi hills and into the district of Sylhet; and it is probably in that direction that the kirgdom must have perished.

Last Came the Aryas

Lastly came the invasion of the Aryas into Eastern India. Their conquering vigour seems to have spent itself by the time they subdued Videha and Magadha, for they had already passed through many generations in the plains of North India, and the enervating climate and easy conditions of life had surely, if slowly, modified the constitution which their ancestors had acquired in colder and hardier climes.

Note and Reference

1. It is in the light of this explanation that I would interpret the curious statement in Sabha-p., xxix. 1078, which Dr. Muir notices *(loc. cit.)*, that Bhima in his conquest of Eastern India went to a *Jalodbhava* country bordering on Himavat *(tato Himavatah parcvam samabhyetya jalodbhavam)*. In such a connexion *jalodbhava* surely cannot mean "of aqueous or oceanic origin", but might well mean "reclaimed from swamp".

2

The Law of Nations in Ancient India

M.K. Nawaz

It has not infrequently been stated by international lawyers that international law is a creation of the modern States of Europe and anyhow a product of Christian civilization.[1] Such an assertion implies that the ancient Nations had no conception of a law of nations. This view held by many writers is not supported by evidence. Historical research discloses that international law, like any law, has its own past and that it took shape among the ancient Nations. Historians of law maintain that the Jews, the Greeks and the Romans had a body of inter-state rules which regulated international relations. The body of rules may or may not be called 'International Law', but the fact remains that those rules governed the conduct of the ancient States.

According to Wheaton and Oppenheim, modern international law originated from the usages and practices of the Greek city States, the Roman Empire and the Jews.[2] The Asian legal system found no place in their treatises.[3] The Asian contribution to the history and science of the law of nations still remains to be assessed. Prof. Nussbaum recently made an effort to fill the gap. His treatise on the history of the law of nations refers to ancient legal practices; the law of nations of ancient India and of China is mentioned therein.[4] But the picture of international law in ancient India drawn by Prof. Nussbaum is far from being either perfect or complete. The learned author overlooks

Kautilya's Arthasastra which is the classic work on international law, and relations in ancient India. Manu's Dharmasastra is mentioned, but it is stated that that the rules propounded therein are not fortified by legal sanctions. It may be pointed out that such an attitude betrays the application of modern legal standards to an entirely different society and may not, therefore, lead to a proper evaluation, An examination of the State practice in ancient Indian Society reveals the existence of a remarkable body of inter-State rules. They were systematically expounded in books on polity, called Arthasastras and Dharmasastras.

Historical and ethnological investigations have testified to the existence of a number of international societies in the past.[5] These societies lived in isolation from each other, separated by geographical factors and racial considerations. Besides, common international interests of the modern type did not exist in the past to unify them. With the rapid progress of technological sciences and various means of the communication, the geographical boundaries and other barriers that separated these ancient societies disappeared and a truly universal family of nations came into existence. But in view of the fact that there existed in the past several international or quasi-international groups, the historian of law would have to study the legal system of each group of nations in order to evaluate their contribution to the growth and development of the law of nations.

The Family of Nations in India

Dr. Vincent Smith[6] writes that the real history of India commences in 327 B.C., the year of Alexander's invasion. He maintains that our knowledge of politico-legal conditions in the pre-Alexander period is based upon the Vedas and the Epics. Since the above-mentioned treatises are not historical or legal works, much reliance cannot justifiably be placed on them, and in case reference is to be made to them, one should make judicious use of the material therein. But nevertheless one can ill-afford to ignore altogether the material found in the Vedas and the Epics, as they alone furnish the source material for the pre-historic period.

The Indo-Aryans who occupied the northern portion of the sub-continent of India were divided into several groups called 'Janas' and formed a homogeneous society, knit together by racial and religious interests. The society depicted in the Vedic literature was tribal in character; it was only after the sixth century B.C. that the concept of territorial sovereignty superseded the tribal concept of State in ancient India.[7]

Historians and Indologists[8] state that there existed several monarchies and republics in India in the 6th cenutry B.C. Prof. Rhys Davids[9] writes that there were sixteen republics in northern India. The Indo-Aryans confined themselves to the territory of the Indus valley and Gangetic belt and only occasionally penetrated into the so-called Dravidistan, the territory occupied by the Dravidians to the South of the Vindhya mountains.

Herodotous, one of the earliest historians, was the first European to speak about the existence of a Family of Nations in ancient India. He wrote: 'The Indians are the last of all nations on the Eastern side of the World. . . . Indians are of many nations each speaking a different tongue.'[10] Similar views were expressed by Robert Ward, a historian of the law of nations of the late 18th century. Ward divides the human family into several international societies: 'the Gentoo (Hindu) Family of Nations' is one of them.[11]

Both the internal and external evidence point to the existence of a Family of Nations in ancient India. Ubi Societas ibi est jus. What were the rules that regulated the institutions of peace and war, neutrality, envoys, and treaties of that international society? And what was the basis of inter-State relations?

Kautilya's Arthasastra and Manu's Dharmasastra

Besides the Vedas, Kautilya's Arthasastra and Manu's Dharmasastra supplied the body of inter-State rules in ancient India. A correct appreciation of the twin sources and the time in which they were written is necessary for the proper understanding of the legal doctrines embodied therein.

Kautilya, also known as Chankya and Vishnugupta, the Chancellor of Chandragupta Maurya, is supposed to have written his treatise 'Arthasastra' some time between 321 and 300 B.C. It deals with the municipal legal system of the period and the rules relating to relations between rulers. It differs from Dharmasastra in that it is completely divorced from rules of a spiritual nature. This difference between the two has led many scholars[12] to regard 'Arthasastra' as the first secular treatise in the field of law. However this view has not remained unquestioned.[13] There are also writers[14] who compare Kautilya to Machiavelli and state that 'Arthasastra' and 'Le Prince' are two political treatises which embody in them 'methods from an amoralistic point of view'[15] and substitute the rule of force to the rule of law in international relations.

Arthasastra as Kautilya says in the very first chapter, is made as a compendium of almost all the Arthasastras, which, in view of the acquisition and maintenance of the earth, have been composed by ancient teachers'.[16] The Arthasastra rules, therefore, are not of Mauryan origin; they date from the pre-Mauryan period. The concluding part of Arthasastra reads as follows: 'Having seen discrepancies in many ways on the part of the writers of commentaries on the Sastras, Vishnugupta himself has made this Sutra and Commentary'.[17-18] From this passage it becomes clear that Kautilya wrote this treatise to remedy the errors of 'Sutra' and Sastra writers.

Many writers on Indian Polity state that the basis of international relations in ancient India is Dharma.[19] The expression 'Dharma' has no precise equivalent in English. It is denned as "the innate quality of the soul".[20] In this sense it may be equated with the law of nature. There is considerable expert opinion in support of the above interpretation.[21] The writers who based ancient international law on the edifice of Dharma declared that the king who infringed the rules of Dharma would entail the wrath of Gods. It is said that the fear of divine punishment acted as a sanction for the maintenance of the rule of law. The International law of the Greeks is also said to be based on similar foundations.

The above view, it is respectfully submitted, is not invulnerable. It is supported neither by Arthasastra nor by State practice in ancient India. It is true that the individual within the society, qua individual, was under the sway of Dharma. Dharma represents a way of life for a Hindu. It is calculated to secure good not only in this world but spiritual benefit after death.[22] But neither Dharma nor the divine sanctions underlying the norm of Dharma prevented a ruler in ancient India from pursuing the game of power politics described so vividly in Arthasastra.

The chapters of Arthasastra dealing with the theory of Mandala, the rules of espionage, Matsyanyaya (the rule of the fish) do not incorporate the rules of Dharma. The doctrine of Mandala was instrumental in the maintenance of what may be called the balance of power[23] and maintenance of peace in the society. It may, therefore, be said that the rules of international law embodies in Arthasastra were not based upon Dharma but upon power. The power-basis kept the several kings, aspiring for imperial status, in check and operated as an effective sanction for the observance of the rule of law. That this is so, becomes obvious by reference to a passage in Arthasastra which declares that strength is power and happiness is the end.[24]

Manu's Dharmasastra, the other important source in the study of the law of nations is said to be composed by Sumati Bhargava in the year 150 B.C. There are two chapters in Manu's Code which embody in them the various rules relating to political wisdom, methods of alliance, rules of chivalry and expediency. These rules do not vary in substance from those of Arthasastra. The passage, 'let him the king so arrange all his affairs that no ally, neutral prince or enemy may obtain any advantage over him; this in a few words is the sum of political wisdom,[25] occurs in Manu's Dharmasastra. The same might have as well occurred in Kautilya's Arthasastra. The uniformity of views and the identity of outlook denote that the ruler in Dharmasastra is as mindful of his territories and as eager to extend his dominions as the ruler or 'Vijigishu' in Arthasastra. International lawyers, if only they divorce rules of municipal law from rules of international law, would be able to discover the true basis of the law of nations in Dharmasastra. The rules of inter-State relations recorded in Manu's Code cannot be brushed aside as rules of 'Indian spirituality'[26] or 'priestly twaddle'.[27] In so far as those rules regulated inter-State relations in ancient India, they belong to the domain of what we describe as public law.

Impact of Buddhism

The precepts of Buddha effected significant changes in international relations in ancient India. Buddhism shook the basis of power-relations in the Indian State system and challenged the traditional legal doctrine. Buddhist literature found in Jatakas[28] and the Rock Edicts of Emperor Asoka furnish the material necessary to assess the impact of Buddhism on the Law of Nations. The Rock inscriptions could be considered part of the national archives of India.

Buddha emphasised the right conduct of the individual; he taught man the eightfold path which made him live in peace with his neighbour. Under the impact of the Dharma of Buddhism the talk about the war and the glory of conquest came to a standstill.[29] Buddha's doctrine of peace symbolised the practical wisdom of Kshatriya king to abolish war. The Dharma of Buddha, like the rule of law, applied to all individuals, whether the ruler or the ruled, and proved to be quite an effective sanction of law of nations. It became the cardinal faith of Emperor Asoka.

Peace and War

Kautilya classifies international relations in six divisions. They are: Sandha (peace), Vigraha (war), Asana (neutrality), Yana (marching), Samraya (alliance) and Dvadhibhava (making peace with one and waging war with another).[30] These divisions may be grouped under the general headings of peace and war.

After enumerating the six phases of international policy, Kautilya enunciates the various rules governing them. The most important doctrine that emerges from these rules is that of Mandala. Prof. Walter Ruben[31] states that the rules of Mandala regulated international relations cf a society of small state entities. They presuppose the State to be in a latent state of hostility. As such a concept implies that every neighbour is a potential enemy, various methods of self-preservation were suggested to meet the eventuality of war, and elaborate rules relating to alliance, neutrality, seizure, march of forces and strategic devices were laid down.

However, Kautilya, the realist as he was, laid emphasis on peace in international relations. He says: 'When the advantages derivable from peace and war are of equal character one should prefer peace; for disadvantages such as the loss of power and wealth, sojourning and sin are ever attending upon war.'[32]

The king is exhorted to adopt the four Upayas (means)—Sama (conciliation), Dana (gift), Bheda (dissension) and Dhanda (war)—to win over his opponent.[33] Resort to war is advised only when all other means had failed. Many institutions supplementary to the rules of war became salient features of the ancient law of nations. For example espionage was a highly developed institution. Arthasastra mentions several kinds of spies; Fraudulent disciple; Recluse; Householder; Merchant; Ascetic; Classmate; and lastly Mendicant woman.[34] The various spies in the employment of the king were required to report to him about the acts, peaceful or warlike, of a foreign king and furnish him with information relating to army, material prosperity and his popularity with the people. Manu says that the 'Charas' (spies) are the eyes of the prince. They are different from 'Dutas' (envoys)[35] and their chief function consists in playing intrigue with the foreign king.

War was a hallowed institution in the practice of the ancient law of nations. The members of the Kshatria community formed the standing army of the State.[36] They were exhorted to show valour and courage in war and maintain their strength and energy. Manu's advice to a king is in the following terms: 'Never to recede from combat, to protect the people and to honour priests; those rulers of the earth who, desirous of defeating each other, exert their utmost strength in battle, without averting their faces, ascend after death, directly to heaven.[37,38,39] These passages are reminiscent of a similar sentiment expressed in the Koran in connection with Jehad (Holy War).

Arthasastra contains several chapters which throw light on how battles should be fought, seizures organised and enemies overpowered. All these rules are anticipatory of Machiavellian precepts. Kautilya, in a significant passage notes: 'Whoever (king) is inferior to another shall make peace with him; whoever is superior in power shall wage war; whoever thinks no enemy can hurt me nor am 1 strong enough to destroy my enemy shall observe neutrality. This passage has given rise to critical comment. It was thought to be evidence for the proposition that there existed no law of nations in ancient India. It may be stated that the above dictum does not portray the universal practice of nations in ancient India. It is simply an advice given to the Vijigishu.[40] Since the underlying concept of Vijay (success) is only subjugation, but not conquest, there is nothing intrinsically reprehensible or unethical about it. An Indian writer[41] on the law of nations says it was only a theoretical proposition meant to inspire a conqueror made of the mettle of Alexander the Great, but not a rule of law evidencing State practice.

Concept of Chakravartin

After laying down the various rules relating to power politics, the author of Arthasastra holds before the Prince the ideal of Chakravartin (emperorship). The whole of India from the Himalayas to Cape Comorin constituted Chakravarti Kshetram[42] (sphere of empire) which could be subdued, though not annexed by the Chakravartin. It is a noteworthy feature of international relations of that period that war did not aim at debilitation, but only served to enhance the honour and dignity of a ruler. Kautilya writes: 'He (king) should never covet the land, things and sons and wives of the king slain by him; he should reinstate in their own estates the relatives of the king slain. . . . All conquered kings will, if thus treated, loyally follow the sons and grandsons of the conqueror.'[43]

The concept of Chakravartin remained engrafted in books of polity and symbolised an ideal. The significane of this concept consists in the role played by it in the several periods of Indian history; it survived the Kautilyan epoch and became the goal of all ambitious kings. The Pathan kings and the Moghul emperors of Hindustan adopted this concept and in their turn aspired to become Badshahs (emperors) of an all India empire.[44] It is a historical fact that the author of this concept installed Chandra-gupta on the throne of Magadha and assisted him in the establishment of a mighty empire, which in turn paved the way for a mightier empire, that of Asoka. Asoka might justifiably be called the first Chakravartin of India. His empire was not a centralised or unitary State; it was only a confederation of States. Within the empire there were States administered by the emperor, and States held in obeisance to him.[45] The relationship between the emperor and the rulers of the States who recognised the title of the emperor was regulated by certain usages and conventions. Those usages and conventions survived the Mauryan epoch and in fact provided the precedent for the doctrine of Paramountcy.

Just and Unjust Wars

Arthasastra never approved of all kinds of invasions. Kautilya classified invaders into three classes: Dharma Vijaya (just conqueror), Asura Vijaya (demon conqueror) and Lobha Vijaya (greedy conqueror), and highly disapproved of the conduct of the Asura and the Lobha invaders.[46] Alexander's invasion of India in 327 B.C. was likewise criticised by Indian jurists. Grotius referred to it in De Jure Belli ac Pacis. He wrote: 'Alexander, if he commenced war with the Persians and other people without cause, was deservedly called a brigand by the Scythians, according to Curtis, as also by Seneca; likewise by Lucan he was styled a robber, and by the sages of India, a man given over to wickedness.[47]

This is one of the earliest references in the classic law of nations in the West to the existence of customs and practices in the law of nations of ancient India. By the expression, 'the sages of India' Grotius might have been referreing to the authors of Sutras and Smritis.

Temperamenta Belli

Manu's Dharmasastra prescribed rules in the nature of Temperamenta Belli. It declares that a warrior should not strike an enemy alighted on the ground, an effeminate man, a person who sues for life with closed palms; one whose hair is loose and obstructs his sight; one who sits down fatigued. The code of Manu also prohibited the killing of non-combatants.[48] The existence of these rules of warfare[49] are corroborated by Megasthenes, the Greek ambassador at the Court of Pataliputra. Megasthenes wrote: 'Whereas among other nations it is usual, in the context of war, to ravage the soil and thus to reduce it to an uncultivated waste, among the Indians on the contrary. . . . the tillers of the soil even when the battle is raging in their neighbourhood are undistrubed by any sense of danger.'[50]

Status of Prisoners of War

The code of Manu proclaims that prisoners of war should not be killed.[51] It is also said in a literary work, Mudra Rakshasa, that Kautilya, the chancellor of Chandragupta set free prisoners captured in war by Chandragupta.[52]

In De Jure Belli, Gentili, one of the greatest international lawyers of the Elizabethan age, made a reference to Indian State practice on the subject of prisoners of war. Gentili wrote: 'When Porus, the most famous of Indian Kings was taken by Alexander and was asked what he wished Alexander to do with him, he replied that he wished to be treated like a king; being then asked what else he desires, he rejoined that everything was included in that speculation.'[53] Gentili in citing the above passage is indirectly giving evidence to the proposition that royal prisoners were treated differently from ordinary prisoners of war. It has already been noted that the kings of ancient India never lost their kingdoms even when they were defeated in a battle. Porus, in the above demand, may be said to be claiming his legal right to the throne of his kingdom based on the law and the usages of India. History records that Alexander reinstated Porus in his kingdom thus respecting the age-long usages of Indian State practice.

No-war Doctrine

The Thirteenth Rock Edict of Emperor Asoka records many important aspects of war in ancient India. It contains among other things the following declaration: 'Directly after the Kalingas had been annexed began His Sacred Majesty's zealous protection of the law of piety (Dhammo Vijaya), his love of that law and his inculcation of that law. Thence arises the remorse of His Sacred Majesty for having conquered the Kalingas, because the conquest of a country previously unconquered involves slaughter, death and carrying away captive of the people.[54] The great king[55] never waged war thereafter.

Indian historians claim that the above declaration is evidence of a 'No War' doctrine in ancient State practice. The policy of the king to renounce war and to propagate the Buddhist Dhamma only amounts to an expression of a sentiment; it cannot justifiably be elevated to the level of a rule of law. But what is significant to us is that the king unilaterally renounced war and in doing so laid down the foundations for a policy of peace in international relations. In one of his speeches on foreign policy, Mr. Jawaharlal Nehru refers to Emperor Asoka and says that the policy of peace which India is pursuing in international relations was laid down by the Great Emperor.[56]

Treaties of Peace and Hostages

Peace treaties are mentioned in Kautilya's Arthasastra. Kautilya writes: 'My teacher says that peace dependent upon honesty or oath is mutable, while peace with a security or hostages is immutable.'

'No', says Kautilya, 'peace dependent on honesty or oath is immutable both in this end and the next world. It is for this world only that security or a hostage is required for strengthening the agreement.'[57]

The passage refers to two legal institutions: treaties and hostages. Kautilya first declares that treaties of peace are inviolable both in this and the next world. Then he says, that, for strengthening an agreement or treaty in this world, a security is required. Does it mean that a treaty is inchoate or invalid in the absence of a security? Such an interpretation is quite plausible. Perhaps, it may also be in conformity with the letter and spirit of Arthasastra.[58]

Foreign Invasions

Alexander's invasion is the first major invasion in the international history of India. The invasion, as such, produced no significant changes in the legal system of India.[59] However, it lifted the veil that had hidden India from Europe. The historians and scientists who accompanied Alexander in his expedition to the East, carried knowledge of Indian philosophy and law, to Greece and made it known in the West. Alexander himself, in the hours of his triumph, was conquered by the soul of the East, says Prof. Humayun Kabir.[60] Will Durant write that Alexander introduced into Europe the oriental notion of the divine right of kings.[61]

The invasion paved the way for further invasions of India.

Seleukos, the successor to Alexander's dominions in India, followed Alexander's example in invading India, but was defeated by Chandragupta. The defeat of the Greek general resulted in a treaty of peace and cession between the two kings. By that treaty Seleukos ceded to Chandragupta the Greek settlements in India. It is also stated that Seleukos gave his daughter in marriage to the Indian Emperor.[62] The above-mentioned treaty, perhaps the first of its kind between an European and an Asian king, bears testimony to the existence of a developed treaty law in India.

Exchange of Embassies

The Greek invasion of Seleukos opened a new era of international contacts. Exchange of envoys between the Indian rulers and the Greek kings became a salient feature of the law of nations of the period. Megasthenes was the first European ambassador to arrive at the Court of Chandragupta. The report of Megasthenes is of outstanding value to the historian of law. It corroborates many of the rules laid down in Arthasastra and Dharmasastra.

The international contacts initiated by Chandragupta were continued by his son Bindusara. Prof. Rawlinson observes that there was regular correspondence between Bindusara and Seleukos. He also notes that when Bindusara asked the Greek king to send a sample of Greek wine, some raisins, and a sophist Seleukos seems to have written to him that he sends the wine with much pleasure but regrets that it is not good form among the Greeks to trade in philosophers.[63]

Asoka, the Emperor of India, sent his envoys to Egypt, Syria Macedonia and Ceylon with the message of Buddha. The Asokan envoys were religious missionaries; they were not much concerned with political affairs. Nevertheless, these missions gave an international character to the activities of an otherwise national religion.[64]

Ambassadors were exchanged between India and Rome in the early centuries of the Christian era. Gentili writes in De Jure Belli[65] that 'ambassadors from India came to Rome. . . .' Strabo, the Roman historian, states that an Indian Embassy came to Caesar Augustus in Rome to promote commercial relations between India and the Roman Empire. Indian luxury goods were in great demand with Roman upper classes during the period and the Roman traders or their agents came all the way to effect purchases.[66] Pliny, another Roman writer, notes in his book on 'Natural History' the drain caused by Indian trade to the Roman treasury.[67]

Foreigners in India

Indian polity displayed a far more liberal and rational outlook in the treatment of foreigners than the Greek legal system. It is common knowledge that the Greeks considered foreigners barbarians and deemed them to be their slaves.[68] In India foreigners enjoyed considerable privileges. Megasthenes wrote: 'Among the Indian officers are appointed even for foreigners, whose duty it is to see that no foreigner is wronged. Should any of them lose his health, they sent physicians to attend him and take care of him, and if he dies they bury him and deliver over such property as he leaves to his relatives.[69]

Foreign Trade

Many foreigners must have found India a good trading centre and settled down in commercial towns of India. Dr. Vincent Smith mentions in his 'Early History of India', that there existed a colony of Roman merchants in Madura, the Pandyan capital.[70]

The legal system of India provided many safeguards to foreign traders. Arthasastra states that foreigners importing merchandise should be exempted from being sued for debts unless they formed or entered local associations.[71] Does it mean that foreign traders enjoyed immunity from civil jurisdiction? Kautilya in another passage states that the superintendent of commerce could grant the remission of trade taxes.[72] The existence of these rules suggest that foreign trade was encouraged and many safeguards were provided for.

Maritime Jurisdiction

The State in ancient India realised the importance of maritime jurisdiction and provided rules to regulate navigation, ports, harbours and piracy.

Arthasastra has a special chapter on maritime jurisdiction.[73] An official, called the Superintendent of Ships was in charge of navigation. One of the first rules in this chapter reads: 'The Superintendent of Ships shall examine the accounts relating to navigation on boats sailing close to the shore (Samudra Samyana), and boats sailing in artificial or natural lakes'. The passage is of considerable significance. We may infer from it that the ancient State in India exercised jurisdiction in territorial waters and considered lakes and rivers as 'national waters'. The extent of the territorial belt was obviously not defined; but foreign ships sailing near the shore were considered to be within the territorial jurisdiction of the littoral State. So were ships in harbours; Arthasastra mentions that ships which touch harbours on their way may be required to pay the toll.

The most important passage of this chapter is the one on piracy. Arthasastra declares that Himsrika (pirate ships) should be destroyed. The rule against pirates is anticipatory of modern international law and is a praiseworthy feature of Arthasastra.

These are some of the rules relating to maritime jurisdiction. They are, however, far from being exhaustive. Kautilya himself states in a passage which occurs in the same chapter that the Superintendent of Ships should strictly observe the customs prevalent in commercial towns. It is difficult, if not impossible, to obtain information about the maritime customs which Arthasastra refers to. But it is certain that the ancient State in India knew a body of customary maritime law.

The maritime States in India are reported to have developed considerable sea power and to have made use of it for oversees colonisation. The Andhras seemed to have assumed the title of Sri Samudradhipati (Lord of three oceans), while the Zamorins of Calicut described themselves as the sovereigns of the sea.[74] The attitude of these maritime States indicates the anxiety of the rulers to assume jurisdiction over open seas also. But in the absence of any tangible evidence, we would not be justified in importing the theory of 'Mare Clausum' in ancient Indian State practice.

Conclusion

The foregoing survey establishes that Arthasastra apart from being a political treatise, contains a wealth of material on international law and that Kautilya was the first international jurist of India and indeed of Asia.

The ancient international legal system, as pointed out earlier, was based upon power relations and not on ethical or moral considerations.[75] State necessity and self-preservation were the paramount considerations in the life of the State.[76] It is but natural that in such a society primacy of place should have been given to the institution of war. War was within the natural order of the society; peace was rather an exception. This state of affairs was not the characteristic feature of Indian society alone; it was a general trait of all ancient societies.[77]

For the first time, it is the precepts of Buddha and the practice of Buddhist doctrines by Asoka that shook the basis of international relations in India. Peace then became the order of the day and war was renounced.[78] This, however, was only a temporary feature in the annals of Indian History. With the disappearance of Buddhism from the land of Buddha, the importance of Buddhist doctrines came to an end and the Arthasastra and Dharmasastra rules revived. Historians agree that the rules of law laid down in those twin sources formed the basis of international relations for the Hindu Kings of India.[79]

The advent of Islam in 712 A.D., opened a new chapter in the History of the Law of Nations in India. The Muslim rulers at the beginning of their career in India showed a propensity to follow the Islamic doctrines of the law of nations. But in course of time they gave up their zeal for Islamic law and adapted many international legal practices of the Hindus.[80] A study of the interaction of the two systems of law deserves separate treatment.

Notes and References

1. Oppenheim: *International Law* (7th edn.), Vol. 1, p. 68. Wheaton: International Law (8th edn.), p. 15.
2. Oppenheim: *op. cit.*, p. 68 et seq. Wheaton: *op. cit.*, p. 15 et seq.
3. The classic writers of International law evinced a keen interest in Asian legal systems. The works of Gentilli, Grotius and Vattel contain references to Asian legal practices. Vide: The Classics of International Law, edited by J.B. Scott (Carnegie Endowment Publications).
4. Arthur Nussbaum: *A Concise History of the Law of Nations* (Revised edn.), p. 3.
5. Dr. Schwarzenberger: *Power Politics* (2nd edn.), pp. 10, 25.
6. Dr. Vincent Smith: *Early History of India* (1914).
7. Beni Prasad: *The State in Ancient India* (1904), p. 23.
8. R. Shama Sastri: *Evolution of Indian Polity* (1920), p. 21.
9. Rhys Davids: *Buddhist India* (1911), p. 23.
10. Quoted by Prof. Rawlinson in 'Intercourse between India and the Western World', p. 21. *Note*: The Greek historian was obviously ignorant of the great civilization of China.
11. Robert Ward: *Foundation and History of the Law of Nations* (1795), p. 139.
12. Jayaswal: *Manu and Yagnavalkya*, p. 15.
13. Prof. V.R.R. Dikshitar: *Is Arthasastra Secular?*
14. Mr. Nehru compares Kautilya to Machiavelli but states that Kautilya was superior to Machiavelli in many respects. Vide: The Discovery of India by Jawaharlal Nehru, p. 93. See also 'Kautilya and Machiavelli' by Prof. Narender Krishna Sinha in Vol. I of this series.
15. Dr. Winterntz in Visvabharati (Quarterly), 1923.
16. *Arthasastra*, translation by Shama Sastri (1915), p. 1.

17-18. *Arthasastra, op. cit.*, p. 520.

19. S.V. Viswanatha, *International Law in Ancient India* (1925), p. 10. See also Prof. K.A. Nilakanta Sastri's '*International Law and Relations in Ancient India*' in the Indian Year Book of International Affairs (IYBIA), Vol. 1.

20 Prof. Rhys Davids: *Buddhist India*, p. 24.

21. Rangaswamy Aiyangar: *Raja Dharma* (1941), p. 25. Prof. Nilakanta Sastri holds the same opinion, vide International Law and Relations in Ancient India (IYBIA), Vol. I.

22. T.V. Mahalingam: *South Indian Polity*, p. 197.

23. Beni Prasad in an excellent dissertation on 'The State in Ancient India' maintains that the system of balance of power was known in ancient Indian State practice even before Kautilya described it in Arthasastra.

24. *Arthasastra op. cit.*, p. 324.

25. Jones, *Institutes of Manu* (1825), p. 214.

26. Nussbaum, *op. cit.*, p. 4.

27. Rangaswami Aiyangar, *op. cit.*, p. 68.

28. Rhys Davids, *Buddhist India*, Chapter 11.

29. The Fourth Rock Edict of Asoka records: 'Now by reason of the practice of piety instead of the war drum, the sound of the drum of piety is heard. Vide: Asoka, the Buddhist Emperor of India, by Dr. Vincent Smith, p. 159.

30. *Arthasastra, op. cit.*, p. 327.

31. Prof. Walter Ruben: *Inter-State Relations in Ancient India*, IYBIA, Vol. 4.

32. *Arthasastra, op. cit.*, p. 331.

33. Prof. R. Bhaskaran: *The Four Upayas of Hindu Diplomacy*, IYBTA, Vol. 3.

34. *Arthasastra, op. cit.*, p. 20.

35. For a detailed study of the institution of 'Duta' see Visvanatha, International Law in Ancient India, Ch. IV and H.S. Bhatia, International Law and Practice in Ancient India.

36. Chandragupta Maurya is reported to have maintained a standing army of 700,000 men. Vide: *Cambridge History of India*, Vol. 1, p. 223.

37-39. *Dharmastra, op. cit.*, p. 200.

40. *Note:* Prof. Ruben writes that the expression 'Vijigishu' connotes success, and not conquest. Vide, Ruben's article on Arthasastra.

41. Bandopadhayaya: *International Law and Customs in Ancient India*, p. 160.

42. *Arthasastra, op. cit.*, p. 412.

43. *Arthasastra, op. cit.*, p. 381.

44. M.K. Nawaz, *Legal Aspects of Anglo-Moghul Relations*, IYBIA, Vol. 5.

45. *Cambridge History of India*, Vol. 1, p. 514.

46. *Arthasastra, op. cit.*, p. 461.

47. *The Classics of International Law* (1925), De Jure Belli ac Pacis, Vol. 2, p. 170.

48. *Dharmasartra, op. cit.*, p. 200.

49. W.S. Armour, *Customs of Warfare in Ancient India*, Transactions of Grotius Society, Vol. 8.
50. McCrindle, *Megasthenes and Arrian*, p. 33.
51. *Dharmasastra, op. cit.*, p. 200.
52. Prof. Dikshitar, *War in Ancient India*, p. 72.
53. *The Classics of International Law* (1933), De Jure Belli Libri Tres, p. 354.
54. Vincent Smith, *Asoka, The Buddhist Emperor of India*, p 24.
55. The greatness of Asoka is referred to by H.G. Wells in the following terms; Amidst tens of thousands of names of monarchs that crowd the columns of history, the name of Asoka shines and shines almost alone like a star . . . 'More living men cherish his memory today than have ever heard the names of Constantine or Charlemagne'. Vide: Outlines of World History by H.G. Wells, p. 402.
56. *The Hindu* (Madras), 30-11-1955.
57. *Arthasastra, op. cit.*, p. 381.
58. Prof. T.M.P. Mahadevan holds the view that treaties of peace were considered inviolable by Arthasastra. Vide: '*Kautilya on the Sanctity of Pacts*', IYBIA: Vol. 5.
59. It should however be noted that it was the invasion which provided the impetus for the unity of India under Chandragupta. It is also said that it was the example of Alexander which inspired Chandragupta. Vide: *Cambridge History of India*, Vol. 1, p. 385.
60. Prof. Humayun Kabir: *The Indian Heritage*, p. 7.
61. Will Durant: *The Story of Philosophy* (Packet edn. 1953), p. 97.
62. *Megasthenes and Arrian* (1877), p. 10.
63. Rawlinson: *Intercourse between India and Western World*, p. 39.
64. B.C. Law: *Indological Studies*, Part 2 (1952), p. 173.
65. *The Classics of International Law* (1933), De Jure Belli, p. 9.
66. *Vishwanatha, op. cit.*, p. 79.
67. K.A.N. Sastri, *Foreign Notices of South India*, 1939, p. 5.
68. Coleman Phillipson: *The International Law and Customs of Ancient Greece and Rome*, p. 40.
69. Megasthenes: *Fragments*, pp. 44, 45.
70. Vincent Smith: *Early History of India*, p. 443.
71. Arthasastra, *op. cit.*, p. 119.
72. *Ibid.*
73. *Ibid.*, pp. 156-59.
74. K.M. Panikkar: *Geographical Factors in Indian History* (1955), p. 64.
75. See Dr. Schwarzenberger, *op. cit.*, p. 205, seq.
76. *The History and Culture of the Indian People—The Age of Imperial Unity* (1951), p. 317.
77. Dr. U.R. Ehrenfels: *Is War a General Trait of Human Nature?* IYBIA Vol. 1.
78. Sunder Kabadi writes in a recent article on Asoka as follows: 'Asoka spoke

from his throne in the Council Chamber. His exact words are not known but in effect this is what he said, "I am sick of carnage: Never again I will draw the sword except to repel an invader. I renounce conquest, I denounce War. I shall give my people peace and not conflict." Vide: *The Indian Express* (Delhi), 18th June 1957.

79. R.C. Majumdar: *Ancient India* (1952), p. 146.

80. C.L. Tupper writes: 'In conceptions of sovereignty we (British) are the heirs of the Moghuls, and they were the heirs of the Hindu Rajas'. Vide: Tupper's 'Our Protectorates' (1893), p. 129.

3

The Village Headman in Ancient India

D.K. Ganguli

The system of carrying on the village administration through a headman, which was a fairly popular institution in ancient India, seems to be as old as the *Rgveda*,[1] for it mentions the term *gramani* twice and uses it in the sense of a village headman at least in X. 107.5.[2] That the office continued throughout the Vedic period appears clear from its references in the later Vedic texts like the *Satapatha Brahmana* and *Taittiriya Samhita*.[3] It cannot be definitely ascertained whether the village headman owed his position to the crown or to a popular election by his co-villagers. The analogy from the primitive society, the absence of any reference to him as a royal servant in the Vedas and the etymological meaning of the term[4] may possibly indicate that the *gramani* was then elected by the community to which he was accountable.

Functions of Headman

Of the functions of *gramani* the Vedas tell us very little. As these texts represent him as leading the villagers to the battlefield, we may infer that one of his duties consisted in defending the village against aggressions from without and rendering military assistance, to the king. There is no indication in the Vedic literature that he was connected with the revenue administration. R.S. Sarma[5] is of the opinion that he did not act in that capacity in those days, as the revenue function in the contemporary period was performed, according to him, by an officer called *bhagadugha*. The observation of R.S. Sarma is applicable to the later Vedic period, but not to the early age when the office of the *bhagadugha* was not yet in vogue. Although the positive evidence is not forthcoming, the *gramani* was probably connected with the fiscal function in the early Vedic age. The nature of his work implies that the headman normally belonged to the Ksatriya caste. That the Vaisyas, too, some time aspired for and obtained this post is testified by the *Taittiriya Samhita*.[6] Despite the meagreness of details about him, it seems that the *gramani*, as one among the *ratnins*, was regarded as an important functionary of the state. That the post carried with it considerable power and position is further evidenced by the *Taittiriya Samhita*[7] which observes that 'the prosperous are three indeed, viz., the learned *brahmana*, the village headman *(gramani)* and the *rajanya* (warrior).[8]

Under Royal Control

The Jatakas[9] and a few Brahmanical texts provide us interesting glimpses into the office of the village headman, mentioned in most of the contemporary texts as *gramabliojaka*, in the post-Vedic period. Then he was no longer an elected official of the villagers but had already been brought under royal control. That he was a royal nominee by this time is borne out by the *Kharasara Jataka*[10] which describes him as an *amacca* of the king and *Kaiuvaka Jataka*[11] which leaves the impression that such an official could be appointed or removed by the crown alone. In the post-Vedic period we find the headman more concerned with the security of the people than anything else. That he could hardly have been indifferent towards the law-breakers is evidently clear from the *Kharasara Jataka*[12] which refers to an officer who was punished by the crown 'as he with his own people went to the forest, leaving the villagers at the mercy of robbers'. Apastamba[13] says that the village officers were to protect the village from thieves up to a distance of one *krosa* on all sides. If any theft occurred within these limits the officer was required to make good the loss. He had hardly any opportunity to act despotically in the discharge of his duties. Sometime the king used to exercise direct control over him as is testified by the *Vinaya Pitaka* which states that king Bimbisara once summoned all the 80,000 *gramikas* of his kingdom to instruct them in worldly things (*ditthadhammike at the anusasitva*).[14] The Jatakas often represent the headman as exercising judicial powers, for we find him in these texts settling disputes, making the guilty pay fine,[15] issuing prohibitions against the slaughter of animals *(maghatan karapesi*) and against the sale of intoxicating liquors.[16]

Status in Maurya Period

The *Arthasastra*[17] shows that in the Maurya period the headman was called *gramika*, *gramakuta*, *gramasvamin* and *gramamukhya*. He is, however, not included in the text in the list of salaried officials[18] and this has given rise to the speculation[19] that the village official was not a royal nominee in the Maurya period. Such a theory does not appear to be tenable, because, the Jatakas, as we have seen earlier conclusively prove that long before the days of Kautilya, the headman had already been brought under royal control. It is interesting to note that the term *gramika*, which is used in the *Arthasastra* as one of the designations for the headman, etymologically means, according to the *Vacaspatya*, an officer, appointed to look after the village. In return for his service to the government he was, no doubt, remunerated, but the early texts leave us in the dark about the ways in which he was rewarded. Kautilya[20] appears to be the first among the ancient Indian writers to deal with this problem, and he prescribes that he was to receive rent-free land for his living. By the time of the Mauryas the *gramika* had evidently no direct contact with the central authority, and he was to work under the direction and supervision of the *gopa*.

The office of the headman continued to be popular in the post-Maurya age. In this period we have for him a variety of designations; Manu[21] calls him *gramasyadhipati* and *gramika*, *Kamasutra*[22] *gramhdhipati*, Sukra[23] *gramaneta*, *Milindapanho*[24] *gramasamika*, *Gatha Saptasati*[25] *gramani* and Mathura Votive epigraph[26] *gramika*. About his appointment in this period we find the continuation of the same practice as in the previous epoch. Manu[27] informs us that the appointment of the *gramika* was a royal prerogative. Visnu[28] also speaks of the appointment of a headman for each village by the king.

Office Becomes Hereditary

Our sources would tend to show that the office of the village headship was normally hereditary in this period. The *Gatha Saptasati*[29] alludes to the succession to the office of the father by his son. A similar case of two generations of *gramikas* is likewise mentioned in a Jain Votive[30] inscription from Mathura of the time of the Kusana king Vasudeva. It would, however, be wrong to suppose that the office of the village headman was always hereditary. The protection of the life and property of the villagers was undobtedly the most important duty of the headman. The *Gatha Saptasati*[31] narrates how a village headman led an expedition against some external forces who had endangered the peace of the locality. The military function of the *gramika* was not always encouraged by the government. Manu,[32] for instance, is not in favour of entrusting him with the defence of the locality. He ordains that in the midst of two, three, five or a hundred villages the king should station military outposts which were to look after the security of villages. Though relieved of his military duty, a village headman could hardly have been indifferent towards the law-breakers. Gautama[33] lays down that when a theft was committed, the king should recover the lost property and return it to the owner, and if he fails to secure the stolen articles, he has to pay its value to the householder. Manu[34] seems to imply that whenever a crime of theft was committed within a village, the headman had to enquire about it and take the necessary steps to detect the culprit. In case of his failure to apprehend the thieves, he, without undue haste, was to report the case to the chief of ten villages for better action. Sukra[35] enjoins the *gramanetr* to be alert in protecting the villagers with paternal care from thieves, robbers and greedy officers.

Village Headman under the System of Manu

In the post-Maurya period the village headman was connected with the revenue administration in most of the localities. Manu[36] definitely assigns to him the fiscel duty, for he was to collect royal dues in the from of grain, drink and fuel. *Milinda-panho*[37] also suggests that the village headman was empowered to realise royal revenue. As it has been shown already, the headman was entitled to get rent-free land for his living in the Maurya period. But the practice of assigning land to him has been opposed by Manu,[38] according to whom, the articles of food, drink and fuel that were payable daily to the king by the villagers should be given to him. A headman could hardly become a tyrant under the system of Manu. From his statement that the *gramika* had to keep the *dasagramapati* well informed of the thefts and crimes *(cauradidosan)* within his jurisdiction, it appears that he had to work under the guidance of the latter. But that was not the only check to the power of the headman. Manu enjoins that the king should appoint a minister to keep a vigilant watch at the activities of this officer *(tesan gramyani karyani prthak karvani caiva hilrajno'npah sacixah snigdhastani pasyedatandritahjj)*. The *Manusanhita* is silent as to the caste of the headman but the *Sukranitisara* declares that the headman should be a Brahmana. It, however, seems that the post of the *gramani* was not preserved for a particular caste, but left open to the member of the three upper castes.

In Gupta Period

The office of the headman was bereft of much of its poplarity in the Gupta period, and confined to restricted areas, as may be inferred from its scanty notices in the contemporary records. The Supia pillar inscription[39] of the time of Skandagupta speaks of a *gramika* named Varga whose father and grandfather were bankers *(osresthin)*. Are we to infer on the evidence of this record that the post of the *gramika* was not hereditary in those days? The case seems to heve been just the reverse, for in the Gupta period most of the posts were bequeathable from father to son. The *gramika* still then continued to play an important role in the revenue administration at least in some areas because his name finds mention in connection with the gift of land in a Damo-darpur copper plate grant[40] of the reign of Buddhagupta and the Maitraka charters from Gujarat, where he is called *gramakuta*.

Saletore[41] holds, on the strength of an inscription of Hastin from Bhumra,[42] that one of the duties of the village headman of the Gupta period consisted in the setting up of boundary pillars. The Bhumra record, however, does not conclusively prove Saletore's contention, because, it mentions that a boundary pillar was erected by Sivadasa, who was not himself a *gramika* but a son of a headman. Even then we may presume that as the state functionary in the village (although the number of such villages was negligible in this period) the *gramika* might have acted as an arbitrator in case of any boundary dispute among the villagers.

Barring the inscriptions of the Rastrakuta kings the records of the later period rarely mention the village headman. The *Harsacarita* and *Rajatarangini* do not contain any reference to him. The inscriptions of the Palas[43] and Senas, which are quite numerous, refer to a large number of officials, but they rarely mention the headman; such is also the case with the Ganga records from Orissa, Pratihara records from Western and Northern India, Calukya records from the Deccan and Cola inscriptions from South India. The paucity of reference to him makes it almost certain that the post of the headman was retained in this period only in a few villages, and since our sources mention him invariably in connection with the grant of land, he seems to have been concerned with the revenue administration in this age also.

Enormous Power and Position Acquired

But the Rastrakuta records present to us an altogether different picture of the village headman, and they show that the office was not only popular but carried with it enormous power and position. Inscriptions reveal that the most important duty of the Rastrakuta headman, called *gramakuta* in Maharashtra and *gavunda* in Karnataka, was to defend the village from the enemies from both within and without. In order to discharge his duty properly he sometimes used to maintain a militia.[44] Inscriptions refer to the headmen and members of the village militia as laying down their lives for the sake of defending their villages. In addition to his military function the *gramakuta* was also associated with the village revenue, as may be guessed from the fact that the Rastrakuta records invariably mention him in connection with land grant. As regards his remuneration we have evidence to show that two systems were followed simultaneously—he enjoyed rent-free lands, in addition to the taxes in kind which were payable to the king.

Ordinarily there was only one headman in charge of each village. The inscriptions of the Rattas of Saundatti and of the later Calukyas,[45] however, show that some localities in Karnataka had several such headmen. It seems that this unusual system was 'probably due to the necessity of accommodating the claims of the numerous branches of the original family.[46]

Notes and References

1. X. 107. 5. D.N. Jha *[Revenue System in Post-Maurya and Gupta Tunes* (Calcutta, 1967). p. 160j opines that the office of the village headman goes back to the latter Vedic period
2. V. 4.4.19.
3. II. 5.4.4.
4. *Vacaspatya*, 2771-2.
5. *Aspects of Political Ideas and Institutions in Ancient India* (Banaras, 1959), p. 108.
6. II. 5.4.4.
7. II. 5.4.4.

8. P.V. Kane, *History of Dharmasastra*. III, p. 153.
9. I. pp. 199, 483; II. p. 135; IV. p. 115.
10. I. 354.
11. I. p. 98.
12. S.K. Maitra, *The Social Organisation in North-East India in Buddha's Time* (Calcutta, 1920), p. 162.
13. II. 10. 26.6-7.
14. I. 483.
15. IV. 115.
16. IV. 115.
17. III. 10; IV. 6; IV. 4.
18. V. 3.
19. H.C. Raychaudhuri, *Political History of Ancient India* (Calcutta, 1953), pp. 292-3.
20. II. 1.
21. VII. 115, 116.
22. V. 5.5.
23. II. 120-21.
24. p. 147.
25. I. 30-1; VII. 24.
26. Luders' List, no. 48.
27. VII. 114.
28. Jolly's Samskrit text, Bk. HI.
29. VII. 31.
30. Luder's List, no. 48.
31. VII. 32.
32. VII. 114. While commenting on this passage Kulluka says *'dvayoriti-dvayor-gramayorammadhye trayanan va gramanan Pacanan va gramasatana va gulman raksitrpurusasmuhan satyapradhana-purusadhisthitan rastrasya sangrhan raksuthanan kuryat.'*
33. X. 46-7.
34. VII. 116.
35. II. 170.
36. VII. 118.
37. pp. 147, 163.
38. VII. 118. Kulluka points cut that he was entitled to get the miscellaneous taxes in kind but not a portion of the annual revenue *(yam anna-panendhanadim gramavasibhih pratyahan rajne deyani, na tu avadakaran—dhanyanamastamo bhagah ityadikan tani gramadhipatih vrttarihyan grhniyatj*). R.S. Sarma, *Aspects of Political Ideas and Institutions in Ancient India* (Banaras, 1959), p. 172 observes, 'But we notice two important changes in the office of the village headman in Manu . . . Secondly, the *gramika* was paid not in the shape of fines realised from the villagers, as in pre-Mauryan times, or in cash salary as the *gramabhrtaka* in Maurya times, but in grant of a piece of land'.

This observation is based on the wrong interpretation of the relevant passages of the *Manusanhita*.

39. *EI*. XXXIII, p. 307.
40. *EI*, XV. No. 7.
41. *Life in the Gupta Age*, p. 298.
42. *CII*, III, no. 24.
43. A *gramika* is mentioned in the Amagachhi grant of Vigrahapala III.
44. A.S. Altekar, *The Rastrakutas and their times* (Banaras, 1934), p. 192.
45. *Ibid*., pp. 189-91.
46. A.S. Altekar, *State and Government in Ancient India* (Banaras, 1955), p. 220. A.S. Altekar (*ibid*., p. 220) distinguishes *gramika* from *gramapati* on the ground that the latter term is used in the sense of 'alienees of government revenues', but this may not be correct. Gramapati literally means the lord of the village *(gramasya patih);* Manu uses a similar term (gramasya-dhipati) in the sense of the village headman. Just as *visayapati* means an officer connected with a *vishaya gramapati* may similarly denote an officer-in-charge of the village.

4

Jails and Jail Administration in Kautilya

B.K. MAJUMDAR

Arthasastra. The Earliest Codification of Laws in India

The Arthasastra of Kautilya, though its date and authorship is still a matter of controversy, must be regarded as a comprehensive work dealing with law, statecraft, economics and military system. The administrative machinery described in Kautilya is considered to be that of a highly organised State. The functions of the state (rastra) in ancient India was not simply protection and policing but also the furtherance of the material needs and happiness of the people. The subject—Jails and Jail administration—forms part of Criminal justice and Police. Before we discuss Kautilya's treatment of the subject, it is necessary to explain the character of the Arthasastra laws. It is often rightly urged that the Arthasastra is the earliest attempt at codification of laws in India. The laws emanating from the Srutis and embodied in the Dharmasutras are for the most part customary laws. The law of crimes was non-existent. Murder and other crimes were offences, mere torts, i.e. compoundable offences and could be expiated by fines. In the Age of Arthasastra, the law come to be divided clearly into two sections, viz., (1) the Dharma, Dharmasthiya of civil law laid down in Book III of the Arthasastra, and (2) the regal, Kantaka-Sodhana or Criminal laws laid down in Book IV of the Arthasastra.

For the administration of the regal Kantaka-Sodhana or Criminal laws there were royal ministers (amatyas) and Kantaka-Sodhana Commissioners. The jurisdiction of these Commissioners was sufficiently wide and one of their functions was the supervision of thefts of all descriptions. With the consolidation of the state in Northern India and emergence of imperial governments and elaboration of royal powers, new offences were created and a Kantaka-Sodhana Code came into existence.[1] In criminal cases the punishment awarded in ancient India was of seven kinds, viz. (1) fine, (2) Imprisonment, (3) whipping, (4) physical torture, (5) banishment, (6) condemnation to work in the mines, and (7) death.[2]

Interesting Jail Regulations

Kautilya has preserved for us an account of the police or security measures to be adopted by the king, although it should be aptly added that in the age of the Arthasastras, there was hardly any distinction between civil and military policing. According to the writer of the Arthasastra in question, police headquarters were set-up in all principal centres of the kingdom where there were also law-courts. There was a *sthaniya* in the midst of 800 villages, a *dronamukha* in the midst of 400 villages, a *kharvata* in the midst of 200 villages and a *Sangrahana* in the midst of 10 villages.[3] Matters relating to jails and jail regulations have only been hinted at in literature both Vedic and post-Vedic. The Arthasastra, however, contains greater details about jails and jail regulations. In the capital city, if not in all important administrative units, there must have been jails for the detention of under-trial prisoners. Kautilya mentions the Superintendent of jails and refers to "Charaka" (lock-up) and bandhangara (prison house). The jail regulations as portrayed in Kautilya are interesting enough. They show elaborate arrangements for the administration of jail affairs. Scrupulous performance of duties by the officers-in-charge of jails has been insisted upon. Their duty to take proper care of the inmates of the jails has been emphasised. The provision of several kinds of punishment for jail officers ill-treating the prisoners and neglecting their duties looms large. Transfer of prisoners from one jail to another was prohibited. Escape from jails was severely dealt with.[4]

Kautilya's statement about fines for offences varied according to circumstances and were proportionate to the gravity of the crime. His first amercement meant a fine ranging from 48 to 96 panas, the middle-most from 200 to 500 panas and the highest from 500 to 1,000 panas.[5]

It is interesting to note that the jail delivery, release and relief of prisoners was not unheard of in the days of the Mauryas. While issuing instructions to Rajukas Asoka speaks of *Danda-amata* (uniformity of punishment) and *Vyavahara-Samata* (uniformity of legal procedure) and enjoins to the condemned men laying in prison under sentence of death a respite of three days.[6] This shows Asoka's anxiety to give relief even to prisoners awaiting capital punishment. As suggested by Hultzsch, Asoka gave amnesty to criminals at the time of the anniversary of his coronation. As many as twenty-five jail deliveries are reported to have been effected by the emperor.

Prisoners Set Free on Auspicious Occasions

Kautilya perhaps records ancient Indian sentiments and practices about the jail delivery when he details the duties of the Nagaraka (Officer-in-charge of the city) corresponding possibly to Strabo's Magistrates in charge of the city.

He writes:

> 'On the days to which the birth star of the king is assigned, as well as on full moon days, such prisoners as are young, old, diseased or helpless (anatha) shall be let out from the bandhanagara, or those who are of charitable disposition or who have made any agreement with the prisoners may liberate them by paying an adequate ransom. . . . Whenever a new country is conquered, when an heir apparent is installed on the throne, or when a prince is born to the king, prisoners are usually set free."[7]

References to jails and prisons are found in the earlier Buddhist Canonical work Mahavagga[8] (The Great Section I. 42) which deals incidentally with thefts, sexual offences, etc. Later works like Manu-Samhita (Chapters VII and VIII) and other Smritis have mentioned the subject in connection with the administration of justice. In the circumstances, there is some scope for a detailed study of this branch of administration which is associated with law and order and forms an integral part of the executive government in any state.

Notes and References

1. Kautilya: Dr. N.C. Banerjee, pp. 71-74.
2. *Public Administration in Ancient India*, Dr. P.N. Banerjee, Chapter XII, p. 166.
3. Kautilya, Bk. II, Chapter 26.

4. Arthasastra, Book IV, Chapter IX, Shyama Sastri's tr., p. 273.
5. *Ibid.*, Shyama Sastri's tr. p. 181 fn.
6. Pillar Edit No. IV.
7. Arthasastra, Bk. II, Chap. XXXIII, Shyama Sastri's tr., p. 179.
8. "As regards the chronology of the different texts constituting the canon, the Mahavagga and Chullavagga are evidently anterior to the period of Asoka, as they are silent about the Third Buddhist Council", *The Age of Imperial Unity*, p. 408.

5

Buddhist India and Rest of the World

I
BUDDHISM AS AN INTERNATIONAL LINK

T.N. RAMACHANDRAN

Indian International History cannot be considered apart from the history of Asia from which peninsular India derived stimulus, nor can the cultural and political history of Asia be considered without reference to the influence of India. Though the Himalayan barrier appears to give India an aspect of geographical exclusiveness, in reality, it was not so. There were and are still routes from China along the Brahmaputra to Assam. From Sikkim it is possible to reach Tibet. Further west were routes from Turkistan to Kashmir which were used by Chinese pilgrims and other travellers who visited all the places in India associated with the life of the Buddha, or who came to study at or visit one or other of the great Buddhist Universities which were founded in ancient India such as at Nalanda, Taxila, etc. The Karakorum Pass was one such route from Asia into Trans-Indus Kashmir. The importance of these routes lay in the fact that they were effective channels for the cultural and political contacts and spread of Buddhism and Buddhist art from India, the place of Buddha's birth, into Central Asia, China, Tibet and Nepal. What looms large in the formation of Indian civilization and international image in the dark centuries before Alexander's invasion of India is the advent of the Buddha, "the supremely enlightened", in the 6th century B.C. the simple human aspect of whose life and teachings appealed spontaneously to the masses and indigenous tribes of India. The teachings of the Buddha were spread by Buddhist envoys not only in Afghanistan, Central Asia, China, Tibet and Nepal, but also in Ceylon, Burma, Siam and Indonesia. These envoys proved to be ambassadors of goodwill and understanding between India and other nations.

Afghanistan and N.W. Frontier

In the early centuries of the Christian era North-Western India and Afghanistan formed a single homogenous cultural and political area. It was the centre of a flourishing Buddhist art represented by sculptures of clay and stucco such as those discovered at Hadda near Jalalabad and at Kunduz on the Oxus Plain. Stucco Buddhas and Bodhisattvas found here present stylistic affinity with Buddhist finds from Taxila in North Punjab. As a result of cultural contacts between India and the Graeco-Roman West in the early centuries A.D. were introduced in North-West India elements from Graeco-Roman art which became a part of the composite Buddhist art of the period. The relevant remains of this art are grouped into two phases: an earlier phase, represented mostly by *stone* sculpture and known as 'Gandhara art' from the ancient name of the frontier-region which centred upon the site of the modern Peshawar; and a later phase, represented mostly by sculptures in *clay* and *stucco*, which has been called the 'Afghan School' from the fact that its geographical centre of dispersion lies in the neighbourhood of Jalalabad in Eastern Afghanistan. The two phases betray an admixture of Western features with an art which was essentially Indian. The Western element is particularly evident in the 'Apolline' rendering of the hair, in the *toga*-like drapery, and in the use of *atlantes*, *putti* and festoons of Hellenistic type. Occasionally the foreign element is uppermost, but the Western features are subordinated to Indian spiritual ideas and expression which are remote from those of the classical world.

Central Asia

Chinese Turkestan, otherwise called 'the innermost Heart of Asia', forms a vast basin 1500 miles by 600 miles, through which passed two great trade-routes from China, a northern route through Kucha, Karashahr (which is the ancient Agnidesa) and Turfan and a southern route through Yarkand, Khotan, Niya, Miran, etc., these two trade routes finally meeting at Tun-huano on the western border of China. These trade routes are also called 'silk routes' and were the principal means of communication between India and China for a thousand years. They were known to Yuan-Chwang who is said to have reached India by the northern route and returned to China by the southern route. The cities along these routes may be described as stages in a pilgrim's progress, the pilgrim being in the present case the Buddhist. Central Asia has been the meeting ground of many different races, arts, trades, national ideas and languages—Graeco-Bactrian, Iranian, Indian and Chinese Archaeological explorations in Central Asia have revealed a wealth of material in the shape of specimens of Buddhist Art and manuscripts in Sanskrit, Chinese, Syriac, Soghadian, Turkish and in unknown languages such as Tocharian and Khotanese. These were truly international meets of economic, cultural and political envoys in the modern parlance.

Sir Aurel Stein's three expeditions to Central Asia are well known. In 1900-01 he worked mainly at Khotan in the southwestern part of the desert. In 1906-08 he proceeded further east across the Taklamkan desert and reached Tun Huang, where he found artificial caves, about 500 cells of various dimensions, known as the "Caves of the Thousand Buddhas". A walled-up chapel of about 500 cubic feet capacity was found packed with a library of manuscripts and hundreds of fine paintings on silk. Some of the silk-paintings recovered are now deposited in the Central Asian Antiquities Museum, New Delhi. During this second expedition, he excavated at Khotan and Domoko, where Sanskrit manuscript-remains of the T'ang period were found, and at Niya, a site abandoned since the 3rd century A.D., where rich discoveries of wooden documents in Kharoshthi script and in a Prakrit dialect were made. The explorations at the Lou-lan site at Miran yielded an abundance of written records in Chinese and Kharoshthi.

During the third expedition (1913-16) he explored these sites again and extended the scope of his operations, visiting on his way back Sistan (ancient Sakasthana or the home of the Scythians) where he discoverd at Kohikhoja in the remains of a large Buddhist monastery fresco-paintings of the Sassanian period. His explorations coupled with those of French, Russian and German archaeologists, have furnished interesting materials relating to the culture of the country which formed the connecting link between the West and the Far East on the one hand and India on the other, and witnessed the intermingling of Indian, Iranian, Greek and Chinese currents of civilization and political philosophies. India played a preponderant role in this cultural and diplomatic relations, mainly through the influence of Buddhism. The artistic remains from Khotan and other places show indeed the progressive diffusion of Buddhist ideas throughout the Far East. Many Buddhist Sanskrit manuscripts, of which the originals are lost in India, have been recovered either in original or in ancient translations from the desert-sands. Local varieties of Indian scripts have also come to light, as also of an Indian Prakrit spoken over a large area of Central Asia.

Some of the more interesting remains include a Kharoshthi manuscript of the Prakrit *Dhammapada* written on birch-bark leaves in a script of the 2nd century A.D., in a Prakrit dialect unknown in any other Buddhist literary work. Numerous wooden documents in Kharoshthi characters were found at the Niya site, showing that Prakrit was the official language down to the beginning of the 4th century A.D., over a wide area in south-eastern Turkestan, extending from Khotan to the western extremity of the Lobnor region.

The Kharoshthi documents from south-eastern Turkestan are written on wooden tablets, leather, paper and silk. The wooden documents are mostly on wedge-shaped tablets known as *kila-mudra*, and were used as short communications of an official nature. The writing was in ink and done with wooden pens and related mostly to state affairs.

Indian Brahmi also figures as one of the scripts widely known in Central Asia. A manuscript of the dramas of Asvaghosha written about the 2nd century A.D., in the Brahmi of the Kushan period, one of *Udanavarga* written in the script of the 3rd century A.D., another manuscript of the book *Kalpana-manditika* by Kumarlata written in the script of the 4th century A.D., and the famous Bower manuscript, comprising several Indian medical texts belonging to the 4th or 5th century A.D., are the most important of the finds from Central Asia which provide proof of the extensive Indian connections with those far-off regions in ancient times.

China

India and China, knew each other from the earliest times. The

Mahabharata refers to China as *China* which is a Sanskrit adaptation of Ts'in, the name of an ancient Chinese dynasty (221-206 B.C.). The Chinese legends speak of the first appearance of the Buddhist missionaries from India in the Chinese capital as early as 217 B.C. under the Ts'in dynasty. According to another authority, Buddhist texts were first presented to the Chinese Court in the 2nd century B.C. by the Yue-che rulers.

The emperor Ming-ti of the Han dynasty (A.D. 26-220) sent ambassadors to India to invite Buddhist missionaries to his court, and accordingly Kasyapa Matanga arrived at the imperial capital in A.D. 65 with a precious cargo of sacred texts and relics. Buddhism was thus the central thread of Indo-Chinese cultural and diplomatic contacts. These increased rapidly during the thousand years following the visit of Kasyapa Matanga. Embassies were exchanged between the kings of India and China; Indian scholars went to China; Chinese scholars and pilgrims visited India in search of Buddhist texts and knowledge, and a vast body of Sanskrit literature was translated into the Chinese language.

The Kushan emperor Kanishka borrowed the title Devaputra, 'Son of Heaven', obviously from the Chinese. According to Chinese annals, Indians often sent messengers to China with presents in the time of the emperor Ho-ti (A.D. 82-105). In A.D. 539, Wu-ti, the first Liang Emperor of China, sent a mission to Magadha to collect original Mahayana texts and obtained the services of an Indian scholar competent to translate them. The Indian king gladly complied with the wishes of the emperor and sent Paramartha from Ujjain to China. Taking with him a large collection of manuscripts, he reached Canton in A.D. 546, where he presented it to the emperor in 548 and died in 569 at the age of 70. It was in Wo-ti's reign, in A.D. 520, that Bodhidharma, the son of a king of Kanchipuram in South India, went to China, where his miracles are even today a favourite subject of Chinese artists.

He advocated "dhyana marga" and leaving Kanchipuram reached Canton in 520 A.D. He spread his faith in North China: this faith was called "Chan by the Chinese and Zen by the Japanese" when his faith spread later on in Japan. He was called *Tamo* by the Chinese, who have included him in their list of 28 apostles. Japanese annals record that after propagating his faith in China, Bodhidharma went to Japan and had religious discourses with Shotoku Taishi at Kataoka Yama. Both in China and Japan temples were built for him. Some exist even today and in them oil lamps burn night and day (c/. Custom in South Indian temples).

Intercourse with China reached its peak in the reign of Harsha, who sent an enyoy to China in 641. In return a Chinese mission was received in India in 643 bearing a reply to Harsha's despatch. In A.D. 795 King Subhakaradeva of Orissa sent his representative to the king of China with a valuable present, a volume of the *Gandavyuha* text from his own palace-library. In the 11th century the Chola emperors of South India exchanged embassies with the emperors of China.

The Muslim emperors also maintained diplomatic relationship with Chinese kings. Thus in 1330 Muhammad Tughlaq sent Ibn Batuta as his envoy to China.

Indo-Chinese past relationship owes a deep debt of gratitude to Buddhist scholar-missionaries who braved great perils in visiting China through the difficult Central Asian and peninsular routes. *Dharmaraksha*, a master of 36 different languages including Sanskrit and Chinese and a scholar of Buddhism was born of Yue-che parents. He was educated at Tun-huang under Indian teachers and after travelling in western parts of Central Asia went to China where he passed the whole of his active career in propagating Buddhism and translating Sanskrit texts into Chinese. But it is *Kumarajiva* who stands as the best symbol of Indo-Chinese cultural unity. He was born at Kuchi in Central Asia of an Indian father who had married a princess of the royal family of Kuchi. He was educated in Kashmir and attained such remarkable proficiency in Buddhist studies that he attracted scholars from all parts of eastern Turkestan. He was taken to China in A.D. 401, and till his death in 413 devoted himself to the propagation of Buddhist philosophy and the translation of Buddhist texts. He acquired an unsurpassed reputation in China as the most efficient interpreter of Buddhism, and of cultural collaboration between India and eastern Asia. Another scholar from Kashmir, named *Buddhajiva*, arrived at Nanking by the sea-route in A.D. 423 and was associated with Fa Hein in translating Sanskrit texts.

Another famous personality was *Gunavarman*, who reached China by the maritime route in the 5th century. A prince of the royal family of Kashmir, he put on the yellow robe of a monk at the age of 24 and afterwards visited Ceylon and Java. His fame spread, and the emperor of China sent a number of monks to request Gunavarman to go to Nanking in A.D. 431, where a new monastery under the name of Jetavana-vihara was constructed to accommodate him.

During the first five centuries of the Christian era Kashmir was the great centre of Buddhist and Sanskrit learning which connected India with Central Asia and China. But other regions of India also played their parts. Thus, Dharmakshema (414-433) and Guna-bhadra (435-468) went from middle India; Jnana-bhadra and Yasogupta (6th century) went from Bengal and Assam; Paramartha from Ujjain; and Buddha-bhadra from Jalalabad, in Eastern Afghanistan. The last travelled with a companion of Fa Hein by the Burma route, going to Tonking on foot and from there by boat to China. Another notable Indian scholar to visit China was *Dharmagupta* of Kathiawad who, after residing at the Kanyakubja monastery, proceeded to northern Punjab, Kapisa, Badakshan, Wakhan, Tashkurgan and Kashgarh whence he took the northern route to Kuchi, Agnidesa (Karashahr), Turfan and Hami and reached the Chinese capital in A.D. 590. There he made a remarkable contribution to the revival of Buddhist traditions in China.

Master of Law

The first two centuries of the T'ang period present an outstanding record of Indo-Chinese contacts. Buddhism was in a flourishing condition, political, diplomatic and cultural relations with India, were intimate, and thousands of Indians were found in the metropolitan cities of China. The University at Nalanda became an international centre of studies in the 7th and 8th centuries and attracted a host of Chinese scholars, amongst whom the name of Yuang Chwang shone with the greatest splendour, equally revered and loved as the 'Master of Law' in India and China.

In A.D. 693 Bodhiruchi, a Brahmin of South India, visited China by the sea-route at the request of a Chinese envoy to the court of a Chalukya king. It is stated in the Chinese annals that Bodhiruchi was commissioned there to translate one of the most extensive works of Mahayana, the *Ratna-kuta*, of which the manuscript had been taken from India by Yuan Chwang. A translation-board was set-up consisting of Indian and Chinese scholars to help Bodhiruchi. The emperor was himself present when the translation was made and took down notes with his own hand.

Chinese Visits to India

As a counterpart to this activity from India, a number of ardent

Chinese Buddhists journeyed to India in quest of first-hand knowledge of their holy land. Of these the following were outstanding:

Fa Hien, who came by the land-route and returned by sea from the port of Tamralipti, *via* Ceylon and Java (A.D. 399-414). India in this period was known in China as Fo-kuo, 'the country of Buddha'.

Sung Yun, who was rent in A.D. 518 as an official envoy by an empress of the Wei dynasty to offer presents to the Buddhist sanctuaries and to bring back Buddhist texts. He followed the southern route through Central Asia.

Yuan Chwang (A.D. 600-654), the most distinguished representative of Sino-Indian cultural relationship. He came by the northern land-route and made personal contact with King Harsha of Kanauj and his ally Bhaskaravarman of Assam.

Silabhadra (518-640 A.D.), the chief disciple of Acharya Dharmapala (528-560 A.D.), the head of the Nalanda Buddhist University and whom he succeeded at Nalanda, took charge of Yuan Chwang and taught him Sanskrit. After his stay in India for sixteen years (629-645) he returned to China and received probably the greatest ovation ever extended to a Buddhist monk.

Yi Tsing (673-693 A.D.), who came to India by sea-routes, halting at Srivijaya (Sumatra) on the way, spent ten years at Nalanda and took back with him a collection of four hundred Sanskrit manuscripts. Jnana-Sundara (671-695 A.D.), another disciple of Acharya Dharmapala and a colleague of Silabhadra figured in the scholastic career (as teacher) of Yi T'sing as the head of *Tilaka-vihara.*

Vajrabodhi (661-730 A.D), a native of Podikai (the place of Agastya) in the Pandya country, was patronised by the Pallava King of Kanchipuram, Narasimhavarman II. At his request, the King sent him to China to spread Tantrayana or Vajrayana or Mantrayana, and conveyed to the Chinese King through him presents and a copy of the famous Buddhist text "Mahaprajnaparamita". Vajrabodhi reached China in 720 after staying on the way in Ceylon and Srivijaya in Sumatra for some time. He translated into Chinese Tantrayana texts and died in 730 A.D. in China.

The inflow of Chinese pilgrims to India reached its climax in the Song period (A.D. 960-1279). Five inscriptions set-up by Chinese travellers of this period have been discovered at Bodha-gaya. The first is dated A.D. 950, the last A.D. 1033. These inscriptions found on Indian soil are a fitting monument of a millennium of active Sino-Indian contact.

The best fruit of China's contact with India is preserved in the Chinese translation of the Buddhist Tripitaka, the sacred canon of the Buddhists in China and Japan. It contains the titles of 1662 different works. The last volume (No. 1662) in this great collection is a record of the titles or catalogue of the Tripitaka as collected under the Ming dynasty (A.D. 1368-1644), and it also contains a record of the names of authors and translators together with their dates.

Indian influence affected China mainly through its philosophy religious ideas and the visible forms of art as conveyed by the Indian ambassador to China. Buddhist motifs and sculpture derived their primary inspiration from Indian sources. The earliest dated examples of Indo-Chinese sculpture are some bronze statuettes of the 5th century A.D., but some of the existing sculptures in the Yun-kang caves are of an approximate antiquity. At first, most of these works were in a Provincial Central Asian style, but as time went on actual Indian works, mainly of the Mathura school of the 5th and early 6th century, served as the model. The beautiful statues of the Gupta period appear to be the prototypes of the statues of Buddhas and Bodhisattvas in the Tien-Lung Shan caves in Shansi Province. These Buddhas are well-modelled and draped in Gupta fashion. The formal treatment as well as the types so closely resemble certain Gupta sculptures that one may be justified in supposing that a direct influence from India had reached the artists. Some influences from south India also found their way into the art of China proper by the sea-route. The reliefs in the Nan-Hsing-T'ang cave temples in Honan showing the Buddha and Paradises reveal South Indian features, similar to the carvings of Nagarjuna-konda and Amaravati.

Tibet

The first recorded contacts between Tibet and India are traceable to the time of Sron-tsan-Gampo, the most distinguished ruler of Tibet, who founded Lahsa in A.D. 639. He introduced Buddhism into his country and devised with the help of Indian scholars an alphabet for Tibet based on the 7th century script of India. Tibet has preserved this script with little change since that time. In this mysterious land of the Lamas, every town, village and monastery has its stupas called *Chod-rten* in the Tibetan language. Outside the city of Leh, the capital of Ladak, a row of 108 such monuments can be seen today.

Tibetan art consists mostly of Buddhist paintings and bronzes. The paintings consist mainly of votive temple-banners. The first group of them showing scenes from the life of Buddha is devoid of Tantric elements and directly based on Indian traditions as derived from Bengal and Nepal. This phase is to be connected with the ministry of the great scholar Atisa who went to Tibet from Sumatra in the 11th century A.D. and introduced religious reforms. The second group is of later origin, showing Buddhas and Bodhisattvas, world-guardians *(Loka-palas)*, local saints and heroes. In the 9th century Tibet was at the height of its military and political power, extending its rule even to Tun-huang on the western border of China, where the oldest known specimens of Tibetan painting were found by Sir Aurel Stein.

In the 13th century the great Mongol Kublai Khan borrowed the Buddhist religion from Tibet. He sent for a scholar from Tibet, named Matidhaja, and asked him to devise a script, for the Mongol empire. Accordingly the Tibetan script, based on Indian script, was presented to the Mongolian emperor and accepted by him.

Tibetan bronzes depicting for the most part, Buddhas, Bodhisattvas and a rich tutelary pantheon maintain a high tradition of execution and artistic skill. Individual figures often show remarkable poise and concentration of energy.

Nepal

Nepal had the honour of being the country where Buddha, 'the Light of Asia' was born. The earliest contact between Nepal and India goes back to the 2nd century A.D., when the Lichchhavis founded a dynasty in Nepal, taking with them from Vaisali in Bihar all the essential elements of Indian civilization. The Nepalese statecraft, language and script, religion and art, have all been deeply influenced by India from very early times. In the time of Samudragupta, Nepal was an autonomous frontier-state paying tribute and owing allegience to the Gupta power. In AD. 6:7 the Chinese mission of Wang-Hiuen-tsi entered India through Nepal, by the the Lhasa route, which was used by many Buddhist pilgrims.

Buddhism was introduced into the plateau by Asoka, and the stupas at Patan are believed to have been founded by him. They are of the old Indian hemispherical type. During the middle ages Buddhism and Brahmanism, combining in the form of a Tantric religion, prevailed in Nepal. As a result, images of Hindu deities, like Vishnu, Siva and Parvati, and those of the Buddhist Tantric pantheon began to be made side by side. In the 11th century, indian princes from Tirhut (North Bihar) controlled the valley of Nepal for some time.

Nepalese art is best known by its metal images, usually in copper or brass and of fine workmanship. A peculiarity of Nepalese bronzes is the use of precious-stone inlay, notably garnet and turquoise. The Nepalese school of painting is related to the Pala School of Bengal, and is illustrated by a number of manuscripts of the 11th century illustrated in the Pala style which have been found in Nepal. With the dispersal of Buddhist centres in Bihar and Bengal in the early 11th century by the Muslim invaders, Nepal gave shelter to many Buddhist monks and scholars, who brought with them loads of valuable Buddhist literature. In this fashion a considerable portion of the Mahayana Buddhist literature has been preserved in Nepal.

The Nepalese school of painting is also noted for its temple-banners *(thanks)*. Early examples with distinct Nepalese affinities were found amongst the paintings at Tun-huang, but most of the available painted banners from Nepal date from the 17th-18th centuries A.D.

Sri Lanka

Ceylon (Sri Lanka) owes to India its faith, Buddhism, its sacred language, Pali, and some of the inspiration for its art, social and political ideas and architecture.

India on the other hand owes a most profound debt to Ceylon in the preservation of the entire Buddhist Pali canon with its voluminous commentaries, which has been preserved with remarkable fidelity in Ceylon, even though it has disappeared from India.

Ceylon is referred to in India under the names of Lanka, Simhala, Tamraparni and Amardvipa, the 'Mango Island', [the last derived from its resemblance to a mango in shape].

The first historical reference in Buddhist literature to Ceylon is found in the second rock-edict of Asoka (272-232 B.C.) who mentions Tamraparni as one of the several countries which received his ethical missions. Ceylonese chronicles say that Ceylon was converted to Buddhism by an Indian mission headed by Asoka's son Mahendra and his daughter Sanghamitra. King Devanampiya Tissa received the royal apostolic diplomats with great honour and in commemoration founded the Great Vihara which has since then remained the headquarters of Ceylonese Buddhism. He also sent a return-embassy to Asoka at Patliputra.

Sanghamitra had taken with her an off-shoot of the Tree of Enlightenment from Bodh-gaya and planted it in the Maha-Vihara in Ceylon. The tree survives under the name of Jaya-Mahabodhi.

The Gupta emperor Samudragupta (326-375) refers in his Allahabad Pillar-inscription to his friendly contacts with the king of Ceylon (352-379). The latter sent a mission to Samudragupta carrying gems and other valuable gifts and asked permission to build a monastery at Bodh-gaya for the Ceylonese pilgrims. When visited by Yuan-Chwang in the seventh century, this magnificent establishment was described by him as being occupied by a thousand monks.

A Sanskrit inscription from Bodh-gaya dated in the year 269 (A.D. 588-89) offers another concrete proof of the intimate contact between India and Ceylon during the Gupta period. It says that a renowned Ceylonese monk named Mahanaman constructed a shrine at the place where Buddha obtained his enlightenment.

A second inscription engraved on the pedestal of a Buddhist image discovered at Bodh-gaya refers to the same Buddhist monk Mahanaman of Amradvipa or Ceylon.

The most valuable fruit of this cultural relationship between India and Ceylon is symbolized in Budhaghosha, a learned Brahmin from Bodh-gaya who arrived in Ceylon in the reign of King Mahanaman (412-34) and wrote voluminous commentaries on the Pali Buddhist canon, famous throughout the Buddhist world. These works have settled the form of Buddhist doctrine which now prevails in Ceylon, Burma, Siam and Cambodia.

Many Acharyas from South India went to Ceylon to spread their faith and to enrich literature there. Most noteworthy are:

1. Sanghamitra, a Tamil Bhikshu of the Chola country, who lived in the early half of the 4th century A.D. He went to Ceylon and converted the king to Mahayana (Vaitulya), and being patronised by his second son Mahasena, destroyed the Mahavihara which was a seat of Hinayana and renewed and enlarged the Abhayagiri Vihara, which became thereafter the strong-hold of Mahayana. He later fell a victim to a treacherous plot hatched by one of the King's wives who was in league with the Hinayana Bhikshu.
2. Thera Buddhadatta (5th century A.D.), a Tamil of the Chola country, held charge successively of Buddhist monasteries at Mahavihara in Anuradhapura, Kaveripattinam, Uragapura, Bhutamangalam and Kanchipura. He has written several works on Buddhist polity and about these monasteries. While at Kaveripattinam he wrote *Buddhavamsattagatha* at the request of his Sishya Buddha-Sikha; and at the request of another

disciple Sumati he wrote "Abhihammavatara". At Bhutamangalam he stayed in a Buddhist-palli built by a Vaishnava Kanna-dasa *alias* Venn (Vinhu) Dasa, and completed another work called "Vinaya-vinischaya". His disciple Buddha Sikha followed him everywhere: Invited to Ceylon, he compiled other works there at the request of a Ceylonese Pontiff Mahathera Saukhapala. They are "Uttaravinischaya", "Ruparupa-vibhage", "Jinalankara" and a commentary to "Buddhavamsa" called "Mathuratta-Vilasini". He met the famous Buddhaghosha in Ceylon and the two had friendly discourse. While the king Kumara Gupta was patron of Buddhaghosha, Thera Buddhadatta's patron was the Kalabhra Achyut Vikkantan (Achyutta Narayana) of the Chola-nadu.

3. Acharya Dharmapala (5th, 6th century A.D.), a native of Tinnavelly, who became successively the head of the Buddhist monastery called Bhataraditta-Vihara at Kanchipuram and the Maha-Vihara at Anuradhapura wrote good commentaries to Buddhist basic texts, such are "Attakatha", "Paramartha-manjusha", "Nettibhakara-nattakatha".
4. Dipanka Thera (1100 AD.), *alias* Buddhapriya Thera, and "Choliya Dipankara, was disciple in Ceylon of Ananda Vanaradana, and later on became the head at Kanchipura of Baladichcha-Vihara". He was the author of the Pali works, Vajjamadu and Rupa-Siddhi, the former on Buddhist art, and the latter on arithmetic. He wrote also a commentary to *Rupa-Siddhi.*
5. Anirudha (12th century A.D.) of the Pandya land, became the head of the Mulasoma-vihara at Kanchipura and became popular in Ceylon and Burma by his works, "Abhidhammatha-Sangraha, Paramartha-vinischaya and Nama-rupa-pariccheda".
6. Dharmakirti (13th century A.D.) of the Pandya country, was invited and patronised by Parakrama Bahu II (1236-68 A.D.). He organised in Ceylon an international conference of Buddhists. Datta-vamsa and Chula-vamsa (latter part of Mahavamsa recording history of Ceylon from Mahasena to Parakrama Bahu II) are works which are ascribed to this Dharmakirti who hailed from Pandya land ("Tambaratte vasamtena Nagara Tanyanamake").

Of the numerous monuments at Anuradhapura, the ancient capital, the following are noteworthy:

(1) Mahathupa—"the Great Stupa" now called Ruanwali Dagaba, built by king Duttagamani (about 100 B.C.). Its dome, 270 ft. high is raised on a square platform decorated with about four hundred elephant figures modelled in terracotta.

(2) Jetavanarama (or Eastern Dagaba) was built by King Mahasena (A.D. 325-52) and completed during the reign of his son Meghavarna. It is the largest building of its kind and stands on a paved platform measuring 600 square feet.

(3) Abhayagiri (or Northern Dagaba), was built by king Vattagamani Abhya (about 29 B.C.). It has an extant height of about 250 feet.

The gigantic stupas of Anuradhapura were derived from early Indian prototypes, but differ from them in that they do not have the railings and gateways and are provided as in the case of Andhra Stupas with four large and elaborately decorated rectangular structures (ayaka-platforms) facing the four cardinal points.

Burma

The religious culture of the Burmese is even today more Buddhist than elsewhere. "Burma" is derived from the word "Mramma" which is the name of a tribe that constituted the Pyus, who (Hinduized) founded the kingdom of Srikshetra in what is now called Hmawza, Old Prome, and the Pyus dynasty continued till the 9th century A.D.

Srikshetra (Hmawza) had been the seat of large scale excavation for over half a century, and the discoveries relate to an earlier group ranging from the 5th to the 7th century A.D., and a latter group from the 6th to the 9th century A.D. They are all Buddhist stupas and consist of religious edifices, sculptures, inscriptions and votive tablets, the last containing the Buddhist creed formulae *(Ye-dhamma)* and sometimes short aphorisms from the *Abhidamma-pitaka*. Terracotta votive tablets from Srikshetra (6th to 7th century A.D.), from Pagan (11th century A.D.) and from Arakan of the 11th-12th century A.D., were discovered in large numbers, all allied to the Indian models and showing Buddha seated in *Vajrasana* or *bhusparsa* or *dhyana* or *upadesa* and with inscriptions of the Buddhist creed formula in Brahmi. The sculptures represent the Buddha and scenes from his life and his pre-births *(jatakas)* and the workmanship is in the Indian style (6th-8th century A.D.). The inscriptions which include gold plates also with extracts from the Pali Buddhist canon, are in Prakrit (Pali), Sanskrit and in an unknown language of the Pyus, but in a script similar to the South Indian script (Vengi or Pallava-Grantha). Images of the Buddha in stone, bronze, and terracotta were discovered in typical South Indian style of the 6-8th century A.D. The stupas exposed are of the pyramidal, cruciform shape *(Sanatobhadra)* as at Paharpur and Mainamati in Bengal, and Lauriya Nandangarh in Upper Bihar and at Borobudur, Java. The best known stupa of Burma is the Shwedagon at Rangoon with its immensely picturesque surroundings.

The Indian script, language, literature and Buddhism as in India spread in Burma. Buddhist works such as "Abhidammatta Sangraha", the author of which was Aniruddha of the Pandya land (12th century A.D.) who was the head of a Buddhist monastery called Mula—some Vihara in Kanchipuram, became popular in Burma and were taught in Burmese monasteries.

The Kalyani inscriptions refer to a great Tamil Buddhist *acharya*, Ananda Thera (died 1245 A.D.), a native of Kanchi, who was taken to Arimarddanapura in Burma by Saddharma Jyoti Pala, where the Burmese king Jayasura received him with great honours and loaded him with presents including an elephant which he sent to his relatives at Kanchi. Ananda was the head of the Burmese Buddhist Church for about 50 years and died in 1245 A.D.

The Kalyani inscriptions of Dhammacheti (1476 A.D.) throw like an oasis in a desert, very refreshing light on the cultural relations between South India and Pegu in the 14th and 15th centuries A.D. Hindusim also spread in Burma but not as vigorously as Buddhism. A part of Sri-kshetra was called Vishnu's city. After the 12th century, the art became local and Indian influence waned.

Siam

The Siamese language has liberally borrowed words from Sanskrit. The "Rama Keun" is the Siamese version of the Ramayana, and the Mahabharata has inspired Siamese literature and stories. Still the Buddhist Pali literature has exercised a more dominant influence on the growth of Siamese literature.

'Dvaravati' (the ancient name of Siam) was part of the ancient empire of Kambuja (Cambodia) and was the seat of a style of art called the 'School of Dvaravati' which flourished at Lobapuri (Navapura) and showed marked Indian influence, closely allied to the Gupta as seen at Sarnath, Mathura and Ajanta. Several stone and bronze images of the Buddha and of Vishnu in Gupta style were found here. Siamese sculptures in the 11th and 12th centuries A.D. are entirely Buddhist and reveal Khmer influence. Also Indian Pala influences passing through Burma were noticeable in developing Buddhist art in North Siam.

The Thais came to possess the Menam delta in the 13th century and the Upper Menam became independent of Kambuja under the name of Svargaloka-Sukhodaya in the time of the great king Suryavamsa Rama Khamhang (1226 A.D.), whose grandson Hridayaraja founded in about 1350 A.D. a new capital called Ayuthia (Ayodhya) which flourished till 1767 when it was superseded by Bangkok. This Sukhodaya kingdom witnessed in the 13th and 14th centuries A.D. a golden age of Buddhist art, when finest examples of Siamese art were developed under Sinhalese inspiration. Noteworthy are 51 Jataka representations on stone at Sukhodaya with accompanying Thai inscriptions engraved in the reign of the king Rama Khamhang.

Takua-pa Inscriptions

To the South Indian, the Takua-pa Tamil inscription on a sand stone stela discovered in an ancient bed of the R. Takua-pa in and near a Buddhist monastery called Vat Na Miang is of exceptional interest. Near it were also found three sculptures in the close grip of a big tree now 20 meters high, whose folds of the bark cover them in part. Two represent Vishnu and Sri Devi. The inscription nearby which is in Tamil of the 8th, 9th century A.D., helps their identification.

Takua-pa inscription of Paliava King Nandivarman III (826-850 A.D) which is in 6 lines reads thus:

> "The tank called Avaninaranam dug by the lord of Nangur is placed under the protection of the members of the Manigramam, the residents of the military camp . . . ."

Avani-Narana or Narayana is a well-known Surname of the Pallava king Nandivarman III (826-850 A.D.). The village Kaveripakkam was named Avaninarayana Chaturvedi-mangalam after him. The Nandikkalambakam, possibly a contemporary work, applies the name Avani-Narayana to the King Nadivarman III the hero of the poem (He is called Aavani-Naranan). The poem also describes him as the master of a navy "Aavani-narana of crowded naval force and the unrivalled lord of the four seas with white foaming waves". The term is interesting as they were members of a merchant-guild belonging to the Malabar Coast of the time of the Chera king, Bhaskaravarman. This *Manigramam* is well-known from inscriptions in South India as a powerful mercantile corporation which prospered for many generations. There were other similar corporations. These merchant-guilds enjoyed extra-territorial rights and were autonomous self-regulating bodies. It is possible that the powerful bodies of this inscription mentioned next to the Manigramattar was an armed camp of soldiers maintained for protection by the colony of South Indian merchants settled there. The Takua-pa Tamil inscription furnishes a peep into an aspect, long forgotten, of the economic relations of South India with the East Archipelago in the 9th century A.D. The author of the lank is Nangurrudaiyan a South Indian, who hails from Nangur. a place celebrated in Tirumangai Mannan's hymns. Periyatirumoli, IV (1, 2. 5, 6; 6:2, 7:1) as the cradle of heroes who distinguished themselves in the wars of the Paliava Kings, whose feudatories the Nangur chiefs were. The name he gave to the tank he dug in Siam was reminiscent of the political allegiance he owed to the Paliava King Nandivarman III.

Cambodia

The first to receive waves of Indian colonisation were the kingdoms of Cambodia (Kambuja) and Annam (Champa) which occupied the eastern belt of French Indo-China. About 400 A.D., Cambodia was fully organised on Indian model under a king Srutavarman. In the 5th-7th centuries A.D. Cambodian art was strongly influenced from India. Both Buddhist and Brahmanical influences are to be seen in the cultural growth of the country. Bi-lingual inscriptions in South Indian Paliava script, in good Sanskrit and perfect palacographical form, appear, equalling the best in India, and revealing a knowledge of the Srutis, Smritis, Puranas and epics. The style of architecture of the temples recalls Gupta influence, the characteristic Gupta form, viz., rectangular cell with flat roof repeats as at Deogarh (Dt. Jhansi, U.P.). More than 50 such brick temples, assignable to the 5th-6th centuries A.D., with wails decorated with architectural reliefs, were found at Prei Kuk. Kompong Thorn, a study of which increases our knowledge of Gupta art. Images of the Buddha with transparent drapery and of Lokesvara Bodhisattva found at Romlok are closely related to the Gupta images of Sarnath.

The history of 7th and 8th centuries is obscure and the Indian art in Cambodia disappears with the rise of the Classic Khmer in the 9th century A.D. But for 5 centuries more, cult and mythology remained essentially Indian, and both Buddhist and Brahmanical pantheon was represented. The most representative and typical of the buildings of this period are the famous temples of Angkor Wat (Yshodharapura in its old name) built in A.D. 1125 as a result of the religious zeal of Cambodia's king Suryavarman II. In the gallery-reliefs of the temples may be noticed battle scenes of the Ramayana and Mahabharata, scenes of heaven and hell and cosmic scenes like the *amrita-manthana*. The Angkor Wat group compares well with another equally famous monument, the Bayon central temple of Angkor Thorn (900 A.D.), which is "a veritable pantheon and portrait-gallery" and enshrines both Hindu deities Siva, Vishnu and Devi and the Buddhist deities of the Mahayana.

The influence of Sanskrit in the ancient place-names of Kambuja is evident, as can be seen from the following:

Angkor Wat	=	Yasodharapura
Benteay-Chhmar	=	Amarendrapura
Phnom Kulen	=	Mahendra-Parvata
Prei Kuk	=	Isanapura
Baphnom	=	Vyadhapura
Ruluos	=	Hariharalaya

Champa

Champa (Annam), the land of the Chams, was for a 1000 years (from 3rd to 13th century A.D.) a land of mixed Indo-Cham culture. It was the earliest theatre of Hindu influence from India. The oldest is a Sanskrit inscription from Vo-Chanh, in the South-Indian script of 2nd or 3rd century A.D. At this time there existed in Central Champa a Hindu kingdom known as Kauthara. Later it was succeeded by the kingdom of Panduranga (modern Phanrang). The Indo-Cham rulers are probably of Pallava origin. They borrowed their ideas of government and details of administration from Indian models.

Saivism was the dominant religion and Siva's consort, Parvati was also commonly worshipped. But the earliest sculpture from Champa is, however, a standing Buddha image in bronze found at Dong-Duong, the only Buddhist site in Champa; the image is so closely related in style to the Amaravati and Nagarjunakonda Buddha figures as to suggest that it may have been imported. The strongest wave of Indian influence seems to have gone to Champa in Gupta period.

Indonesia

Java is referred to in Valmiki's Ramayanam. Early Indian colonisation of Java appears to date back to the first century A.D. Sanskrit inscriptions of the 4th-5th century A.D., in Pallava-Grantha script, speak of a Hindu kingdom of Taruma and a king Purnavarman. But early Hindu rule has left few traces and did not persist after the 5th century.

In 414, Fa Hian, was caught in a storm, while on his voyage home from Ceylon, and landed at an island which he calls Ye-po-ti (Java or Sumatra), and where, according to him, the law of the Buddha was not known, heretics and Brahmans alone flourishing in the island. Buddhism appears to have been introduced into Java in 423 A.D. by Gunavarman, a prince of Kashmir; the new faith received very little attention till much later, for we find that up to the 8th century A.D. it was Brahmanism that was having its sway over the isle. Buddhaditva, whose time is not known, was a Bhikshu poet from Kanchipuram who has in Tamil several verses in praise of a King of Java.

During the Sailendra rule (732-860 A.D.) Java witnessed the growth of Buddhism. The Sailendras were rulers of Srivijaya in Sumatra a mighty kingdom comprising Sumatra, Java and the Malay Peninsula. They were zealous Buddhists, who founded sanctuaries not only in their kingdom, but also at Nalanda, where a C.P. inscription states that a Sailendra king Balaputra-deva built a monastery at Nalanda and endowed it with 5 villages. The Sailendras had international contacts with the kings of India. Two other Sailendra kings, Maravijayottungavarman, and Samgramavijayottungavarman established contacts with Rajaraja I and Rajendra Chola I, the Chola kings of Tanjore.

The greatest surviving Buddhist monument in Java is the Borobudur. The Borobudur is a stupa, a monument of the piety of the Sailendra monarchs, and was built probably in the latter half of the 8th century.—Derived from the simple relic shrines of India, it is a pyramidal edifice built on the top of a hill on a succession of 9 terraces, supporting a relatively small central stupa surrounded by 72 much smaller perforated stupas arranged in three concentric circles. The ground plan of six lower terraces is square with re-entrant corners (Sarvatobhadra), while that of the three upper terraces circular. Its four lower terraces are perambulation galleries on the walls of which are long series of reliefs, as at Nagarjunakonda, Amaravati and

Gummadidurru, illustrating the life of the Buddha according to Lalitavistara and stories from Divyavadana. Gandavyuha, Jatakamala and other sources. The total number of sculpture panels along the 4 galleries amounts to 1300, which if placed end to end would extend for over 3 miles. Indian in design and inspiration, the Borobudur well represents the development of Mahayana Buddhism in the South-east. For sheer sculptural rendering of Buddhist lore and doctrine it has no parallel in India, except at Amaravati and Nagarjunakonda. It may rightly be said that in the Borobudur the stupa attains its final development and greatest perfection.

After A.D. 919 Central Java was deserted, and the centre of art shifted to east Java. Here the indigenous art of Indonesia asserts itself but the subjects are mostly Brahmanical Buddhist. The reliefs of Chandi Jago near the town of Mallam illustrate the Krishna story, an unexpected theme in a Buddhist temple. In the 11th, 12th centuries a profound intermixture of Brahminical and Buddhist cults took place in Java, as in Nepal and Cambodia, and its effects are still surviving in Bali.

Nagapatam (S. India)

As a result of maritime commerce between Eastern India and the Malay Peninsula, there existed at Nagapatam, in the days of the Cholas (87-1250 A.D.) a colony of Malay Buddhists,. particularly from Srivijaya, who appear to have given a new lease of life to the declining Buddhism of South India by erecting Buddhist temples at Nagapatam with the aid of subsidies granted by their kings, the Sailendras. Being patronised by the Chola monarchs, they built at least two temples at the beginning of the 11th century, called 'Rajaraja-perum-palli' and 'Rajendrachola-perum-palli' or 'Chola-perum-palli'. The former was named after Rajaraja I and the later after Rajendra Chola I, during whose reigns they were respectively built. The former was evidently the chapel of a Vihara, known as the "Chudamani-varma-vihara" which including its chapel, was built during the reign of Rajaraja I by Sri Mara-vijayottunga-varman, son of Chudamanivarman of the Sailendra dynasty, King of 'Kataha' (Kadaram) and Srivishaya or Srivijaya.

II
THE HIERARCHY OF THE DALAI LAMA (1398-1745)

SARAT CHANDRA DAS

The ruler of Tibet Sron tsan-Gampo who founded Lhasa in 639 A.D. introduced Buddhism into his country which flourished during the reigns of successive riders. E-chan Gotan, grandson of Jenghis Khan, to whose share fell both Tibet and China, hearing the fame of the Pandit *hicrarch of Sakya named Kungah Gyai tshan, invited him to China and received him in audience at his palace of Tulpai De. Thus the learned Buddhist Hierarch of Tibet gained the opportunity to implant in the mind of the dreaded monarch the doctrine of Buddha—to have compassion over all living beings and to effect one's own salvation by loving others. So the hierarch quietly effected the spiritual conquest of the Tartars. On the death of E-chan Gotan Khan, Kublai Khan became emperor of China. He removed his residence to Peking and renewed his contacts with the Buddhist scholars from Tibet. The author has compiled this article from Tibetan histories such as Pagsamjonzang, etc. Dalai Lama, the supreme religious leader of Tibetans is in India since 1959, when he was forced to flee from Tibet. In early 1950's New Delhi persuaded Dalai Lama to accept Chinese annexation of Tibet on the basis of certain assurances extended by Peking. The Geneva-based International Commission of Jurists in a voluminous report have rejected Chinese assertions that Tibet was historically part of China and have added that Tibet was an independent country when China invaded it in 1950 (Ed.).*

The reformed Buddhist Church called *Shwaser* the school of yellow-cap Lamas, founded by Tsongkhapa acquired such a celebrity within a few years of its birth that in the year 1406 Yunglo, the third Emperor of the Ta Ming dynasty, sent an invitation to the great reformer to visit Peking. Finding his time fully necessary for scriptural as well as monastic reformation, Tsongkhapa was unable to comply with Yunglo's wish. He, however, sent his principal disciple to enlighten the devout monarch in the mysteries of Lamaism as developed in the reformed school, in the following year.

On his arrival at Peking, Cakya Yeces found the Emperor suffering from a serious illness. He performed several religious ceremonies, which were believed to have effected a speedy recovery. Under his direction a huge image of Maitreya, the coming Buddha, called Chamchen, was constructed and placed in the monastery of Yung-ho-kung[1] founded by Yung-lo himself. Cakya Yeces was appointed high priest of this monastery and given the title of Chamchen Choije. He founded the great monastery of Hwang-sze or Yellow Temple in one of the imperial gardens situated to the north of Peking.[2] On his return journey to Tibet he took the circuitous Mongolian route and paid a visit to his tutor and chief Tsongkhapa, making large presents to him. Shortly, after his return to Lhasa, in the year 1418, he founded the great monastery of Sera Theg cheling with the wealth which he had amassed during his residence in the capital of China. Sera, in time, rose to great distinction and was resorted to by Lamas as a seat of learning. It now contains 5,500 monks and is second only to Dapung in rank.

In 1408, shortly after establishing the grand annual congregational assembly called *Monlam chenpo* (literally, the great prayer meeting) at Lhasa, Tsongkhapa founded the great monastery of Gahdan with 3,300 monks at a place some 20 miles to the East of Lhasa, and presided over it as the minister of the reformed Church till his death. He laid down the rule that his successors in the ministerial chair of Gahdan should be elected from among the most pious and learned of the brotherhood irrespective of their position in birth. Constitutionally, therefore, the Gahdan Thipa (chairman) became as his successor in the ministry, the hiearch of the Yellow-cap Church.[3]

From that time Gahdan became the chief seat of the reformed Church, the monks of which put on the yellow-cap to distinguish themselves from the followers of the older sects who generally wore the red-cap *(shwa-mar)* and were, therefore, called Shwa-ser Ge-luga-pa, i.e., the order of which the religious badge was the yellow-cap. They were also called *Gahdan-pa* from the name of their monastery.

In 1415, one of Tsongkhapa's disciple named Jam-yang Choije founded Dapung now the premier monastery of Tibet with 7,700 monks under the patronage of Namkha Zangpo, the then ruler of Tibet. In the year of the foundation of the monastery of Sera, the great reformer, whose real name was Lozang Tagpa but who is better known as *Tsongkhapa* from the name of his birth-place *Tsongkha* (onion bank), in Amdo, passed away from mundane existence.

In 1446, Gadun dub one of the later disciples of Tsongkhapa founded the grand monastery of Tashilhunpo in Tsang. The establishment of these four great monasteries.—first Gahdan, then Dapung and Sera, and, lastly, Tashilhunpo,—which have played such an important part in the political administration of the country, made the provinces of U and Tsang the headquarters of the Yellow Church. On account of his profound learning and holiness, though of humble and obscure parentage, Gadundub was regarded as a saint. He himself never pretended to have been of saintly origin, but people believed that he must have possessed in him the spirit of *Bodhisattva* Avalokitecvara—the guardian saint of Tibet. About three years alter Gadundub's death the possibility of the reappearance of the spirits of deceased Lamas for the first time dawned in the minds of the members of the reformed Church. The monks of Dapung over which Gadundub had laterly presided thought that the spirit of one who had loved his country and all living beings so much could hardly have become freed from his longings, to work for them even when he had passed out of his mortal tenements. They, therefore, sent emissaries to the different places which the Lama had visited during his lifetime, to inquire if there was born, seven weeks after his demise, any child in whom could be traced the signs of its indicating any incidents of Gadundub's life. They also consulted their tutelary deities for guidance in the right identification of Gadundub's spirit should it have re-appeared in any child.

At last, a child was discovered at Tanag born in the family of Sreg-ton Darma, who had settled in Tsang from Lower Kham. It revealed some signs of having been the re-embodiment of the Lama's spirit and successfully claimed as his own certain articles for which Gadundub used to evince much liking and which were kept mixed up with other people's properties. This fortunate child was removed to Tashilhunpo for religious and monastic education. His father, who was a lay *Tantrik* priest of the Ninma sect, instructed him in the *Tantrik* cult. When twelve years old he took the vows of an *Upasaka* (lay devotee) from Panchen

Lungrig Gya-tsho of Tashilhunpo; after which he was admitted into monkhood by the abbot of Ne-nin. When he passed all the examinations in the sacred scriptures he was elevated to the highest rank in the order of monkhood, after being given the name of Gadun gya-tsho and placed on the high priest's chair in 1511. He ably presided over the monastery of Tashilhunpo for a period of five years. He received instruction in the Buddhist scriptures and metaphysics from such eminent scholars as Ye-ces zang, hierarch of Gahdan. Yontan

Gya-tsho of Tsang and Panchen yeccs tse of Tashilhunpo. He founded the monastery of Choikhor Gyal in the plain of Metog thang in 1508. In the 43rd year of his age, in the year 1516, he was appointed to the abbot-ship of Dapung where he was better known by the title of Dapung *Talku* or *Avatar*. In later times this *Avatar*, in his successive incarnations, received the titles of *Gyal-wa Rinphche*, *Gyalwai Wangpo*, *Talc Lama*, *etc.*

With him, in fact, *originated the institution of incarnations in Tibet* which was but little known before and which since then has become general all over Tibet and Mongolia.

In the 52nd year of his age the Lamas of Sera elected him as their high priest, which office he held till his death in 1541. Since Kyisho, the district of which Lhasa is the chief town, had passed under the ruler of Tsang named Rinchen-Pung-pa, for a period of nineteen years, the Lamas of Sangphu and Karma sects presided over the annual prayer assembly of Lhasa called the Monlam Chenpo. Under the auspices of Gadun Gya-tsho the Lamas of Sera and Dapung regained their lost authority over the grand institution. Gadun wrote several works on the different branches of the sacred literature. At the age of 68, in the year called *Water-tiger*, he departed from this life.

His spirit was discovered in a lad of four years born in the family of Ma Rinchen Chog at Toilung in the year 1546. When this boy was ten years old the Lamas of Dapung placed him on the chair of their high priest under the title of Sonam Gya-tsho. Formerly, when the Tartar Emperor Khublai Khan made rich presents to his spiritual tutor Lama Phag-pa, the latter had predicted that in time to come he would reappear on this earth as a Lama bearing the name—"Ocean", which in Mongolian was called Tale—*Dalai*, while the Emperor himself would reign as a king of the name *Altan* signifying gold—in Mongolian.

Altan, the powerful Khan who ruled over Thumed Mongolia, being told by an astrologer that in a former life he was the great Khan of China, wished to know what became of the spirit of the Lama who had exercised so much influence over Emperor Khublai. Being informed that he too was reborn in the person of Sonam Gya-tsho, the incarnate Lama of Dapung, the monarch sent his general Tashi Rabdan to bring him to Mongolia.

In 1557, Sonam Gya-lsho became High Priest of Sera. Being in charge of both Sera and Dapung, he exercised great influence at Lhasa.

In 1563, he took the final vows of monkhood. In 1573, he founded the monastery of Namgyal Ta-tshang on Potala, but the *Shwamar* (red-cap) Lamas whose power was again ascendant under the auspices of the ruler of Tsang, dispossessed him of this institution, converting it at the same time to a monastery of their own school. In 1574, the Tsang army under Rinchen Pung-pa invaded U and after subjugating it, withdrew to Tsang. About this time, the messenger of Altan Khan arrived and Sonam Gya-tsho was but too glad to accept the invitation for the purpose of converting the Mongolians to his creed. He set out on his journey to Mongolia in the company of the Khan's messenger, but owing to the numerous, invitations he received on the way from the various chiefs and nobles of Tibet and who importuned him for his blessings, his journey was retarded. Tashi Rabdan, therefore, parted company with him at Radeng and proceeded to Mongolia, in advance of the Lama. Being informed that the incarnate Phagpa was coming, Altan Khan deputed three of his generals to welcome him. While passing through Arig-thang, Non-tsho and upper Mongolia, the Lama received the deputations which brought the tidings of the welcome that would be accorded him by the Khan. Altan himself advanced up to Tshab-cha, at the source of the Hoangho, a palace situated to the South-East of Lake. At the first meeting the Khan addressed the Lama by the title—Tale Lama *Vajradhara* (the holder of the unchangeable state, i.e., *Nirvana*) *Tale* being the Mongolian equivalent of *Gya-tsho* which signifies "Ocean". But the Lama's real name was Sonam Gya-tsho which signified "The ocean of merit". Thus originated the name Dalai (from *Tale*) Lama by which the Buddhist hierarchs of the line of Gadun-dub came to be known in Mongolia, China and Tibet. From that time *Gya-tsho* became a necessary and inseparable part of the name of Gadundub's successors. The Mongolians readily embraced Buddhism and became devout followers of the Yellow cap Church. With a view to commemorate his visit to Mongolia, Sonam Gya-tsho, under the auspices of the Khan, founded the monastery of Choikhorling in the Mongol capital. About this time the monastery of Kumbum[4] was founded at the birth place of Tsongkhapa in Amdo.

On his return journey Sonam Gya-tsho visited Khukukhukto Lithang, Chamdo, Kham, Lithang, Apo, Chakhyungtag, Ngan-tig Jomokhan, Chambabomling, etc., thus propagating the Buddhist faith in Mongolia and the border lands of Tibet. Having been worshipped by all classes of people—from the Khans of Mongolia down to the barbarians of Ulterior Tibet, he returned to Tibet, full of glory. He died in 1587. The spirit of Sonam Gya-tsho was discovered in Mongolia, the favourite place of his sojourn, in the family of Sumi Thaiji, a direct descendant of Jenghis Khan, the great Tartar conqueror. The child was named Yontan Gya-tsho the 'ocean of good quality'. This happy incident made the Mongolians firmly attached to the Yellow Church. They kept him in their country till the 15th year of his age. The authorities of Dapung, fearing lest the morals of their incarnate Lama might get stained by his continued residence in a country where chastity in the fair sex was unknown, brought him to Tibet at the budding of his youth. They gave him a good religious education before entrusting him with the duties of the high-priest of their monastery. About the time of Sonam Gya-tsho, the Kalmuk Tartars of Khalkha had set-up a third hierarch of the Yellow-cap sect under the name of Je-tsun-Dampa at Urga—the city of tents. A question arose as to the relative position, in spiritual rank, of the high priest of the Mongolian monastery of Gahdan and the Khalkha hierarch. The Tartars of the upper and lower Mongolia were about to go to war for its soulution.

In 1605, the young chief of the Oeleuth Mongols effected reconciliation between the Kalmuks and his own tribe who had been quarrelling for some time on the question of precedence between Gahdan and Urga. For this service the Emperor of China conferred on him the Buddhist title of Ta Kau-sri, from which circumstance he became known by the name of Gushi Khan.

In the year 1609, the armies of Tsang again invaded U, but encountering much opposition they were forced to withdraw from there. In 1611, Phun-tshog Namgyal who patronized the *Shwa-mar* (red-cap) Lamas, became the supreme ruler of Tibet. In the beginning of the 17th century the province of Tsang came to prominence on account of the power of its *Deba* or chief. He belonged to the Karmapa hierarchy known by the name of *Shwa-mar* which had its headquarters at Tshorpu and Ralung. With a view to put to shade Tashilhunpo they erected a large monastery in its immediate vicinity.

In the year 1615, Yontan Gya-tsho died, an event which was followed by the seige of the monasteries of Sera and Dapung by the armies of the *Deba* of Tsang in which several thousand yellow-cap Lamas were killed. The news of this disaster to the Yellow Church enraged the Oeleuth Mongols, whose general marched with a large army to Tibet and fought a fierce battle with the Tsang army at

Kyang-thang-gang, and killed several thousand Tibetans. In 1620, the Mongolians retired after restoring the lost territorial endowments of the Yellow Church to the monasteries of Sera, Dapung and Gahdan. About this time Sera and Dapung were presided over by the grand Lama of Tashilhunpo. In 1621, the boy Lozang Gya-tsho, in whom the spirit of Yontan Gya-tsho had passed in 1616, was brought to Dapung. In 1623, he was ordained and installed as the high priest of Dapung. About this time the *Shwa-mar* Lamas had regained their lost position and were vigorously persecuting the Yellow Church.

They had, in the meantime, influenced the Kulmuk Mongols whose chief had become a convert to their creed. In the year 1636, Gushi Khan espoused the cause of the Yellow Church and entered Kokonor with a large army. At the outset of this invasion he had to encounter with the Kulmuk Mongols who had taken up the side of the *Shwa-mar* Lamas. He completely defeated them after several engagements. From Kokonor, while proceeding towards Tibet, he heard that king Beri of Kham, who was a follower of the Bon[5] religion, was preparing to invade Tibet. He, therefore, marched against him and reduced him to subjection. He again invaded Kham in 1639; this time, putting Beri to death, he annexed his territories to his Mongolian kingdom.

In the year 1641, at the invitation and earnest entreaty of the Dalai Lama Ngag-wang Lozang Gya-tsho, he entered Tibet with 30,000 Tartars and fought several battles with the Tsang army led by the powerful *Deba* of Tsang. After capturing Lhasa and other towns which had been in the occupation of the *Deba*, he put him to prison, annexed Upper Tsang[6] of which Gyan-tse was the chief town, and proclaimed himself the supreme king of Tibet, assuming the Tibetan name of Tanzing Choi-Gyal—the upholder of Religion or *Dharma Raja*.

He appointed Sonam Choiphel as *Desrid* (governor) to rule over the country in his absence. Henceforth Tibet became a dependency of the Mongolian kingdom founded by Gushi Khan, the Oeleuth chief, who owed but nominal allegiance to China. In 1643, six great nobles of China conspired against the last Ta-ming emperor Khrungtin (Tungtin), and their leader usurped the imperial authority for some time. Shortly after, Shun-ti (also called Shunchi), a Mantchu chief, seized the throne and displaced the Ta-Ming dynasty. So, owing to troubles in China and confusion during the period which preceded this dynastic change, no armed protest came from Peking against

Gushi Khan's military operations in Tibet and Kham. In 1644, Gushi Khan built a castle on the famous hill of Potala for the accommodation of his court.

As soon as Shun-ti found himself secure and firmly seated on the imperial throne, he took up the foreign affairs in hand. With a view to bring Tibet again under his direct control he sent an invitation to the Dalai Lama to visit Peking. In 1651, Ngag-wang Lozang reached Peking where he was feted and loaded with honours. The Emperor, who with his whole family embraced the Lamaism of the Yellow Church in prefrence to that of the red-cap school to which the Ta-Mings were attached, decorated him with the exalted title of Ta-kausri. On this occasion, the Dalai Lama was greatly impressed with the power and splendour of the Emperor's court as well as the vastness of his dominions. With a view to make the position of his church secure in Tibet he prayed to the Emperor that China might take over the protectorate of Tibet in the manner it was done by Khublai Khan, the founder of the Ta-Yen dynasty, when the Emperor himself had embraced the Lamaism of the Sakya-pa school. He also explained that the Ta-Mings from the time they had displaced the Tartar dynasty proved themselves very staunch supporters of Lamaism and became pledged to the tenets of the Red-cap sect of the Karma-pa hierarchy Shun-ti very gladly acceded to the prayer. From that time the Mantchu dynasty became vouched, under solemn promises, to the protection of the authority of the Dalai Lama in Tibet.

Shortly after this, Shun-ti proceeded to Mukden, his Mantchu capital, for offering prayers in the tombs of his ancestors. Lozang Gya-tsho accompanied him thither. At the end of the year 1652 the Lama returned to Tibet, visiting on way the great monastery of Gonlung in Amdo, then a flourishing Yellow-Church institution with 10,000 monks.

In 1653, Gushi Khan was succeeded by his son Da-yen Khan who appointed Lama Tin-leh Gya-tsho as *Desrid* of Tibet. The government having passed from the hands of a Tartar General to those of a Lama, the power of the Dalai Lama, who had lately returned from China, full of glory, greatly increased. Lozang Gya-tsho, besides being a scholar, well read in the sacred literature, was a shrewd stateman of great ability. He made Tin-leh unconsciously subservient to his wishes in the government of the country. In 1668, the *Desrid* died leaving the Government in the hands of a layman named Choipon Deba, an incident which afforded Lozang Gya-tsho a still better opportunity to exercise his influence more effectually in the affairs of the state.

In 1670, Da-yen Khan died leaving the throne to his son Ratna Talai Khan. On the retirement of Choipon Deba in 1674, Lama Lozang Jin-pa was appointed *Desrid* of Tibet. Since the conquest of Tibet by Gushi Khan, the internal administration of the country, which was vested in the *Desrid*, had been practically directed by Lozang Gya-tsho, who, since his return from China, was considered as the holiest man on the face of the earth on account of his having become the spiritual tutor of the Emperor of China. He was reverentially called Gongsa-nga-pachenpo, the fifth supreme Lama, the four who preceded him being Gadundub the founder of the hierarchy, Gadun Gya-tsho, Sonam Gya-tsho and Yontan Gya-tsho.

Talai Khan having become powerless in Mongolia itself, his *Desrid* became a non-entity in Tibet. In the year 1678, Lozang Gya-tsho assumed the supreme control of the country and appointed Sangye-Gya-tsho, a layman of great wisdom and learning, as *Desrid* in the place of Lozang Jin-pa. Thus the sovereignty over Tibet and Kham practically passed from Talai Ratna Khan, the great-grandson of Gushi Khan, to the *Tale Lama* Nag-wang Lozang Gya-tsho, the supreme hierarch.

The ancient castle of Srontsan-Gampo, the first Buddhist King of Tibet, which stood on the hill called *Marpoi-ri* (the red hill), was selected by Lozang Gya-tsho for his court. He transferred his residence and court called Chyog-le Namgyal from Dapung to there, and laid the foundation of the famous palace of Phodang Marpo, now called *Gahdan Phodang Chyogle Namgyal.*

The name of the hill at the same time became changed into Potala, because the residence of *Bodhisattva* Avalokitecvara, the patron saint of Tibet, whose spirit was believed to have appeared both in King Srongtsan Gampo and himself, was mentioned in the sacred books to have been on the top of a hill called Potala-giri (the habour-hill)[7] somewhere in the south of India. Henceforth, from this circumstance, Potala became the chief place of pilgrimage of the Buddhist of the northern school who regarded the Dalai Lama as the holiest of holies. His young *Desrid*, an adept in statecraft, than whom a greater statesman has not appeared in Tibet, in course of three years, firmly established the grand Lama's temporal authority all over the country, including Kham and Amdo. In 1681, Lozang Gya-tsho died, but the wily *Desrid* managed to keep the occurrence secret from the public.

He gave out that the Dalai Lama, whose spirit was in communion with the gods, had entered into a *samadhi* (deep-meditation) under a solemn vow not to come out to public view for a period of twelve years. He now dressed himself in *lamaic* robes, and assumed a holy character, for it was not desirable for a *Desrid* not to be looked upon as a holy man. He was regarded as a wise minister and efficient ruler: in 1683 he wrote a valuable work on astronomy, astrology and chronology called *Vaidurya Karpo*. In 1693, he completed the nine-storeyed building called Phobrang Mar-po (the red-palace) on Potala, and entombed the remains of Gongsa-nga-pa chen-po, in the central hall, in a golden Chorten *(chaitya)*. In the same year he installed, under the name of Tshang-yang Gya-tsho, a child, three years old, as the incarnation of the deceased Dalai who had passed out of his body at the termination of his twelve years trance in profound *samadhi*. During this long period the *Desrid* had consolidated the Dalai Lama's authority, having governed the country with consummate skill. He being the central figure in the government, and a layman, too, was called *De-ba*, and his government came to be known by the name of *shung* (signifying the central). At the close of the year, with a view to commemorate the accession of his late master to the sovereianty of Tibet, he inaugurated the Tshog-choi the congregational service in connexion with the annual prayer meeting called *Monlam Chenpo*, of Lhasa, founded by Tsong-khapa. In 1697, he wrote the work called *Vai Ser-Choijung*, the history of the rise of the Yellow Church. The boy Dalai Lama, as he grew up in age, shewed indifference to the performance of his religious duties. He failed in almost all the examinations that he was required to pass through, before his ordination. He, however, displayed a tendency towards love-literature in which he acquired some proficiency. He selected from among the monks of Namgyal Ta-tshang young men for his companions. He composed love songs and generally spent his time in the royal groves in the suburbs of Lhasa, where men and women of all classes and age came to receive his blessings. Here he got facilities for indulging in the pleasures of life, the enjoyment of which was strictly prohibited to monks. His attention to young ladies alarmed the Lamas. At first the courtiers interpreted this unholy tendency of the youthful Lama as a mark of his communion with the *Khan-do* (female angels) who, it was given out, paid him secret visits in the guise of young maidens for initiating him in the mysteries of *tantrik* Buddhism; but later on, when the grand Lama ran to excesses, and sung love songs and behaved in utter disregard of the canonical rules, the public became undeceived. The Lamaic authorities of monasteries of Sera, Dapung and Gahdan took steps for his removal from the hierarchial throne.

About this time the Chungar or the left branch of the Oeleuth Mongols under the leadership of Tshe-wang Rab-dan had become very powerful, in consequence of which the influence of Gushi Khan's line over the Tartars greatly waned. The ambitious Tshe-wang Rubdan, who had made his power felt even in Russia in the north, was waiting for an opportunity to overrun Tibet.

The friends of the *Desrid* now courted his help against the enemies of the government who had reported the matter to the Emperor of China. In the year 1701, the abbots of the great monasteries with the help of the *Desrid* induced the prodigal youth to formally renounce the vows[8] of celebacy and monkhood which he had taken from the grand Lama of Tashilhunpo. An incarnate Lama named Yeces Gya-tsho, who had come to Lhasa for that work, now took up the spiritual business appertaining to the Dalai Lama.

In 1702 *Desrid* Sangye Gya-tsho resigned his office and retired to private life In 1705, the unfortunate Dalai Lama was removed from Tibet under a Chinese escort. He died on the way near lake Kokonur. When this news reached Peking, Emperor Kanghi ordered that a child in whom the spirit of Nag-wang Lozang may be discovered should be reported to him. In 1703, Lhabzang, son of *Talai* Ratna Khan, declared himself ruler of Tibet. He dismissed the militia and raised an army from among the Tartars. His first act was to surround the residence of the retired *Desrid*, his former chief, with a number of armed men and to kill him with four hundred of his devoted followers. In 1704, orders came from the Emperor to deport Tshang yang Gya-tsho to China. The faction in the Yellow-Church which was inimical to Lhabzang took immediate steps to elect a new Dalai Lama. They gave out that Nag-wang Lozang Gya-tsho, who was reported to have entered *Samadhi*, had actually died in the year 1681, and his spirit reappeared in one Pakar dsin-pa Ye-ces Gya-tsho in 1685, whose claim to the hierarchical throne was set aside by the *Desrid*. Pakar dsin-pa. who was an ordained monk of pure morals, was, however, was holding the office of the high priest of Dupung. Accordingly, they set him up as the real Dalai Lama in 1706, but the public hesitated to accept the new pretender as their grand hierarch.

Lhabzang submitted to Chinese authority. The Lamas of the

Yellow-Church were now on their wit's end, being required to solve a problem of a novel nature. Emissaries were, therefore, sent to the different great monasteries of the Yellow Church in search of a new incarnation of the Dalai Lama. Applications came from the parents of different child-pretenders to the exalted office, which were carefully examined. At last the real embodiment of the Dalai Lama was found at Kumbum—the birth place of Tsong-khapa, the founder of the Yellow. Church. The council of Buddhist cardinals comprising of the abbots of Sera, Dapung and Gahdan, with the Tashi Lama as president, on whom devolved the responsibility of the right identification, resorted to all manner of religious rites and consultations with the gods for the purpose. All evidence having pointed towards and in favour of the discovery at Kumbum, in a child born in 1707, the matter was reported to the Emperor. Sanction having come, the princely child named Kalzang Gya-tsho was declared Dalai Lama, but, on account of his tender age, the child could not be brought in state to Tibet and installed on the throne of Potala. Kanghi, however, invested him with the insignia of an imperial order in 1709. But fresh dangers had in the meantime sprung forth which threatened Lhasa and also taxed the energies of the Emperor.

Tshe wang Rabdan, the powerful chief of Chungar or the left branch or the Oeleuth Mongols who had risen to eminence on the downfall of Gushi Khan's kingdom, had espoused the cause of the Tibetans. The friends of *Desrid* Sangye Gya-tsho, with a view to avenge his death and to overthrow Lhabzang, had communicated to him all that had happened in Tibet. Accordingly, Tshewang Rabdan sent a large army to Tibet for punishing the enemies of the Yellow Church. In 1716 the Chinese and Tibetan troops fought a great battle with the Chungar army but were defeated, Lhabzang being slain in the field. In 1717, the victorious Chungars, at the instance of the yellow-cap Lamas, sacked the monasteries of rival sects such as Tshur-phu, Samding, Namgyaling, Dorje Tag, Mindolling and others, situated in the valley of the Tsangpo. In 1718 they returned to Mongolia.

About the time of the Chungar invasion the Tibetans had endeavoured to be independent, but Kanghi was determined to re-establish his authority over the whole of Mongolia and Tibet. In 1718, when order was restored in Tibet, the Chungar Mongolians being fully subjugated by the victorious Chinese, the young Dalai Lama was brought back to Lhasa from Kumbum by the command of the

Emperor, who sent two high Commissioners ostensibly to protect the Dalai Lama but really to form an imperial residency at Lhasa which had been controlling the political and military affairs of the country.

In 1722, the Chungars and the Oeleuth Mongols of Kokonur fought with the imperial forces and were defeated. The Chinese killed upwards of seven hundred monks of all grades, including the abbot of Ser-Khog-Gon, called Chuzang-Rinpo-che, and destroyed many religious objects and burnt down many shrines and congregation halls. They demolished the great monastery of Shwa-khog. Many aged monks of Kumbum were also killed by them. In Amdo, in the following year, the Chinese generals Kung and You then destroyed the temples and grand congregation halls of the Gon-lung monastery. In 1725 and 1726 there arose internal dissensions in the Government at Lhasa, the *Kahlons* or ministers having risen against the *Desrid* Shang Khang Chenpo and killed him. About this time, general Phola Theji[9] who had gone to Upper Tibet returned to Lhasa with troops from Ladak, Nagahri and Tsang. He slew upwards of one thousand men who had been drawn from U and Kong-po by the rebel ministers, and for a time restored order in the country. In 1727, Chinese troops came to his help and he was enabled to suppress the rebellion of U by killing the three ministers who had headed it. He removed the Dalai Lama to Kahdag or Kathog monastery in Kham, thinking it would be unsafe to keep him in Lhasa at the time.

Notes and References

1. This monastery is now (1904) presided over by an incarnate Lama and contains about 1,000 monks, mostly, Mongolians. I visited it several times during my residence in Peking, in 1885.
2. During my residence in Peking I was accommodated in this monastery as the guest of Kusho Kudub-pa, agent of the grand Lama of Lhasa. It contains the marble tomb of great artistic workmanship and beauty erected by Emperor Kuenlong in honour of the *Taslii Lama* Paldan Yeces, Warren Hasting's friend, who died of smallpox in Peking.
3. In the recent negotiations with the British Government at Lhasa the Regent who signed the Treaty with Colonel Younghusband, was Gahdan T'hipa (incorrectly named as Te-Iama) in whose hands the Dalai Lama, at the time of his flight from Lhasa, had left the keys of the palace of Potala.
4. Kumbum, it may be remembered, was visited by Abbe Hue and Gabet and later on by Mr. W.W. Rockhill.
5. The pre-Buddhistic religion of Tibet, called Yun-drun Bon, a form of fetischism in which exorcism and incantations were the chief features. It now

prevails in some parts of Tibet, particularly, Kham, but in a greatly modified and partly Buddhicised form.

6. He left lower Tsang, with Shiga-tse as its capital, to the possession of the Grand Lama Tashihunpo which continues to belong to that hierarchy up to this day.
7. The Sanskrit name *Potala* in Tibetan, is Gru-hdsin meaning 'harbour'. The Chinese Buddhists have located Potala the residence of their favourite saint Kwan-yin (Avalokitecvara in his Chinese form) in the island of Putoshan, situated on the coast of China about 200 miles off Shanghai, N.N.F., where pilgrims from China and Mongolia go annually in large number.
   Alex-Csoma de Koros, by mistake, located Potala in the neighbourhood of the town of Khara Tata in the mouth of the Indus in Sinde.
8. It is customary with the incarnate Lamas of Tibet to take religious vows from their seniors in the order. The grand Lama of Tashilhunpo being spiritually of equal rank with the Dalai Lama is competent to ordain him in the holy order. In the same manner the Tashi Lama, when junior in age, receives his religious vows and ordination from the Dalai Lama. They are related to each other as spiritual brothers and called (Gyalsras or *Jinaputra*) sons of Buddha.
9. On account of his gallant and meritorious services Phola Theji was invested with the title of Chun-wang and appointed *Desrid* by Emperor Yung-ting. Henceforth he became known in Tibet by the name Gyalpo Mi-wang. In 1734, by the command of the same Empiror, Chankya Rinpo-che brought back the Dalai Lama Lhasa from Kahdag (Ka-thog) and thereby restored peace and prosperity in Tibet and Kham.

6

Foreigners in Ajanta Paintings

Rajendra Lala Mitra

In a preceding chapter on "Buddhism as an International Link", it has been shown that ancient India had cultural, economic and political links with the outside world. In the following article, the learned author confirms these international links by pointing out that a few paintings in the World-famous Ajanta caves depict scenes from private life, or state pageantry, which afford interesting details regarding the manners, customs, habits, social conditions, and intercourse of foreigners with the people of Western India, two thousand years ago. (Ed.)

The Ajanta Pass first came to the notice of Europeans during the great battle of Asayi, which broke down the Marhatta power; but the caves near it were not visited by any Englishman until several years afterwards. According to Mr. Burgess, some officers of the Madras army were the first to visit them in 1819, and Col. Morgan of the Madras army wrote a short notice of them which appeared in Mr. Erskine's 'Remains of the Buddhists in India'. Then followed Lieut. J.E. Alexander in 1824, and his account was published by the Royal Asiatic Society in 1829.[1] Dr. Bird visited the place by order of Sir John Malcolm in 1828, at the same time when Capt. Grisely and Lieut. Ralp were at the place. The account of the former appeared in his "Researches into the Cave Temples of Western India", a meagre and faulty account, utterly untrustworthy for all historical purposes. The description of the latter appeared in this Journal.[2] It is graphic and enthusiastic, but calculated more to rouse than to allay the curiousity of the reader. Mr. Burgess says, "A somewhat interesting and correct topographical account of them, was subsequently (1839) published in the "Bombay Courier", and republished in pamphlet form, but I have not seen the brochure. Soon after, came out Mr. Fergusson's description in his Memoir on the "Rock-cut Temples of India." (1843) and laid the foundation of a critical study of these remarkable works of art. It drew to them the attention of the Court of Directors, and Capt. Gill was, six or seven years after, deputed to prepare facsimile drawings of the fresco paintings which adorn most of the caves. His report was published in 1855, but it was meagre, like the works of his predecessors, and subserved, like them, only to whet the desire for further information. Dr. Wilson's account, in his paper on the "Ancient Remains of Western India", published in 1850, in the Journal of the Bombay Asiatic Society,[3] is a mere resume of what was then known, and Dr. John Muir's subsequent notice professes to give nothing more than a foretaste of what may be seen at the place. Dr. Bhau Daji came to Ajanta in 1865, and took facsimiles of most of the inscriptions, some of which had been previously noticed by James Prinsep, and published translations of them in the Bombay Journal.[4] The translations are generally correct and of great value, but the general remarks on the nature of the caves and their ornament are brief and not always satisfactory. The learned gentleman had the intention of writing a separate paper on the subject, but his untimely and lamented death prevented his carrying out the intention. Since his death several notices have appeared in the 'Indian Antiquary' which are highly interesting, but none of them is exhaustive.

When Major Gill's copies of these curious works of art were sent to Europe, it was expected that antiquarians in England would take them in hand, and submit to the public a full and comprehensive critical account of their character, and the subjects they portray. But the copies were destroyed by fire in the Sydenham Crystal Palace, and nothing came of them. In the meantime the originals suffered greatly from leakage in the caves and want of care, and it was apprehended that in a few years more they would be totally lost. A representation was accordingly made to Government to adopt some measures for their preservation. Thereupon a party of draftsmen, under the superintendence of Mr. Griffiths, Principal of the Art School at

Bombay, was deputed in 1872-73 to prepare copies of all the printings which were still legible. The result was a "collection of excellent copies of four large wall-paintings covering 122 square feet of canvas, 160 panels of ceiling, aggregating about 280 square feet, 17 moulds from the sculptures, and several drawings". In reporting on these Mr. Griffiths says: "The artists who painted them, were giants in execution. Even on the vertical sides of the walls some of the lines which were drawn with one sweep of the brush stuck me as being very wonderful; but when I saw long delicate curves drawn without faltering with equal precision upon the horizontal surface of a ceiling, where the difficulty of execution is increased a thousand-fold, it appeared to me nothing less than miraculous. One of the students, when hoisted up on the scaffolding, tracing his first panel on the ceiling, naturally remarked that some of the work looked like a child's work; little thinking that what appeared to him up there as rough and meaningless, had been laid in by a cunning hand, so that when seen at its right distance, every touch fell into its proper place.

"The condition of mind in which these paintings at Ajanta were originated and executed must have been very similar to that which produced the early Italian paintings of the fourteenth century, as we find much that is in common. Little attention paid to the science of art, a general crowding of figures into a subject, regard being had more to the truthful rendering of a story than to a beautiful rendering of it; not that they discarded beauty, but they did not make it the primary motive of representation. There is a want of aerial perspective—the parts are delicately shaded, not forced by light and shade, giving the whole a look of flatness—a quality to be desired in mural decoration.

Admirable True to Life Paintings

"Whoever were the authors of these paintings, they must have constantly mixed with the world. Scenes of every-day life, such as preparing food, carrying water, buying and selling, processions, hunting-scenes, elephant-fights, men and women engaged in singing, dancing, and playing on musical instruments, are most gracefully depicted upon these walls; and they could only have been done by men who were constant spectators of such scenes, by men of keen observation and retentive memories. . . . In every example that has come under my observation, the action of the hands is admirable and unmistakable in conveying the particular expression the artist intended."[5]

Adverting to the second picture he says: "Parts of this picture are admirably executed. In addition to the natural grace and ease with which she is standing, the drawing of the woman holding a casket in one hand, and a jewel with a string of pearls hanging from it in the other, is most delicately and truly rendered. The same applies to the woman seated on the ground in the left hand corner. The upward gaze and sweet expression of the mouth are beautifully given. The left hand of the same woman is drawn with great subtlety and tenderness."[6] "The third picture", he remarks, 'contains eight figures and portions of three others, all of which are seated or standing upon large lotus flowers with nimbi round the heads. The action of some of the figures, especially the standing ones, bears such a very striking resemblance to what is characteristic of the figures in Christian art, that they might have been taken from some mediaeval Church, rather than from the caves of Ajanta. The delicate foliage which tills in the spaces between the figures will give some idea of the power of these old artists as designers, and also of their knowledge of the growth of plants."[7]

Unsurpassed in the History of Art

Referring to a picture in cave No. 16 he observes: "This picture, I consider, cannot be surpassed in the history of art. The Florentine could have put better drawing and the Venetian better colour, but neither could have thrown greater expression into it. The dying woman, with drooping head, half-closed eyes, and languid limbs, reclines on a bed the like of which may be found in any native house of the present day. She is tenderly supported by a female attendant, whilst another, with cager gaze, is looking into her face, and holding the sick woman's arms, as if in the act of feeling her pulse. The expression on her lace is one of deep anxiety, as she seems, to realize how soon life will be extinct in one she loves. Another female behind is in attendance with a panka, whilst two men on the left are looking on with the expression of profound grief depicted in their faces. Below are seated on the floor other relations, who appear to have given up all hope, and to have begun their days of mourning,—for one woman has buried her face in her hands, and, apparently, is weeping bitterly."[8]

No Better Examples for Art Education

And he sums up the value of the whole by saying—"For the purposes of art-education, no better examples could be placed before an Indian art-student than those to be found in the caves of Ajanta. Here we have art with life in it, human faces full of expression,—limbs drawn with grace and action, flowers which bloom, birds which soar, and beasts that spring, or fight, or patiently carry burdens: all are taken from Nature's book-growing after her pattern, and in this respect differing entirely from Muhammadan art, which is unreal, unnatural, and therefore incapable of development."[9]

It is to be regretted, however, that as yet no attempt has been made to secure for the public a detailed, descriptive, critical and historical account of these relics. At one time a proposition was made to place the drawings at the disposal of Mr. Fergusson for the purpose; but, I believe, it has since fallen through.

The Government of India has, however, in the meantime, caused photographic impressions to be taken of Mr. Griffiths' drawings, and copies thereof sent to Societies interested in Indian Archaeology. Three batches of these photographs have, from time to time, been received by the Asiatic Society of Bengal, and they fully bear out Mr. Griffiths' remarks regarding their value.

A large number of the photographs represent architectural details and floral scrolls of much importance as illustration of ancient art-designs in this country, and are well worthy of careful study. There are others representing scenes in the legendary life of Buddha, which are of considerable value in connexion with the antiquity of the legends which they illustrate. While a few depict scenes from private life, or state pageantry, which afford interesting details regarding the manners, customs, habits, social condition, and intercourse of foreigners with the people of Western India, two thousand years ago.

First to Note Foreigners in Ajanta Paintings

Messrs. Ralph and Grisley were the first to notice the existence of foreigners in these frescoes. In their animated and scenic correspondence, mention is repeatedly made of foreigners as distinct from the natives. In one place they say: "Here is a lovely face, a Madonna face. What eyes! She looks towards the moon. Observe, these are Hindu faces—nothing foreign".[10] Elsewhere, "Observe that Abyssinian black prince seated on a bed—remark his ornaments. Now the woman seated on his left knee whom he embraces is as fair as you or 1. Did these fellows get Georgian slaves?" Again: "Here are evidently three beauties in this apartment—one an African, one copper-coloured, one of a *European* complexion. Yes; and how frequently we see these intermixed. See this, R. is a fair man, a eunuch." Again, "How often we see people of three complexions in the same panel! Now this is the most extraordinary thing we have found. Here are three placid portraits—they are *Chinese.* Nothing can be plainer;—observe the style of their hair;—the women have locks brought down in ringlets over their faces, and falling on to the neck, like some of the Hampton Court beauties." The writers did not, however, attempt to define the character of these foreigners, in any detail. It will not be uninteresting, therefore, to examine at length the peculiarities of a few of the figures shown in the photographs.

The first picture I have to notice is a court-scene on the south side of the cave No. I. In Messrs. Ralph and Grisley's paper it is thus described: "Here is a fair man of full age, dressed in a robe and cap, like some monk or abbot. Here is, next to him, a half-naked Brahman, copper-coloured, with shaven crown, and the single lock on his head. Here is a man presenting him with a scroll on which *something is written*. He is in a crowded court,—he has come to an audience." In the original this picture measures 15′×6′-6″ (Plate I). It represents a large audience chamber with colonnaded side aisles, and a large portal in front. The room is carpeted with some stuff bearings spring on a black, or dark-coloured, ground. On the centre is a *charpai* or bedstead, which serves the purpose of a throne. It has four feet of the ordinary modern make, with a tape-woven top, such as is to be met with in every decently furnished house in northern India in the present day. Over it is a mattress of striped cloth, and on the off side a large pillow or *takia*, having behind it an ornamented head-piece shaped like a corona. A king or chief is seated, squatting on this throne in the usual oriental style, dressed in a flowing *dhuti* or body-cloth, a *chadar* lied round the waist, and a tunic of some kind whose character is not apparent. He wears a rich heavy crown, bracelets and necklaces, one of the last being worn athwart the chest, very like a Brahmanical cord. The face and parts of the arms and chest are destroyed or smudged over. In front of the throne there is a man seated, holding an ox-tail *chauri*, and having in front of him a curious ornament, shaped like a cornucopia. To the right there are four other persons seated on the ground, one of them having in front a tray placed on a tripod stand. The pose of the person is like that of a Brahman engaged in worship. Behind and on the two sides of the throne, there are several persons,— officers, of state, courtiers body-guard, and menials,—standing in different attitudes, some dressed in *dhuti* only, others with tunics or made dresses, the character of which, owing to the smudgy condition of the picture, cannot be satisfactorily made out, except in one case in which a pair of close-fitting trousers and a *chapkan* are unmistakable. Some are armed with clubs, and one, near the entrance to the hall, upholds a standard. Their shaven chin, oriental head-dress, dark complexion, and characteristic features leave no doubt in my mind that they are all Indians. Among them there are four females, one standing behind the throne, and three seated on the carpet on the left side. In marked contrast to these are three persons standing in front of the king, and four others at a little distance. The foremost among them has a sugar-loaf-shaped hat with a black band, a large flowing gown of white stuff, a striped jacket, and a dagger held in a cloth girdle. The lower part of the gown or long coat is partially covered by the figure of the Brahman engaged in worship, but from the portion which is visible, it is evident that it extended below the middle of the leg. Between the girdle and the lower edge of the jacket there is a waistband buckled in front. Round his neck there is a necklace with a large locket. He is in the attitude of making a courtesy to the king, with his right hand passed under the jacket and placed on the left breast, and the left holding out a folded letter. The second person, dressed in the same style, but with a black jacket, is standing with folded hands in token of respect. His hat has no band. The third has a Persian helmet, with a crescent on top and a rosette on one side. He is bearing a tray full of presents of some kind. At a little distance from the last, just entering the hall, there is another person of the same nationality, bearing a tray, and outside the door there are two or three others who are evidently servants of the persons who have entered the hall, and belonging to the same nationality. The lower part of the gowns of these is not visible, but it must be the same as in the case of the foremost figure. The coat of the man with a helmet is probably short.

The complexion of these persons, except the first, is markedly fair. Studying the group carefully the conclusion appears inevitable that it represents an embassy from a foreign country. The foremost person is the ambassador, who is presenting his credentials in open court to the Indian potentate. Behind him is his secretary, and then follow the bearers of the *nazr* or presents from the foreign court.

But whence is this embassy? and what is the nationality of the persons who compose it? We are aware of no Indian race or tribe which differed so materially and markedly in complexion, features, and dress from the natives of the country as represented in the court. From beyond India on the north and the east, there was no nation which, two thousand years ago, could have presented such a group. We must look to the North-West, therefore, for the birth-place of the ambassador and his suite. Now on that side we had the Afghans, the Bactrians, the Scythians, and the Persians. But the Afghans never had the peculiar sugar-loaf hat, nor the flowing gown, nor the crescented helmet. Their features too, were, as shall be presently shown, coarser and rude. The Bactrian and the Scythian dresses, to judge from numismatic evidence—the only evidence available in the case,—were also different. The coat was short, the trousers tight-fitting, and the head-gear very unlike a sugar-loaf hat. The Persian dress, however, as we now have it, is the exact counterpart of what appears in the picture. The hat, the gown and the jacket are identically the same.

Persian Embassy in Indian Court

The helmet appears repeatedly in the sculptures of Khorsabad and Nineveh, and the features and the beard are in no way different. We may, therefore, safely conclude that the picture represents a group of Persians, either merchants, or an embassy from Persia to an Indian court, probably the latter, as the letter in the hand of the foremost person would be redundant in a merchant. I am not aware of any mention of such an embassy in Buddhist religious history; but I have read but a small portion of Buddhist literature, and as it is abundantly evident that the frescoes of Ajanta were not confined to representations of religious history, it is not necessary to hunt up any relationship with it of Buddhist legends. Nor is it material to know whether the representation is historical or an ideal one. In either case it shows that the Indians of old had free intercourse with the Persians, and were thoroughly familiar with their features and dress. Literary evidence on this subject may be had in abundance in Sanskrit literature, but it is not necessary to adduce it here.

Man of Central Asiatic Race

The second scene I have to describe is a domestic one, and three editions of it occur in the collection of photographs before me. There is no indication, however, to show whence they have been taken. The scales attached show them to be of large size, about 30x28 ft. In its simplest version (Plate II) it represents a divan placed in front of a cloth screen, and covered with cushions and a check pattern coverlet; and on it are seated a big, stout, burly-looking man and a lady by his side. The man is seated cross-legged, and is in an amatory mood, perhaps somewhat befuddled with wine. His face is heavy and square, and he has both a beard and a moustache. He wears long hair covered by a thick conical cap with a turban, or a fur band around it like the Qilpaq cap of the Central Asiatic races of the present day. On his body is a coat or tunic reaching to the knee and trimmed with, what appears to me, patch-work decorations; knee-breeches and striped stockings complete his dress. He holds a cup in his left hand, and before him, on the ground, in front of the divan, there is a covered tray. The lady beside him has a gown reaching to the knee, a shell-jacket, (both set-off with patch work trimmings), and a pair of striped stockings. She has a skull cap on her head, and earrings. Her right hand is lifted as in the act of telling something interesting to her lord. To the right of the man, in front of the divan, there stands a maid, arrayed in a long flowing gown which leaves only the tips of her shoes visible, and holding a flagon, shaped like a soda-water bottle with a long narrow neck, ready to replenish the cup of her lord. Behind the mistress there is a second maid with a wide-mouthed covered jar in her hand.

In the second version the man holds the cup in his right hand, and a stick or straight sword in his left. He has also an elaborately-worked belt, and the trimmings of the coats and gowns are of different patterns. The lady leans on the shoulder of her lord by her right hand, and by her attitude expresses great solicitude to please him. There is also a third maid, squatting in front, and ready to serve out edibles from the covered tray beside her.

Negro Looking Servants

The third version is even more developed (Plate III). The screen behind the divan is set off with floral designs. The coat of the hero and the gown of his lady, and also that of her maid, are set-off with triangular striped streamers flying from the back. The features of the lady are vivid with life, and the expression of endearment on her face is truly admirable. The second maid holds a *surahi* or goglet instead of a jar. The lady has, instead of a cap, a fillet round her head with an aigrette in front, and the maids similar fillets, but without the jewel. The third maid is replaced by two bearded, thick-lipped Negro-looking servants who are serving out dishes from the covered tray. The stockings in the last two versions are white. In two small panels the male figure is reproduced in company with another male,—two jovial companions, engaged in some pleasantries and pledging their faith to each other over a cup of liquor. The striped stockings are distinctly seen in these, as also a pair of check-pattern trousers, not striped.

There are more than five hundred representations of Indian men and women in the photographs, but they appear totally unlike the human figures shown in these plates, and, bearing in mind the fact that the artists of these frescoes were most faithful in delineating the peculiarities of their subjects, it is impossible to deny that they took their models for these from other than Indians. It is difficult, however, to determine what nationality they had in view. The features, the cap and the turban of the principal figure, are the exact counterparts of what may be every day seen in the Kabulese fruit-sellers in the streets of Calcutta; but the coat is different. I have never seen an Afghan woman in her native dress, but the gown and the jacket of the female figures appear very like those of Jewesses. The patch-work trimmings are peculiar to them, and the best specimens of the kind of work I have seen are of Jewish make. The Afghans, however, are in no way inferior in this art: they bring to Calcutta every year a number of rugs and other articles of patch-work, which are remarkably beautiful. Knowing how such domestic arts as needle-work and patch-work are perpetuated for generations, and looking at the complexion, the cap and the turban, I was first disposed to believe that the figures on these plates represented Afghans, the thick-lipped servants being Negroes.

Bactrian Greeks—The Authors of Ajanta Caves?

In the Zodiac Cave (No. XVI) Dr. Bhau Daji found an inscription which once "contained the names of seven or eight kings of the Vakataka dynasty, but only that of Vindhyasakti, the oldest and most eminent, was preserved intact". "By a strange fatality", says the writer, "the inscription has been obliterated wherever a royal name existed, so that one is tempted to suppose that the destruction was intentional. But, he adds, "the destructive influence of the rainy weather is sufficient to account for the gaps".[11] The name of this Vindhyasakti's country is mentioned in the Seoni copper-plate; but the chief himself is not named there. Dr. Bhau Daji identifies this Vindhyasakti with a chief of the Kailakila Yavanas who, according to the Vishnu Purana, once ruled in India. Having advanced thus far, he takes Kailakila to be identical with an ancient city and citadel named Ghulghuleh near Bamian, mentioned by Mr. Masson in his paper on the Antiquities of Bamian (*ante*, v. 708), and Vakataka with Bactria, thereby suggesting, though not positively asserting, that the Bactrian Greeks were the authors of the Ajanta caves. If this reasoning be admitted, the figures we have shown would be those of Bactrian Greeks. But there are various difficulties to overcome before we can accept the identification. The name Vindhyasakti is too thorough a Sanskrit word to be the name of a Bactrian Greek, and there is nothing to connect him with the princes of the Seoni plate, except the word Vakataka, which, as given in the Seoni plate, is unmistakably the name of an Indian, and not of a trans-Indian locality, particularly Bactrian, for which the usual and very extensively-employed term is Valhika. In the Puranas these Valhikas are said to have reigned after Vindhyasakti. Denying, however, the accuracy of the identification of Vakataka with Bactria and of Vindhyasakti having been a Bactrian, it might still be said that the figures under notice are Bactrians. In some Kenerki coins the cap is conical, and surrounded by a turban or a band of fur like the Qilpaq cap; the cut of the coat is of the same style, and the close-fitting trousers and stockings are, as far as can be made out in coins, the same. The coarse square face of the Mongolian type is particularly remarkable, and, as the Bactrians exercised supremacy for some time in India from a little before the commencement of the Christian era, to nearly a century after it, it would be much more reasonable to suppose the representations to be of Bactrians, rather than those of Afghans, who attained to no political distinction at the time, and were to some extent included among the Hindus.

The stockings of the peculiar pattern which has hitherto been thought to be the outcome of modern European art, are remarkable: I have noticed them nowhere else in Indian paintings or sculpture. The Hindus seem to have borrowed the stockings from their neighbours; for in a panel in Cave No. 1, there is a representation of an Indian bacchanalian scene, unmistakable from the features and dress, in which they have been reproduced on the legs of a man and his lady-love. Before the importation of stockings from Europe, the Indian got their supplies from Kashmir. I do not, however, know when knitted stockings were first introduced into that country. To England they first came in the reign of Henry VIIT, and it is extremely doubtful if they were of much more ancient date in Kashmir. And after all what I take to be stockings might be sewed hose of cloth or milled stuff of some kind.

The indulgence in spirituous drinks was common all over India, Bactria and Persia in ancient times, and the evidence of it in the frescoes does not call for any notice.[12] That the cup and the flagon indicate something more potent than sherbet, I believe, none will question.

The curtains behind the divan suggest the idea that the sites of the Bactrian domestic scenes were tents, and that the people shown had not become settled inhabitants of the country. But the evidence in this respect is too meagre to attach any importance to such an idea.

Looking to the made-dresses of the Persians and the Bactrians, it might be supposed that the Indians got theirs from those sources; but, as I have shown in my "Antiquities of Orissa", such was not the case, at least when the Ajanta frescoes were painted. In the Indian bacchanalian scene above noticed, the dresses of the Indian man and woman are quite different, and by no means such as to justify the assumption that they had been designed from foreign models. In the very affecting picture of the death of a lady of rank in Cave No. XVI, the bodices shown on some of the maid-servants engaged in grinding corn in hand-mills, are quite unlike the jackets of the Bactrian women.

In an Indian scene in Cave No. I, where a large number of sable beauties are exhibited, there is a figure seated cross-legged, whose dark features, punchy belly and style of sitting, leave no doubt in my mind of his nationality; and he is dressed in a *dhuti* which leaves a part of his thigh exposed, and a *mirzai* of flowered muslin which is thoroughly Indian, and the like of it has nowhere been seen out of India. The *mirzai* is in use by the Hindus to this day all over northern India, and its make seems not to have changed in the least since the time of the fresco.

Two Thousand Years Old Ajanta Paintings

It is not my intention to enter into a discussion here as to the date of the Ajanta Caves. The late Dr. Wilson of Bombay took them to extend from the third or second century before, to the fifth or sixth century after Christ.[13] Mr. Burgess, after a careful study of the Caves, states "that the oldest of them cannot be later than the second century before the Christian era". Long before him Mr. Fergusson came to the same conclusion in his 'Rock-cut Caves of India,' and in his 'History of Eastern Architecture' remarked that Cave No. XII, "the facade of which so much resembles that of the Nasik Chaitya (B.C. 129), cannot be far off in date" (p. 122). The latest are supposed to be of the 5th or 6th century. Accepting this opinion for my guide, and there is not much to show that it is untenable, and bearing in mind that Cave No. I is one of the largest and richest in paintings which long preceded sculpture, I may fairly come to the conclusion that the scenes I have described above represent phases of Indian life from eighteen hundred to two thousand years ago.

Notes and References

1. Transactions Rl. As. Soc, I, p. 557.
2. *Ante* V.
3. Vol. III, pp. 71ff.
4. Vol. VII.
5. *Indian Antiquary*, III. 26.
6. *Ibid.*, loc. cit.
7. *Loc. cit.*, p. 27.
8. *Ibid.*, p. 27.
9. *Ibid.*, p. 28.
10. *Ante*, Vol. V, p. 558.
11. Journal, Bombay As. Soc, VII, p. 65.
12. *Vide passim* my paper on 'Spirituous Drinks in Ancient India,' *ante*, XLII, pp. 1 ff.
13. Journal, Bombay As. Soc., III, p. 73.

I. A Persian Embassy to an Indian Court (From Ajanta)

II. A Bactrian Domestic Scene from Ajanta

III. A Bactrian Domestic Scene from Ajanta

7

Foreign Influences in Ancient India

RAWLINSON

Prehistoric Trade Ties

Trade between India and the West, both by land and sea, stretches, no doubt, beyond the dawn of history. But for a long time it was fitful and intermittent. By land the journey was beset with perils, deserts, mountains,[1] and hostile tribes. By sea, navigation was hindered by bad ships and want of enterprise on the part of the sailors. It was not until the Phoenicians, the greatest maritime nation, perhaps, in all history, undertook the task of exploring Eastern waters, that anything serious was achieved in this direction. Curiously enough, this important step was not due to any of the powerful nations of Asia Minor, the Egyptians, or Assyrians, but to the enterprising actions of Solomon, the ruler of the tiny Hebrew Kingdom of Israel, some time in the twelfth century B.C. Solomon, upon coming to the throne, found his country in a state of almost unexampled prosperity, and determined to make Jerusalem as magnificent as the capitals of his great neighbours. Unable, however, to obtain in sufficient quantities locally the gold, silver, and rare woods required for his purpose, he requested his ally, Hiram of Tyre, to lend him some of his skilled seamen to build a fleet for use in Eastern waters. Making their headquarters the port of Ezion-Geber, the modern Akaba, at the northern extremity of the right arm of the Red Sea, these sailors fitted out a number of vessels, in which with characteristic boldness they soon passed the Straits of Bab-el-Mandeb. Their final destination was the port of Ophir, from which they brought back as much as "four hundred and twenty talents of gold," as well as almug-wood, ivory, apes, and peacocks. The voyage to Ophir and back occupied a space of three years.[2]

Indus Valley—A Mine of Gold

There are many reasons for thinking that the port of Ophir was somewhere on the Indian coast.[3] The mention of the vast quantities of gold exported from it, seems to favour an identification of it with the "Barbarikon" of the Greek traders, which stood at the mouth of the Indus. The Indus valley, in anicent days, produced an enormous amount of gold; it paid Darius three hundred and sixty talents weight of gold-dust yearly in tribute;[4] and every one in Greece had heard of legends of the miners of Dardistan and their fierce yellow mastiffs, which travellers in some extraordinary fashion mistook for huge ants! Again, the fleet of Solomon took three years to sail from Ezion-Geber and back. The voyage, then, took about eighteen months, and this was exactly the length of the voyage of Scylax of Caryanda from the Indus to the Gulf of Suez.[5] Ivory, apes, and peacocks would naturally come from an Indian port; and the Hebrew word for "ape", *koph*, is suspiciously like the Sanskrit *kapi*.[6] The "peacock", on the other hand, appears to have reached the West from a Dravidian port, perhaps Mangalore. the Roman Muziris, for the Hebrew word for a peacock, *thuki*, is, apparently, derived from the Tamil *tokei*, whence also the Persian *tavus* and the Greek *Tafws*. Many other commodities appear to have been introduced by these traders and their successors, to judge by their names. Thus the Greek word meaning (sandal, perhaps the "almug" of Solomon) is the Sanskrit *chandana*;[7] the Greek word meaning linen, may be derived from the "Sindhu", or Indian country,[8] and may have been brought by Hebrew traders to the West; for we find *Sadin*[9] used as "fine linen" in Isaiah, and *Satin* is the Arabic for a "covering". The word is also found in Assyrian. In a similar fashion, rice was brought to Europe by Arabian traders from Dravidian ports, for the word *rice* is a shortened form of the Spanish *arroz*, derived from the Arabic *aruz*, from which, too, the Greek and the Latin *oryza* also come; and the Arabic word is simply a corruption of the Tamil *arisi*. The rich fields of Southern India must have borne rice crops for immemorial ages.[10]

Intercourse Between India and Soloman's Judaea

But the strangest and most interesting evidence of intercourse between India and Judaea in the time of Solomon is afforded to us by a Buddhist birth story called the *Mahosada Jataka*.[11] Here we have the story of a Yakshini, or female ghoul, who has carried off a poor woman's child in order to devour it. The mother claims her offspring, and the two women are summoned to the judgment hall of the Buddha (at that time incarnate as the wazir of the Rajah of Benares), to have their dispute adjudicated. The Buddha tells one woman to take the child's legs and the other its head, and decide the matter by a tug-of-war. The Yakshini consents, but the rightful mother will give up all her claims rather than put the baby to such torture. The Buddha then gives her the child. No one, I think, can doubt that this is an Indian version of the famous story of the Judgment of Solomon,[12] nor will anybody who has studied the extraordinary history of the migration of the Jataka Tales, be surprised at this odd occurrence. There can be no doubt that the Indians borrowed the tale from the Jews, and not *vice versa*. The Jatakas were collected from all sorts of prae-Buddhistic folk-legends. The only question is whether the Indians got it direct from Hebrew traders long before the birth of Gautama, or whether it came from Babylon, whether it had been brought by the Jews during the Captivity (597-538 B.C.).[13]

After the death of Solomon, the Persian Gulf became the chief trade route between India and Asia Minor.[14] At the mouth of the Euphrates lived the Chaldeans, a restless, seafaring race; the prophet Isaiah speaks of the "Chaldeans whose cry is in their ships,"—a vivid phrase, describing exactly the bustle and turmoil of an Oriental port. About 695 B.C., however, Sennacherib, King of Assyria, replaced them by Phoenicians, probably in order to punish the Chaldeans for helping the Babylonians in a rising against the Assyrian Empire. The advent of the Phoenicians had the same magical effect upon the trade of the Persian Gulf as it had formerly produced in the Red Sea. These bold navigators soon pushed on to India, and rounding the Indian coast, even visited the Malay Archipelago and China. A whole colony of Phoenician sailors sprang up in the Persian) Gulf. The Bahrein Islands were especially popular as a port of call for vessels to take in water and provisions before setting out on their long run across the Indian Ocean, and recent excavations have revealed remains of a large settlement there.[15] Strabo says that in his day the islands of the Persian Gulf were dotted with Phoenician temples.[16] Their less skilful rivals, the Chaldeans, disconted at their supersession, appear to have rebelled again. This time they were banished to Gerrha, a terribly hot, barren spot, where they had to use blocks of salt to build their houses.[17] This must have been an unwelcome change after the humid climate of Chaldea.

Overland Route Between India and the West

Of the overland route between India and the West, we hear little before the time of Darius the Great, probably because the journey was rendered difficult and dangerous by the wild tribes who beset the road. Even in the remotest days, however such a route must have existed; an axehead of white Chinese jade was found in the second city of Troy.[18] Caravans came and went, no doubt, both from Tyre and from the ports further north. In any case the route taken must have been ultimately the same,—past the Caspian Gates, and north of the Carmanian Desert to Balkh, where the roads running to China and India converged. Shalmaneser (858 B.C.) has representations of Indian elephants and apes[19] and Bactrian camels on his obelisk, and these animals the elephants at any rate, must have been imported overland. After the defeat of Assyria by Nebuchadnezzar in 606 B.C., Babylon became the leading city of Asia. In its market-places met the nations of the world,—captive Jews, Indian traders, Egyptian ambassadors, Phoenician sailors from the Far East—in short, as Berosus says, "a crowd of men of all nationalities". We hear in one of the Jataka Stories of the adventures of the merchants who took the first peacock to Babylon; on the other hand, there appears to have been a settlement of Babylonian traders at the frontier town of Taxila in India, for Aristobulus of Cassandria[20] found at that city a "marriage-market" being carried on in Babylonian fashion, just as is described by Herodotus.[21] What was the result of the contact been India and the Semitic races? Not very great, I think. Casual traders do little towards the real opening up of a country. From the Jews India learnt practically nothing; from the Chaldeans she may have borrowed part of her prae-Alexandrian system of Astronomy;[22] from the Babylonian merchants may have come the idea of striking rude, punch-marked coins, and perhaps a system of weights and measures. It is, I think, useless to attempt to trace early Indian architecture to Babylonian or Assyrian sources. "The culture of Assyria, and still more of Babylonia, was essentially literary; we miss in it the artistic spirit of Egypt or Greece. In Babylonia the abundance of clay and want of stone led to the employment of brick; the Babylonian temples are massive but shapeless structures of crude brick, supported by buttresses."[23] The absurd stories of Ctesias about an Assyrian invasion of India, narrated by Justin,[24] are a gross fabrication, and Semiramis is a product of the imagination. The Semiter merely prepared the way for the momentous Iranian invasion, with which we shall presently deal.

Buddhism at Variance with Hinduism

While thrones were rising and falling in Western Asia, a revolution of another kind was taking place in North-Eastern India. Gautama Buddha (568–488 B.C.)[25] was formulating the doctrines which were destined, to use the picturesque of the phrase of the Pali commentator, to re-echo "like a great bell set in the heavens" throughout the East. Gautama Buddhạ is the one personality of the prae-Alexandrian period of whom we can really say that we *know* something. Was he really an Aryan, or are we to class his remarkable creed among the "foreign influences" which affected India during this period? The question is a startling one, and has never, I think, been adequately considered. But every one must have noticed the many striking features of Buddhism, so utterly at variance with anything to be found elsewhere in Hinduism, the *stupa*, the worship of relics, the abolition of caste as a religious factor, contempt for penance and ceremonies, and the discouragement of abstract metaphysics. Many of these peculiarities may, of course, be merely the products of a powerful and far-reaching mind, bent on religious reform; but relic-worship, and its concomitant the *stupa*, are quite un-Indian.[26] Gautama belonged to the Sakya clan: were they an early offshoot of the Sakas, the Sacae or Scyths, who, as we know, followed the Aryans from time to time into India in successive waves? The word *stupa* signifies a "barrow", or "tumulus", a Sanskrit name for a Scythian object. The Scythian chieftain was buried under a tumulus of this kind, and not, as in India, cremated. Herodotus, for instance, tells us how the Gerrhi, a tribe on the Borysthenes, buried their kings in huge square tombs, over which the people raised a high mound of earth, each vying with his neighbour to make it as tall as possible.[27] In Southern Siberia may be seen to this day the *kurgans* of the primitive Scythian tribes. The round shape of the *stupa* shows that it was originally an earthen structure,[28] just as the pyramid, a kindred type of building, must have been always constructed of stone. And so the massive Sanchi

Stupa, with its elaborately carved stone railing, is very probably the lineal descendant of the rude earthen mound covering the tombs of the Scythian chieftains on the Central Asia steppes, fenced in by a rough palisade of huge logs, decorated with fetish-symbols to scare away the evil spirits which might otherwise disturb the peace of the inmate.

When the Saka tribes migrated to India, and were received into the fold of Hinduism, a kind of compromise must have been effected, in the case of notable personages, between the rival customs of burial beneath a barrow and cremation. The body was first cremated and then the ashes were buried. The custom of relic-worship—not a Hindu custom[29]—led to the practice of dividing the ashes (and other remains) of a deceased teacher among several claimants, each of whom enshrined his portion under a *stupa* of his own. Thus the *stupa*, or burial mound, became a *dagoba*, or relic-holder. The earliest record of such a division relates to the ashes of Gautama Buddha himself.[30] Eight tribes sent delegates to claim, on the ground of kindred with the deceased teacher, a share of his remains. The possession of such relics was, of course, an asset of great material value; the dagoba beneath which they lay became a *tirtha*, or place of pilgrimage, and rapidly grew rich and famous.

Buddhism among the Products of Early Foreign Influence

Among the tribes claiming, as kinsmen, a right to a portion of the ashes of Gautama, were the Vajjis of Vaisali. They are depicted[31] in early Buddhist sculptures as wearing Scythian garb. Whether Vajji is simply a variation of *Yue-chi*, and whether the Lichhavi clan, said to be an offshoot of the Vajji, are to be identified with the Litsavi, a Mongolo-Scythic tribe in Thibet, is uncertain, but probable. Another tribe, the Gandharas, must have originally come from the distant North-West Frontier, where Scythians would naturally be found. If these two tribes were Scythian, the tribe of Gautama must have been Scythian too. And so, perhaps, we are justified in including Buddhism among the products of early foreign influence in India.

When Darius Occupied Panjab

In 538 B.C., Cyrus the Great took Babylon by storm, and became Master of Western Asia—"King of Babel, Sumer, Akkad, and the four quarters of the world". Twenty years later, his equally great successor, Darius, crossed the Carmanian Desert to claim the allegiance of

Eastern Iran. Darius was, a splendid organizer and financier—his abilities in that latter direction had gained him the contemptuous title of "The Pedlar", from the Persian nobility,—and he was struck with the brilliant idea of annexing the Indus Valley to his eastern possessions. The scheme was carried out in a most methodical fashion: the Panjab was occupied, and an expedition was sent under a Greek named Scylax of Caryanda to explore the Indus Valley and to travel home by sea from the mouth of the river.[32] The explorers accomplished their task with complete success; they returned by the old route followed by Solomon's trading fleet, and landed eighteen months later near the modern port of Suez.

Marriage Market

We know so little of the history of Persia, that there is not much to record of the "Satrapy of India" during the two centuries which preceded the invasion of Alexander. That the country fully realized the expectations of Darius is shown by the enormous tribute which it paid to the imperial coffers. Indian contingents fought in the Persian campaigns against Greece. Perhaps Taxila was the capital of the province, for Alexander's soldiers found there traces of Persian and Babylonian customs; the people held a marriage-market every year in their city, like the Babylonians, and exposed their dead for the vultures to devour instead of cremating them.[33] Darius was the first monarch to have both Greek and Indian subjects under his rule. Of the mainland of Greece, India knew nothing; the Ionians of Asia Minor, employed in the Great King's service, or traders of the same nationality who put in at Barbarikon or Barygaza, were the only Greeks with whom they were acquainted. Hence we may dismiss at once any theories about the influence of Greek literature on India before Alexander's invasion. The Sanskrit *Yavana, 'Iafwv*, dates from the time when the digamma was still in use. The Prakrit *Yona*, is, of course, later.[34] There seems little doubt that the Persian occupation of the Panjab made a great impression upon India; Persian customs and Persian architecture were probably adopted at the courts of some of the local rajas. One unmistakable trace of Persian influence lasted in Western India for many centuries after the Persian Empire had disappeared. This was the Kharoshthi script, introduced by the officials of the Achaemenids, which was not entirely replaced by the Brahmi writing till the fourth century A.D. The Kharoshthi is undoubtedly Aramaic in origin, reading, like other kindred scripts, from right to left.[35] The last hope of Persia perished with the gallant young Cyrus on the field of Cunaxa (401 B.C.). After this the great Empire began to break up. Eastern Iran became a practically independent kingdom under the Satrap of Balkh, who was always a member of the Royal family. We cease to hear of Indian troops in the Persian army, and probably the annual Indian tribute seldom found its way to the Imperial coffers.

Greek Influence

In 329 B.C. Alexander entered the Panjab. He found Western India governed by a number of independent princes, controlled by no sort of central government. In this disunited condition, they fell an easy prey to the Macedonian forces, in spite of the desperate resistance which was offered from time to time by the gallant natives. Alexander marched across the Panjab in a south-easterly direction to the river Bias, where he was compelled to turn back. He then retreated to the banks of the Jhilam, and sailed down that stream to its confluence with the Indus, and thence to the coast, subduing and organizing the country as he went. The conquered lands were put in charge of governors, native and Greek; elaborate arrangements were made for building a harbour at Pattala; Nearchus was sent to explore, and re-opened the old Phoenician trade route between the mouths of the Indus and Euphrates. Unfortunately, these far-seeing plans came to nothing. In 323 B.C., two years after leaving India, Alexander died. The empire collapsed like a pack of cards; at the same time a great national movement under Chandragupta united all Aryan India under a single leader, and the Macedonian governors were glad to hurry away to the further side of the Hindu Kush with such booty as they could lay hands on.

By 321 B.C., Macedonian power was at an end in India; only those settlers remained who cared to throw in their lot with the people.[36] The effect of the great invasion was practically *nil*, unless the example of Alexander inspired the enterprising Chandragupta with the idea of making himself master of Northern India.

Period of Renaissance

We now come to the age of the enlightened and powerful Maurya dynasty, which may be compared with the age of the Antonines in Rome for wisdom, progress and moderation, though there is a certain spirituality about the great Asoka which is hardly found in Marcus

Aurelius himself. It was a period of Renaissance in India: a great religious revival was accompanied by a magnificent artistic outburst. Shrines and palaces of stone suddenly replaced the wood and plaster erections of earlier days; clemency of a type unknown in India prevailed in the government; free communication with the hitherto despised "barbarian" was welcomed and encouraged. The difference which organization could make to a country's powers of resistance was seen when Seleucus Nicator tried in 305 B.C. to repeat the exploits of Alexander. The "Victorious" monarch quickly found it prudent to come to terms with his adversary. A friendly agreement was made, ceding a large portion of Eastern Iran to India, and the compact was sealed by a marriage between Chandragupta and a Syrian princes. The relations between the Mauryas and their western neighbours was of the most cordial kind. Chandragupta was an enthusiastic admirer of Greek customs. Envoys from the West were in attendance at Pataliputra, and the presence of a Greek *rani* must have enhanced the philhellenic tendencies of the court. Among the ambassadors, the most famous was Megasthenes, the Syrian envoy to Chandragupta; in the reign of Bindusara he was suceeded by Deimachus. We also hear of a Dionysius from the court of Alexandria, who appears to have been in residence in the reign of Asoka.[37] A friendly and often amusing correspondence between the Maurya kings and their Syrian neighbours testifies to the intimate character of the relations between India and the Greek world at that time. Chandragupta sends Seleucus some powerful Indian drugs; Bindusara requests of Antiochus a consignment of "figs, Greek wine, and a sophist"; to which that monarch replies, that while delighted to send the wine, he regrets that it is not "good form for Greeks to deal in sophists." After his conversion to Buddhism, Asoka's first thought is for his friends, the Greek rulers of Syria and Alexandria. And yet, in spite of the intimacy between India and the West under the Mauryas, we can discern very few actual traces of Greek influence on Indian civilization during that period. The court of Chandragupta, as described by Megasthenes,[38] was conducted in Persian fashion. As in Persia, the king lived in strict seclusion, and observed Persian festivals like the curious "hair-washing festival" held on the king's birthday.[39] Offences were punished by mutilation, a Persian practice abhorred by the Greeks. The country was split up into provinces, like the Persian satrapies. Asoka, when he determined to use a more lasting material than the wood and plaster of his predecessors for architectural purposes, set his workmen to erect buildings and monuments of stone in the Persian style, but adapted an Indianized in characteristic Hindu fashion. At the same time, we may discern traces of Scythian influence in the sculpture of the period. The grotesque, broad shouldered figures of the Sanchi carvings are certainly not Aryan in type. The same type of figure appears even in the semi-Hellenic sculptures of the Gandhara school.

Irrigation Schemes and GT Road Built by a Bactrian

We may take it for granted that the inhabitants of the Aryavarta at the time of the accession of Chandragupta were already a highly civilized people. No remains, alas, of the early architecture of India have survived, owing to the fragile nature of the materials employed, but we can see that the beautifully carved and inscribed pillars of Asoka are not the crude efforts of a primitive nation. At the same time, their essentially Indian appearance seems to prove that they are not the work of foreign artizans, like the Gandhara sculptures. The numerous "sermons in stone" erected by Asoka, show that reading was a common accomplishment,[40] otherwise their erection all over the country would have been pointless. For two centuries constant intercourse with Persia, combined with the indigenous culture of the people, had produced an advanced civilization to which the rude Macedonian could add nothing, and upon which even Hellenistic refinement had comparatively little influence. Already, when Megasthenes arrived at Pataliputra, he found it as splendid as Susa or Ecbatana; and it was from Susa, *via* Taxila, that foreign influence had influenced the country. A Persian official, Tushaspa,[41] carried out Asoka's irrigation schemes in Kathiawar, doubtless on the model of the famous Babylonian works; the great trunk road, built from Pataliputra through Delhi to the North-West Frontier, was suggested, no doubt, by the Royal road of Darius in Persia.

Panjab—Meeting Place of Nations

A great deal has been made of the sudden introduction of stone as a building material by Asoka. It may be, of course, that he learnt from foreigners, perhaps Greeks, to use stone instead of wood. But it seems clear that he employed native craftsmen to work in this material, and allowed them to treat it very much in their own fashion. Thus, any one examining the carvings of the Sanchi Stupi will recognize that the workmen employed were used to working in wood. The famous "Buddhist rail" at Sanchi is built of stone blocks elaborately hewn into the likeness of wooden logs, and a significant inscription records that one of the gates was the work of the "ivory carvers of Vidisa."[42] The truth is, that stone was not extensively used for building purposes till a much later period. Even four centuries later, Hiuen Tsiang regards the deserted ruins of Asoka's stone palaces with superstitious awe, as "the work of no mortal hands". Kanishka's great relic tower at Peshawar was of wood,[43] and wood was used for the fortifications of Pataliputra. The huge wooden arches in the Karla Caves show to what use wood could be put by Indian builders, and no doubt the vast majority of the buildings of the time were of wood and plaster, built on brick foundations, such as are still popular in Western India. Asoka's more ambitious schemes were partly due to religious enthusiasm, and partly, no doubt, to the great access of wealth which resulted from the excellent organization of his vast empire. Persian influence may be detected in the bell-shaped pillars and "lien-capitals" of the Buddhist architecture of the Maurya period, but it is so adapted and transformed that we cannot help tracing its first introduction back for many years before the accession of Chandragupta, to the time when the Persian, Indian, and Central Asian races first encountered one another in that strangle meeting-place of nations, the Panjab.

Bactrian Conquest and Influence

The "Yellow Peril" was no new thing to the ancient world. The Assyrian Empire had been menaced by the threats of Scythian incursions; and Scythians assisted at the sack of Nineveh. Cyrus the Great fell in battle against these traditional foes of the Aryan race, and Alexander, though compelled to destroy Cyropolis, the fortress built by the Persian monarch to guard the passage over the Jaxartes, replaced it by an even greater stronghold in the shape of Alexandria Eschate. But the chief safeguard for the Aryans of Western Asia was the ancient Iranian province of Balkh or Bactria, the great buffer-state between the Persian Empire and the peoples of the steppes of Central Asia. Alexander had realized the strategic importance of Balkh to his eastern possessions, and had established there a large military colony. After his death this colony had grown into the dimensions of an important kingdom, the veterans having freely intermarried with the Iranian and Scythic populace. In 250 B.C. they revolted against the Syrian Empire, and their independence was recognized some forty years later by Antiochus the Great. That monarch had marched against the revolting province and laid siege to the capital, but he was induced to abandon his design by the plea that if he weakened this outpost of the Greek world, the Scythians would burst in and overrun the whole of the West at once.[44] Unfortunately, the Bactrians did not confine themselves to the *role* of guarding the Oxus; the disorders which followed upon the break-up of Maurya Empire, left the Panjab as a tempting prey to an ambitious conqueror, and the Bactrian monarchs were unable to resist the opportunity. About 190 B.C. the Bactrian king Demetrius invaded the northwest of India, and made himself master of a considerable portion of territory. This he made into a separate kingdom, with its capital at Sagala,[45] which he renamed Euthydemeia after his father Euthydemus. This left Bactria proper in a precarious condition. Harassed by internal dissentions, and by continual quarrels with their old rivals the Parthians, the Bactrian Greeks could ill-afford to send the flower of their troops on distant expeditions to the far South. As Justin says, they were literally "drained of their life-blood."[46] In consequence, the Scythians at last managed to cross the Oxus, and overrun the country. Heliodorus, the last Greek king to reign north of the Hindu Kush, hastily evacuated Bactria, and fled, with such of his followers as did not care to submit to the invaders, to find a home in the province of Sagala, which his predecessors had established. This was about 140 B.C. Unfortunately, the Greeks were continually quarrelling among themselves, and spilt up into a number of independent principalities. Only once, under the great Menander, did they unite for a brief time; and by 20 A.D. they dissappeared altogether, though little isolated Greek states probably struggled on here and there till a much later period.[47]

Indo-Greek Culture

These Greeks had really very little Western blood in their veins when they settled in India, and their influence upon this country was very slight. They issued, however, some very beautiful and remarkable coins, one or two of which will compare with anything produced in the ancient world. It is impossible to explain this outburst of artistic genius in the furthest confines of Hellenic influence. These Bactrian coins were imitated extensively by the few Indian rulers who showed any taste in this direction, the Kushans, the Guptas, and the Western Kshatrapas, especially Nahapana, the ruler who issued the coins found in such immense numbers near Nasik, some years ago.[48]

The Greek word *drachma* has passed into the vernacular language of to-day: from it came the Prakrit *dramma* and the modern *dam*.[49] Otherwise it appears that the Greeks were rapidly absorbed in the native population. The process may be traced in the coinage, where Indian figures and inscriptions replace by degrees the Greek types of the earlier monarchs, and the workmanship becomes more and more debased. The few remains we have of the Indo-Greeks seem to show that they quickly lost all traces of their individuality, and adopted the religion, and even in many cases the names, of their neighbours. Thus the Karla Caves contain many inscriptions recording donations from the "Yavanas". These must be Bactrian Greeks; but they have Hindu names, and are Buddhists. The pillar recently discovered at Besnagar[50] bears an inscription to the effect that it is the work of "Heliodorus, a worshipper of Krishna, sent by the Yona King Antialcidas". The pillar is in the Indo-Persian style, and contains no traces of Greek.workmanship. Probably the Greek language was only used at the court of Sagala, and among a few of the ruling class who had not intermarried with the natives. The Indo-Greek kingdoms reached the height of their power under the Buddhist prince Menander, who for a brief space carried the Greek arms to the walls of Pataliputra. Of his court and capital we find a delightful picture in the Buddhist *Questions of Milinda*[51] which describes them as follows:

> "There is in the country of the Yonakas a great centre of trade, a city called Sagala. . . . Wise architects have laid it out, and its people know of no oppression, since all their enemies and adversaries have been put down. Brave is its defence, with many and strong towers and ramparts, with superb gates and entrance archways; and with the royal citadel in its midst, white-walled and deeply moated. Well laid out are its streets, squares, cross-roads, and market-places. Well displayed are the innumerable sorts of costly merchandise with which its shops are filled. It is richly adorned with hundreds of almshalls of various kinds, and splendid with hundreds of thousands of magnificent mansions, which rise aloft like the mountain-peaks of the Himalayas. Its streets are filled with elephants, horses, carriages, frequented by men of all sorts and conditions—Brahmins, nobles, artificers, and servants. They resound with cries of welcome to the teachers of every creed, and the city is the resort of the leading men of each of the differing sects." In the unoppressive government, the white-walled acropolis, and the "welcome given to

teachers of every sect,"[52] we may perhaps discern echoes of the old Greek spirit; but Menander was essentially an Indian raja, and not a Greek ruler. A Siamese tradition affirms that he took the yellow robe in his old age, and died an *arhat;* and Plutarch relates a story[53] to the effect that at his funeral, as at that of Gautama Buddha, seven nations disputed for a share of his ashes, which they carried away and buried beneath *stupas* in their own countries. As far as we can tell at present, the Indo-Greeks exercised very little intellectual influence upon India, though excavation on the site of the ancient Sagala may modify this view. If, however, Menander used the same flimsy materials for his great palaces and fortresses as his Indian contemporaries, not much remains to be unearthed.

Saka's Arrival and Influence

In the meanwhile, bodies of Sakas were beginning to appear in the Panjab and to settle in the vicinity of Taxila, Mathura, and other places. One isolated tribe eventually reached Kathiawar.[54] Great numbers somewhere about this time flocked into the modern Sistan (Sakastan), giving the country its modern name. These immigrants appear to have been accompanied by a certain number of Parthians, but in spite of the ingenuity of modern numismatologists, very little can be said with certainty about these petty chieftains. Whether there was an actual Parthian invasion of the Panjab is unknown, and, after all, not very important; but coins and inscriptions show that a powerful Saka dynasty was succeeded by a line of monarchs bearing Parthian names, who employed satraps to govern the more distant parts of their realms. The Greeks, who were continually quarrelling among themselves, could offer no resistance to these new-comers. Hindu writers speak contemptuously of the "Sakas, Yavanas, and Pahlavas," as a set of barbarians with little to distinguish them. There is little doubt that the sudden incursion of Saka tribes was caused by pressure from the North. After a series of obscure movements, a powerful Mongolian tribe called the Yueh-chi had treated the Sakas of Bactria precisely as the latter had formerly treated the Bactrian Greeks, and thus the Sakas were in their turn compelled to seek new homes south of the Hindu Kush. In the meanwhile, the nomads who now held Bactria, settled down in that fertile country and rapidly became a powerful and civilized nation. In their new abode they acquired a certain amount of culture; from the remnants of the Scythian and Iranian peoples of Balkh they adopted a debased form of Zoroastrianism; while from the Greeks of the country, or perhaps the Parthians, they took over the Greek alphabet, and possibly a certain modicum of the Greek language. Finally, about the first century A.D., the Yueh-chi began, like their predecessors, to cast envious eyes upon the Panjab, and a Yueh-chi monarch named Kadphises, belonging to the dominant Kushan clan, quietly overran the decadent Indo-Greek and Saka principalities in North-western India.[55] That the Greeks submitted without a struggle appears from the fact that the last Greek prince, Hermae, issued coins in conjunction with Kadphises until his death, when Kadphises appears alone. The Kushans rapidly made themselves masters of Northern India. Kanishka, their most powerful prince, must have ruled from the Jaxartes to the mouth of the Ganges. He appears to have sent an embassy to the Emperor Trajan, and for the next two centuries the trade between Rome and India reached very large dimensions. Some idea of the extent of the commerce between the two countries may be gathered from the immense finds of Roman coins which have been made from time to time in India. Five cooly loads of *aurei* of the reign of Nero were found some years ago near Cannanore, and this is by no means an isolated instance.[56] Pliny complains bitterly of the "drain" caused by the shipment of Roman gold and silver to India in return for useless and unproductive luxuries, and anticipates the gravest results therefrom.[57] Perhaps this export of Roman money really had something to do with the disastrous financial paralysis which finally overtook the Roman Empire. Similar complaints about the absorption of money by India are not unknown in modern times, the Kushans, having no indigenous culture of their own, were forced, as they became a settled nation, to borrow from their neighbours. The result, as seen in their coins, is a curious medley. From the Parthians they took over the titles of *Kshatrapa*, *King of Kings*, etc., probably because no change in the government of the subordinate provinces was made when they conquered the country. From the Parthians, too, they borrowed the Greek script generally in vogue, modifying it, however, to express certain sounds not known to the Greek tongue. Thus P on the Kushan coins represents not *r* but *sh;* KOPANO KANEPKI is "Kanishka the Kushan," and the title PAONANO is the Pahlava *Shahan-shah.*[58] It does not follow, of course, that the Kushans spoke Greek because they employed the Greek script. The Greek script is frequently used by various rulers of time, indifferently with the Brahmi or Kharoshthi, to express Prakrit coin-legends. A curious example of the confusion of Greek and Indian ideas by these semi-barbarous tribes is a coin of Kanishka bearing a *male* figure of the moon, and inscribed ΣΑ Λ ΗΝΗ.[59] The Goddess NANAIA appears on many Kushan coins. She is the Zoroastrian Anaitis, the tutelary deity of Balkh, and it appears probable that she and many other Zoroastrian deities,[60] were imported by the Kushans from their ancient home on the Oxus. In some cases, no doubt, the Kushans merely continued the local coins of the districts over which they ruled, and it is possible that the Zoroastrian coins of the Kushans were issued for circulation in Pahlava settlements and satrapies. The deity on a particular coin very often represents the religion, not of the king who strikes it, but of the district for use in which it is minted.

Greek Artists from Asia Minor

Far more important, however, was the importation by Kanishka of Greek artists from Asia Minor to decorate the numerous shrines, monasteries, and other buildings with which, in the first enthusiasm of his conversion to the Buddhist creed, he covered the district round his capital town, Peshawar. The productions of these workmen and their Indian imitators still cover the ancient country of Gandhara in vast quantities, and their influence upon Buddhist art was very considerable. It is a curious thing that it was left to a Scythian, and not to the Indo-Greeks, to introduce Hellenic art into India. Of the artistic value of the "Gandhara school" of sculpture, very varying estimates have been formed. Many Europeans, educated on Greek models, have found them more familiar and intelligible then the purely Hindu work of the following period, and have, in consequence lavished upon them a duite disproportionate amount of praise. On the other hand, the recent school of Indian critics, which has done so much for ancient Hindu art, condemns them as utterly worthless attempts on the part of fifth-rate Hellenistic workmen to represent subjects they do not in the least comprehend. This, I think, is a little exaggerated. No one in his senses would compare the work of Kanishka's semi-barbarous Indo-Scythian mechanics, or the decadent Syrian sculptors imported from Ephesus and Pergamum, with the Elephanta bas-reliefs, or the magnificent Mahayana Buddhist statues of Java, or the South Indian bronzes. They are obviously second-rate; they are not even up to the average standard of the Hellenistic art of the period. They are evidently "made to order," and show comparatively few traces of higher artistic feeling. It is, after all, impossible for any one to represent purely Eastern ideas by Western methods. The result is always lamentable.[61] On the other hand, we could ill-afford to lose these interesting, realistic, and often pretty representatives of Indian life in the first century A.D.[62] To the student of Buddhism they are a mine of information, an entrancing record of the beliefs of the time. We should beware of under-estimating their value and interest. Their importance, too, in the history of Buddhist art is very great. The Greeks first taught the Indians to represent the Master in human form; it is possible that they are responsible for the introduction of sculptured representations of the gods of the Hindu Pantheon as well. The conventional Buddha of modern Buddhism originated from the Gandhara sculptures. Buddhism has now become very largely the religion of the Mongolian nations, and the Modern type of the Buddha has Mongolian features; but in the hair, the halo, and the arrangement of the drapery, we may discern clear traces of his Indo-Greek origin. The Gandhara school, no doubt, influenced the Far East through Khotan, where abundant remains of semi-Mongolian culture, strongly tinged by Indo-Greek ideas, have recently been discovered. The amount of Hellenistic influence in the Gandhara sculptures varies considerably. Some of the statues and bas-reliefs are obviously the work of Greek artists: Zeus does duty as Kubera, Pallas Athene as an Indian attendant. Purely Greek themes like Hercules and the Lion, Ganymede and the Eagle, Tritons, Centaurs, and so forth, are reproduced with no attempt at concealment. Others, again, are much less Greek, both in type and subject. They represent scenes from the Jataka Stories, treated with a humorous realism which takes us back to the older Maurya sculptures. The short, broad-shouldered figures appearing in these sculptures are Scythian rather than Aryan. Probably they were the work of native craftsmen working under Greek overseers. In the later remains of the period, we find debased Corinthian pillars, bearing figures in the foliage, which are Roman rather than Greek. Some of them are "finished" with stucco in a similar fashion to the pillars of the Baths of Caracalla (217 A.D.).[63] As we have already mentioned, there was a considerable intercourse between Rome and India in the first three centuries after Christ.

The most unpleasing remains of the period are the repulsive Mathura sculptures, which probably belong to a local Tantric cult, as Mr. Vincent Smith supposes. The finest work of the time, on the other hand, is found at Amravati. The Amravati bas-reliefs show very little Greek influence, having beep executed under the orders of the

Andra princes, who were not, like the Kushans, foreigners without a culture of their own. On the whole, the influence of Greece on the Gandhara and kindred schools of culture has been exaggerated; we may find a good many traces in Kushan art of the ancient traditions of the Maurya period, partly Indo-Persian, and partly Central Asian. The critics who are determined to find an origin for every striking artistic type, trace to Alexandria the practice of executing long bas-reliefs of an anecdotal character; in that case we must, perhaps, look for Greek influence, transmitted from Western India, in the wonderful mural sculptures of Java as well as in the Gandhara friezes.

Revival of Brahmanism and Hindu Art

After the collapse of the Kushan Empire, attention reverts to Eastern India, where the great indigenous dynasty of the Guptas arose about 300 A.D. With the Gupta monarchs India begins once more to discard foreign influence; Buddhism, the creed of the cosmopolitan settlers of the Panjab, is slowly replaced by the more conservative Brahmanism; a great revival of Sanskrit literature takes place. In art, a very noticeable change is observed, both in style and subject. The short, broad-shouldered type of figure gives place to the long-limbed, graceful forms which are characteristic of later Hindu art. Hindu subjects replace Buddhist ones. Did even this great conservative reaction owe anything to Western influence? The Guptas, while adhering strictly to national ideals, were a singularly enlightened dynasty. They encouraged foreign trade, and, like the Kushans, issued a gold coin in imitation of the Roman *aureus*. Indian philosophy began to make itself felt in the West; Neo-platonism undoubtedly bears traces of contact with Eastern ideas. Even Christianity borrowed something in the course of its development from Buddhism; relic-worship and monasticism found their way into the Church from the East; and Gautama Buddha, under the title of St. Josaphat, is still, *mirabile dictu*, recognized as a Christian saint. On the other hand, the East borrowed something in her turn from Western schools. Astronomy, which has a ritual as well as a scientific importance in India, was about this time very largely re-modelled upon the lines suggested by the researches of the Alexandrian mathematicians. Indians were quite frank about their indebtedness to Greece in this respect. "The Yavanas are indeed barbarians", says the *Gargi Samhita*, "but astronomy originated with them, and for this they must be venerated as gods." Of the five *siddhantas*, or astronomical systems, two, the

Romaka siddhanta and the *Paulina Siddhanta* (the latter is named after Paul of Alexandria, *c.* 387 A.D.), are manifestly Western in origin. The word *jamitra*, used by Kalidasa (*Ku-marasambhava*, vii. 1), is Greek.[64] Many of the names of the planets, as well as of the signs of the zodiac, are derived from the Greek.[65] Hindu medical science, in a similar fashion, is said to show distinct traces of Western influence, though this may have been introduced in Kushan times.[66]

Indian and Greek Dramas

We now come to a much more disputed question. Does the Indian drama, which reached its height of perfection under the Guptas, owe anything to Greece? If the Greek language was ever known to any extent in India, it would be easy to suppose that the Indian dramatists had read Menander and the other Greek writers. But can we infer this from the actual evidence which we have? A corrupt Greek was no doubt spoken at the Court of Sagala by the successors of the Bactrian Greeks, but the coins show that it was in moribund condition.[67] Still more corrupt, if we may judge from the coins, was the Greek in use at the court of the Kushanas; indeed, it is doubtful whether it was used at all, except for intercourse with foreigners, as the language of diplomacy and commerce. Traders at Barygaza must have picked up a little of the language, and so must the stonemasons who associated with Kanishka's foreign workmen. But this does not imply a knowledge of the literary, written language of classical Greece. Nor can we rely much upon the fact that Indian astronomers and doctors were acquainted with Greek astronomy and medicine. The knowledge was brought to India by students who had studied abroad. In the same way, medieval Europe owed a great deal to Arabian astonomers and scientists but this does not imply that Roger Bacon or other students knew Arabic. As a matter of fact, we know they did not.

Only one Indian play, the *Toy Cart.*, shows any real resemblance to a Greek comedy. Even Mr. Vincent smith would hesitate to find likenesses in *Shakuntala* to any classical drama. Indeed, we might very well show the futility of making too much of such resemblances by comparing the Indian and Elizabethan dramas.[68] The Fool (*Vidusaka*) certainly plays a prominent part in the plays of Shakespeare; *Shakuntala* resembles for more closely romantic comedies like the *Winter's Tale*, or the plays of Beaumont and Fletcher, than any Greek drama. Then, again, Greek plays were acted in public, open-air theatres; Indian and Elizabethan plays in halls and courtyards. The small amphitheatre discovered by Dr. Bloch at Ramgarh[69] is unique, and may be, like the *Yavanika*, or Greek curtain,[70] the work of an ingenious Greek workman in Indian employ. Indian like Elizabethan playwrights, show a sublime disregard for the unities, and mingle prose and verse indiscriminately. The *Natya Sastra* of Bharata, it is true, lays down a rule limiting the number of the persons appearing upon the stage to five, and the Sanskrit, like the classical drama, avoids the representation of violent or unseemly actions. But these conventions may very well have arisen independently. It is possible, of course, that the author of the *Natya Sastra*, like the Indian writers on astronomy and medicine, *may* have derived some of his rules from Alexandria. The writer of the *Toy Cart may* have witnessed or read a Greek comedy. But the ingenious arguments of Weber and Windisch are merely clever special pleading; there is really no reason why the Indian drama should not have arisen, like the Greek, from primitive religious celebrations, quite independently of foreign influence. Mr. Vincent Smith, who is always anxious to deprive India of the credit of all her achievements in Art and Literature, thinks there is sufficient evidence to warrant our believing that Kalidasa could read, not only Menander, but Terence!. He also finds Greek influence in the typically Indian sculptures of the Gupta period.[71] The rhetorical statements of writers like Clement of Alexandria and Aelian, that there were Hindus who knew Homer and the Greek tragedians, need not be taken seriously. They probably arose from vague stories of the purely fortuitous points of resemblance between the Greek and Indian Epics.[72]

East and West, Interaction

After 400 A.D., the Western world, in the throes of her last struggles with the barbarian, ceased to have commerce with the East, and India remained a vaguely known and legendary land to Europe until it was rediscovered by Vasco de Gama. The results arrived at in this essay are mainly negative; for the duty of the historian is, I conceive, to overthrow groundless assumptions and hasty conclusions before building up theories of his own. I hope I may have succeeded in showing how unjust are the theories which attribute any lasting influence upon India to Greece. To sum up, we may trace three distinct currents of foreign influence in India. Firstly, the influence of Babylon and Chaldea, which is visible in early Indian weights and measures and computations of time; secondly, Persian influence, which is very apparent in the court of the Mauryas; and, thirdly, Greco-Reman influence. This last dates from the time of the Kushan kings only (the Macedonian and Bactrian Greeks exerted no influence worth mentioning), and is to be seen in the Indo-Greek school of sculpture found in North-Western India, in coinage, and in works on technical subjects, such as astronomy and medicine. It did not affect the literature. On the other hand, India Influenced the West very considerably, from the time of the Phoenician traders to the adoption of certain Indian philosophical ideas and religious customs by Greeks and Christian thinkers. The latter question, however, has not yet been fully investigated: it awaits unbiased and patient research.[73]

Notes and References

1. Ibn Batuta, the Moor, who did the journey in the thirteenth century, said that the Hindu Kush Mountains (i.e. Hindu-slaying Mountains) were so called because so few Hindu captives survived the journey over them.
2. See 1 Kings ix 26 and 2 Chron. ix. 21.
3. Perhaps, however, it was at the mouth of the Persian Gulf, and was an entrepot visited by Indian traders, where they bartered their goods with the Phoenicians.
4. Herod, iii. 97. A huge sum, equal to 4680 talents in Eubocic mony; about £1,300,000 sterling. The mines were quickly exhausted, but gold is still extracted in small quantities.
5. Herod, iv. 44.
6. Egyptian *kafu*. The Hebrew *shen-habbin* (elephant's teeth) is the Skt. *ibha-danta*, Egyptian *ebu*, Latin *ebur*. The Greek word is the same word with the Arabic *el* prefixed. The Greek words (Skt. *kastira*) are both found in Homer, which points to an early (indirect) trade between Greece and India.
7. For *ch* = Σ, *cf.* Chandragupta, Sandracottus.
8. Like *Calico* (Calicut), *Muslin* (Mosul), etc.
9. Isaiah iii. 23. See Sayce, Hibbert Lectures, 1887, p. 138. So, too, *cotton* is *karpasa* in Sanskrit, *karpas* in Hebrew, and in Greek words.
10. Another plant known to Europe by its Tamil name was *the jack fruit* (Latin *pata*, Tamil *pala*). The dictionaries translate *pala* as "plantain," but Pliny's description of the tree is conclusive. "Fructum cortice emittit, longitudine trium cubitorum." (*N.H.* 12. 6.) Fancy a plantain three cubits long growing out of the bark of a tree ! Dr. Caldwell in his *Dravidian Grammar*, has made a list of the Tamil words thus taken by traders to the West. Hebrew *anal*, "aloes," Tamil *aghil;* "cinnamon" (Ctesias), Tamil *karppu; inchiver* (ginger), etc. Spices have always been a favourite export from the East, perhaps, till tea, coffee, and rubber took their place, the principal one. The Dutch made a fortune out of *cinnamon*. *Pepper* was, curiously enough, consumed in huge quantities in Rome. Alaric demanded as part of his ransom 3000 lbs. of

pepper. (Mukerji, *Indian Shipping*, p. 127). The Zamorin of Calicut wrote to the King of Portugal, when Vasco de Gama visited him, "In my kingdom there is an abundance of cinnamon, cloves, ginger and pepper". Most of these came from the Dravidian ports.

11. Rhys Davids, *Buddhist Birth Stories*, p. xiv. Cowell and Rouse's translation, vi. 163 (Cambridge, 1907).
12. I Kings iii. 16.
13. During Gautama's lifetime. See, too, the story of the merchants who took crows and peacocks to Babylon. (*Baveru Jataka*, Cowell and Rouse, iii. 83.)
14. For the facts about the I hoenicians and Babylonians, I am indebted to Mr. Kennedy's article on *Early Commerce of India with Babylon: J.R.A.S.*, 1898, and Professor Mukerji's *Indian Shipping*.
15. The last Report of the Archaeological Department gives details of these. Some of the remains have been put in the Prince of Wales's Museum, Bombay.
16. *Geog.* xvi. 3. 3-5.
17. Strabo, *Geog.* xiv. 33. This is not a traveller's tale. Ibn Batuta, the Moorish traveller, tells the same story about the negroes in the Sudan.
18. The "Swastika" sign has, I believe, been found in Troy.
19. For methods of trapping apes (apparently for export), see Aelian, *apud* McCrindle, p. 149.
20. *Apud* Strabo, *Geog.* xv 62-1
21. I.196.
22. It has been also suggested that the story of the Tortoise Incarnation of Vishnu is a Hindu version of the story of the Flood, which first appears in Babylonian legend. Dr. Vogel attributes to Babylon the practice, in India and modern Europe, of naming the days of the week after the Sun, Moon, and five planets. This is a very interesting explanation of a remarkable coincidence.
23. *Encyc. Brit.*, XIth Edn., "Babylonian Art."
24. Justin, i. 1-3, etc.
25. Dr. Fleet's date.
26. The Babylonians, of course, practised urn-burian.
27. Herod, iv. 71.
28. Fergusson thinks it was copied from the conical Tartar tents. But it is difficult to account for such an imitation. And the early stupas are more dome-shaped. Professor Rapson (Hastings' *Dictionary of Religion*) traces it to the funeral pyre. But the resemblance is not very close.
29. Perhaps a survival of the old barbarous rites paid to the "Manes" of deceased ancestors by various nations, particularly Mongolian nations. If the Scythians were Mongolian in origin, we have another interesting piece of evidence in this custom.
30. *Mahaparanibbana Sutta*. S.B.E., xi. p. 131.
31. Cunningham, *Anc. Geog. of India*, 447, Beal, in *J.R.A.S.*, xiv. 39.
32. He started from an unidentified city called "Caspatyrus in Pactyica," somewhere in the North-West Panjab. Pactyica is the land of the Pachtu or Pashtu, the Pathans or Afghans.

33. A Median custom, borrowed from the Scythians, who gave their dead to "dogs and birds" to devour. At Bactria, the home of Zoroastrianism, a special breed of dogs, called "lintombers", were kept for the purpose. The Persians buried their dead. The tomb of Cyrus at Pasargadae, for instance, is a proof of this.
34. Compare Milton's "Ionian gods of Javan's issue held". *P.L.*, i. 508, and *S.A.*, 715-6. Milton got the word from Isa. lxvi. 19, but he mixes up Javan with Javan son of Japheth (Gen. x. 2), The Greeks heard of India from the Persians. Greek word is Hendu, the Avesta word, and not Sindava (Skt.). Otherwise we should have Greek word, as Max Muller points out. Hecataeus (520 B.C.) is the first to mention India among surviving Greek writers. Some of the stories in Herodotus—e.g. the story of Hippocleides—have been traced to India, through Persia, Tawney, *Journal of Philology*, xii. 112.
35. A highly amusing article by Prof. Lacouperie, in the *Bobylonian and Oriental Record*, 1886, p. 58, ascribes this script to Cyrus (Khusru). Unfortunately Cyrus never visited India.
36. Quite possibly considerable Yavana colonies remained behind. They are mentioned in Asoka's inscriptions, and probably the king Apollodotus whose coins are so difficult to place, belongs to this race, and not to the Bactrian dynasties.
37. Strabo, 2, i, 9. Pliny, *N.H.* 17.
38. V.A. Smith, *Early History of India*, Ch. v.
39. "Royal Festival is held once a year on the birthday of Xerxes. It is called *Tycta* in Persian. The king washes his head and makes presents to the Persians." Herod, ix. 110.
    "When the King (Chandragupta) washes his hair, they celebrate a great festival and send him presents." Strabo, xv. 69.
40. The common legend that writing was not practised in India arose from the fact that most Sanskrit *literature* was transmitted orally, and legal disputes were settled by unwritten local custom. Strabo, xiv. 53, 67, etc. Writing was confined to secular purposes: even in the fifth century A.D. Fa Hian had the greatest difficulty in getting MSS. of Buddhist works. Perhaps Asoka borrowed from Persia the idea of inscribing long records upon the surface of rocks where they would meet the eye of the passer-by.
41. Called, however, a *Yona*, in the Girnar Inscription. No doubt he spoke Greek. He may have been a Greek half-breed from Bactria.
42. So, too, in the *Toy Cart*, the Palace has a "high ivory portal". V.A. Smith, *Hist. Fine Art*, x. 8.
43. Beal, *Buddhist Records*, i. 103.
44. Polyb. xi. 34.
45. Probably Sialkot.
46. *Exscingues*. Justin, xli. 6.
47. Thus Gautamiputra (after 130 A.D.) talks of subduing Yavanas (Rapson, *Coins of the Andras*, Section 44, Indtroduction).
48. See the *Journal B.B.R.A.S.*, Vol. xxii. 224.

49. The Kushans and Guptas also imitated extensively the Roman coins which poured into India in the first and second centuries A.D. *Dinar* is the Roman *Denarius.*
50. *J.R.A.S.*, 1909, p. 1092.
51. *S.B.E.*, xxv. The book is so replete with detail that it must have been written soon after the time of Menander, by one who knew the country.
52. Cf. Acts of the Apostles xvii. 21.
53. In the tract *Reip. Gerend.* p. 121.
54. The modern Jats are perhaps descendants of the famous Scythian tribe, the Getae.
55. The invasion was no doubt quite a peaceful one; the "Kshatrapas" merely acknowledged their new overlords and remained undisturbed.
56. An immense amount of trade passed between India and the West in the first century B.C. It was stimulated by Augustus suppression of piracy, and by the discovery of the monsoon by Hippalus, *c.* 48 A.D. The goods were sent to Myos Hormus on the Red Sea, and transhipped at Alexandria. Strabo saw 120 ships leave Myos Hormus for India. The chief port was Muziris (probably Mangalore), and it was a run of only forty days from Aden to that port in the monsoon. Indian Rajas often had Greek bodyguards, and Greek girls in their harems. The Greek janissary was useful because he could form no plots, being ignorant of the language of the country. *Yavana* hence, like *Suisse* in the eighteenth century, comes to be used very vaguely. Nowadays it means any Westerner, even a Mahom-medan. So *Roumi* among the Turks and Arabs.
57. "Minima computatione milies centena milia sestertium annis omnibus India et Seres peninsulaque illa imperio nostro adimunt." *N.H.* 12. 18.
58. For the whole question, see Stein's *Zoroastrian Deities on Indo-Scythian Coins.* (Babylonian and Oriental Record, Vol. i. p. 133.) Perhaps in this letter we have a revival of the Σαν, the Indian S, used at one time by the Dorians. It may have survived in a remote corner of the Greek world.
59. B.M. Cat. xxvi. 1.
60. Also represented on Kushan coins.
61. Take, for instance, the atrocities of Ravi Varma, unhappily so popular in Western India.
62. See the Indo-Greek Buddha, for instance, on p. 5.
63. These pillars are ornamental and not structural. The *buildings* erected by Kanishka must have been of the conventional Indian type, and to judge from the way in which they have disappeared, must have been mostly of wood and brick. It should be mentioned, by the way, that faint traces of Hellenistic influence before the Kushan era may be found, notably in the coins and other remains of Azes, and other Saka and Indo-Parthian rulers. Mention should also be made of the wonderful vase containing the Buddha relics, discovered in 1909, at Peshawar. It was the work of "Agesilaus, a workman of Kanishka."—*J.R.A.S.*, 1909, p. 1058.

64. It is the seventh place on the horoscope, by which the astrologer predicts the happiness of married life for a person.
65. *Vide* Dr. Vogel's article in *East and West*, Jan. 1912.
66. Dr. Vogel finds in the works of Charaka, "said to have been Kanishka's physician", very strong traces of a knowledge of Hippocrates.
67. It has even been held that the corrupt Greek inscriptions on Kushan and other coins are survivals of a dead language, like the Latin ones on our own coins.
68. Dean Milman, in an article in the *Quarterly* for 1831, compared the Indian and Spanish dramas.
69. *Arch. Survey of India*, 1903-4, p. 123.
70. *No* curtain was used on the Greek stage, hence this apparatus was *not* imported from Greece. Dr. Rapson says *Yavanika* merely means "made of Greek (or Western) material."
71. *Hist. Fine Art*, vi. 1.
72. Like the supposed resemblance between the *Ramayana* (the story of Sita) and the *Iliad* (the story of Helen) of which Weber absurdly makes so much.
73. It would be interesting to deal with the influence of India through Alexandria upon the early Christian Church. Monasticism and relic-worship may have been borrowed from Buddhism. Then we may ask whether Christ Himself owed any of His teaching to the Essences, and they to the Buddhists of Balkh and Persia? Eastern thought influenced Neo-Platonism and Gnosticism, and possibly Origen. Saint Josaphat, Prince of India, still regarded as a saint by the Roman Church, reached Europe from Antioch. The presence of Indian fables in the *Gesta Romanorum*, Boccaccio, and in Chaucer is also a remarkable fact. See, for instance, Tawney's remarks in the *Journal of Philology*, vol. xii. pp. 112 and 203*ff.*

8

Sailors of Sixty Centuries

CHAMAN LAL

The art of navigation was born in river Sindh 6000 years ago. The very word navigation is derived from Sanskrit word Nav (or Nav-ship) Gatih.—Dr. Radha Kumud Mookerjee

Nowadays we hear so much, and see so much of foreign shipping, and of the progress made in the nautical sciences, that we are apt to forget that India too in ancient times carried on an extensive trade by means of her shipping. A peninsula cut-off from the Northern world by the Himalayas, and from the Eastern and Western, by vast expanses of water. India had to take to shipping, if she wanted to export her surplus goods.

Literature as well as art expresses the life of a people, and evidences from Indian literature and art, prove that in ancient times, India had developed her own shipping. Professor Bubler, the German Orientalist, said, "There are passages in ancient Indian works which prove the early existence of a navigation of the Indian Ocean, and the somewhat later occurrence of trading voyages undertaken by Hindu merchants to the shores of the Persian Gulf and its rivers." These references, however, supply indirect evidence, and contain no direct information regarding the existence of a national maritime trade, to which they refer. No commerce can thrive unless fostered by national shipping.

When Indians went to America

The world's leading anthropologists Dr. Robert Heine Geldern and Dr. Gordon F. Ekholm have strongly supported my claim that Indian ships went all the way to Mexico and Peru centuries before Columbus. In the "civilisations of ancient America" (1951) they state:

> "*There appears to be little doubt but that ship-building and navigation were sufficiently advanced in southern and eastern Asia at the period in question to have made trans-Pacific voyages possible.* As early as the time of Ptolemy, in the second century A.D., Indian ships sailed to the Malay Peninsula and Indonesia not coastwise, but across the Bay of Bengal. *In the third century, horses were exported from India to the Malay Peninsula and Indo-China, an indication that there must have been ships of considerable size.* The recent discovery of a large metropolis in Cochinchina yielding Roman objects of the second century A.D. testifies to the intensity of see traffic. When the Chinese Buddhist scholar Fahien returned from India *around A.D. 400 he embarked on a ship which carried more than two hundred sailors and merchants and which therefore must have been larger than the ships of Columbus and other early Spanish explorers. This ship sailed directly across the ocean from Ceylon to Java. From Java, Fahien travelled in another merchant vessel which again carried more than two hundred persons. This ship too sailed not along the coast, but right across the China Sea to northern China. Ships of that size able to cross the Indian Ocean and the China Sea with their dangerous cyclones could certainly cross the Pacific as well.*"
>
> (And yet some pessimists doubt my thesis of "Hindu America".—The Author)

Migration in Third Century

"Although it would be too much to expect any definite analysis of the chronological problem at this stage of the investigation, we wish to offer a few tentative suggestions in this respect. *As already mentioned, there are indications that the contacts in question may have begun between A.D. 100 and 600. As seen from Asia, third to fifth centuries would seem most likely.* On the basis of the American evidence, the establishment of contacts must have taken place not later than the middle of the Classic period of Middle America since some traits of Hindu-Buddhist affinity appear in the Maya area at that time. *This does not, however, preclude an earlier date.*

"Contacts with Southeast Asia seem to have been either intensified or renewed around the end of the Classic period and the beginning of the Mexican or so-called New Empire period. This indicates that they may have continued through many centuries."

Evidence from Sanskrit Literature

Yuktikalpataru, a Sanskrit manuscript by Bhoja Narapati, which is now in the Calcutta Sanskrit College Library, is something like a treatise, on the art of ship-building in Ancient India. It gives, according to Vriksha-Ayurveda ("Botany"), an account of four different kinds of wood. The first class comprises wood, that is light and soft, and can be joined to any other wood. The second class is light and hard, but cannot be joined to any other class of wood. The third class of wood is soft and heavy. Lastly, the fourth kind is hard and heavy. There may be too the Dvijati class of wood, in which are blended properties of two separate classes. According to Bhoja, a ship made out of the second class of wood, brings wealth and happiness. Ships of this type can be safely used for crossing the oceans. Ships made out of timbers containing different properties are not good, as they rot in water, and split and sink at the slightest shock.

Bhoja says that care should be taken that no iron be used in joining planks, for they would be subjected to the influence of magnetism; but they are to be fitted together with substances other that iron. Of course, this direction was required in ancient times, when the onward march of science was not yet made. Bhoja also gives names of diffierent classes of ships: (1) River-going ships—Samanya; (2) Ocean-going ships—Visesa.

The measurements in cubits of the "Ordinary class" of ships are the following:

		Length	*Breadth*	*Height*
1.	Kshudra	16	4	4
2.	Madhya ma	24	12	8
3.	Bhima	40	20	20
4.	Chapala	48	24	24
5.	Patala	64	32	32
6.	Bhaya	72	36	36
7.	Dirgha	88	44	44
8.	Patraputa	96	48	48
9.	Garbhara	112	56	56
10.	Manthra	120	60	60

Bhima, Bhaya, Garbhara are liable to bring ill-luck because their dimensions are such as not to balance themselves in water.

Among the "Special" are two classes.

1. DIRGHA

		Length	*Breadth*	*Height*
a.	Dirghika	32	4	31/5
b.	Tarani	48	6	44/5
c.	Lota	64	8	62/5
d.	Gatvara	80	10	8
e.	Gamini	96	12	92/5
f.	Tari	112	14	111/5
g.	Jangala	128	16	124/5
h.	Plavini	144	18	142/5
i.	Dharini	160	20	16
j.	Begini	176	22	173/5

2. UNNANTA

a.	Urddhva	22	16	16
b.	Anurddhva	48	24	24
c.	Svarnamukhi	64	32	32
d.	Gharbhini	80	40	40
e.	Manthara	96	48	48

Lota, Gamini, Plavini, Anurddhava, Gharbhini, Manthara bring misfortune, because of their dimensions, and Urddhva much gain.

The "Yaktikalpataru" also suggests the metals to be used in decorations, e.g., gold, silver, copper and compounds of all three as well as the colours. A vessel with four masts is to be painted white, the one with three masts is to be given a red paint, a two-masted vessel is to be coloured yellow, and a one masted vessel is to have a blue colour. The prows are to be shaped into the form of heads of lions, buffaloes, serpents, elephants, tigers, ducks, pea-hens, parrots, frogs, and human beings, thus arguing an advanced progress in carpentry. Pearl and gold garlands are to decorate the prows.

Three Classes of Ships

According to cabins, ships are to be grouped into three classes:

(1) Sarvamandira ships, having the largest cabin, from one end of the ship to the other. These are to be used for the transportation of royal treasury, of women and horses. (2) Madhyamandira ships,

with cabins for the rainy seasons. (3) Ships with cabins near the prows, are called Agramandira, and are for sailing in the dry seasons as well as for long voyages, and navel warfare.

It was in these ships, that the first naval battle recorded in Indian literature, was fought, when Tugra, the Rishi King, sent his son Bhujyu against his enemies inhabiting some Island, and Bhujyu, on being wrecked was rescued by two Asvins, in their hundred oared galley. Of the same descriptions are the five hundrded vessels, mentioned in the Ramayana.

Carried 1000 Passengers

In Rajavalliya, the ship in which Prince Vijaya and his followers were sent away by King Sinhala of Bengal, was large enough to accommodate seven hundred passengers. The ship in which Prince Vijaya's bride was conveyed to Ceylon, was big enough to accommodate eight hundred people of the bride's party. The ship which took Prince Sinhala to Ceylon contained five hundred merchants besides himself. The Janaka Jataka mentions a ship-wreck of seven hundred passengers. The ship by which was effected the rescue of the Brahmin mentioned in Sankha Jataka was 800 cubits in length, 600 cubits in width, 20 fathoms deep, and had three masts. The ship mentioned in the Samuddha Vanija Jataka was big enough to transport a village full of absconding carpenters, numbering a thousand, who had failed to deliver goods paid for in advance.

Early History

An ancient couplet betrays the spirit with which the Indo-Aryans were imbued and which accounts for their wonderful achievements on land, beyond seas and across mountain barriers. There is indeed evidence to show that even before their advent in India, the sons of the soil were adept at navigation both riverine and oceanic. Right from the dawn of history, therefore, Indians have been engaged in plying boats and ships, carrying cargoes and passengers, manufacturing vessels of all types and dimensions, studying the stars and winds, erecting lighthouses and building ports, wharfs, dockyards and warehouses. From rustic-beginnings they developed a precise science of navigation and composed regular manuals as well as elaborate treaties on the subject, some of which survive to this day. Thanks to the research conducted during the past century mainly in the fields of literature and archaelogy, we have gathered a mass of information, on the subject, which is, moreover, constantly being augmented.

It is noteworthy that the very term navigation is derived from nau, which is the Sanskrit word for 'ship' or 'boat'. The same nau or nav as well as its synonym or diminutive nauka is even now commonly used in Hindi and other cognate languages. Thus navi gatih 'going in a boat' amounts to 'navigation'. Note also the Sanskrit term yanapatra, which connotes a 'ship', though literally it means 'sailing pot', comparable to the English term 'Vessel'.

Literary Evidence

Sanskrit literature is full of references to river transport and sea voyages Sometimes we have graphic descriptions of fleets, even of ship-wreck. The Rigveda is taken as the earliest extant work of the Aryans, though there is no general agreement as to its exact age. Tradition ascribes it to a hoary past, while the archaeologists place it between 2500 B.C. and 1500 B.C. Anyway, it mirrors the life of early Indo-Aryans faithfully, wherein rivers and seas, boats and ships play an important part. At one place, Rishi Kutsa Angirasa prays to Agni: "Remove our foes as if by ship to the yonder shore. Carry us as if in a ship across the sea for our welfare". Here the reference to a ship and the sea is only by way of similitude. At another place, we have what appears to be an historical fact recorded by Rishi Kakshivat. It is an episode of Bhujyu, son of Tugra, undertaking a voyage in the Indian Ocean, experiencing a shipwreck and rescued by the Asvins. The terms denoting the manned ship (naubhir atmanvatibhir) and the vast expanse of the fathomless ocean (anarambhane . . .agrabhane samudre) in this context are significant indeed.

In Ramayana

In Valmiki's Ramayana, we come across beautiful descriptions of large boats plying on the Ganga near Sringiberapura, King Guha of that place arranges a magnificent boat for Rama accompanied by Laksmana and Sita, in exile, to enable the party to cross the river.

When Bharata comes later to the same place, with the whole royal household, citizens of Ayodhya and a large army, with the intention of bringing Rama back to Ayodhya from exile, the same King Guha, suspecting Bharata's intentions, takes precautionary measures by ordering five hundered ships, each manned by one hundred youthful mariners to keep in readiness, should resitance be necessary.

When Guha is convinced of Bharata's good intention, however, the same fleet of five hundred ships transports Bharata and his army to the other shore. The description of the ships is noteworthy:

> "Some (of the ships) reared aloft the swastika sign, had tremendous gongs, flew gay flags, displayed full sails and were exceedingly well built."

The ship chosen for Bharat, Satrughan, Kaushalya, Sumitra and other ladies of the royal household had special fittings and furniture such as yellow rugs. It also displayed the insignia of swastika.

In Mahabharata

In the Mahabharata too there are many references. The ship contrived by Vidura for the escape of Pandavas had some kind of mechanism fitted in it: "the ship strong enough to withstand hurricanes, fitted with machinery and displaying flags".

Panini, who flourished about the 7th century B.C., in his Ashtadhyayi, the most commented upon work on Sankrit grammar, has incidentally recorded certain usages which reflect in a way the maritime activity before and during his days in India. According to one sutra various types of small river craft were in use, and their names were *utsagna*, *udupa*, *udyata*, *utputa*, *pitaka*, etc. A large boat was called *Udavahana* or *udakavahana*. Of special interest is the distinction made between the cargoes coming from an island near the coast and those coming from midocean islands: the former were called *dvaipya*, and the latter dvaipa or dvaipaka. Certain other sutras speak of ferry charges, cargoes, marine trade and the like of those days.

Chandragupta Maurya's minister, Vishnugupta Chanakya alias Kautilya, the celebrated author of the treatise on statecraft, *Kautilya Arthasastra*, of about 320 B.C. devotes a full chapter on the state department of waterways under a *Navadhyaksha* 'Superintendent of ships'. His duties included the examination of accounts relating to navigation, not only on oceans and mouths of rivers, but also on lakes, natural or artificial, and rivers. Fisheries, pearl-fisheries, customs on ports, passenger and mercantile shipping, control and safety of ships and similar other affairs all came under his charge.

Jaina scriptures, Buddhist *Jatakas* and *Avadanas*, as well as classical Sanskrit literature, abound in references to sea-voyages. "They acquaint us with many interesting details as to the sizes, and shapes of ships, their furniture and decorations, articles of import and export, names of seaports and islands, in short, everything connected with navigation."

Evidence from Sculpture

Evidence from Sculpture and Paintings—The Sanchi sculptures dating back to the second century B.C. also represent Indian ships. On the Eastern Gateway of Stupa No. 1 at Sanchi, is sculptured a canoe of rough flanks fastened together with hemp. In the canoe are three ascetics, two of whom are rowing the canoe, and the central one is facing four other ascetics below, who are standing in a reverential attitude, at the water's edge. This sculpture represents the departure of some ascetics, on some mission or expedition. On Stupa No. 1 of the Western Gateway, is sculptured another boat with a prow like a winged gryphon, and a stern terminating into the tail of a fish. In the boat is a vacant throne and in the water are fresh water flowers, and a large shell, and there are five men floating about on inflated skin bladders, while a sixth is asking for help of the oarsman, who is steering the boat. This sculpture, perhaps represents a Royal State barge.

In the Kenri caves near Bombay, are sculptures belonging to the second century A.D. which represent different persons in distress praying to God Padmapani for deliverance. One of the last sculptures in the second cave, depicts two figures praying to be rescued from a ship-wreck at sea, and the God Padmapani sends two winged messengers to comfort them. This is considered to be the oldest representation in Indian sculpture, of a sea voyage.

Temples give Proof

In the temple of Jagannath at Puri, a stately barge is sculptured in relief. The oarsman paddle with all their strength, the water is thrown into waves, and the whole scene is one of desperate hurry. The boat is of the Madhayamandira type, as denned by Bhoja in the "Yuktikalpataru".

Lastly, the Ajanta paintings are rightly interpreted by Griffiths as a "vivid testimony to the ancient foreign trade of India". Of the many paintings one is of "a sea-going vessel with high stem and stern with three oblong sails attached to as many upright masts. Each mast is surmounted by a truck and there is carried a big sail. The jib is well-filled with wind. A sort of bowsprit, projecting from a kind of gallows on deck is indicated with the outflying jib, square in form", like that of Columbus ships. The ship is of the Agramandira type, as described in the "Yuktikalpataru" (mentioned above). Another painting is of a royal pleasure boat which is "like the heraldic lymphad, with painted eyes at stem and stern, a pillared canopy amidships, and an umbrella for the steerman being accommodated on a sort of ladder, which remotely suggest the steerman's chair, in the modern Burmese row boats, while a rower is in the bows. "The barge is of the Madhyamandira type. A third painting commemorates the landing of Prince Vijaya in Ceylon in B.C. 543

Sculptures at Boro-Budur

The temple of Boro-Budur in Java contains sculptures recalling the colonisation of Java by Indians. One of the ships "tells more plainly than words, the perils, which the Prince of Gujarat and his companions encountered on the long and difficult voyages from the west coast of India." There are other ships tempest tossed on the ocean, fully trying the pluck and dexterity of the oarsmen, sailors, and pilots, who, however, in their movements and looksimpress one with the idea, that they are quite equal to the occasion. These sculptured types arq of the 6th and 7th century Indian ships.

What Historians Say

Nicolo Conti wrote: "The natives of India build some ships larger than ours, capable of containing 2,000 butts, and with five sails and as many masts. The lower part is constructed with triple planks, in order to withstand the force of the tempests to which they are much exposed. But some ships are so built in compartments, that should one part be shattered, the other portion remaining whole may accomplish the journey." Mr. J.L. Reid, member of the Institute of Naval 'Architects and Shipbuilders, England, and the Superintendent of the Hongli Docks, has stated: "The early Hindu astrologers dare sai to have used the magnet as they still eus the modern compass, in fixing the north and east, in laying foundations, and other religious ceremonies. The Hindu compass was an iron fish, that floated in a vessel of oil, and pointed, to the north. Fact of this older Hindu compass seems placed beyond doubt by the Sanskrit word "maccha-yantra".

India's Extensive Sea-Borne Trade

The historian Strabo says that in the time of Alexander, the River Oxus was so easily navigable that Indian wares were conducted down it, to the Caspian and the Euxine sea, thence to the Mediterranean Sea, and finally to Rome. Perhaps at that time, the Caspian Sea and the Aral Sea into which the Oxus flows, were one. Between the years 130 B.C. to 300 A.D., there was a colony of Indians in Armenia. There were also ship wrecked Indians, living in slavery among the Suevi and the Boii who were merchant victims of the Caspian Sea storms. The discovery of the Caspian Sea trade by Pompey, was the real cause of the rivalry between Rome and Parthia, over Armenia, which was receiving large quantities of Indian merchandise, from the Parthian as well as the Caspian regions.

Indo-Roman Trade

Julius Caesar contemplated the deepening of the Ostia and the Tiber, and the cutting of a canal across the Isthmus of Corinth in order to help the Indian trade, but he was murdered before the realisation of his plans. His successor Augustus after conquering Egypt, established a prosperous sea-trade between Egypt and India; the Mediterranean Sea was cleared of pirates; large maps were to be seen in Rome, and Horace's references to the East reflect the prosperity of the sea-trade. Greeks and Indians began to meet at the newly established sea ports, and finally all these activities culminated in Indian embassies being seat to Rome from several Indian States, for Augustus himself says that Indian embassies came "frequently". These embassies were encouraged by the Greeks in order to cut-off the Arabs from the trade. From the very start, the whole wealthy Roman Empire under Augustus, was unable to counterbalance the inflow of Indian products by a return of imperial goods, with the result that the Romans sent out coined money, which never returned to them, not even in the form of Indian money. Abundant Roman coins from Augustus right down to Nero, have been found in India. Indian tigers, lions, rhinoceroses, elephants, and serpents were brought to Rome for exhibition; Indian birds were kept as pets, especially parrots; Indian spices were used for flavours; Indian ivory, tortoise-shells, and precious stones were all rapidly bought up by the Roman ladies. Much of the Indian luxuries came to the notice of the Romans with the death of Cleopatra, who greatly rejoiced in importing Indian luxuries, and with the Battle of Actium began Rome's most luxurious period. Though

Augustus conquered Cleopatra, he could not smother in the hearts of his countrymen the love for Cleopatra's luxuries. Tiberius tried to check the extravagant tastes of the Romans, tastes which, he said, were sending Roman gold into India. The discovery of coins in India justifies his fears; the total number of gold coins of Tiberius unearthed in India being 1007 as against the 453 of Augustus. There must be thousands more lying buried in Indian soil.

Discovery of the Monsoons: The reign of Emperor Caludius is interesting as it was during his time that the proper use of the trade winds and the monsoons was discovered. Hitherto the voyages had been all coasting voyages. Pliny says that after this discovery, men would sail from Ccelis in Arabia to Malabar, in forty days, by the help of these winds, if they started in July. The Indians sailed from India either late in December or early in January, when their ships were carried to the Red Sea, by the North-East monsoons. The Arabs and the Somalis had known the secret of the monsoons but had not divulged it, and they had excluded as a rule, the Indians from competing with them in the Red Sea. It was the Romans, who on entering the Red Sea allowed the Indian ships to sail up its whole length. The Greeks and the Romans, however did not directly touch at Ceylon ports, but were contented to receive from Indian ports and ships, the goods exported from Ceylon which was "a great resort of ships from all parts of India".

Turning from the people to the rulers of India and Rome, we find that the latter, too, encouraged the seaborne trade. The Indian kings cleared the estuaries and maintained special service there, built official marts and seaports all over the coasts, and issued special coinage to facilitate exchange. The Roman Emperors, too, encouraged the Indian trade, though they failed to establish a favourable balance, for Pliny states that the Indian trade brought a good profit. "Indian wares cost a hundred times more in Roman markets than they did in Indian markets."—(By Alice Siqueira)

Archaeologist's Testimony

Dr. Bahadur Chand Chhabra, formerly Joint Director General of Archaeology writing in the 'March of India' (October, 1961) provides valuable evidence from Archaeology:

> Archaeology amply supports literary record. We start with the Harappa Culture which, according to archaeologists, predates Vedic

Culture in India. Excavations at Mohan-jo-daro on the Indus have yielded, among other things, a potsherd and a couple of steatite seals, each bearing a representation of a boat or a ship incised on it. "The vessel portrayed on the seal has a sharply upturned prow and stern, a feature which is present in nearly all archaic representations of boats." Commenting further, Mackay observes in his book, "Further Excavation at Mohan-jo-daro": "It will be noticed that this boat is shown as lashed together at both bow and stern, indicating perhaps that it was made of reeds like the primitive boats of Egypt and the crafts that were used in the swamps of southern Babylonia. The hut or shrine in its centre also appears to be made of reeds, and fastened at each end of it is a standard." Regarding the boat depicted on the potsherd, he says: "Boats of this type must have been very familiar to the people of Mohan-jo-daro living as they did beside the Indus or a branch of it. The high prow and stern, would be especially suitable to a riverboat in that cargo could by this means be safely landed on a shelving bank."

By far the most substantial proof is afforded by the recent discovery of a dockyard at Lothal in the Ahmedabad District of Gujarat, where extensive ruins of the Harappa Culture have lately been laid bare'. The remains of the dockyard testify to the water-borne trade, particularly of the Harappan people in that region. It was roughly trapezoid in plan; its eastern and western embankments were each 216 m (710 ft) long; the northern embankment measured 38 m (124 ft) and the southern embankment 35.4 m (116 ft).

It may here be pointed out that the designation Harappa Culture replaces the one that was commonly used till very recently—Indus Valley Civilization—because subsequent finds have shown that it was not confined to the Indus Valley alone. It is now called Harappa Culture after the ancient site of Harappa on the Ravi in the Montgomery District, now in West Pakistan, because of the circumstance that the first relic, a steatite seal, of the concerned culture was picked up there by Cunningham in 1872-73. This provisional or sentimental designation may later on have to give place to a more appropriate one when we come to know the exact name of the people concerned which depends on the correct decipherment and interpretation of the legends on the typical Harappan seals, hundreds of which have already come to light. These legends still remain an enigma.

There is a long gap after the Harappan period, archaeo-logically speaking. And there are few remains that throw light on navigation in India in subsequent times until we come to the Andhra period of Indian history. The sculptures at Sanchi and similar other sites show vivid scenes of river and sea journeys. They attest the continuity of old traditions of navigation in India. In this connection the ship-type coins of the Satavahana rulers in South India deserve special mention. The one illustrated here belongs to King Yajna Satakarni. It clearly shows a two-masted ship on the obverse, and the so-called Ujjaini symbol on the reverse. A fish, a conch and a snake or eel below the two-masted ship are indicative of the sea. The four circles of the Ujjaini symbol on the reverse are also supposed to represent the chatur-udadhi, 'four seas', that encircle the earth. The legend, running along the edge on the obverse, is in Brahmi characters and Prakrit language. It contains the king's name: Sami Siri Yans Satakani.

Then, there is a stone inscription, likewise in Brahmi and Prakrit, of about the second or third century A.D. which mentions a 'sea-captain' or 'master-mariner' (Mahanavika) named Sivaka. This inscription was found at Ghantasala (ancient Kanta-kasola) in the Krishna District of Andhra Pradesh. This place was a sea-port in olden days. Ptolemy mentions it as "the emporium Kantakossyla", immediately after the mouths of Maisolos, that is the river Krishna.

Similarly, a Mahanavika, called Buddhagupta, a resident of Raktamrittika, indentified with Rangamati in Bengal, is mentioned in a Sanskrit stone inscription, discovered in Province Wellesly of Malay Peninsula, now kept in the Indian Museum at Calcutta. This inscription belongs to about the fifth century A.D. and affords an evidence of sea-voyages between India and the Far East in those days.

In Old Paintings

A fresco painting on Cave II at Ajanta of about the same time (500 A.D.), depicts the sea-voyage of Bhavila, described in the Purna-avadana of the Divyavadana an early Buddhist Sanskrit text. The story in short is as follows:

> "Purna, whose mother was a slave-girl, was the youngest and favourite son of a rich merchant of Surparaka. After the father's death he and his eldest brother Bhavila were deprived of their property by the other two brothers, but by the judicious marketing of some sandalwood Purna restored their fortune and became

eventually the chief merchant of the country. He made six succssful ocean voyages, and was then inclined to rest content, but some merchants from Sravasti persuaded him to embark a seventh time. On the way he heard them reciting verses in praise of the Buddha, and was filled with a desire to embrace the faith. When the voyage was over, he obtained the permission of his brother Bhavila to abandon wordly life, and received instruction from the Buddha at Sravasti. To show that he had now no care for the body, he chose to live in the land of the Sronaparantakas, a notoriusly fierce and dangerous people, and converted many of them. Meanwhile Bhavila had gone to sea and arrived at a land where was a forest of Gosirsha sandalwood; his men proceeded to cut down the trees, whereupon the owner, the Yaksha Mahesvara, raised a hurricane of the kind no ship can withstand. Bhavila was helpless, but his companions called to Purna for help. Purna, by his supernatural power, appeared on the ship, the storm ceased, and the Yaksha had to yield. Upon his return to Surparaka, Purna built a sandalwood vihara, and with the cooperation of his brothers and the king, prepared a reception for the Buddha. The rest of the Avadana relates the miracles associated with the Buddha's journey from Sravasti to Surparaka". These two places are represented by the modern Seth-Maheth in Uttar Pradesh and Sopara in Maharashtra.

The details of the story depicted on the wall-painting are not all clear, owing to the damage it has sustained. Yet, what can be made out of the illustration has been set out clearly by Dr. G. Yazdani. "The boat itself seems to be massively built, and the presence of twelve large pictures of fresh water in its bow may indicate the strength of the crew, or suggest that the vessel is bound for a long voyage. A pair of oars is visible, each of which is attached to the side of the boat by a loop, the ends of the latter for security being passed through two rings fixed to the boat. Dragons' heads are carved both in the front and hind parts of the boat, and there is a lip-like projection at each end which adds to the picturesqueness of the design, and might have been useful for steering purposes as well, especially in shallow waters.

Near the oar, on the starboard side, there is a plank frame, which apparently marks the place where the captain of the boat regulated the steering. There are the masts, apparently of timber, from which sails are hung. There is a post fixed to frame in the stern of the boat as well, from which another sail (jib-sail?) fully blown by wind, may be seen.

On the boat we notice Bhavila looking up to heaven for succour, raising his hands in prayer. An angel (?) is painted as if coming down from heaven to the rescue of the boat. The wings of the angel have a remarkable similarity to those shown on a fresco in Sir Aurel Stein's Collection of Central Asian Antiquities at Delhi."

The scene depicted at Ajanta is a forerunner of elaborate sculptured representations on a number of fine reliefs of the world-famous Buddhist stupa at Boro Budur in Central Java. This stupendous monument was built by the Sailendra monarch of Srivijaya, a Sumatran empire about the 9th century A.D. The sculptured relief reproduced here is a telling example of the plastic art of those days, showing strong Indian influence, and, at the same time providing an evidence of how merchants and monks travelled between India and Indonesia, and how a brisk cultural intercourse existed between them.

When India Ruled Waves

The eminent Indian Archaeologist Dr. B.C. Chhabra concludes:

> "It may be a surprise even to an Indian today to be told that in the ancient world India was in the forefront in the field of shipping and ship-building Her ships, flying Indian flags, sailed up and down the Arabian Sea, the Indian Ocean and far beyond. Her master-mariners led the way in navigation. Riverine traffic within the country, shipping along the entire length of India's coastline, and on high seas were brisk until as recently as the days of the East India Company. Owing, however, to historical competition by the British, ancient Indian shipping was wiped out without a trace. No wonder then the common man in India today readily believes that Indians are only now learning the ABC of navigation.

It would have been odd indeed if, bounded on three sides by great oceans, and gifted with a remarkable spirit of enterprise and invention, India had registered no advancement in the sphere of navigation while she had gone far in other arts and sciences. *Recent research has firmly established the obvious: in olden days India's navigation system was second to none in the world."*

This is the glorious story of India's 6000 year history of shipping.

9

Ancient Hindu Geography

Akshoy Kumar Mazumdar

Ephinstone makes the following remarks on the Hindu Geography:

"The Hindus have made less progress in this than in any other science. India and some other countries nearest to it, appear to be the only part of the earth at all known to the Hindus. Within India, their ancient books furnish geographical divisions, etc.—that can be recognised. But all beyond India is plunged in a darkness from which the boldest speculations of modern Geographers have failed to rescue it.

The names of places beyond the Indus, do not coincide with those of Alexander's historians, though many on the Indian side do. It would seem, therefore as if the Hindus had, in early times, been as averse to travelling as most of them are still; and that they would have remained for ever unconnected with the rest of the world if all mankind have been as exempt from restlessness and curiosity as themselves." *History of India*, BK. III, Chap. II, pp. 145-46.

Doubtless, our geography, like several other subjects, has suffered terribly from mythological fables and priestly obscuration. Yet a good deal may be rescued and reconstructed from the Vedas, the Brahmanas, the Upanishadas, the Sanskrit Epics, the Puranas, the Tantras and the astronomical works.

Two Kinds of Hindu Geography

Hindu Geography is of two kinds, viz., Kha-gola, i.e., Mathematical/Astronomical Geography and Bhu-gola, i.e., Political Geography.

Regarding the Earth

They knew the following points regarding the earth:

(i) It originated from the gradual condensation of the 'primal waters' (ambhah apraketah of the Rigveda).

(ii) It is very large in extent. Of. Prithvi.

(iii) It is over 80,000 years (lunar) old since the dawn of human civilization.

(iv) It is round. Of. Brahmanas—the Mundane egg or ball. "The rotundity of the earth appears from the circular shadow cast on the moon"—Mahabharata. Bhaskaracharya (12th century A.D.) compares the earth to a Kadamva flower,—a very apt simile.

(v) "The sun is the upholder of the earth"—Rigveda; Self-poised, it rests in the sky—Bhaskara.

(vi) "The earth moves, though it appears still"—Aryyabhatta. Modern Geography speaks of the two motions of the earth. Hindu Geography admits its daily motion and states that the yearly motion is only a product of the first and not a separate motion.

(vii) It draws all objects towards its centre.—Aryyabhatta.

(viii) Vishuvat (equator) is the middle part of it. It is spoken of as a Vritta i.e. circle. The equator passes through Lanka (Ceylon), where days and nights are equal all the year round. No shadow on the equator. Hindus knew of the unequal lengths of the days and nights. Valmiki in his Ramayana speaks of the sunless North and refers to the Northern streamers. The Rigveda also states similar phenomena in the Arctic region. Bhaskara says "When it is morning at Lanka, it is midnight at Rome." They knew the equinoxes and the solstices. They knew of the alternate progress of the sun towards north and south. They knew of the precession of the equinoxes, being 54 bikalas a year, or one day in about 6 years. They could explain an eclipse. They recognised six seasons and knew their cause. They knew the ocean currents, the tides and their cause. They knew badavanala (submarine volcanoes) etc.

(ix) North Pole was their Sumeru (not to be confounded) with the Sumeru mountain of Central Asia); South Pole was their Kumeru. Longitude was reckoned from Ujjain in Malwa.

(x) The earth was formerly uneven.

The Mahabharata speaks of the earth as composed of numberless islands of which 49 are chief.

In a daily Hindu prayer occurs the following: "O Mother Earth, composed of the three land-masses, viz., Aswa Kranta, Ratha Kranta and Vishnu Kranta, take away all the sins from me." The Aswa Kranta—"The Horse-shaped Land"—is most probably Eurasia. Ratha Kranta—"The Car-shaped Land"—is perhaps Africa and the Vishnu Kranta is perhaps the two Americas.

In the Mahabharata, the minister Sanjaya describes the earth at some length to the blind Raja Dhrita-rastra. There the earth is described as having seven continents. We think Jambu is Asia. Saka (the Powerful Continent) is Europe. Salmali is Africa. Plaksha is the Indo-African continent now submerged. Pushkara is North America. Kusa is South America. Krauncha is Australasia.

Knowledge of Asia

Hindu knowledge of Asia—"Jambu Dvipa"—appears to be full. It is surrounded by salt seas. In shape, it looks like a large lotus-leaf.

Asia—Jambu Dvipa

Attached Islands—Svarna-prastha. Chandra Sakta, Abartana, Ramanaka, Manda harina, Panchajanya (Papuan?), Sinhala (Ceylon) and Lanka (a small island), now a part of Ceylon. The last two only are now recognised.

Lakes—The Mahabharata, describing the conquests of Arjuna in the North, speaks of the Caspian Sea as Kshiroda Sagara. The Kaushitaki Upanishad, page 146-47, mentions the lake Aral as Arar. The Manasa Sarovara is our modern Mansarowar. The other small lakes of Central Asia are called Rishi-kulyas.

Rivers—The Vedic Wakshus is our Oxus. Sita (Hsito) = Sira is now Yarmond. Yei-nei-sei is Hiranwati (Mahabh). Ob or Obei is our Vedic Yavyawati. Su wahini—is modern Huang-ho.

Mountains—Himavat = Himalaya. Suktiman = Sulaiman. Hema-kuta=Hindu kosh. Gandha-madan = Belurtag. Kailas = Kailas. Nishadha = Nyssa. Sveta (White Mt.) = Sofedkoh. Malyavan = Insan and Khanghan.

Nine Principal Divisions of Asia

Asia was divided into 9 principal divisions called Varshas:

1. Bharata Varsha=India. 2. Ketumala Varsha = Afghanistan, Persia, Turkey, etc. 3. Bhadraswa Varsha = China. 4. Kimpurusha = Tibet. 5. Hari Varsha = Tartary. 6. Ila Varsha = Mongolia, 7. Ramyaka = South Siberia. 8. Hiranmaya = Central Siberia. 9. Uttar Kuru = North Siberia.

The countries of India according to the Sakti Sangama Tantra, Chap. 7:

1. Anga=East Behar (now Bhagalpur Division). 2. Banga = Bengal. 3. Kalinga—between Orissa and R. Krishna. 4. Kalinga —Kalinga and its south up to 104 miles. 5. Kerala. 6. Kashmir. 7. Kamarupa—north of Garo Hills. 8. Maharashtra—Bombay Presidency down to Kolhapur. 9. Andhra—S.W. of Orissa. 10. Saurashtra=Cathiawar. 11. Gujrat. 12. Tailanga. 13. Malayala=Malabar Coast. 14. Karnata—between Ramanatha and Seringapatam. 15. Avanti—a part of Malwa. 16. Bidarbha = Berar and a part of Hyderabad. 17. Maru = Marwar. 18. Abhira —On the R. Taptee near the Vindhya range. 19. Malwa—East of Ujjain and north of R. Godavari. 20. Chola—Between Dravira of Delhi. 22. Kamboja—is noted for its horse: in the N.W. India. 23. Virata=Jaipur. 24. Pandya—south of Kamboja and west of Delhi. (Perh. a part of the Panjab). 25. Videha = North Behar. 26. Balhika = Bulkh. 27. Kirata—a small country in the Vindhya Range. 28. Multan—between R. Karatoa and Hinglaz: said to be full of mlechchhas, i.e., unclean beings. 29. Khorasan (Persia)—Between Hinglaz and Makkesa. 30. Airaka—North of Persia. 31. Bhotanta = Bhotan. 32. China = S. China. 33. Maha China—N. China. 34. Masesa=Manchuria(?). 35. Nepal. 36. Silahatta—Perth. E. Assam or Indo-China. 37. Gaur—Perh. modern Fyzabad. 38. Kosala—modern Oudh = Seat of the Solar Kings. 39. Magadh—a country in the United Provinces. 40. Kikata=Gaya Province. 41. Magadh—South Behar. 42. Utkala—Orissa. 43. Sri-kuntala—Prob. a part of Gujrat. 44. Hoona Desa—North of Marwar and South of Kashmir. 45. Konkana—a coast strip, south of Bombay. 46. Kekata—in N.W. India. 47. Saurasena—South of Magadha and West of the Vindhya. 48. Kuru Desa—South of Carnal and East of Panchala. 49. Sinhala—said to be the best country in India. East of the

Indian Desert and south of Kamagiri. 50. Pulandhri—East of Silahatta: Perh. Lusai Hills. 51. Kachchha Desa—Kachar: North of the Bay and east of Garo Hills (Skr. Ganesa Giri). 52. Matsya Desa (country of fish): North of Pulinda and East of Cachar: Prop. Sylhet, Mymensingh and parts of Rajsahi Division. 53. Madra—between Virata (Jaipur) and Pandya. 54. Sauvira is a sea-board tract between Sindh and Gujrat. But the S.S. Tantra fixes its locality between Muttra and R. Gandaki. 55. Nata—is perh. modern Baroda State. 56. Barbara (a large tract), from Hardwar to Sapta Sringa Hill. 57. Saindhava=Sindh (The work states that the hilly tracts in the coast from Sindh to Mecca are known by the name). Ancient Pushkarany is modern Mukran or Mekran Coast. 58. Kaleswar—? 59. Traipura—Central Province. 60. Swetagiri—Sikkim?

Countries of India as per Astronomical Work

The Ancient countries of India according to the astronomical work entitled 'The Lyotistatvam':

(i) In the middle—Sarasvata (a part of the Panjab), Matsya (Jaipur), Surasena and Mathara—Muttra Districts, Panchala—a long narrow strip on either sides of the Ganges: the northern half is now called Rohilkhanda. Salva (a part of Panjab), Mandavya (?). Kurukshetra (Carnal), Gajahwa (ancient Hastinapur on the Ganges); Maru (the Desert)—prob. Sindh and West Rajputra, Naimisha—a large forest tract near ancient Hastinapur. The Vindhyas, Pandyaghosha (a part of Panjab), Yamuna (Delhi), Kasi (Benares), Oudh, Prayaga (Allahabad), Gaya, Videha (North Behar), etc.

(ii) In the East—Magadh (South Behar), Sona (a country on the R. Sona), Varendra (North Bengal), Rarhaka (the Gangetic Delta), Burdwan, Tamalipta (Midnapur, etc.), Pragjyotisha (Assam), Udayadri (Hill Tippera and the Chittagong Division).

(iii) In the South-East—Anga (East Behar), Banga (N.W. Bengal), Upa-Banga—East Bengal, Traipura (Teori in the Central Provinces), Koshala, Kalinga (Northern part of the Madras Presidency), Odra=Orissa, Andhra, Kisbkindhya (Bellary District), Bidarbha (Berar, etc.), Savara—a forest tract, etc.

(iv) In the South—Avanti, Mahendra, Malaya (Malabar), Rishya—Mukaka (part of Hyderabad).

Chitrakuta (Bundel Khand), Maharanya (?), Kanchi (Chola),

Sinhala (not Ceylon), Konkana, Kavery (South India), Tamraparni (Ceylon), Lanka and Trikutaka are small islands to the North-west of Ceylon.

(v) In the South-west—Dravira, Anarta (Cathiawar), Maharashtra (Bombay), Raivata (a part of Gujarat), Javana (?), Pahnava, Sindha (Sindh), Persia, etc.

(vi) In the West—Haihaya (countries about the mouths of the Nerbuda), Tadrai (?), Mlechchha—Vasa (?) Prob. on the right bank of the Indus. Saka is Perh. modern Seistan.

(vii) In the North-west—Gujarat, Nata (Prob. the Baroda State) Jalandhara, etc.

(viii) In the North—China, Nepala, Hoona, Kekaya, Mandara (?) Gandhara (Candahar), Himavan (the Himalayan States) Karauncha (?), Gandhamadana (now Belurtag), Malwa (?) Kailas, Madra, Kashmir, Mlechchha Khasa, Balhika (Bulkh) Kirata (a part of Tibbet), Darada (Dardistan), etc.

(ix) In the North-east—Svarna-Bhauma (Golden Chersonese) Ganga-Dvara (a part of Trans-Gangetic Peninsula), Tankana (?) Brahmapura (Burma), etc.

The Matsya Purana also gives a list of the ancient Indian countries The curious readers will obtain much profit and pleasure from a stud of General Cunningham's Ancient Geography of India.

Hindu knowledge of and communication with, all countrie between India and the Arctic Ocean, will appear from the Ramayana Kishkindhya Book, Canto 43, Verses 53-58; Mahabh. Book I, Chap 120, Slokas 1-20. The Vayu Purana, Chap. 45, sl. 11-16-42. Th Chhandogya Upanishad, p. 358 to 360. Do, p. 171 to 181. Th Vayu Purana, Chap. 39, sl. 76-81. Bhaskara's Siddhanta Siroman Charaka's Medical Work, The Vishnu Purana and other works.

Though the political relations of the Hindus with the Nort became gradually less and less, yet trade relations with the Centr Asia, the Caspian Sea, Black Sea and the Mediterranean Sea, continu for ever. A Hindu colony is still extant at Astrakhan on the Volg The Hindu fire-temple of Baku, on the western shore of the Caspia Sea, is well-known. From the close of the third century B.C. onwar the Buddhist preachers carried the Indian wisdom, arts and religi to the different countries of the world. They not only gave, but al brought much knowledge of new things from abroad. Hindus ha preserved records, however brief, of all foreign invasions.

Travels and Voyages of the Ancient Hindus, Latin, Greek and works of other nations furnish ample proofs of Hindus going abroad on commerce, culture, political and other purposes.

Arab Countries

Hindu writings also corroborate this. Hindus, Buddhists and Jains lived in large numbers in Arabia, Syria and other parts of Asia Minor. Lucian tells us that at Nineveh he once saw a great many travellers who had come there only for the sake of worshipping images. He further tells us that to that Sacred City, Hindus came every day in large numbers because they regarded that city as a place of pilgrimage. Many other Hindu idols with broken noses and ears told the tale of the influence of Brahmanical culture and worship on the ancient religion of that land. Baharam and Astrakhan, Cairo and Moscow were the centres of trade in ancient times. Indian merchants flocked to those cities every year to earn money.

Some of the Hindu families permanently resided in those cities. In the same way, Baku and Kongo also held a great many well-to-do Hindu families. Travellers to those regions reported that they were famous there for their honesty and learning. Numerous books on astrology written by them are still extant. The great astronomer Yavanacharya was born of a Brahman family in Arabia and was educated in the University of Alexandria. He was the author of several treatises on astrology. It is said that in those days, there were in Arabia a great many Brahmans well-versed in Sanskrit and Yavanacharya learned Sanskrit from one of them. Dr. Buchanan, when he was in India, saw several tribes of Jainas who insisted that they came originally from Mecca or Arabia and that they were expelled by the successors of Muhammad. After the rise and success of Islam, the Hindu temples were pulled down and the great stone image of Siva was placed at the entrance to the Great Mosque containing the tomb of Muhammad.

Some Hindu families embraced Islam. Some came back to India. Some Brahmin families still remained at Mecca, without changing their faith. It is said that their children are known as Hussani Brahamans who look like Muhammadans in their habits and manners but wear a sacred thread and worship in their own way.

10

Guilds in Ancient India

V. NATESAN

Trade Guilds in Ancient India—such would be the exclamation of a few students of Ancient Indian History, who, while admitting and admiring the vast amount of research-work that has been brought to bear on the study and elucidation of Ancient Indian History, still sound a note of warning that we should not read into the facts of Ancient History ideas and institutions essentially modern. For, they say, such a reading would destroy the individuality and the uniqueness of Indian ideas and culture. Without falling into that alleged pitfall, I shall bring out a few salient features of the Ancient Indian trade-guild system and in doing so I shall try to bring out its unique features which distinguish it from the Guild-system of the West in mediaeval times.

Composition of the Guilds

The Guilds of Ancient India are often referred to by Sanskritic writers as the "Srenya". By this term, all authors on Hindu Polity and on economics mean a fraternal organisation of a group of labourers or artisans. A Srenya is thus primarily a combination of manual workers for some common purposes. Thus the early Hindu, Jain and Buddhistic traditions often refer to the Srenyas. We find frequent references in the Jataka stories of several such organisations.

Once when king Ajatasatru met the Buddha at his court, the king asked him. "What in the world is the good of your renunciation, of joining an order like yours? Other people, by following ordinary crafts, get something out of them." Then king Ajatasatru is reported to have given a list of such crafts the most important of which were: (1) Elephant-riders, (2) Cavalry, (3) Charioteers, (4) Archers, (5-13) Different grades in the army, (14) Slaves, (15) Cooks, (16) Barbers. (17) Bath attendants, (18) Confectioners, (19) Garland-makers, (20) Washermen, (21) Weavers, (22) Basket-makers, (23) Potters, Clerks, etc.

The detailed cataloguing of the list of crafts by no means implies that all the crafts were organised. Perhaps the component parts of the royal army, the clerks and accountants had no organisations of their own. But the other crafts seem to have been organised in guilds and the account of the Jataka stories is corroborated by a Sanskrit verse in the Samasa Kusumavali.

The meaning of the sloka is clear enough. "The guilds of potters, weavers and metal-workers should be located in the neighbourhood of villages." Thus it is evident from this sloka as well as from the reference to the crafts in the Jataka stories, that manual workers organised themselves into guilds in those ancient days.

Origin of the Guilds

The earliest associations of manual workers should have been due to the communalistic spirit of Indian civilisation. Men of the same professions, and so of the same caste had that common caste-feeling, which brought them together. Besides, the inherent advantages of association and of collective bargaining might have been one of the prompting motives. When once these organisations came into being, the cohesive forces added strength and they became corporate bodies with a separate existence and personality of their own. These bodies had for their existence the sanction of religion and hence they occupied such a large place in the socio-economic structure of the Hindu states. These bodies gradually acquired some influence in the political affairs of the tribes to which they belonged. Thus we hear in early times of the Chola kings convening primary assemblies of, what Megasthenes calls, the five castes; among them the artisans being one. We again find references in early Tamil Literature, especially in Mani-Mekhalai and Chilappadhikaram, to primary assemblies wherein the artisans seem also to have had some right of representation. Thus it is highly probable that in the early period of Indian History, i.e., before the 6th century B.C., before the rise of big empires, the trade-guilds would have fulfilled some political functions also.

The period of Government by primary assemblies however was a short-lived one in the History of Ancient India. For with the extension of territory in a state and the appearance of big kingdoms or empires. Assemblies could not be convened so easily and so frequently and thus the Assemblies gradually died out. Along with the disappearance of Assemblies the guilds would also have lost their privilege of representation in the old Assemblies.

When the transition from small petty kingdoms to huge empires had taken place, the political organisations had also to change. There was more of centralisation and all political power tended to be concentrated in the hands of the King and of the Royal Council. The territories of the Empire were often so wide as to preclude effective supervision by the King from his far-off capital. Hence a certain amount of administrative decentralisation was necessary. Throughout the history of ancient Indian polity, we witness this almost unique fact of an extreme legislative centralisation coupled with an extreme administrative decentralisation.

Out of this decentralising process, the guilds would have gained something. By reason of their corporate character and organisation, they would have been vested with a certain amount of administrative functions. Thus often the King would have endowed the guilds with judicial functions. We know as a matter of fact from contemporary evidence that the guilds in the 4th and 3rd centuries B.C. settled disputes among their members. From its sentence however there was an appeal to the Royal Court. Disputes between several guilds were settled by means of arbitration. The settlement of disputes between or within the guilds by arbitration is a characteristic feature of the ancient trade-guilds system of India. Even to this day where vestiges of such guilds remain arbitration usually plays a good part. Thus in a village near Kumbakonam, there is yet a guild consisting of weavers. The traditional history of that guild is still preserved by its members. Thus in that tradition, we hear of a certain Govinda Dikshit who was usually appointed by them as the arbitrator and his judgment have even now been preserved by some families. And many a family lays its claim to a piece of land or house-site by virtue of the award of that Dikshit. Who that Dikshit was or when he lived is matter for another topic. Suffice it here to say that he was always resorted to for settling disputes and his awards were always regarded as final, so much that even to this day the weavers of that village usually settle there disputes by arbitration. The disputants give a certain sum of money, often paltry, not exceeding, 1 Rupee in a temple and then invoke the spirit of Govinda Dikshit to settle their disputes. They then appoint an arbitrator, on whom, they believe Govinda Dikshitar's spirit comes down and dictates the judgment This rather queer procedure of settling disputes illustrates very well how the ancient trade-guilds would have exerted a beneficial influence on the settlement of disputes.

Thus we see that in the judicial arrangements of the State, the guilds occupied a prominent place and should have performed the duties of a subordinate judicary subject to the supervision of royal authority. In this lies one of the unique features of the Indian trade-guild system and a characteristic point of difference between the guilds of the West and of India.

Functions of the Guilds

In tracing the origin of the Guilds, we anticipated to some extent, the functions usually performed by the Guilds. We have seen that the Guilds of artisans became important bodies exercising political functions. But the political functions of the Guilds were only secondary; their primary functions were economic and social. The guilds of artisans guaranteed efficient production and maintained equitable distribution in the industries which they controlled. They guaranteed also the quality of the wares produced. They fixed prices also. Thus industrial production was in the hands of a syndicate of producers and consequently regulation instead of competition should have been the dominant characteristic of production.

Not only was the regulation of production and trade in the hands of the guilds but also often the duties of maintaining the currency. Thus among the coins which passed current in Ancient India there were some that were muted and circulated by the Srenyas (Cf. Rapson). Presumably these coins had to conform to certain standards prescribed by the central power. It is highly likely also that the state superintendant of coinage and currency maintained an effective control over this function of the Srenyas. We have however proofs positive to show that in the discharge of economic functions, the Guilds were supervised by the state superintendant of industry.

Constitution of the Guilds

It is evident that the trade-guilds occupied a very prominent and indispensable place in the economic and political structure of ancient Hindu states. The Guilds were not separate organisations of workers, unrecognised by law, but formed part of the political and economic machinery of the State. Hence, their organisation was largely a matter of some imperial concern, though the actual organisation was a local business.

The business of the Guilds was usually conducted in an Assembly consisting of all the artisan members. At the beginning of every year the Assembly elected its officers styled the Panchayet. Direct election by lottery would perhaps have been the probable mode of nominating the Panchayet. The Panchayet was an executive council at the head of which was a Pramukha or Nayaka who was the official president of the Guild. These presidents had often to act in a two-fold capacity: they were the nominees of the artisans as well as imperial officers. Thus they owed responsibility to both the guildsman and the King. The Pramukha was official link between the Guild and the state. The Pramukhas were also influential persons in the royal courts.

Comparison

What we have seen hitherto of the organisation and working of the Guilds in Ancient India enables us to understand that they were unique and have nothing in common with their compeers of Mediaeval Europe. Thus the Guilds in Ancient India, though at the outset formed voluntarily by the artisans, are yet recognised by the state and accepted as an essential part of the state's political and economic system. The mediaeval guilds, on the contrary remain purely private organisations, safeguarding the interests of the workers. Again the trade-guilds of Ancient India are purely democratic in their organisation and remain so till the very end, unlike those of Mediaeval Europe. The trade-guilds of Ancient India are political as well as economic institutions while the guilds of Mediaeval Europe were organised for economic ends alone. The Guilds of Mediaeval Europe are not merely fraternal organisations but they present a militant aspect also: while the Indian guilds presented no other except the fraternal. Thus the Guild-system of Ancient India exhibits peculiar features which make it unique: and because of its importance in the state-system, it deserves close investigation and study.

11

Medical Sciences and Industries in Vedic India

JYOTIR MITRA

Ayurveda—the ancient Indian science of medicine is a very comprehensive science. It is the science dealing with the life of plants, the life of animals and the life of human beings [and comprising the study of botanical, zoological and human anatomy, physiology, pathology, therapeutics, as well as minerology, chemistry, physiography, climatology and other physical sciences that directly or indirectly touch the sphere of life or world of living beings. To be a specialist in Ayurveda, the practitioner, in addition to all the medical qualifications, had to receive a little more of humane and liberal culture, e.g., lessons in philosophy, metaphysics and theology along with the healing art. (*Ed.*)

Ayurveda is the name which the ancient Indians gave to their science of Medicine. Ayus means life and veda to know or attain. It is the only applied science which is still in practice having the unbroken continuity. The three ancient *Sambitas* of the *Ayurveda* unanimously owe their allegiance to the *Atharvaveda*[1] but the *Mahabharata* (II. 11.33) on the contrary speaks of the *Upavedas*, and Nilakantha explaining it states that there are four *Upavedas*, the *Ayurveda* is attributed to the *Rgveda* and *Arthasastra* to the *Atharvaveda*. However, it is utterly explicit that the science possesses the great antiquity.

The *Ayurveda* has been divided into eight schools in Ayurvedic Samhitas[2] and elsewhere[3] and they are as follows: 1. *Salyatantra* (Surgery), 2. *Salakyatantra* (Diseases of Eye, Ear, Nose, Throat and Head), 3. *Kayacikitsa* (Internal Medicine), 4. *Bhutavidya* (Bacteriology and Psychiatry), 5. *Kamarabhrtya* (Pediatrics), 6. *Agadatantra* (Toxicology), 7. *Rasayana* (Geriatrics), and 8. *Vajikarana* (Science of Aphrodisiacs). It is surprising that the term "*Ayurveda*" does not occur at all in any of the works of Vedic literature. Perhaps the *Astadhyayi* of Panini is the oldest work, where this word has been cited twice.[4] Besides, the *Mahabharata*[5] puts forth the term *Ayurveda* along with its eight-fold divisions. Hence, we can assume that this science could not get the sound footing in spite of possessing the rudimentary knowledge of the above branches during the Vedic period. No doubt development was in course and some of the branches were in vogue and in practice. Medicine is a such type of civil science which has been needed by every body since the creation. That is why, the *Caraka Samhita* (belonging to school of *Kayacikitsa*) announces that this science is eternal and beginningless.[6]

If we review the development of Medical science, it becomes quite apparent that the Aryans of Vedic India were originally anchorites. Their livelihood was entirely based on the animals. In other words, the herdsmanship was the means of life of the Rgvedic Aryans.[7] Having seen the catties grazing in pasture ground they detected the utility of various herbs grown there and most probably became aware of the poisonous plants when the catties died caused of feeding. In the beginning they were helped towards the observation made from the therapeutic point of view by the virtue of natural instincts found in animals. Now a days a medicinal plant is compulsorily tried on animals in order to watch its toxic efficacy prior to use on human beings. Such primeval effort is traceable in the Atharvaveda,[8] where the physician (*Bhisaj*) becomes acquainted with the therapeutic properties of the some plants through the association of animals like the bore the ichneumon, the serpent, the eagle, the falcon, birds, oxen, goats, cows, sheep, etc. So far as the treatment is concerned in the beginning of the Vedic period, the use of single drug seems to be initiated against a few diseases like *Yakshma*,[9] *Apva*[10] (Dysentry or Diarrhoea), *Durnaman*[11] (Haemorrhoids], *Rajaya-kshma*[12] (Pthysis), *Vandana*[13] (Eruption on the body), *Vidradha*[14] (Abscess), *Suram*[15] (Alcoholism), *Hrdroga*[16] (Heart disease) and *Hariman*[17] (Jaundice) mentioned in the *Rgveda* only. Compound reparations, did not come into being even up to the time of *Atharvaveda*. From the references[18] we come to know that there were hundreds of medical practitioners and thousands of medicines.

In fact Vedic medicine was magico-religious and did not distinguish between medicine, magic and religion. It believed that diseases were caused by supernatural agents, such as the sorcery of enemies, possession by evil spirits and demons or the anger of certain gods. Amulets, medicines, philters, witchcraft and other devices of magic were the methods used in the treatment of diseases. In the *Atharvaveda* itself, only a few midicines are mentioned such as *Jangida*,[19] *Audumbara*,[20] *Darbha*[21] and *Satavara*[22] and these are all to be used as amulets for protection, not only against certain diseases, but also from the witchcraft of enemies. The effect of these herbs was of the same miraculous nature as that of mere charms or incantations. This tradition is still in vogue in India. By the time of the *Atharvaveda* the number of herbs increased to about more than hundred.

A primitive sort of surgery is as old as warfare. The Aryan invaders of India had to wage fierce war with the inhabitants of the Indus valley before they conquered them. During the wars, surgeons were frequently requisitioned to attend on the wounded. Thus in the *Rgveda* we read of the amputation of legs and the fitting with artificial limbs of *Vispala*,[23] joining the limbs of Atri and others,[24] bringing back to life of Syavasva, who was cut to pieces by enemies,[25] joining the head of a horse to Dadhyanci and rejoining his own head to him[26] restoring the eye sight to Rjrasva[27] and to Kanva,[28] enucleation of eyes to Paravrja,[29] hearing to Narsada[30] and walking to the lame Srona[31] by Asvin-Twins, the heavenly surgeons. Besides, Rudra-cut off the head of Daksa. Then the gods called on the twins to repair the damage and they successfully united the head to the trunk and restored Daksa to life.[32]

To some extent it would be a mistake to assume that the Vedic Indians possessed any surgical skill,[33] and it is also a fact that they applied merely simples to the wounds and their medicines and their surgery were very primitive, that they had very little scientific outlook of things.[34] In one context of *Rgveda* (VIII. 1. 12) Indra is praised for binding the wound in the neck without medicine to stanch the flow of blood. The *Atharvaveda* mentions the surgical skill of joining of fractures,[35] probing of the urethra,[36] some sort of operation in difficult labour[37] pricking of the boils of scrofula through the needle[38] along with washing of operated boils with astringent lotion.[39] Thus we can assume that the surgery was successively developing in the time of the *Atharvaveda*.

In the field of *Salakyatantra* (Eye & E.N.T.), the *Vajasaneyi Samhita* of the *Yajurveda* supplies the material regarding the physiology[40] of teeth, gums, tongue, lids and lashes of eyes and ear in rudimentary form. The *Atharvaveda* mentions the diseases of head and ear.[41] Sirsakti[42] and *Sirsamaya*[43] are treated separately. There is also a mention of *Alaji*[44] (Pterygium) an eye disease in the *Atharvaveda.* A prayer has been made to keep the urdhvangas in normal function.[45] Hence, it must be accepted that this branch was not clearly distinguished in the Vedic period.

The basis of the above two branches lies on the knowledge of anatomy and without it, both the branches cannot be practised. The existence of an anatomical tradition can be traced back to the Vedic period. In the Rgvedic hymns we find mention made of the lungs, the heart, the stomach, the intestines, the kidneys and other viscera. The *Atharvaveda* evinces a thorough knowledge of the coarser anatomy of the human body. Thus in the Book X.2 we have a hymn entitled "the wonderful structure of man" in which the several parts of the skeleton are carefully and systematically enumerated, in striking agreement with the Atreya school. In Book II.33 almost all the important organs mentioned by the Atreya and Dhanvantara schools are enumerated. *Samhitas*[46] and *Brahmanas*[47] count the bones of man as 360 which is supported by the *Caraka Samhita* and it seems that Osteology was developed through the sacrifice of animals and men and which is evident from the reference of *Yajurveda.*[48]

Kayachikitsa is the only branch of medicine which gets exhaustive treatment in the *Atharvaveda.* The *Rgveda* is acquainted with a few diseases which are already told in the beginning. The Av. mentions nearly a hundred diseases—minor and major; known and unknown and in clear terms or vaguely. The hymn IX.8 presents a classified list of diseases and they may be broadly put into five groups:

1. Some Atharvanic people recognise a three-fold classification of diseases produced by wind (*Vataja*), by Water (*Abhraja*) and by Fire (*Susma*) which corresponds to the latter classification of all diseases as due to three doshas—Vayu, Pitta and Kapha.
2. Diseases produced by possession by demons and evil spirits.
3. Diseases due to worms (*krimis*) well known, both in man and cattle.
4. Diseases due to sorcery.
5. Hereditary (*ksetriya*).

No proper methodology of diagnosis is indicated throughout the *Rgveda* and the *Atharvaveda* except supernatural agents. *Yakshma* is the general term used for diseases[49] in the *Rgveda* and in the *Atharvaveda.* Only when *Yaksma* takes the prefix Ajnata or Papa, it acquires a special meaning.

The *Atharvaveda* mentions the diseases like *Takman*[50] (fever), *Asrava*[51] (Haematuria or Polyuria), *Mutrarodha*[52] (retention of urine), *Nadivrana*[53] (Sinus), *Jalodara*[54] (Ascitis), *Kasa*[55] (cough), *Kilasa*[56] (Leucoderma), *Jayana*[57] (Tuberculosis), *Apacita*[58] (Adenoids), *Balasa*[59] (consumption), *Harima*[60] (chlorosis), *Hrdaya-maya*[61] (heart desease). Besides, there is also indication of minor diseases in the *Atharvaveda* and which are *Palita, Papayaksma, Ajuatayaksma, Aksata, Udyuga, Visara, Prstyamaya, Asrika, Visrika, Visalpaka, Vidradha, Ksipta, Hrdyota, Alaji, Snla, Paman, Paksaghata, Arista, Trsna, Asthibhauga, Jambha, Samhanau, Bhaya, Angabhcda, Angajvara, Ajnatam, Lohita, Samilunakes'a, Rudhirasrava, Kaha baha, Visncika, Apa,* etc. *Viskandha*[62] and *Grahi*[63] are in fact two terrible diseases.

Besides some specific medicines for particular diseases, the Naturotherapy was also in practice during Vedic times. Germs[64] were responsible to cause the diseases and this was known to Atharvan people. Sun's germ killing power[65] was recognised and the efficacy of sun light for curing diseases like *Harima* (chlorosis) was also known.[66] Similarly, Agni was thought of as the best physician.[67] It cures the diseases and provides the long life.

Water[68] is indicated as a curative medicine in the *Atharvaveda.* The medicinal water is to be understood here as ice-water, river water or mountain water, i.e. natural water. Water bath, washing, cleansings, sprinkling, drinking of water are all recommended for giving the strength.[69] It is a remedy because it expells the diseases.[70]

The existence of *Bhutavidya* as a separate science appears in the *Chandogya Upanisa*[71] and *Dighanikaya* of *Suttapitaka* and it was amalgamated with *Ayurveda* in later period. The credit goes to *Atharvaveda* for establishing the relation between *Bhutas* (germs) and diseases. In the Ayurvedic Samhitas the various *Grahas* like Raksasa,[72] Pisaca,[73] Gandharva,[74] Daitya,[75] etc. and Putana,[76] Skanda,[77] etc. mentioned under the heading of *unmada* (insomnia) and *Balagraha* (children diseases) respectively can be treated as the causes of diseases. In the *Rgveda* the duty of physician was also to destroy the demons and Amiva.[78]

The *Atharvaveda* describes the four main groups of *Bhutas* viz.

Pisaca, Raksasa, Atrins and Kanvas. Pisaca devour the flesh of their victims.[79] So do Atrins. Kanvas prey upon the child in the womb.[80] Raksas steel away the senses,[81] catch at joints,[82] Gandharvas[83] are doglike. Some glimpse expressing the connection between *Bhutas* and diseases are also found in the Rgveda.[84] The spirit of the dead was considered to cause the diseases,[85] therefore, the Sun,[86] Agni[87] and Brhaspati[88] are said to be the dispeller of diseases. These were supposed to enter the human-body through food.[89] The *Atharvaveda* indicates some amulets[90] to dispel them.

Kaumarbhrtya includes obstetrics and gynaecology both apart from the children diseases. The *Atharvaveda* gives a long list of charms starting from the conceptions up to the nourishment of child. Under the *strikarmani sukta*, the *Atharvaveda* gives the mantras for Garbhadrmhana,[91] Garbharaksana,[92] Sukhaprasuti[93] and to remove the evil effect of the inauspicious moment at birth.[94] Many prayers have been offered to Prajapati and other gods to prevent the miscarriage[95] and abortion. No particular gynaec disease is indicated except the *Rudhirasrava* (Pradara or Metroregia Haemorrhagica).

The knowledge of toxicology was developed during the forest-dwelling life of Aryans. The *Rgveda* gives the hymn VII. 50, against snake poison and scorpions and venomous vermins. The *Atharvaveda*[96] introducing many charms against the above, provides the same treatment against poisonous plants and arrows. *Kairats*, *Prsna*, *Upastrnya*, *Babhra*, *Taimata*, *Aligi*, *Viligi*, *Urugula* seem to be varieties of poisonous snakes.[97] Kankaparvan, *Sarkota*, *Vriscika* and *Babhru* are terms for scorpion. Mosquito[98] (*Masaka*) and Ant[99] (*Upajika*) are also considered to be poisonous insects. Among the plants *Taudi*, *Ghrtaci*,[100] *Kandavisa* seem to be the poisonous roots.[101] The *Atharvaveda* makes a clear reference to the poisoned arrow.[102] Beating of drum[103] anointed with antidots is also referred to in order to avoid the poisonous air which is followed by Susruta.[104]

Rasayana is that which rejuvenates the olds and cures the diseases. The *Vaj. Samhita* (XII. 81) mentions four kinds of plants—*Asvavari*, *Somavati*, *Urjayanti* and *Udojasa* are plants, among the last two stand for *vrsya* and *Rasayana*. In the Av. water[105] is considered the best *rasayana* among all. If the story of the rejuvenation of sage Cyavana by Asvins is true, it is quite apparent that the process was known to Vedic people. When the civilisation of Aryans was urbanized, they might have felt the need of taking the Rasayana in order to attain the longevity. Many hymns belonging to it are mentioned in the

Atharvaveda.[106] The last attempt might have been made by the settled Aryans addicted with prosperity and all sorts of happiness to promote the virility. The Atharvaveda[107] safely recommends the plant named Ucchusma (Kapikacchu=Maeuma pruritus) as rejuvenating agent which is still regarded one of the cheapest and best herbs. In the same period they might have also discovered the plants as *Saubhagyavardhaka,*[108] *Saundaryavardhaka,*[109] *Kesavardkaka,*[110] and *Kesadrmhana.*[111]

NOTES AND REFERENCES

1. (a) Caraka Samhita. I. 30.21; (b) Susruta Samhita. I. 1.6.: (c) Kasyapa Samhita. III. 1. p. 42.
2. (a) C.S.I. 30 (b) S.S.I. 1.6.
3. Mahabharata, II. 5.61; 11.25; and Harivamsa P. Ch. 29.
4. (a) Kratukthadisutrantatthak. IV. 2. 60.
   (b) Kathadibhyasthak. IV. 4. 102.
5. (a) Kaccid vaidayas cikitsayam astangayam visaradah. MBH. II. 5.61.
   (b) Ayurvedas tatha stango dehavans tatra bharata. Ibid. IE. 11.25.
6. C.S.I. 30. 27.
7. IV. 15.6; VIII. 22.2; VII. 55.3.
8. VIII. 7. 23-26.
9. X. 161.1.
10. X. 103.12.
11. X. 162.2.
12. I. 161.7.
13. VII. 50.2.
14. IV. 32.23.
15. X. 131.5.
16. I. 50.11.
17. I. 11. et seq.
18. Satam te rajan bhisajah sahasram urvi gabhira sumatiste'stu. Rv. I. 24. 9. cf.
    Adhitiradbyagad ayam adhi jivapura agan.
    Satam hyasya bhisajah sahasram ut virudhah. Av. II. 9.3.
19. Av. XIX. 34. 1-10; 35. 1-5.
20. Av. XIX. 31. 1-14.
21. Av. XIX. 28. 1-10; 29. 1-9.
22. Av. XIX. 36. 1-6.
23. I. 116.15.
24. I. 117.19.
25. I. 117.24.
26. I. 116.12; 117.12.
27. I. 116.16.
28. I. 117.17.
29. I. 112.8.

30. I. 117.8.
31. I. 112.8.
32. Satapatha Brahmana. VIII. 1.8.18.
33. Macdonella and Keith: Vedic Index Vol. II. p. 1057.
34. Karambelkar's the Atharvaveda and the Ayurveda, p. 34.
35. Av. IV. 12.7.
36. Av. I. 3.
37. Av. I. 11.5.
38. Av. VII. 74.2.
39. Av. VII. 76.1; VI. 57.
40. Yajurveda XXV. 1.2.
41. Av. IX. 8.
42. Av. I. 17.
43. Av. IV. 22.
44. Av. VI. 16; IX. 8.20.
45. Van me asannasoh pranas' caksur aksnoh srotram karnayoh.
    Apalitah kes'a asona danta bahu Bahvorbalam... Av. XIX. 60.1.
46. Rv. I. 164. 48 = Av. X. 8.4.
47. Vaj. Samhita XXX. 10.
48. Satapatha Brahmana X. 5.4.12; Tait. Bra. III. 4.4.1.
49. Av. I. 2.4; II. 3.3; IX. 8.1-5; 21.22.
50. I. 25; V. 4. 22; VI. 20; VII; VII. 116; XIX. 39.
51. I. 2; II. 3; VI. *44*.
52. I. 3.
53. VI. 57; 109.
54. I. 10; VI. 22; 24; 26; Rv. I. 50. 11-13.
55. I. 17; VI. 12.
56. I. 23, 24.
57. VII. 76. 2.
58. VI. 25; 57.
59. VI. 14; 127.
60. I. 22; VI. 24.
61. I. 22.
62. I. 16; III. 9; II. 4.
63. VI. 112; 113.
64. II. 31, 32; V. 23.
65. VI. 3.
66. III. 7. 7.
67. I.28. 1.
68. Av. V. 28.1; 30.14.
69. II. 29.5.
70. VI. 91.3.
71. VII. 1.2.
72. C.S. VI. 9. 20; S.S. utt. 60.40; Ast. Hr. utt. 4. 26-29.
73. C.S. VI. 9.20; S.S. utt. 60.15; Ast. Hr. utt. 4. 30-34.

74. C.S. VI. 9.20; S.S. utt. 60.10; Ast. Hr. utt. 4. 18, 19.
75. S.S. utt. 60.9; Ast. Hr. 4. 16, 17.
76. S.S, utt. 27.12; Ast. Hr. utt. 27.9.
77. S.S. utt. 27.6; Ast. Hr. utt. 3. 9-11.
78. X. 97.6=Vaj. S. XII. 80.
79. IV. 36. 3; V. 29.5.
80. II. 25. 3.
81. VI. 111.3.
82. II. 9.1.
83. IV. 37. 11.
84. III. 15.1; VII. 1.7; 8.6; 38.7; VIII. 35. 16-18.
85. X. 85.31.
86. I. 35.9; 191, 8, 9; X. 37; 3; 100.8.
87. I. 12. 7; 189. 3.
88. X. 98.3.
89. Rv. III. 22. 4.
90. IV. 10. 1-7; VIII. 5. 1-22 X. 3.1-25; 6. 1-35.
91. V.25; VI. 81; III. 23 = Rv. X. 162.
92. VI. 17 = Rv. V. 78.
93. I. 11.
94. VI. 110; 140.
95. Av. n. 25. 3.
96. IV. 6; 7; VI. 100; V. 13; VI. 12; VI. 56; VII. 88.
97. V. 13; VII. 56.
98. VII, 56.2.
99. VI. 100.
100. X. 4.24.
101. X. 4.22.
102. VI. 6.
103. Av. v. 20.
104. S.S. Kalp. 6th Chapter.
105. I. 4.5; 6; 33, III. 7.13; IV. 33; VI. 22, 23, 24.
106. II. 28. 1-5; VIII. 1. 1-21; 2. 1-28; I. 30. 1-4, 35. 1-4.
107. VI. 4.3.
108. Av. VI. 139. 1-5.
109. *Ibid.*
110. Av. VI. 21. 1-3.
111. VI. 136. 1-3.

12

Woman in the Ayurvedic Literature

H.G. Ranade

The present paper is an attempt to delineate the position of women in the Ayurvedic Literature. Many scholars have thrown light on the status of women in the Vedic, Buddhist and later period of ancient Indian History, and have also made a study of their position in the legal literature of the times. However, no attempt seems to have been made so far to examine the status of women in the Ayurvedic literature, "which is regarded as the oldest of Indian Sciences and has been proved to be the science in which the Indians specialised first."[1] There is also a need today for a dispassionate and impartial study of the background of the position of women in India, since this is an age of reform, when the position and status of Indian women in society is undergoing a vast change.

It could thus be found that while the literary and other works have thrown light on her position either as a colourful unit of the society or as a heir to the property, etc., the medical treatises of the Hindus have viewed her from the pathological point of view. Her status as a mother, as wife and Dhatri, as an agent for the cure of diseases, as one being the cause of diseases is the subject for the ancient treatises on Ayurveda.

Of all the treatises the Caraka Samhita and the Susruta Samhita are the oldest and basic. It is mainly their views that the works of the later period elaborate and elucidate. The period to which the Ayurvedic works belong ranges from the later vedic period to the late middle ages of the Indian History.[2]

General Treatment

The Ayurveda has expressed a very high regard towards women. As a mother she shoulders a very big responsibility of the society. Caraka Samhita speaks very highly about the woman. "It is she in whom the virtues have gathered together. It is she who is lovable and who gives birth to an issue. The Dharma and Artha are, thus, in her, incarnate. Her qualities supply eddification to the man. (Caraka Sam, Cikitsa 2, 4 to 9).

Her beautiful form and graceful gait are also not lost sight of. It is, however, warned that her attractive character should not be allowed to cause harm to the general health. If not properly cared for, she is dangerous like wine.

Physiological Peculiarities

In the treatment of 'Salyatantra she is taken on par with a young boy, an old-age, very tender in age and a fearful'.[3] Her menstruation cycle functions between the age of twelve to fifty. In the loss of blood in the body if the cycle is irregular, it shows loss in quantity and causes pain in the pubic region. In the excess the discharge is excessive and with a bad smell.[4] The blood of a woman which does not stain the cloth is praised by Susruta.[5] Rakta-gulma or the blood-tumour is a disease which is peculiar to women.[6]

The presence of milk (after conception) in the breasts causes enlargment.[7] In the excess of breast-milk the breasts are enlarged excessively and pricking pain is caused.[8] The breast of a woman (eighteen angulas approx) is of the size of the man's waist and the hips of a woman agree with the size of a man's chest.[9] Semen and breast-milk are the effects of the same type of *dhamanis* in a man and a woman respectively.[10] The semen is also related to the menstruation-blood.[11]

In the ear-piercing ceremony the Susruta Samhita prescribes that the left ear should be pierced first in the case of a girl while it is the right in the case of a boy.[12]

Ethics

Caraka Samhita lays down that one should not desire for another's wife and indulge in a misbehaved woman.[13] One should not disrespect a woman.[14] Killing of a woman causes leprosy.[15] In the general principles of healthy behaviour 'Hemanta' is regarded as the proper time for enjoyment with a woman.[16] Caraka prescribes that one should control the discharges if they causes trouble to others.[17]

Disbelief is expressed in a woman appointed in the kitchen. She should be appointed only after a proper test to avoid poisoning of food.[18] She could be the agent of the enemy (Caraka Cikitsa 23, 233).

The patient should avoid taking food with a *ganika*.[19] Contact with a *Visakanya* may cause danger to life.[20] Caraka prescribes that one should not indulge in a prostitute.[21] In this case she is to be on par with wine and dice-play. Ugly women with ill-shaped breasts are condemned by Caraka.[22]

Woman and the Bhisaj

It is prescribed that the medical practitioner should not indulge in sitting or staying with the woman. He should avoid joking them.[23] It is a good omen for him if he sees a woman with a son or a girl wearing ornaments, when he is on his way to the patient.[24] Caraka lays down that a student of Ayurveda should use his knowledge to cure diseases of his parents, brothers and teacher. Except food he should not accept any gift from women.[25] The doctor should not desire to copulate with another's wife even in a dream.[26]

Relationship of a Patient with a Woman

Contact with a woman from a distance causes loss of virility in a wounded. It is prescribed that the wounded should avoid looking at the approachable (*gamya*) woman, talking with her and physical contact with her, because that may cause discharge of semen.[27] The possibility of the breast-milk being poisonous is expressed in Susruta Samhita Sutra, (27. 5) and it is prescribed that such breast-milk should be sucked out by mouth or by a horn (visana). If a patient is dragged to the south in a dream by a black, loose-haired, laughing dancing woman wearing red dress the patient dies, if not, is further attacked by a disease.[28] The breast-milk is useful for curing the diseases of the eyes and ear.[29] The piles 'disease is caused due to a sexual intercourse with a woman'.[30] So is the case of a number of other diseases.[31] A woman having blood affected by leprosy gives rise to leprous issue.[32]

The food and drink with the nails, hair, urine, blood, of a

misbehaving woman causes dangerous diseases of abdomen.[33] Upadamsa, a disease of the male organ is caused due to excessive intercourse with a woman who has given up for a long time discharging the menstruation, having long, rough, short hair, not desiring for intercourse, who has washed the vagina with dirty water, and one having diseases of the vagina.[34] A patient of leprosy can get rid of it by avoiding contact with a woman, flesh and liquor.[35] A man gains in flesh if he stops sexual intercourse with a woman.[36] A typical treatment is suggested in Ayurveda for the curing from fever. The fever could be lowered down by the embraces of beautiful and largebreasted women, who apply perfumes and sandal to their bodies and please the mind of the patient. But the patient is to be removed from them as soon as the fever is diminished.[37] The use of beautiful and attractive woman is also prescribed for curing the diseases caused by overdrinking.[38] But these two prescriptions seem to be possible only in the case of kings and rich people. Sexual intercourse with a woman could also cure 'udavarta' disease with regard to semen.[39]

Woman as Mother

The texts of the Ayurveda take immense care to safeguard the life of a mother during pregnancy. Kasyapasamhita is almost an independent work on the care of mother. Caraka discusses in details the controversy regarding the theory that the virtues and vices of the delivered child belonging to the mother and father or the *either* one of them.[40] At one place the leprosy of a child is traced to that of mother and father.[41] A brahman versed in Atharvaveda must ward of by 'Santi the demonic', influences in the sutikagrha (a room for the delivering).[42]

It is prescribed that the pregnant woman should not be treated with purgatives,[43] enima[44] and smoking.[45]

Diseases of Woman and Remedies

There is nothing more difficult in *surgery* than removing the stillborn foetus.[46] The Bhisaj should by all means rescue her from the hands of death in such cases. Swelling of the mouth and concealed parts of a woman are indicative of death.[47]

Buffalo's flesh is useful for increasing the quality and quantity of the breast-milk.[48] It is remarkable that the application of approdisiacs is also prescribed for the women who are desirous of the real love from man.[49] Measurment is given for women of the syringe in the treatment of *'uttarabasti'* a kind of enima for clearing the urinal passage. It should be 4 angulas long for them. For women the insertion is 2 angulas, while for the girls it is 'angula',[50] There is a special section in the Susruta Samhita on the diseases of the female organ of generation. It is indicative of the misbehaviour of the women at the time.[51]

Woman as a Wife

The marriageable age according to Susruta Samhita is twenty-five for men and sixteen for the bride.[52] The man should not cause conception in too young a girl.[53] If the delivered wife gives birth to a son after six years the son lives only a short time.[54]

The husband is treated on par with wife so far as the reference to the semen and breast-milk or menstruation are respectively concerned.[55] The significance of 'Bralunacharya' for the wife as well as the husband is particularly stressed and it is pointed out that they should couplate only for the purpose of '*praja* progeny, especially, the son.[56] Conception does take place if the copulation takes place in the period of menstruation cycle.[57] If the copulation is of the reverse type the daughter born will be manly in her behaviour.[58] If she does sexual intercourse during a dream a foetus is born to her in her abdomen.[59] Superiority of semen gives birth to a son, that of blood a daughter and the equality an impotent.[60]

The ideal conditions of a wife are depicted in the Susruta Samhita sarirasthana 24.131. She should be matching to the husband in age and form, she should have good behaviour, she should be from a good family and desirous of the husband. She should use ornaments which enhance her beauty.

Polygamy was in vogue is clear from the words *bahubharya,* etc.[61] There is also an indication that women used to live unmarried throughout life.[62]

Woman's Role as Dhatri

The importance of a Dhatri is very greatly recognised by the Ayurvedic text. She should be of the caste as the mother, of middle size, of middle age, devoid of any disease, well-behaved, not cunning, not greedy, not thin, not fat, with pure breast-milk, with not very long lips, not with long and raised breasts, without any physical defects, without additions, having a living child, affectionate, not doing low deeds and born in a good family. She should take the utmost care of the child. Her milk should be tested in water. If there it looks shell-like and becomes solidified it should be taken as pure.[63] She should clean the breasts from time to time avoiding thereby the defect of inflammation, etc.[64] It appears that only rich families could afford to appoint Dhatris for their children.

King and Women

It appears that the kings had employed women at their services. Because, it is stated that women have to suffer from diseases which are caused by checking of natural discharges from the body due to bashfulness and compulsion.

Lastly, the importance of the old lady in the family is also recognised. Her advice was accepted specially in connection with pregnancy.

Notes and References

1. Kashikar (Tr.) of 'Indian Medicine' by Julius Jolly, Poona, 1951, p. 1.
2. The Atharvaveda could be regarded as the first work on Ayurveda with its medicinal plants and magical spells. In the Caraka Samhita and Susruta Samhita it is often quoted, Susruta Samhita I. 1.6 also denotes the Ayurveda as the Upanga of Atharvaveda. Caraka Samhita roughly belongs to the 1st Cent. A.D. while the Susruta with its developed surgery is later in period.
3. Susru, Sutrasthana 8.5; 10.8; 13.3; Caraka. Su 10.15.
4. Susruta Su 15.12.
5. *Ibid.*, Sarirasthana 2.17.
6. *Ibid.*, Uttaratantra 42.19.
7. Susru. Sutra. 15.5.
8. *Ibid.*, 15.16.
9. *Ibid.*, 35.12.
10. *Ibid.*, Sarira 9.5.
11. *Ibid.*, 9.7.
12. Susruta Sutra 16.3.
13. Carka, Sutrasthaṇa 8.20; see also 13.53.
14. *Ibid.*, 8.23.
15. Susruta Samhita, Nidanasthana 5.30.
16. Susruta Uttaratantra 64.26; for Caraka it is Sisira Sutra, 6.17.
17. Caraka, Sutrasthana 7.29.
18. Susruta, Kalpa 1.13.
19. Susru, Cikitsa 24.98.
20. Susru, Kalpa 1.6.
21. Caraka, Sutra 8.26.
22. *Ibid.*, Cikitsa, 30.35.

23. Susru. Su. 10.9.
24. Caraka Sam. Su 30.27.
25. Susru Su., 10.9, 29.28; see also Caraka Vimana 8.11.
26. Caraka Vimana 8.11.
27. Susruta Sutra 19-14-15.
28. *Ibid.*, 29.57.
29. *Ibid.*, 45.103
30. Susruta Nidana 2.4.
31. *Ibid.*, Cikitsasthana 6.22.
32. *Ibid.*, Nidana 5.28.
33. Susruta Nidana 7.11.
34. *Ibid.*, 12.7.
35. *Ibid.*, Cikitsa 23.13.
36. *Ibid.*, Cikitsa 24.113.
37. Susruta uttara 39.276 to 280; Caraka Vimana 6.15; Cikitsa 3.266; also see 4.108.
38. Susruta uttara 47.43-44.56, Caraka Cikitsa 24.155.
39. Caraka Cikitsa 8.186.
40. Susru Su. 25.18
41. *Ibid*, 24.5, Nidana 8.11.
42. Caraka 4.8.30.
43. Susru. Cikitsa 33.29.
44. *Ibid.*, 32.48.
45. Caraka Su 5.42.
46. Susruta Cikitsa 15.3.
47. *Ibid.*, Su 31.19.
48. Susru Su 46.96.
49. *Ibid.*, Cikitsa 26.4.
50. *Ibid.*, 3.7, 103, 104.
51. *Ibid.*, Uttara ch. 38.3, 4, 10d ch.
52. Susru. Su. 35.13.
53. *Ibid.*, Sarira 10.55.
54. *Ibid.*, 10.66.
55. Susruta Su 46.299 for example.
56. Susruta Sarira 2.27, 28.
57. *Ibid.*, 2.30.
58. *Ibid.*, 2.43.
59. *Ibid.*, 2.48.
60. *Ibid.*, 3.5; also 3.12.
61. *Ibid.*, 26.5, Caraka Cikitsasthana 2.10.
62. Caraka Cikitsa 8.5.
63. Susruta Samhita, Sarirasthana 10.24 to 31; Caraka Sarira 8.54.
64. Susruta Cikitsa 17.47.

13

Modern Light on Ancient Law

PROF. B.M. GHOSAL

Contrary to the general belief, the Manu-smriti or 'Code of Manu' does not necessarily deals with jurisprudential laws only. The purely legal parts in it comprise about one-third of the treatise. The other two-thirds deal with other subjects including some mundane. For example, the following article deals with injunctions of Manu with the mode of taking meals. (Ed.)

Experiments on the influence of emotions on digestion have revealed certain facts which are interesting in as much as they throw a flood of light on some injunctions of Manu.

Everybody takes his meals daily, but very few persons know what they ought to take. Still fewer people know how to take a meal.

Eating is so common an affair that nobody takes any special care to learn the principles that must be followed in order to derive the maximum benefit from what is eaten.

In our Shastras there are rules about eating. Not to speak of observing them very few families even know them.

In families, the elder members of which still stick to the old ways, younger ones, either students in schools and colleges or adults with English education, are not uncommon who care very little for such things. In some cases positive disregard and hatred is evinced when such youths are asked by their mothers and other superiors to follow these rules.

In most cases this apathy arises from want of reason to support the shastraic injunctions. When properly explained and supported by reason, such rules may find favour with some, but for a full belief shastraic injunctions must enlist the support and confirmation of modern science, at least in those cases in which it is possible to do so.

Cases for which scientific data are available ought to be made known to all so that the right course may be adopted.

In this article we shall consider a few rules in connection with the mode of taking meals as enjoined by Manu in the light of modern scientific researches:

> The twice-born should wash hands, feet and mouth every day before sitting at a meal, and eat with an undistracted mind.—Manu II, 53.

Though only a part of this line seems to be directly connected with the theme we have proposed, yet a little thought will show that a wash applied to the hands, feet and mouth helps indirectly to bring about that equanimity and the pleasant mood insisted on by Manu and modern scientists with equal emphasis.

Moreover in a hot country like India, the body is always soiled with perspiration; and as food is touched and taken with the hand, it is a matter of necessity, for ensuring cleanliness, to wash the hand. A wash applied to the face with a few gargles gives a refreshing tone to the whole body and removes all the dirt and undesirable matter that may have accumulated in the mouth.

Hence, we find that the preliminary wash serves the physical purpose of removing dirt and giving a refreshing tone to the body; and the mental benefit that arises from this is a part of that undistractedness and pleasantness of which we shall say more in what follows.

Manu goes on to enjoin in the next couplet:

> Receive the meal every day with a hearty welcome and take it without censure, evince a hearty joy at its sight and wish that every day you may get one.—Manu II, 54.

It is a painful sight to see many youths of the present day disregard this wholesome rule, perhaps through ignorance, not only to the detriment of their digestive system but also to a corresponding deterioration in their moral nature.

Of course food prepared at hostels may sometimes deserve censure and the cooks rebuke, for they are only mercenary hands having very little care for the health of those for whom they work but the stormy scene, that some youths are in the habit of creating almost every day over their meals, even when the food is cooked and served personally by the mother than whom there can he no greater well-wisher of anybody and than whom nobody would prepare food with greater purity, greater care and devotion, should be severely condemned.

Such as inconsiderate person little knows or feels the injury he inflicts on his digestive system and to his moral nature. He is deprived of the benefit derivable from the meal and renders positive harm to the digestive mechanism; and by wounding the feelings of one, whose debt nobody has yet been able to repay, he lays the axe at the very root of his moral nature.

Now the question may arise why one should welcome food and express joy at its sight. The answer is given in the next couplet, which runs:

> Strength and energy can be gained by thus welcoming the meal every day. Food taken without being worshipped destroys both these.—Manu II, 55.

The purport of this couplet is that food, though wholesome or otherwise and properly prepared, cannot serve the purpose for which it is taken, if it is not taken in a spirit of welcome and worship.

It may be argued, however, that a particular substance is sure to react chemically on another substance in a particular way whether we wish it or not. Food taken by an individual is sure to be digested and assimilated by the system and the inevitable result of this process is the nutrition of the muscular and nervous matter in which strength and energy reside potentially.

Such an argument may appear to be sound at the first sight, but it cannot bear close examination. Of course, if digestion be independent of the emotional condition of the individual when at his meal, there is nothing to say against the above argument, but Manu's injunctions point to the opposite direction, namely, emotion exercises an enormous influence on the process of digestion.

Manu's injunctions appear to be dogmatic and hence are liable to be neglected and overlooked by those who have a rational and scientific turn of mind. What scientific or empirical knowledge is crystallised into these commands is not known. These couplets are mere assertions without being supported by positive experimental facts or proper reasoning.

We shall presently see that Manu's commands are based on scientific principles though these are not enunciated to prop up the commands.

It is necessary to understand the process of digestion before we can understand the validity and utility of these commands.

The human body consists of several kinds of tissues, namely, bone or osseous tissue, muscular tissue, nerve tissue, etc. The tissues, get their nutrition from the food that is taken by the individual. All tissues suffer waste, and nutrition makes good the loss. The different chemical substances required for the repair and replenishment of the different tissues are all derived from the food. The different constituents of the different tissues are distributed to them through the blood. The blood receives these from the food through the process known as digestion. For being changed into blood all food materials have first to be brought to a liquid condition. An insoluble solid has to be changed into a soluble substance before being digested. Digestion begins in the mouth. A piece of bread or a morsel of rice taken alone and masticated for a sufficient length of time gives a distinct sweet taste, due to the change of insoluble starch into soluble sugar which is absorbed through the mouth. After being thoroughly masticated, the food enters the stomach where it is stirred and shaken with a juice, which is called the gastric juice, secreted by tiny vessels lining the inner walls of the stomach. This juice is essential for digestion in the stomach. This is only the simplest possible description of the complicated process up to what happens in the stomach; but this will serve the purpose of understanding Manu's commands.

The activities of the human body are due to the emotions of the muscles and the nerves. Muscles are under the control of the nerves which are themselves controlled by the brain. The nerves which control the blood vessels (heart, etc.) and the digestive system are independent of the will, and form a separate system altogether known as the sympathetic system. Though independent of the will, this system is intimately connected with the emotional nature. For example, there is a rush of blood to the face when there is a feeling of shame. This disturbance in the automatic ordinary circulation is independent of the will. The individual does not deliberately wish that there should be a rush of blood towards the face, but it so happens automatically due to the response of the sympathetic system to the feeling in question.

Persons of irritable temperament admit that they not only lose appetite and power of digestion during an acute fit of anger, but also the same effect is felt, sometimes, for two or three days.

The analogous case cited above and the experience of choleric persons sufficiently support Manu's injunctions for preserving attention and equanimity of the mind during a meal. But evidence of a more positive nature, hence more satisfactory and convincing, is available now.

The actual condition of the stomach while at work has been brought within the jurisdiction of the naked eye by means of the X-rays. It is now possible, thanks to the superhuman achievements of modern science, to arrange for an ocular demonstration of the influence which emotions excite on digestion by withholding the flow of the gastric juice and checking the contractions of the stomach.

The following is an extract from an article headed, 'Influence of Mind on the Body,' that appeared in the *Statesman*, dated Sunday, 15th October 1922:

(For the) *Statesman*, London, September, 21,

> The influence of mind on the body has been . . . emphasised . . . by the teaching of M. Cone. . . . It appears, however, from a lecture delivered the other day by Dr. Hadfield at the Nations' Food Exhibition at Olympia on the Psychology of feeding that mental processes are much more extensively associated with eating and drinking than has hitherto been imagined to be the case.
>
> To show the connection between the flow of the gastric juice and emotions, such as anger and fear, the help of the X-rays has been enlisted, and it has in this way been made evident that when the mind is under the sway of these emotions, the digestive contractions of the stomach cease to take place.
>
> It follows that when we sit down to a meal we should in the first place turn our backs on all our cares and worries, and in no circumstances should we allow ourselves to be involved in a heated argument at table.

Did not Manu predict the findings of modern science? Certainly the facts were known but the proof is not given in the couplets quoted above. At any rate when science confirms' Manu's commands, there is no reason why they should not be obeyed in the interest of one's health.

Dr. Hadfield's wholesome advice, based on experimental facts, tells us not to do certain things; Manu's commands include this negative aspect indirectly and ask us positively to be calm, quiet, and undistracted, to welcome or worship food, to be pleased at its sight and so on, for such emotions promote the very process which is hampered by emotions like anger and fear.

The above considerations lead us to think that irritable persons have a greater tendency to dyspepsia.

We have learnt therefore that emotions like anger, fear, etc., interfere with digestion. Undigested or ill-digested food is a burdensome load on the system and a mere waste from which escape lies in following the advice of Dr. Hadfield and better the commands of Manu.

The Hindu Conception of Moral Judgment

PROFESSOR CHARU CHANDRA SINHA

NECESSITY OF JUDGMENT (UDYOGA PARVAN)

Characteristics of Moral Judgment

Moral judgment is regulative (Vana Parvan).—It aims at destroying the attributes of Darkness and Passion. Eight-fold path of regulating action—(a) Right views—Duhkha, Duhkha-samudaya, Duhkha-nirodha, Duhkha-nirodhagamini-pratipad, (b) Right aspirations, (c) Right speech, (d) Right conduct, (e) Right living, (f) Right effort, (g) Right mindfulness, and (h) Right meditation.

Moral judgment refers to the highest good (Sankhya Prava-cana Sutram). Three kinds of Siddhi—(a) Pramoda Siddhi—prevention of Adhidaivika pain, (b) Mudita Siddhi—prevention of Adhibhautika pain, and (c) Modamana Siddhi—prevention of Adhyatmika pain.

Postulates of Moral Judgment

Moral judgment presupposes (1) Self-determination (Anu-sasana Parvan). (2) Discrimination, which is classified as (a) Svabhava Nirdesa, (b) Prayoga Nirdesa, and (c) Anusmrti Nirdesa. (3) Moral standard—Dharma, Artha, Kama and Moksa (Visnupuranam). (4) Personality (Gita, Smrti, and Karika).

The Object of Moral Judgment

Is consequence the object of moral judgment? Arguments for (Udyoga Parvan, Devi Bhagavatam). Arguments against (Santi Parvan) Story of Valaka and Kausika.

Is motive the object of moral judgment? Arguments for (Santi Parvan; Devi Bhagavatam). Arguments against (Devi Bhagavatam). Motive alone cannot be the object of moral judgment—means also should be taken into consideration (Santi Parvan).

The principle, "The end justifies the means". Arguments for the principle (Santi Parvan). Arguments against the principle (Santi Parvan). Story of the great Rsi Visvamitra. Cases in which the end appears to justify the means (Siva Puranam). But such means being productive of greater good cannot properly be regarded as evils (Siva Puranam). That any means which involves pain is to be discarded, should not be regarded as a Universal law (Siva Puranam). Story of Sankha and Likhita. Criminal means, however insignificant, ever tolerated are soon preferred, as presenting a shorter cut to the object than through the highway of moral virtues (Santi Parvan). Character is not a trivial thing and it should not be trifled with (Santi Parvan).

An action, therefore, should be judged not by its motive alone, not by its actual results, but by its intention, i.e., both motive and means (Udyoga Parvan, Santi Parvan, Bhisma Parvan).

Necessity of Moral Judgment

The man, who, after duly reflecting in his mind, and ascertaining his own ability, accomplishes righteous actions, is sure to obtain what is for his benefit. Actions done without reflection, without the aid of understanding, will not become beneficial; but, on the other hand, actions done with careful judgment will remain with undiminished excellence and will yield happiness as their natural consequence (Mahabharatam).

The nature of the act itself and of its consequence must be taken into account. Before we proceed to perform an action or before we refrain from doing it, we must determine what will happen to us if we perform the action, and what, if we omit to do it.

To say that such and such action is or has happened is one thing, but to state that what has happened is good or bad is a different thing. In this judgment we judge the value or worth of the action by reference to a standard or *norm* that is beyond the act itself. A moral judgment is normative as opposed to the judgment dealt with in the positive sciences which is merely factual. The moral judgment does not state a relation that exists, a mere fact that such and such events have occurred, but states the relation as it ought to be. "The man has committed murder" is a mere statement of a fact, "the man ought not to have committed murder" is our judgment upon the fact. This latter is a moral judgment.

Characteristics of Moral Judgment

It is evident that every judgment will involve these constituents:

(1) A subject who judges.
(2) An object which is judged.
(3) A standard according to which it is judged.
(4) A faculty of judging.

In having a subject, an object, a standard and a faculty moral judgment agrees with other judgments. It differs, however, in the following respects:

(1) Moral judgment is regulative.
(2) Moral judgment refers to an ultimate good.
(3) Moral judgment makes the subject responsible.

Moral Judgment—Regulative

As man is a rational being, he, by exercising his own intellect, knows that oil may be had from sesame seeds, curds from milk, and fire from fuel, and he also knows the means necessary for accomplishing such actions. And thus when the action and the end and the means are known, he sets himself with proper means to accomplish it (32. 28. Vana Parvan).

Similarly when man comes to know that he is subject to desire on account of wrath; that cupidity, delusion, vanity and pride and selfishness spring from desire; that selfishness is the root of many evil actions; that from acts spring diverse bonds of action; and that from those bonds spring sorrow and misery; then he regulates his actions in such a way as to enable him to escape from those evils; then he makes an attempt to purify his soul, to discipline his character and to ennable his heart by destroying the attribute of passion, the cause of delusion, and the attribute of darkness, the source of wrath and fear and cupidity and pride; and thus in this way when perfect purity is obtained, he succeeds in arriving at the knowledge of the Supreme Soul which is resplendent with effulgence, which is incapable of deterioration, which is without change and which is all-pervading. He then begins to regulate his life and action by following the eight-fold path, namely:

(1) Right Views:
- (i) Duhkha—Knowledge of suffering.
- (ii) Duhkha-samudaya—Knowledge of the origin of suffering.
- (iii) Duhkha-niroda—Knowledge of the cessation of suffering.
- (iv) Duhkha-nirodhagamini-pratipad—Knowledge of the path leading to the cessation of suffering.

(2) Right Aspirations:
- (i) To renounce worldliness.
- (ii) To renounce ill-feeling,
- (iii) To renounce doing injury to others.

(3) Right Speech:
- (i) Abstention from lying.
- (ii) Abstention from slander.
- (iii) Abstention from unkind words.
- (iv) Abstention from frivolous talk.

(4) Right Conduct:
- (i) Abstention from destroying life.
- (ii) Abstention from taking away what is not given.
- (iii) Abstention from wrongful gratification of the senses.

(5) Right Living:

(6) Right Effort:
- (i) To put a stop to the rise of evil and sinful tendencies of mind which have not yet risen.
- (ii) To renounce the will and sinful states of mind which have already arisen.
- (iii) To evolve good states of mind which have not yet arisen.
- (iv) To continue and realise and repeat and extend the good states of mind that have already arisen.

(7) Right Mindfulness:
- (i) To regard the body as body.
- (ii) To regard the sensations as sensations.
- (iii) To regard mind as mind.
- (iv) To regard the mental stages as mental.

(8) Right Meditation:

Right rapture arising from right meditation or self-concentration (Dharma Sangraha).

Moral Judgment Refers to the Highest Good

Moral judgment not only determines what actions should be, but judges them as means to an ultimate good. The ideas of Tightness and obligation suggest the idea of an ultimate end or highest good to which all actions must be conducive in order to be right and obligatory.

Man is subject to pain which is threefold:

(1) Adhyatmika—arising from bodily and mental processes.
(2) Adhibhautika—arising from created beings.
(3) Adhidaivika—arising from supernatural forces.

He always works with an end in view. He takes medicine for the prevention of bodily pains; he seeks wife and wealth for the prevention of mental pain. Similarly he takes recourse to suitable means for the prevention of Adhibhautika and Adhidaivika pains. But it is found that where pain is prevented by means of men, money and medicine, and the like, it comes back again afterwards on the disappearance of the visible means adopted. Therefore, the moral judgment declares that such visible means, though they have their uses, should be rejected, for, they do not exist in all places and at all times, and even if they do exist they cannot bring about permanent cessation of the three-fold pain. What man desires is not the temporary absence but the permanent prevention of the three-fold pain. (1.1. Sankhya Pravachana). The disappearance of the Adhidaivika pain is a means to the attainment of Pramoda (hilarious) Siddhi; the removal of the Adhibhautika pain is a means to the attainment of Mudita (delighted) Siddhi; and lastly the prevention of the Adhyatmika pain is a means to the attainment of Modamana (joyful) Siddhi.

And again, the end of our action is:

(1) Dharma, acquistion of merits.
(2) Artha, acquisition of wealth.
(3) Kama, satisfaction of desires.
(4) Moksa, attainment of release.

These are the objects of volition, but the ultimate object is neither Dharma nor Artha nor Kama—for they are perishable and the pleasure that is found in it is derived from the objects of senses—but it is Moksa, since it is eternal and has the form of illumination. Hence, this is the ultimate standard to which all other standards must be made subordinate as means to ends (1.5. Sankhya Pravacana Sutram).

Moral Judgment Implies Freedom

The ideas of right and good, of duty and obligation, carry with them the conviction of responsibility. Man works to regulate his conduct, to improve his character, to attain the end of his life because he is conscious, he is a free being, he is responsible for his action. Because man is a free agent, because he is himself the cause of his work, he is praised and applauded when he attains success; and he is blamed and censured when he meets with failure. If a man be not a free being, he cannot certainly be held responsible for his action, he cannot be praised or blamed for his success or failure (32. 31. Vana Parvan).

Postulates of Moral Judgment

The preceding remarks make it plain that every moral judgment presupposes the following factors:—(i) Self-determination, (ii) Discrimination, (iii) Moral standard, (iv) Personality.

Self-determination

A man always exerts himself:

(i) To retain good states of mind already existing.
(ii) To produce such not yet in existence.
(iii) To destroy sinful states already existing.
(iv) To prevent such states from coming into existence. (Dharma Sangraha).

But he exerts because he believes that a man wanting in personal exertion can secure nothing through destiny alone; because he knows that everything can be acquired by exertion, that by devoted application he can secure beauty and fortune and riches of all kinds, and that by well-directed individual exertion he can attain to heaven, can procure all the objects of enjoyments and can satisfy the cravings of his heart. He acts in vain who does not pursue the human modes of action but surrenders himself to destiny. Man can determine his own destiny. Perform good actions, and happiness will be your reward; perform bad actions, and pain will be the natural consequence of your actions (6. 12. Anusasana Parvan).

Discrimination

There must be an apprehensive faculty in us giving us a knowledge of the circumstances in which we perform an action. The discernment of all the circumstances, necessary for determining the moral quality of an action, depends mainly upon the discriminative function of mind which is thus classified:

(1) Svabhava Nirdesa—Natural Discrimination.
(2) Prayoga Nirdesa—Actual Discrimination.
(3) Anusmrti Nirdesa—Reminiscent Discrimination.

The first is intuitive, the second is inferential, and the third is reminiscent. The first deals with the present, the second with the present, past and future, and the third with the past only.

Moral Standard

Without the admission of an objective standard, moral judgment loses its significance and importance. This standard has been variously regarded by various persons. Some hold virtue as the standard of moral judgment; some regard pleasure as the standard of moral judgment; some consider wealth and some emancipation as the standard of moral judgment.

Virtue

Study of the various scriptures, practice of asceticism, performance of sacrifices, sincerity of disposition, right regulation of the lower passions and sentiments, charity, forgiveness, compassion and truth constitute virtue. It is by virtue that great sages have crossed the ocean of the world with all its difficulties and dangers; it is by virtue that gods attained to their position of superiority; it is upon virtue that all the worlds depend for their existence, it is virtue that supports and holds together the peoples of this universe (69, 59, Kama Parvan).

Virtue, therefore, should be regarded as the standard of judgment. Virtue is the basis of pleasure and wealth. In point of merit, virtue is foremost, profit is middling, and desire lowest (167-8, Santi Parvan).

Wealth

Wealth is the universal object of adoration. As all creatures worship Brahman, the Supreme Person, so persons, even of superior birth, worship a man possessed of wealth. They that are dressed in deer-skins, they that bear matted locks on their heads, they that are self-restrained, they that smear their bodies with mire, they that have their senses under complete control, they that have bald heads, they that live separated from one another, in short, they that have discarded everything, cherish a desire for wealth. They that are attired in yellow robes, they that bear long beards, they that are graced with modesty;

they that are possessed of learning, they that are freed from all attachments, cherish a desire for wealth. They that follow the practices of their ancestors, they that are observant of their respective duties and they that are desirous of heaven, also cherish a desire for wealth. Wealth, therefore, according to some, should be regarded as the standard of judgment, because all persons, the believers and the unbelievers and even the rigid practisers of the highest Yoga, all certify to the excellence of wealth. The persons of impure souls, if possessed of diverse kinds of wealth, are able to perform the highest acts of virtue and gratify desires that are apparently difficult of being gratified. Thus, with the acquisition of wealth both virtue and the objects of desire may be won (16-19; 13-15. Ch. 167. Santi Parvan).

Pleasure

Both virtue and wealth are based upon pleasure. As butter is the essence of curds so pleasure is the essence of profit and virtue. Oil is better than oil-seeds; ghee is better than sour milk; flowers are better than wood; so pleasure is better than virtue and profit. Pleasure is the soul of virtue and profit. Pleasure is the foremost of the triple aggregate. Without pleasure no one would give sweets or wealth to another. Without pleasure the various kinds of action that are seen in this world of ours would never have been seen (35-37; Ch. 167. Santi Parvan).

Virtue, Wealth and Pleasure

Virtue is the cause of wealth and pleasure is its consequence. Wealth, virtue and pleasure—all the three have their root in will. Will is concerned with objects, and objects again exist for gratifying the desire of enjoyment. Virtue is sought for the protection of the body, wealth for the acquisition of virtue, and pleasure for the gratification of the senses. All the three, therefore, have the quality of passion. Virtue's dross consists in the desire of rewards; the dross of wealth consists in hoarding it. When, of course, they are purged of these impurities they are productive of great results. But the man who abandoning virtue and wealth pursues only pleasure causes the annihilation of his intelligence, which is followed by headlessness, which again brings ruin to both virtue and wealth. Therefore, when man of pure hearts endeavors to achieve wealth with the aid of virtue, then those three, viz., virtue, wealth and pleasure, may be seen to coexist in a state of union as regards time, cause, and action.

Various other Goods

Thus there are many things which are considered best, as well as those which are the great ends of life. To him who, by the worship of gods, seeks for wealth, prosperity, children or dominion, each of these is respectively the best. Best is the rite or sacrifice that is rewarded with heavenly pleasures. Best is that which yields the best recompense, although it be not solicited. Best is self-contemplation to the devout ascetics. But the best of all is the identification of soul with the Supreme Spirit. Hundreds and thousands of conditions, in this way, may be called the best, but certainly these are not the great and true ends of life. Wealth, for instance, cannot be regarded as the true end of life, for, it may be reliquished for the sake of virtue, and moreover, expenditure for the gratification of desire is the most important characteristic of wealth (Visnupuranam, II. 2. Sl. 12-17).

Desire can never be satisfied. A man obtaining affluence hankers after sovereignty, which being obtained, he hankers after the state of gods, which again, if achieved, makes him wish for the chiefdom of the celestials. So desires can have no end, and in no condition a man can get contentment from the acquisition of desirable objects. The man who pursues pleasure for the sake of pleasure is a man of lost self (40-9, Bhisma Parvan).

Virtuous acts again, from which no recompense is sought, cannot be regarded as the true end of life, for, such acts are the means of obtaining liberation. Meditation on self again is said to be for the sake of supreme truth, but it is not so, as the object of this is to emphasise the distinction between soul and body and the great truth is without distinction. Can union of self with supreme spirit be regarded to be the great end of all? No; for, the substance cannot become substantially another. Thus infinite are the objects which are considered most desirable. What the great end of all is will be considered in its proper place.

Personality

There must be an agent or personality capable of apprehending moral principles. Such an agent or person is ourself, is the doer of Karma, the Karta, he is the enjoyer, he is the prompter, the stimulator within to do the Karma and enjoy the fruits thereof. Weapons cleave it not, fire burneth it not, waters wet it not, and wind drieth it not (Gita II 20).

Light is in the self and nowhere else. It is the same in all beings.

It can be seen by itself, by one whose mind has been concentrated completely by means of meditation. The self in me in the form of knowledge is as great as it is in another's self. He who constantly bears this in mind is never perplexed (Smrti).

"Purusa exists: since a structure of manifold parts (which the world is) is for the benefit of another of a different character; since the reverse of the nature of the three Gunas must exist; since there must exist a superintendent; since there must be an experiencer; since activity is with a view to isolation." (Karika).

Consciousness is the characteristic of personality. The self must be a conscious agent. He is the cognisor of everything. But who cognises the cognisor? It cannot be something else, for that something else again would require another cognisor and thus the result would be non-finality (Br. Aran Up.).

Therefore, on the ground of simplicity the self must be assumed to be of the form of light. Purusa, therefore, like the sun, is truly and essentially of the form of light, of the nature of cognition (Smriti).

Self is that which feels, thinks and wills. Its marks are:

(1) Desire, aversion and conation.
(2) Pleasure and pain.
(3) Knowledge. (Nyaya 1. 10)

It has three attributes:

(1) Sattva or purity—corresponding to intellect.
(2) Rajas or activity—corresponding to volition.
(3) Tamas or passivity—corresponding to emotion.

(Gita XIV. 5-8)

Consciousness is the principal characteristic of self. Consciousness is continuous and indivisible. Its continuity is never broken even in dreamless sleep. Knowing is always inseparable from the knower.

(Pancadasi I. 7 and Br. Aran. Upa. IV. 3.23-30)

The states of consciousness are:

(1) Jagrat or waking.
(2) Svapna or dreaming.
(3) Susupti or dreamless sleep.
(4) Turiya or transcendental.

The waking state is externally cognitive with seven members with nineteen inlets and with the fruition of the sensible. The dream-consciousness is internally congnitive with seven members, with nineteen inlets and with the fruition of the ideal. In dreamless consciousness, the soul desires nothing, it dreams no dream, is one in itself, is a mass of cognition, is pre-eminent in bliss, is with the fruition of beautitude, is of transcendent knowledge, and thought is its inlet. And in pure consciousness one becomes, as if one with Brahman, the Absolute.

The Object of Moral Judgment

Now as regards the object of moral judgment, we know already that it is voluntary action or action for the realisation of a foreseen and desired end. But a voluntary action passes through the following principal phases:

(1) The mental states and processes out of which it springs.
(2) The movements in which it embodies itself.
(3) The results which it produces.

Thus there are three stages of every voluntary action, viz., the incipient stage—the stage of motive; the motor stage—the stage of movement; and the final stage—the stage of consequence. Of these three phases we may leave the physical movements out of account, for we do not ascribe moral quality to them. Now the question is: On which of these factors of action does its moral quality depend? on its mental antecendents or its external results?

Consequence, the Object of Moral Judgment

Do we judge an action according to its actual results? It is desirable no doubt that while passing judgment on an action we should determine the nature of the act and its consequence, otherwise the action may lead to the destruction of the agent (33. 12. Udyoga Parvan).

Those actions should be performed which destory sufferings and give rise to happiness. Those actions, the consequence of which is pain, are to be avoided, and those actions the consequence of which is bliss and peace should be performed (5. 26. Devi Bhagavatam).

Virtuous actions are generally performed with the belief that their consquences are good. It is believed that sin is burnt by pouring libations on the sacred fire; it is believed that tranquillity is obtained by the study of the Vedas; it is believed that pleasures and objects of enjoyment are secured by gift; it is believed that the blessed heaven is acquired by penances, and that is why these virtuous actions are generally adhered to.

But so many circumstances interfere with the carrying out of our intentions that actual results are often different from, and sometimes entirely contrary to, what was originally intended. If our intentions invariably corresponded to actual results, then all actions undertaken for our welfare would certainly be crowned with success. The object of none of them would remain unfulfilled. But what is generally observed is this that persons, though struggling their utmost, fail to effect the suspension of that which is not desired and to effect the occurrence of that which is desired (222. 19. Santi Parvan). Man naturally wishes to attain to a gradual superiority of position and he tries to the best of his ability to satisfy his wish, but the result unfortunately does not always agree with his wish (331. 38. Santi Parvan).

What wonder, therefore, is there in this that a man of wisdom by prepetrating an act which is apparently cruel may obtain a great merit just in the same way as Valka did by the slaughter of the blind beast? What wonder, again is there in this that a man of ignorance, even with the desire of winning merit, may earn a great sin just as Kausika did among the rivers? (69. 37. and 39. 38. Kama Parvan).

Thus we see that actual consequence does not always correspond to the motive or intention of the agent. It is seen that an ordinary person commits unrighteousness while apparently achieving righteousness and an extraordinary person again may be seen to achieve righteousness by committing acts that are apparently unrighteous (259.6. Santi Parvan).

Motive—The Object of Moral Judgment

We should not, therefore, judge the moral worth of actions by their actual results. Do we judge actions then, by their subjective spring or motive for the sake of which the action is performed? The learned have declared that the motive from which an act is accomplished is an indication of Tightness. (258. 3. Santi Parvan).

It is said that if the motive is bad the action is bad and if the motive is good the action is good. In all cases of morality the motive is said to be the object of desire. If the motive be impure and sullied the action also becomes so; for, the impurity of one's motive is the cause of one's ruin in every respect. (Devi Bhagavatam IV. V. 8).

If a sacrifice, for instance, be done from a bad motive, say, for the destruction of one's enemy or from a personal motive or for one's gain, it converts auspicious results into those that are inauspicious and ultimately leads to destruction. For, the motive here is selfish, and selfish persons are unable to ascertain which actions are good and which are not. (Devi Bhagavatam IV. 4. 47).

But if the motive alone be the indication of Tightness, it would lead us to assume the dangerous principle that the end justifies the means. In that case, in seasons of distress, a man by even speaking a falsehood will acquire the merit of speaking the truth; he may by performing an unrighteous act acquire by that very means the merit of having done a righteous act. A thief will be justified in robbing a man of his property if he spends the produce of his theft in acts of apparent virtue. But it should be borne in mind that if things, acquired by bad means e.g., acquired by injuring others, be utilised in any auspicious act, they yield contrary results at the time of fruition. (Devi Bhagavatam IV. 4. 42).

The motive alone cannot be the object of moral judgment; means also should be taken into consideration; for, the criterion that has been kept in view in declaring the indication of righteousness and inequity is the nature of means of which the help is taken in the accomplishment of objects. A conduct is righteous if the means adopted for its performance is agreeable, otherwise not. Righteousness can never be acquired by unrighteous means. A person who wishes to acquire righteousness, should never earn wealth, for instance, by means that involves injury in others. He should accomplish his acts according to his abiltity without jealously pursuing wealth. A king should incur the sin of theft if he snatches thousands of kine from their lawful owners and gives them away to deserving persons. (293. 9. Santi Parvan).

The End Justifies the Means

Once the great Rsi Visvamitra, urged by pang of hunger, engaged himself in a search after food and endeavoured his best to find something to eat, but unfortunately could secure nothing to appease his burning hunger. When he busied himself in thinking of the means by which he could avoid immediate death, he happened to see a large piece of flesh of a dog spread on the floor of a Candala's hut and determined to steal it reflecting that theft is allowable in a season of distress for even an eminent person. (141.38—41. Santi Parvan).

Thus when the end in view is the preservation of life itself, a high-souled person possessed of learning and well-acquainted with means is perfectly justified in rescuing his own cheerless self, when afflicted with distress, by any means he can safely take the help of. That by which life may be preserved should certainly be accomplished without a scruple. Life is better than death. A person, if alive, can win religious merit, can enjoy happiness and prosperity. (141.100, 101. Santi Parvan).

If the action of the Rsi taking away the dog's haunch for saving his life, which is so horrible and which, like falsehood, should never be an object of regard, be cited as an example of duty, then what action is there in this world from which man should abstain? Why should not then robbers and murderers be respected? If such be the ideal of morality, will not then the sense of man be stupefied? Will not then the heart of man be deeply wounded? Will not then the tie that binds man to morality be hopelessly loosened? (142.1, 2 Santi Parvan).

Such a mode of conduct has, from the very nature of the case, whatever may be the motive, effects which are extremely dangerous to human welfare. If such conduct became general, if the end would justify the means, if people behaved falsely towards one another, then chaos and confusion would prevail in society. Such means, therefore, should be adopted as would not lead to confusion; such means should be followed as would benefit men in every respect; and such means should be practised as are not harmful in their consequences. No attempt should be made to support life by deceit and fraud, and no wealth, however great, should be earned by unrighteous means. 106.1—3, Santi Parvan).

And yet it must be admitted that there are cases in which the end does appear to justify the means. Does not the prevention of evil habits in children justify the infliction of pain? Yes, it does. But the means used here, though evil in themselves, are for the greater good of those that suffer from them and are the outcome not of cruelty but of kindness. (Siva Puranam—27.35).

Does not, in the case of the Government, the defence of rights and liberties of the people justify chastisement with all its evils? Yes, it does. A king is justified in using the rod of chastisement to root out his foes, to maintain law and order, and to safeguard the peace and prosperity of his subjects. If the rod of chastisement be withheld, all wholesome restraints will disappear, all truths in respect of righteousness will be disturbed and confounded, men will become stupefied in respect of their duties, they will have a cause of fear in every direction in consequence of lust and coveteousness and folly;

they will slay one another by deceitful means and deceive one another in their mutual dealings. And that is why, of the four requisites of the Government, viz., conciliation, gift, disunion and chastisement, chastisement has been so highly applauded by men possessed of learning. (Santi Parvan—130.6).

But such means being productive of greater good cannot properly be regarded as evil. That which disturbs the peace of a people is certainly to be condemned by men of wisdom. Chastisement, if it be not the product of envy and revenge, should not be regarded as an evil. (Siva Puranam—27.34).

That any means which involves pain is to be discarded should not be regarded as a universal law. The physician is perfectly justified in amputating the diseased organ of a person in order to save his entire system. (Siva Puranam—27.38, 39).

The above considerations, therefore, should not lead us to believe that a good motive may justify evil means, for, the cases cited above are only apparent.

A story is told of Sankha and Likhita who were two brothers of rigid vows and who had two separate dwellings adorned with trees always burthened with fruits and flowers. Once upon a time Likhita came to the residence of his brother Sankha. At that time, however, Sankha had gone out of his asylum on no fixed purpose. Arrived at that asylum Likhita plucked some ripe fruits and began to eat them without any qualms of conscience. Sankha, when he came back to his retreat, found his brother eating the fruits, and coming to learn that they had been obtained from his retreat, became mad with rage, and asked him to approach the king and confess to the king that he had committed theft by appropriating what was not given to him. Accordingly Likhita approached the king and addressed him.

Then Sudyumna, the ruler of the earth, caused the two hands of the high-souled Likhita to be cut-off. After receiving the punishment Likhita returned to his brother Sankha in great affliction and requested him to pardon him for the offence he had done and for which he had been duly punished. Sankha then said, "I am not angry with thee, nor hast thou injured me, O, foremost of all persons conversant with duties. Thy virtue however, had suffered a shock. I have rescued thee from that plight." (23.38, Santi Parvan).

Now the question is, why so severe a punishment for an offence so trivial? The only offence which Likhita committed was that he took some fruits from the orchard of his own brother without his permission, but he had certainly not the least intention of concealing the fact from his brother, knew as he fully well, that he would be received by his brother Sankha with due hospitality. If Sankha was not angry with his brother Likhita, if Sankha incurred no loss from Likhita's action which he characterised as theft, if there was no chance of Likhita's conduct being imitated by others as it was performed in a place which was solitary, then why was so terrible a punishment inflicted on a person who acted from no dishonest motive and with no insincere purpose? Likhita's conduct might not have injured others, might not have injured the person robbed, but assuredly it would have injured at least one person, and that is the agent himself, by polluting his character; and do you think character so trivial? There is danger in excusing wrong actions in private life at least. The doing of wrong actions, though at first indifferent, soon becomes a habit of doing them independently of the original ends and thus a criminal disposition may be acquired.

"Criminal means once tolerated are soon preferred, as presenting a shorter cut to the object than through the highway of moral virtues" (Burke) Sankha, has, therefore, rightly said, "Desire naturally arises from the perception of objects of senses such as form, taste, scent, sound and touch. For the acquisition of what is liked and for the avoidance of what is disliked man strives and works, and endeavours his best for repeatedly enjoying that which appears agreeable. Gradually, then, attachment and aversion, and greed and consequently errors of judgment take possession of the mind; and it is a well-known fact that the mind of one smitten with grief and affected by attachment and overwhelmed with errors of judgment is never directed to virtue. He then begins to do acts, that are good, with hypocrisy; with hypocrisy then he seeks to acquire virtue, and with hypocrisy he likes to acquire wealth; and thus when he meets with success on one or two occasions he sets his heart on such acquisition wholly. He then gradually takes courage and begins to commit sinful acts. The admonitions of well-wishers and the wise are of no avail. He makes an attempt to meet such admonitions with answers that are apparently and plausibly consistent with reason and seemingly conformable to the injunctions of the scriptures. His sins, born of attachment and error, now go on rapidly multiplying. He now thinks sinfully, speaks sinfully and acts sinfully. It is thus that one becomes sinful. No one becomes sinful with the object of becoming so. (172. 4-11. Santi Parvan).

Character, after all, is not a trivial thing and it should not be trifled with. There is nothing impossible of attainment by a man of moral character. Character is the embodiment of righteousness; character is the embodiment of truth; character is the embodiment of good deeds; character is the embodiment of might; character is the embodiment of prosperity. (124.62, Santi Parvan).

Intention—The Object of Moral Judgment

It follows, therefore, that falsehood, deceit, murder, etc. are not justifiable or even meritorious, if they are supposed to have beneficial effects upon the welfare of humanity. An intentional falsehood, if it is supposed to have only beneficial effects should still be regarded as a reprehensible lie; and the act of depriving a man of his property, if it resulted in the greatest good, should still be considered as an act of theft. It is not, therefore desirable to set one's heart upon those means of success that are unjust and improper. (33.7. Udyoga Parvan).

An action, therefore, to be judged rightly according to the moral standard, must be judged not by its motive alone, not by its actual results but by its whole intention, i.e., both motive and means. In other words, it must be judged not by the one end for the sake of which alone the action is performed but by this principal end in conjunction with the subordinate ends which are sought only as means towards this principal end. Righteousness consists in the accomplishment of objects with the help of means which are agreeable. Intention is the criterion which should be kept in view while trying to determine the indications of righteousness and inequity. (258.25, Santi Parvan).

Intention, then, is the true object of moral judgment. Our motive for its success depends on means, and means again are dependent on the nature of the motive which is sought to be accomplished. Success, therefore, depends not on the motive alone, not on means alone, but on both the motive and the means, as they are intimately connected. (36.38. Bhisma Parvan).

To say that we judge actions by intention is equivalent to saying that we judge them by their intended results. An action should be regarded as good if it has a tendency to produce good results. A man of intelligence, therefore, should not give way to grief, if his motive, notwithstanding the application of fair and proper means, does not meet with success. (33.7, Udyoga Parvan).

For, the conduct of the good, that is fraught with excellence, is subject to many restraints for acquiring righteousness which depends upon many delicate considerations. As success depends on the union of many circumstances, man should not give way to despair and despondency if he meets with failure. (32.51, Vana Parvan).

Success of failure depends on the nature of acts in respect of their circumstances and place and means and motives. (62.8. Santi Parvan).

Overt Act is the Object of Moral Judgment

It is said that mere intention, if it be not embodied in an overt act, cannot be regarded as an object of moral judgment. Those who are acquainted thoroughly with moral science know very well that if a person having intended mentally to commit a sinful act does not do so actually then the demerit of that action can never affect him. (32.7, Udyoga Parvan).

But purity of mind is all in all. If the mind be vitiated by desire, wrath and other evil passions, it will then have a tendency to run towards sin, for mind is the source of virtue and vice. (321. Devi Bhagvatam).

The intention, though not embodied in an overt act, is still the object of moral judgment; for, in all cases where the conservation of moral affairs is concerned the original wish or desire is the real cause. If this desire be impure and sullied, morality also becomes sullied, for verily the impurity in one's desire is the cause of one's ruin in every respect. (4. 5, Devi Bhagvatam).

Nothing can properly be called good but purity of mind. There is no natural good in things; it is the mind which makes a thing either good or bad. Purity of body is no purity, if the mind itself remains sullied and defiled, and no salvation will ever be possible so long as our mind is not thoroughly purified. External purification will be of no avail without internal purification. (Skanda Puranam).

The act, however, in which the intention is embodied, is not indifferent from a moral point of view.

Agent—The Object of Moral Judgment

Judgment upon intention is also judgment upon character and upon the agent himself; for the intention of the agent is determined by the character of the agent. We have seen already that there are three kinds of quality, and the character of the agent is determined by the predominance of one of these qualities. The three Gunas reside in a mixed way in all persons, but sometimes the Sattva predominates and sometimes the Rajas and sometimes the Tamas, and sometimes they live together, the three balancing one another. (6. 15, Devi Bhagavatam).

So the nature of intention is determined by the character of the agent who intends. The man of Sattvika disposition, for instance, intends to perform sacrifices without any desire for fruits, and the only motive of his action is the sense of duty for the sake of duty. The man of a Rajasika disposition intends to perform an action in expectation of fruit and even for the sake of ostentation. (Bhagavadagita).

There are three kinds of penances:

(1) The penance of the body.
(2) The penance of speech.
(3) The penance of the mind.

The penance of the body consists of reverence to the gods, regenerate ones, preceptors and men of knowledge, of purity, uprightness, the practices of a Brahmacarin and abstention from injury. The presence of speech consists of the speech which causes no agitation, the speech which is true, the speech which is agreeable and beneficial, and the diligent study of the Vedas. The penance of the mind consists of serenity of the mind, gentleness, taciturnity, self-restraint and purity of disposition. A man of Sattvika disposition intends to practise the three-fold penance with perfect faith, with due devotion and with no desire of fruit. A man of Rajasika disposition intends to perform penances for the sake of respect, honour and reverence and he performs them with hypocricy. A man of a Tamasika disposition, on the other hand, intends to do the same under a deluded conviction, with the torture of one's self and for the destruction of another. (41. 17-19. Bhisma Parvan).

A man of a Sattvika disposition gives a gift beause he thinks that it is his duty to give, and he gives to one from whom he expects nothing in return, and he gives it in a proper place and at a proper time and to a deserving person. A person of a Rajasika disposition makes a gift reluctantly and in return for services past or expected and even with an eye to fruit. A person of a Tamasika disposition makes a gift in an unfit place and at an unfit time and to an unworthy object without respect and in contempt. (41. 10-22. Bhisma Parvan).

Faith and Action

Thus we see that the object of moral judgment is either the

intention or the character of the agent as revealed in the intention of the agent himself. The intention of the agent is the reflection of the character of the agent and it is largely influenced by his faith which again is the outcome of his disposition. The faith of a man is of three kinds. It is also born of his individual natue. It is Good, Passionate and Dark. (41.2. Bhisma Parvan).

त्रिविधा भवति श्रद्धा देहिनां सा स्वभावजा।
सात्विकी रामजी चैव तामसी चेति तां श्रृणु।।
भी.प. 41 । 2 ।।

The Sattvika faith is the only one of the three that yields entire results and it is very rare in this world; the Rajasika faith yields half the results; and the Tamasika faith is fruitless and inglorious, and such a faith arises with those persons that are overwhelmed with lust, anger, greed, etc. (6. 13. Devi Bhagavatam).

सात्त्विकौ दुर्लभा लोके यथोक्तफलदा सदा।
तदर्द्ध फलदा प्रोक्ता राजसी विधिसंयुता।।
तामसी त्वफला राजन्तु कीर्त्तिकर पुनः।
कामक्रोधाभिभूतानां जनानां नृपसत्तम।।
देवोभागवतम्। 6 । 13 । 2-3 ।।

15

The Concept of 'Samrambhayoga' in Hindu Thought

Dr. K. Raghavan Pillai

Peculiar to Hinduism

The purpose of this paper is to discuss a concept which, I think, is peculiar to Hinduism among the world's religions. This is the concept of 'samrambhayoga' also somtimes described as 'vairayoga'. By 'samrambhayoga' is meant the choice of the path of hostility to God to reach him. By describing this as a yoga it is not intended to convey the impression that it has been included among the great yogas or has been advised to be followed by anyone by choice. The emphasis in the literature on this yoga is rather one of concession. That is, it is conceded that where a set of circumstances have so developed that hostility is the only path which can be followed there, the doors of liberation from the bondage of samsara and of union with God can be opened through following that path. There are, again, no Acaryas who advocate and expound this yoga, as there are for jnanayoga, karmayoga and so on, because it is largely something like an apaddharma or making the best of a bad situation.

Salient Features

We get the clearest declaration of samrambha as a yoga in the Mahabhagavata, Canto III, Chapters 15 and 16. The occasion is the condemnation of Jaya and Vijaya by the Brahmarsis Sanaka and others. The sages were on a visit to Vaikuntha when they were stopped by Jaya and Vijaya who were gods guarding the gates af Visnu's abode. The enraged sages cursed the two attendants that they will have to go down to the world where there were the three enemies of lust, anger and greed (kama, krodha and lobha). Ultimately Visnu appeared on the scene and while he agreed that the attendants deserved the punishment meted out to them, he also made the sages relent towards the wretched gods. After the sages left Visnu, compassionate towards Jaya and Vijaya asked them to get back to him soon, through following samrambhayoga with him as the objective. I quote below the relevant passages in order to bring out what I think are the salient features of samrambhayoga. When the sages pronounced their curse on the attendants Jaya and Vijaya asked them one boon. That was that in the period of their exile in the world of passions, forgetfulness of Visnu should not occur to them. The passage reads as follows:

bhuyadaghoni bhagavadbhirakari dando
yo nau hareta surahelanamapya esam
ma vo'nutapakalaya bhagavatsmrtighna-
moho bhavediha tu vrajateradho'ghah.

(MBH Canto III, Ch. 15. Verse 36)

It is well that punishment has been imposed by your Lordships on this sinful one. That punishment will wash-off the sin of having insulted the Brahmarsis. Let us not, by your grace, be afflicted by the error which is charactised by the forgetfulness of the Lord (Visnu) during our existence down below. The words of Visnu to the attendants asking them to follow the path of samrambhayoga are as follows:

'mayi samrambhayogena nistirya brahmahelanam
pratyesyatam nikasam me kalenalpiyasa punah.

(MBH III-16-31)

'Concentrating on me through the yoga of hostility remove the sin of having insulted the Brahmarsis and get back to me in a short while!'

Earlier while describing the method that the attendants were to adopt in order to get to Him, Visnu uses the expression 'samrambhasambhutasamadhyanubaddhayogau' to describe the attendants in their new discipline. (MBH III-16). That is, they should be, in the Lord's view, following the discipline of the samadht generated from hostility.

More Light on the Concept

I may also quote here a passage from a comparatively late work which throws additional iight on the concept under discussion. The passage is from the 'Rajasuyam Prabandham' a Campu from the pen of the celebrated sixteenth century grammarian and poet of Kerala, Melputtur Narayana Bhattatiri. The passage reads as follows:

> 'ata eva niravagraha-nugraha-tvaraya-vaira-yoga-bhajam bhoja-raja-dinam vyoma-vada-narada-vacanadina vaira-dipana-vega-kari.........

'That is why through the employment of words from the sky, from Narada and so on He (The Lord Krsna) has increased the anger of King of Bhojas and others who were following the yoga of hostility. He did so because he was anxious to speed up their union with him.'

Essentials of 'Samrambhayoga'

These passages from the Bhagavadgita and the Rajasuyam Prabandham give the essentials of the concept of samrambhayoga. They are the following:

(1) The element of constant unflagging attention on God is common to samrambhayoga and to the other kinds of yoga like the yoga of devotion, knowledge and so on. Notice the prayer of Jaya and Vijaya to the Brahmarsis that they should not be cursed with forgetfulness of the Lord. The central character of yoga is satisfied in this position. In karmayoga the devotee does all actions as an offering to God and as such God is constantly in the mind of the yogi. In Bhaktiyoga the emotions of the devotee, indeed his total personality is directed with supreme concentration on God. In the yoga of knowledge the yogi employs a discipline of cognitive union with the Absolute to realise the fact of his already existent union with It. We recognise that in samrambhayoga too a similar single-pointed direction of the personality towards God is needed. The integrity is seen in their emotions, actions and indeed in their total personality. Thus we are told in the Puranas that Jaya and Vijaya in their three lives in this world of passions as Hiranyaksa and Hiranyakasipu, Ravana and Kumbhakarna, and Sisupala and Dantavaktra, really lived to hate Visnu.

Path of Concentrated Hostility

(2) The passage in which Krsna enjoins on the attendants to follow the path of concentrated hostility to Him in order to get back to Him shows that as far as the Lord is concerned brickbats and bouquets are the same to him. Indeed as Bhattatiri says the Lord sometimes purposefully intensifies the anger of the samrambhayogi to speed up his progress. Perhaps in the concept of 'samrambhayoga' we find an exemplification of the truth that the Absolute is above the distinctions we show such fondness for in our relative ways of thinking. Hindu thought does not build up an antithesis between good and evil. Good and evil, according to it, are only two aspects of a totality. Together, they represent a system of relative values and in one of our systems of Philosophy, namely, the Advaita the good is as much a part of error as evil is. Even in those Bhakti systems where considerable emphasis is placed on the good life and on the performance of good works, and God is described as 'sakala-kalayna-gunakara' (the abode of all good qualities) evil is not entirely unrelated to God. After all, matter and souls in Ramanuja's system constitute the body of God and are controlled by him.

(3) In 'samrambhayoga' is represented not just and kind of hostility but hostility which is love frustrated at least temporarily. Here then clearly is a philosophical position which gets ample justification from the Freudian theory of emotional ambivalence. The essential mutability of human emotions rubs off the distinction between opposites like hatred and love, so sacred in those systems of thinking where dichotomy is ultimately valid.

Passion in Spiritual Life

(4) Another point which becomes clear on a study of 'samrambhayoga' concerns with the position of passion in spiritual life. We know that more views than one are current on this topic, and these views range from whole-hearted support of the severest asceticism to the acceptance of the need for extreme indulgence. Side by side with Buddhist, Jaina and Hindu ascetic practices we have also the extreme vamacara practices condemnable at least in their later corrupt forms. Which of these views does 'samrambhayoga' represent?

The absolute repression of passion or the expression of it? It is obvious that the latter view is represented in it and in respect of this 'samrambhayoga' can be grouped with bhaktiyoga, although we might as well note a distinction between the two. Whereas in 'bhaktiyoga' it is passion purified through devotion to God which is offered to Him, in 'samrambhayoga' raw passions are directed as such towards God. There is something significant in this philosophy which believes in the utilization of the very elemental forces in man towards ultimate spiritual purposes.

(5) Elsewhere in this paper I have discussed the question of 'samrambha' in the framework of evil and good in general terms. A necessary distinction has to be made here between 'samrambha' and any mere evil. 'Samrambha' being hostility must have an object and it has the potential to become a yoga because of this. There are of course other manifestations of hostility which are directed towards no high purpose and as such are spiritually non-productive at best and disastrous very often.

Glorious End and Liberation

Before concluding this paper I may ask a question whether a concept like 'samrambhayoga' is possible in Christian and other foreign dualistic systems, with their rather rigid framework of ethics. If we take the Christian framework, for example, its rigid system of good and evil would bar a doctrine like this which raises the status of evil and makes it spiritually productive. Something very similar to 'samrambhayoga' we do indeed see in the life of Satan and in his attitude to God. But the significant fact is that his hostility towards God leads him to no salvation. It is not spiritually productive. The difficulty in this position seems to be that there is such rigid dichotomy built up between good and evil that a deliberate hostility towards God just cannot lead to Him, who is the ultimate good. If God may not always be on the side of big guns he certainly is not on the side of the bad guys. Even the exercise of divine compassion is preceded by repentance and it confers salvation on the sinner as a divine gift. The glorious end of a 'samrambhayogi' is not through such cleansing and consequent divine munificence. He dies as he lives and through death at divine hands reaches the end of the road and achieves liberation.

16

Some Mathematical Achievements of Ancient India*

H.S. URSEKAR

Ancient India is regarded by a section of Western scholars like Maxmuller as a nation of philosophers. The materialistic West talks always of its counterpart as the mystic East. The dichotomy of mind and matter is reflected according to them in the terms East and West and probably this was one of the misunderstandings which inspired Kipling's notorious aphorism that East is East and West is West and never shall the twain meet.

India's spiritual heritage has overshadowed her material achievements. Apart from the derisive note underlying the notion of being a nation of philosophers, it cannot be overlooked that India was equally a country of the tailor, the tinker and the candle-stick-maker. Their gamut of the Vedas included even the Ayurveda and the Dhanurveda. They were equally at home with Music as with Metaphysics. Ethics and Economics were grist alike to there mill.

Concededly the Western nations are far advanced on the runway of modern Scientific airfield but quite a good spade work was done in this land. Like the poet-seers Atri, Vasistha, Vishwamitra of the Rgveda, India produced mathematicians and astronomers like

*Paper read before the All India Oriental Conference, Srinagar, 1961.

Aryabhata, Varahamihira, Brahmagupta, Mahavira, Bhasakaracharya, etc.

Eminent Mathematicians

Aryabhata was one of the oldest writers on Mathematics. According to Smith, Arya-Bhata was the first of the great writers whose name has come down to us. He was born at Kusumapura and lived in the 5th Century A.D. His work Aryabhatiyam is an original treatise on Mathematics. Astronomy was one of the six essential auxiliaries of the Vedas, its earliest exponent being Lagadha. But Aryabhata was the first writer to insert the mathematical section in Astronomy. Out of the five Siddhantas viz. Surya, Paitamaha, Vasistha, Romaka and Pulisha, Aryabhata is recognised as the inventor (Upadnya) of the Pulish Siddhant. Though he hails from Bihar, yet the earliest extent manuscript of the Aryabhatiyam as discovered by Dr. Cairns is in Malyalam.

Aryabhata was followed by Varahamihira (6th Cent. A.D.) the doyen of astronomers in ancient India. He is supposed to be one of the nine jewels in the Court of King Vikrarn of Ujjain. His Pancha Siddhantika is a well-known work. He was such an enlightened scholar that he frankly conceded that the Yawanas (Greeks) have developed the science of Astronomy and. therefore, they are adored like the sages.[1] Alberuni has specially cited this remark of Varahamihira.

Varahamihira was followed by Brahmagupta (7th Cent. A.D.). He lived and worked at Ujjam like Varahamihira. He wrote the Brahma Siddhanta. Thereafter, Mahavira, a follower of Jina is believed to have writer. Ganita-Sara-Sangraba. He probably lived at the Court of one of the old Rashtrakuta monarchs who ruled over Mysore, Mahavira flourished in the 9th Century A.D. The last of the great mathematicians of ancient India was Bhaskaracharya who also lived in Ujjain though he was born in Khandesha (Maharashtra) in 12th Cent A.D.

According to some scholars considerable pioneering work in various branches of Mathematics like the Arithmatic, Algebra, Geometry and Trigonometry was done by the Indian scholars. It is believed that the Arabs carried this knowledge to the West round about the 12th century and they can be considered as the cultural liaisons between the East and the West.

Arithmetic: Mathematical Notations

Man has an eternal fascination for numbers. In the field of Arithmetic it is now more or less accepted without serious challenge that the numerals 1 to 9 were invented in India. Professor Gamow points out that the Hottentots in Africa do not still have numbers beyond 1, 2 and 3. Every count beyond 3 is denoted by the omnibus term 'many'.[2] On other hand, in the Rgveda one comes across the words for the numbers one to ten. We have also Sahastra (1000) and Ayuta (10000). In Taiteriya Samhita numbers up to the 18th order—(Parardha) are mentioned. The earliest documentary proof of the use of numerals is found in the Naneghat inscription situated about 75 miles from Poona. This inscription is believed to be a century later than the—edicts of Ashoka, i.e. of 2nd century B.C. Similarly, numbers are found carved in another inscription in the caves near Nasik in the Deccan (1st or 2nd Cent. A.D.) These numbers may be deemed to be the Adam and Eve of the modern Arabic numerals. These numbers of Indian origin were relayed to Europe by the Arab scholars and hence they came to be known as Arabic numerals. This inference is fortified by the name Hindasi by which the numerals are called in Arabic even today. This process is not unprecedented. To-day we have a category of cattle as the Brahmin cattle in America as the forefathers of that breed were imported from India into that country. One of the possible reasons for the absence of the early recognition of Indian origin of these achievements in Europe seems to be the slowness of Indians to cross the sea-frontier, probably out of regard for the ban thereof.

Zero

As with the numbers 1 to 9 so with zero too now it is almost well established that the cipher is one of the most significant contributions of India to the world of Mathematics. The science of Numerology could not have progressed but for the invention of She cipher. It is a naught fraught with aught. It is the apex of creative imagination of man in the field of numbers. It is difficult to say accurately as to who was the inventor of the cipher, but that he was an Indian is now certain. It is equally difficult to assert as to how or when the zero was evolved, It might have flowed from the circle, I may venture a suggestion in this behalf. In ancient Indian Mathematics a negative number used to be denoted by a circle placed on its top, e.g. $\overset{\circ}{5}$ = — 5. Possibly due to some fortunate slip of pen this circle might have slipped from the top of the number by its side, as a result of the carelessness of the scribe and in that heaven-sent moment like Arnold's Scholar Gypsy, some genius might have seen and seized the infinite potentialities in that accident. What a world of change by a single slip. That is why when I think of the Zero I recall Marlowe's line "infinite riches in a little room". Metaphorically speaking, the number is like the husband, while the zero may be compared to the wife. If a wife dominates the husband, the latter is reduced to a negative entity, but on the other hand, if she cooperates with him on equal footing, she does enhance his prestige ten-fold and so on.

The earliest inscribed proof of the use of cipher is discovered in the Gwalior inscription of the 9th Century A.D. In that stone carving in denoting the sums of 50 and 270, the cipher is used. It is safe to assume hence that the place value was also given to the zero by Indians in the past.

It may be asked whether before the cipher was rubbed into other countries were there no numbers involving the tens, hundreds and thousands. To say so would be presumptious. These numbers used to be expressed then by letters or picturesque signs. For example, the number *ten* used to be written by different people as follows:

Babylonians:	L
Chinese :	+
Egyptians :	∩
Greeks :	K
Romans :	X

We still use the Roman letters such as X for 10, L for 50, C fox 100 and so on. The Arabs on the other hand denote the number 5 by Δ notation akin to zero and write a dot for the cipher.

Additions, Substractions, etc.

The process of Additions, Substractions, etc., were known to Indians as can be seen from Lilavati of Bhaskaracharya. The way of setting a prosaic sum was quite charming.

> 'Oh dear talented Lilawati, if you are adept at sums add the following ...'

In one of the commentaries on Lilawati the units, tens and hundreds are written in separate horizontal lines and are then added. The remarkable thing is that even in those times the modern system of writing the figures of sums to be added one below the other was prevalent.

Fractions

According to some scholars one of the significant contribution of the Indians to Mathematics is the fraction of numbers. Brahmagupta has written the fraction $^2/_3$ as $^2/_3$ without the dividing dash. It is believed that it was introduced by the Arabs later on.

Negative Sign

The idea of the negative number is considered to be a progressive landmark in the march of mathematics. The negative sums are found in the Brahma-siddhantika of Brahmagupta. It was indicated as stated earlier by a circle on the top of a number ($\overset{0}{6}$) or sometimes it was shown by a dot atop $\dot{6}$ (see Lilawati). Sometimes the negative number used to be written in a circle. In the Bakshaali manuscript (8th or 10th century A.D.) found near Peshawar the negative number is shown by putting a cross after the number, e.g. 7 +. Thus paradoxically here we find the plus sign used to denote the negative, of course with a change of position. It seems that there was no uniform practice of writing a negative number in ancient India.

Plus Sign

It appears the plus sign was not known in the hoary past, A number having no sign either preceding, succeeding or atop was regarded as an unqualified positive number. The present plus sign, is claimed to have been involved from the Latin word et.

Square Root

The method of deriving the square root of a sum is found in Lilawati.

Tallying

According to Paul Tanery, another important contribution of Indians is the method of tallying the correctness of the results of sums, multiplications, etc., with the help of the number 9.

Rule of Three, etc.

The rule of three, the rule of five and the rule of the polynumbers (Bahurashik) are remarkably Indian methods. Brahmagupta uses the terms Praman, Phal and Ichcha to indicate the ingredients of the rule of three. Mahavira has given the rule of three as follows:

Phal multiplied by Ichcha and divided by Praman yields the desired results.

On these lines examples of simple interest are set by Mahavira and Bhaskara.

Dust Abacas

The dust abacus is of definite Indian origin. Arithmetical sums could be easily done with its aid. In the introduction to Lilawati, Taylor has observed that the dust abacus was in the use in India till the end of the last century.

Algebra

Like Arithmetic the Indians were quite well-versed in Algebra. They are credited with a considerable amount of pioneering work in Algebra. Arithmetic studies the numbers of known values, while Algebra studies the number of unknown values. In Algebra man unlocked the unknown with the key of the known. That is why Ahms (1650 B.C.) described Algebra as the Science of unrivalling the mysteries of numbers in the world.

The term Algebra originated in Arabia. It gained currency from the title of the book "Al-jabra Va Al-Mukabla" composed by Al-Khowarijmi who flourished in Arabia in the 9th century A.D. The essence of Algebra lies in the transposition of a negative entity to the other side of the question so as to give positive value to the negative entity.

The Greeks treated Algebra as part of Arithmetic and so did ancient Indians. Brahmagupta calls it Kuttak, while Bhaskaracharya describes it as Awyakta Ganita or Bij Ganita. The name Avyakta also emphasizes the unknown aspect dealt by Algebra. Aryabhata calls Arithmetic as Vyakta Ganita or Pati Ganita or Anka Ganita.

Aryabhata, according to Colebrooke is nearly as anicent as the Greek Algebrist Diophantus (c. 275). Aryabhatiyam includes problems in series, permutations and linear and Quadratic equations. That is why Colebrooke observes:

> "Assuming Hindu and Alexanderine authors to be equally ancient, Aryabhata, it must be conceded was more advanced In the science."[3]

Brahmasiddhanta of Brahmagupta contains a satisfactory rule for solving the quadratic equation. A term was called Pada. Co-efficient was called Ansha or Prakruti by him. The unknown quantity was denoted by Ya (Yavat Tawat), by Brahmagupta. Thus Ya stood for the first unknown quantity corresponding to X in modern Algebra. The terms of unknown quantities after Ya were coined by taking the initial letter of colours by Brahmagupta.

K (Kalak) (Black) for 2nd unknown quantity.
Ni (Nilak) (Blue) for 3rd unknown quantity.
Pi (Pitak) (Yellow) for 4th unknown quantity.
Pa (Pandu) White for 5th unknown quantity.
Lo (Lohit) (Red) for 6th unknown quantity.

He denoted the absolute or known numbers by Ru a contraction of Rup. Root is mentioned by Ka (Kami). Va stood for Varga, i.e. Square number. Thus X^2 was expressed by Yava.

Mahavira's Ganita-Sara-Sangraha contains a large number of problems involving series, radicals and equations. From the works of pre-Arabic mathematicians like Aryabhata, Brahmagupta and Mahavira, it will be seen that the Indians were far advanced in Algebra. Colebrooke remarks:

> "The age when Brahmagupta flourished, seems then . . . as antecedent to the earliest dawn of the culture of the sciences among the Arabs, and consequently establishes the fact that the Hindus were in possession of Algebra before it was known to Arabians."[4]

At another place, Colebrooke has given an unqualified assessment of Indian achievement thus:

> "This science (Algebra) in a more advanced state subsisted among Hindus prior to the earlier disclosures of it by the Arabians to Modern Europe."[5]

He has also stated that Arabs were 'avowed borrowers'.

Bhaskaracharya's Bija Ganita (1150) contains nine chapters and extends the work up to quadratic equations. He uses the expression, Samya Karanartham to denote the words to equate. He has given examples of quadratic and cubic equations. The following example of Geometric series is very illuminating:

> "A gave 2 *couries* to a mendicant, next day he gave double the number to him, the day after that double of that number and so on. Find out how many *couries* A denotes per month."

According to Colebrooke and Keith, Indians were far in advance of the nations in the field of Algebra.

Geometry

Like numbers, the various figures in nature has an attraction for man from earliest times. In Arithmetic and Algebra man studied the known and unknown numbers, while in Geometry he learnt the properties of figures.

It is said that Science and Religion are at loggerheads in modern times. However, Dr. Keith has observed that:

"In India Science arises in close connection with Religion."

In the Vedic times, for performing sacrifices, knowledge of Calendar and Mensuration was a necessity. According to Keith, the science of Geometry arose in India out of the functions of measuring and constructing the sacrificial altars. In the famous Shulvasutras (5 Cent. B.C.) of Apastamba, we come across the elements of this science. From this, it can be reasonably deduced that the use of Geometry was known to the Indian Engineers of yore.

Geometry used to be applied first for measuring distances. The properties of various figures like the triangles, square, circle, pyramid (Shanku) were known to the ancient Aryans.

The three principal problems before the ancient Greek mathematicians were: (1) trisection of angle, (2) calculation of the height of a cube with double the volume of a given cube, (3) squaring a circle.[6] The last problem was considered to be a prestige problem. The obvious method to solve it was to calculate the length of the circumference of a circle. Now this process was obvious but by no means simple. It was necessary to evaluate w.

The Indians were also aware of this problem. In the 5th Century, Aryabhata gave the value of π as 3,1416, with rules to derive it. Brahmagupta has cited that an astronomer called Pulish had calculated the value of—up to five decimal places, viz. 3,14153. According to him, the square root of 10, yields the value of π. Bhaskaracharya has given the well-known value of π viz. $^{22}/_{7}$. Let us turn from the value of π to the theorem of Pythagorus. This theorem crystallizes the properties of a right-angled triangle. Thus, in a right-angled triangle, the squares described on the hypotenuse is equal to the sum of the squares described on the other two sides. This formula was known to Indians, at a very early stage of human civilization. In the

Shulastras, we find the length of sides of triangles to construct right-angled triangles of various sizes given as follows—e.g. (1) 3, 4, 5; (2) 5, 12, 13, etc.

Aryabhata has given the formula to calculate the volume of a cube as follows: Base of a cube multiplied by height and the result divided by two. It may be pointed out that in Indian Geometry, we do not find definition of terms, nor there are mention of parallels.

Trigonometry

If Geometry originated in measuring of distances on the earth trigonometry evolved out of the man's effort to measure the distances in the sky. The ancient Egyptians used to measure time by erecting a stick called Gnomon in the sun. Time was measured by refering to the shadow of the gnomon. They observed the angle made by the stick with the ground and in studying its functions, came to know the properties of angles. Out of these efforts developed the idea of sines etc. Aryabhata uses the term 'Jya' to denote sine. First he called it Ardhajya (half-chord) but subsequently he uses the term Jya (chord). He has divided circle into 360° like Ptolemy. Sine is called Kramajya by Brahmagupta. It is believed that the Arabic word Karajya for sine may be a distortion of the Sanskrit term Kramajya. Such decadent uses of Sanskrit words in Arabic are not unusual. Alberuni has pointed out that it is difficult for a foreigner to learn Sanskrit. According to Keith in the Pulish Siddhana Aryabhata has made important contribution to Trigonometry. Aryabhata has also given the sine and versed sine tables familiar to the students of Mathematics. Varahamihira has also cited the sine tables in the Surya Siddhanta.

From the above discussion it will be clear that the ancient Indian mathematicians did make a significant contribution to the development of Mathematics. Dr. Kane has pointed out that the knowledge of Aryans of Algebra was of a superior order, they invented the decimal place value system for numbers and propagated it and the sign of Zero to Europe through the Arabs in the 12th century A.D.[7]

Dr. Keith has also fairly conceded that:

> "The mathematical achievements of India lay in field of Algebra and in the invention of a valuable system of notation."[8]

However, it is difficult to close this paper without mentioning the appreciation of Indian Mathematicians as given by Severus Sebokht who lived in the 7th century A.D. in Mesopotamia.

> "Their subtle discoveries in the Science of Astronomy, discoveries that are more ingenious than those of the Greeks and Babylonians, their valuable methods of calculating and their computing that surpasses description."[9]

Notes and References

1. Chapter II, V. 15. Varahmihira.
2. Gamow's 'I, 2, 3 to Infinity' page 15.
3. Colebrooke's 'Miscellaneous Essays', Vol. II, p. 439.
4. *Ibid.*, p. 425.
5. *Ibid.*, p. 418.
6. Smith's 'History of Mathematics', Vol II, p. 297.
7. Kane's 'History of Dharma-Sastra', Vol. V, Part I, p. 518.
8. Keith's 'History of Sanskrit Literature', p. 408.
9. Smith's 'History of Mathematics', Vol. II, p. 64.

17

Disposal of the Dead and Funeral Ceremonies in Ancient India

The archaeological evidences, unearthed at Mohanjodaro and Harappa exhibit cases of burial of three types, complete, fractional and post-cremation. An examination of the habits of the Aryans in some regions shows that they practised burial. But the Rgveda and Atharvaveda indicate the prevalence of both burial and burning among the Vedic Aryans. Sir John Marshall in his "Mohanjodaro and the Indus Civilization" (Vol. I, p. 89) concludes that cremation was the general way of disposing of the dead during the period of Indus culture. According to Mahaparinibhana Suttanta the dead body of the Buddha was first burned and then its relics were buried. (Ed.)

I
DISPOSAL OF THE DEAD IN ANCIENT INDIA

K. KRISHNAMURTHY

References to the disposal of the dead in the early Indian literature are plenteous and the earliest of them we find in the Vedas.[1] The physical need combined with religious superstition necessitated the disposal of the dead inevitable and indispensable. The purification of the corpse rendered it impossible to keep the dead body in a house for a long time. Besides, the disease and the death of persons caused pestilence and contagion in the family. However, the main object of the disposal of the dead seems to be release of the survivors from the pollution of death and accord rest to the dead. It has been the general belief that the performance of the funeral ceremonies would secure a befitting place to the soul in the next world. Significantly similar mystic importance came to be attached to the funeral ceremonies among the ancient Greeks and Egyptians.

Various Modes of Disposal of the Dead

The *Rg Veda* alludes to two modes of disposal of the dead namely *Agni-dagdha* (cremation) and *Anagni-dagdha* (burial).[2] However, the earliest method of disposing the dead seems to be the sub-aerial deposit or leaving the body on the ground. This was required among the primitive people who were nomadic. As they had to ramble from place to place seeking food and fodder, the dead and the diseased proved to be onerous on the wandering family and they had to resort to the method of the exposure of the dead as the means of disposal. In this connection the reference to two words *paropta* (casting out) and *uddhitah* (exposure of the dead) in the Atharvaveda (xviii, 2, 34) need mention here.[3] Again Brhad Aranyaka Upanisad[4] informs us that when the heart departs from the body the dogs eat it and the birds tear it into pieces. The body gets such an end due to the absence of the heart. This may indirectly refer to the custom of casting out the deadbody to be devoured by the birds and beasts. But it becomes difficult to comprehend how the Upanisads speak of it when the *Samhita* of the Rg Veda is silent about it. In Mahabharata, another mode of disposing the dead namely tying the dead body on the top of the tree is indicated. In Vanaparva it is stated that the Pandavas concealed their weapons on *Sami* tree. In order to save it from the disclosure they told the people that they were tying the corpse of their mother, who died on the way, on the top of the tree. This would incidentally indicate the mode of disposing the dead in vogue at the time. But nowhere the cave burial has been cited among the funeral ceremonies of the Hindus;[5] whereas references to water burial are available. It is said that small children, ascetics, mendicants and in certain cases married men and women who died of epidemics were given water burial.[6]

Inhumation or burial proper prevailed in the Rg Vedic times.[7] References to them in Vedic literature are profuse[8] and in fact one complete hymn is set aside to the ritual attending it.[9] It was the hoary practice to bury the dead man in full attire with bow in his hand. Sometimes the wife of the deceased committed *Sati*,[10] the practice which was commonly prevalent among the savage tribes. This practice underwent a modification in the Vedic period. The son had to take the bow from the hand of the dead man and the widow was taken away from her husband by his brother or nearest kinsman. A stone was set to demarcate the separation between the dead and the living.

Raising a Mound Over the Grave

Among the funeral ceremonies of the Hindus, reference is made to *Pitrmedha* or *Smasana* (i.e.) the building of a mound over the remains of a dead person. There should have been a great fillip for erecting a mound or tomb over the grave. In the Vedas we have no direct reference to this custom. However, *bhumi-grha* (house of earth) and *Vrksa* (a coffin) are referred to.[11] But the *Satapatha Brahmana* gives a graphic description of the *Smasana* ceremony. It gives different opinions regarding the mode of the construction of *tumili*.[12] It prescribes a four cornered mound facing the south-east on ground inclined to the North, afar from the village in a tranquil spot or on barren ground.[13] In this connection we get a word *camu* meaning a trough made of either solid stone or consisting of bricks used to protect the body of the dead from contact with earth similar to the stone-lined graves.[14] At the time of the *grhya sutras*[15] the custom was not universal. It was in vogue with some modifications in the procedure in the *Satapatha Prahmana* period. Among the Buddhists, however, this custom of raising a mound was very popular[16] and the Hindu Sastrakaras restricted this honour to the great saints, monks, etc.

Embalming the Dead Body

Preservation of the dead body in the house with or without desiccation or mummification has not been mentioned anywhere in the ritual literature of the Hindus.[17] But it appears that embalming the dead body for a short time was known in ancient India. Interestingly the *Satyasadha Srauta Sutra* and the *Vaikhanasa Srauta Sutra* insist that the corpse of the *Ahitagni* should be placed in a tub or trough filled with seasame oil and brought home in a cart.[18] It is said in the *Ramayana*[19] that the body of Dasaratha was kept for several days in a tub filled with oil till the arrival of Bharata. The *Visnupurana*[20] reveals that Nimmi's body did not decompose and looked fresh owing to its coverage with oil and redolent substances. Sayana mentions the custom of putting the bones of the dead into an urn (*Asthi sancayana*)[21] and urn burial should be regarded as a relic of ancient custom of burial which was being replaced by the custom of cremation.[22]

Burning—The Most Accepted Mode

The cremation or burning of the dead body is the most accepted mode of the disposal of the dead among the Hindus from the time of the Vedas. The most puissant factor that gave the custom of cremation a lasting position was the religious belief of the Indo-Aryans. Fire was regarded by them as messenger of the gods on earth and the carrier of the oblation offered to them.[23] It was also believed that the evil spirits mostly originated from the iniquitous souls of the dead persons buried in the earth.[24] So the people resorted to cremation to avoid such contingency. Moreover the funeral *mantras* of the *Vajasaneya samhita*[25] direct to the contemplation of burning. The body was wrapped in fat and a goat was also buried along with it in accordance with the rules laid down in the *Rg Veda*. The belief was that the goat would act as a guide to the dead body on the way to the next world.[26] It was expected that the dead would revive with his whole body and all his limbs (*Sarva tanuh sanghah*).[27]

Practice in the Jain Period

The Jain literature accords ample information about the various ways of disposing the dead practised in the Jain period. The Jain texts speak of the custom of leaving the dead bodies to the mercy of wild beasts and birds.[28] A reference is made to *gidaha pithaka* a kind of death in which a person threw himself among the corpse of human beings, elephants, camels, etc., allowing his body to be devoured by vultures. It is said that the bodies of the criminals and the indigent were thrown away to rot and to be devoured by jackals and vultures.

The Jains knew water burial also. At times it appears, under the instructions of the kings the ascetics were buried in a hollow (*agadha*), lakes, rivers, or by the side of these places.[29] The mlecchas buried their dead in the stipulated burial ground (*madagagiha: Madagalna*). Such burial houses were in plenty in the country of Diva and Jova.[30]

The Jain monks were cremated and shrines and stupas *Tubalena* were erected over them. The *Tittira Jataka*[31] informs that the bodies were cremated with sandal wood, aguru the *Rukka*, ghee and honey.

When the fire consumed the flesh and blood from the body, the bones were collected and consecrated in *Ceiya tubas*. The *Cheda-Sutras* elaborately prescribed the rules for disposing the dead body of the Jaina monks.[32] In the event of the death of a monk a bier to carry the cropse should be made ready and the proper place for the cremation in the *tandila* (the cremation ground) had to be demarcated. Wrapped with pure white cloth the corpse should be carried by monks or by laymen in a cart or with the help of the Mallas or Candalas.[33] At the cremation ground the cropse should be disposed of duly with the permission of the keeper of the cemetery.

Thus the Jains honoured the dead greatly. The ceremony of taking out the dead body, *Niharana*, was performed by them with great ostentation and splendour *iddhi skhara* and the many funeral rites were attended to with great solemnity.[34] Paying homage to the dead *madagapuyana* and mourning are referred to invariably in the Jain literature.[35]

Two Modes in the Buddhist Literature

Likewise, much can be known about the disposal of the dead from the Buddhist literature also. The early Pali texts refer to two kinds of grounds viz. *Alahana* (*Ardhamagadhi, Adahand*) and *Sivathika* or *Amakarusana* for the disposal of the dead. *Alahana* (*Ardhamagadhi, Adahana*) was the place where the dead bodies were cremated. In *Sivathika* or *Amakarusana* the corpse were thrown away to undergo the natural process of decay or to be devoured by wild beasts. *Susanagopakas* who were generally Candalas were in charge of *Smasana*.[36] The texts also refer to an aboriginal custom of burning the dead and washing the bones (*atthi dopana*).[37]

Cremation of Buddha

The dead bodies of persons of high rank and honour like great rulers and teachers were cremated and Tupas were erected over the ashes or relics.[38] The *Mahaparinibbana Sutta*[39] vividly describes death and cremation of the great teacher, the Buddha. His dead body was wrapped with five hundred alternative layers of new cloths and carded cotton wool and was kept in a closed iron vessel on the funeral pyre made of different kinds of odourous wood. Towards the sunrise the four chieftains of Mallas bathed and set fire to the body of the Perfect One. Buddha's body was cremated before the city gates of Kapilavastu with all honour and pomp that was given to and Universal monarch.

Later when the fire was extinguished the bones were collected and distributed among many who wished to erect stupas over them.

Kautilya Refers to Cremation

Kautilya in his *Arthasastra*[40] also indirectly refers to the modes of disposal of the dead. He states whoever inters or cremates the dead body beyond the demarcated burial or cremation ground, should be fined with twelve *panas*. Similarly whoever throws the human corpse inside the city limits other than the cremation ground he should be penalised with fifty *panas*.

The Sangam literature of the South also alludes to the three methods of the disposal of the dead, namely complete burial, partial burial and cremation.

Bana's *Harsacarita* informs us that Harsa's father, Prabhakaravardhana, was cremated on the banks of the river Sarasvati where a pyre befitting an emperor solemnly consumed all but his glory in the flames.[41] But Kalidasa commended death at a holy place like Prayaga, the confluence of two rivers like Yamuna and the Sarayu (Ganga).[42] The interment in the wild prevalent at Taxila probably was then current among the Hunas.[43]

Chinese Travellers' Accounts

The later accounts left by the Chinese travellers also mention the ways of the disposal of the dead in vogue during the period. Yuan Chwang who visited India in the 7th century A.D. speaks of the funeral customs like water burial, cremation and interment in the wilds. In water burial the dead body was put into a stream to float and dissolve.[44] Besides, Yuan Chwang also refers to another method of disposal of the dead akin to the water burial. The persons who were old, nearing mortality or afflicted with incurable diseases desired to caste off humanity. Such persons were made to sit in a boat and were taken to the middle of Ganges where they drowned themselves with great expectancy of next birth in the heaven.

Thus the literary references to the disposal of the dead in ancient India are copious and are discernible through ages which clearly indicate different methods adopted by the people in disposing the dead.

Notes and References

1. *R.V.* VIII, 1,2,3,4; *A.V.* XVIII, 2-34; Taittiriya Brah. iii, 1.1.7.

2. *R.V.* X, 15, 14; Hopkins, *Journal of the American Oriental Society*, 16. CHI; *Winternitz: Geschichtedzr indischam* 1, 84, 85.
3. Zimmer quotes a similar custom among the ancient Germans (Zimmer; *Act Laben*, 326-328), He also speaks of the practice of casting out the dead to be devoured by the beasts among the Iranian (Zimmer, *Altindisches Laben*, 425); Whitney refers to the expression—exposure of the dead body on a raised Platform (Translation of the *Atharvaveda*, 841). Kaegie interprets certain *Rg Vedic* verses as indicating the prevalence of similar customs among the Rg Vedic Aryans (*Vedic Index* 1. 351, 352). His theory has been refuted by Pandey R.B., *Hindu Samskaras—A Socio-religious study of the Hindu Sacraments* pp. 414-15 *Man in India*, vol. xvii, nos. 1 and 2, pp. 1-68.
4. Chapter III, *Brahmana*, ix. 25.
5. In Rome it appears that more than four thousand monks are preserved in the walls of the subterranean burial chapels in the Capuchin church near the Piazza Barber. See also Puckles': *Funeral custom*, p. 136.
6. Pandey; R.B., *op. cit.*, p. 417; see also Hartland, E.S.: *Encyclopaedia of Religion and Ethics*, Vol. IV, p. 421.
7. X, 18-10-13; x, 15-4, vii, 89.1.
8. *Ibid.*, A.V. 5.30-14; 18.2.34; xviii, 2-25; In *Candogya Upanisad* (*viii*, 8.5) a reference is made to burial; vide Scharder: *Aryan Religion*, *E.R.E*, Vol. II, p. 115-57.
9. X. 18.
10. For the origin and development of the *Sati* sacrifice see author's article in *Orissa Historical Research Society Journal*, Vol. XI, (1963), no. 4, pp. 201-5.
11. *R.V.* vii, 89. 1; *A.V.* V. 30-14; XVIII, 2.52; *A.V.* XVIII, 2, 25, 3, 70 cf. *Brahaddevata* v. 83 with Macdonell's note (d).
12. XIII. 8,2, 1.
13. XIII. 8. l, et seq. cf. Eggeling, *Sacred Books of the East* 44, 525 et seq. cf. Zimmer, *Altindisches Liben*, 407; Hopkins, *Journal of the American Oriental Soctety, 16* CIII.
14. XIII, 8, 2, 1; Eggeling, *Sacred Books of the East,* 44, 430, n. 1.
15. *A.G. S.* iv. 5.
16. Author's article "Caityas not exclusively Buddhistic in origin" in *Poona Orientalist* (in press).
17. *Mary Levin's* hypothesis advanced in Mummification and cremation in India in *Man* Feb. no. 18, 1930 that the mummification was practised before the mode of cremation came into use.
18. 29. 4. 29; 31-23.
19. *Ayodhya*, 66. 14-16, 76.4.
20. IV. 5. 7.
21. References to the rite we get in *San. Sr.* IV. 15, 12-18, *Sat. Sr.* 28, 3, *ASV. Gr.* iv 5. 1-18, *Gaut. P.S.* 1. 5, *Visnu Dh. S.* 19-10-12, *Baud P.S.* 1-14, *Kausika sutra* 82-29-32, *Vaik Smarta Sutra* v. 7; *Yama* 87-88, *Samvarta* 38, *Gobhila-Smrti* III. 54-59.
22. A.G.S., IV-5.

23. *R. V.* x, 14.8.
24. Macdonell, A. A., *Vedic Mythology*, p. 10 cf. Oldenburg, *Religion des Veda*, 62-2; Villiamy, *Immortal Man* p. 34, opines that one of the purposes of cremation may have been the complete destruction of the human aspect of the ghost or its transference to a region from which contacts with mankind in any material sense, was impossible, Kane P.V., *History of Dharmasastra,* Vol. iv, p. 232 foot note 2.
25. XXV. cf. also *Kausika Sutra*, 80 et. seq; which treats the *Atharvaveda* hymns, xviii, 1-3, as intended for burning only.
26. *R.V.* x, 16, 4.
27. *Satapatha Brahmana* iv, 6, 1.
28. Matra Ni, p. 25, cf. *Lalitavistara*, p. 265.
29. *Brh. Bha*, 3, 48, 24.
30. *Nisi-cu.* 3, p. 330; *Aca. Cu.* 370.
31. The *Tittira Jataka* (no. 438) III, p. 537 mentions topes of Sarid (Valuka tupa); also Parama thadepani the com. on the *Udena*, p. 97, cf. the funeral ceremonies in the *Ramayana* (iv. 25, 16 ff).
32. See *Visavagbha-vana Prakrtâm;* Brh. Su. 4.29 and its *Bhasya* 5497-5565.
33. *Vya. Bha 1. 449*, p. 79ff. According to *Manu* also the candalas to carry the corpse of persons who have no relatives.
34. *Vya-Bha* 7. 442, p. 76ff; also *Ava Nir Dipika*, vol. II, 95ff, *Ava cu.* II, pp. 102-9; *Bhagvati*. Aradh 1974-2000.
35. *Brh. Su.* 1.47 and the *Bhasya* (1. 3139-3206) and also *Aca* 11. 1, 2, 3, 236ff; *Das* 7. 36 f.
36. *Dhammapada* commentary, i. p. 59.
37. *Anguttara* V, p. 216; *Sumangala vilasini* i, p. 84; see also Pathak, K.B., *Commemoration volume;* Law, B.C., *Social, Economical and Religious conditions of Ancient India*. According to Buddhist Texts, p. 7, 3, Govt. Oriental Series Class B. No. 7. The Bhandarkar Oriental Research Institute, Poona.
38. But there is some difference between the stupas of an ordinary man and exalted person as is minutely described in Vinaya *text-Samyuktavastu*, chap. xviii.
39. Krishnamurthy, K., "The Great decease (death) of Buddha" in *J.A.H.R.S.* Vol. XXXIX, parts 3 & 4, pp. 51-54; see also *R.A.S.* for 1906, pp. 655-671 and 881-913; I-Tsing: A Record of the Buddhist Religion as practised in India and the Malaya Archipelago (A.D. 671-695) translated by Takakusu, I, pp. 81-82.
40. Shyamasastri, R., *Arthasastra*, Chap, xxxvi, p. 163.
41. Bana, *Harsacarita*, p. 164.
42. *Raghu*, vii, 95, p. 182.
43. Strabo, xv, 714; *J. A.* 1915, p. 75; cf. Tarn, *The Greeks in Bactria & India*, p. 137.
44. Yuan Chwang, *On Yuan Chwang's Travels in India* (A.D. 629-45) edited by Rhys Davids, T.W. and Bushell, S.W. London, 1904, p. 174; Hiuen Tsiang: *Buddhist Record of the Western World* (*translated from the Chinese*) by *Beal* S, I. 86.

II
FUNERAL CEREMONIES OF THE ANCIENT HINDUS

RAJENDRA LALA MITRA

Few papers have appeared on the funeral ceremonies of the Hindus. Dr. Max Muller is of opinion—"These burial ceremonies have been described in detail by Asvalayana only, and it is possible that the burial was not considered as an essential part of that class of rites which is comprehended under the name of *Samskara*." Such, however, does not seem to be the case; for the whole of the funeral ceremonies, including those required to be observed at burials, are given in detail in the sixth chapter of the *Aranyaka* of the Black Yajur Veda, aphorised by Baudhayana and Bharadvaja in their Sutras, and commented upon by Sayana Acharya. I find that Hiranyakesi also has written on the subject, but I have not his work at hand to refer to, nor has Sayana noticed him. A hand-book for the performance and funeral ceremonies, professing to be founded on the rules of Hiranyakesi, exists in the Society's Library and is entitled: *Hiranyakes yanteshti-prayogamani;* but it is a compilation by a modern author, Abhayankara Bhatta, and does not correspond with the rules of the other Sutrakaras. It treats of the whole of the rites due on the first thirteen days after death, but it does not anywhere quote the rules of Hiranyakesi, and so simplifies the operations detailed in the works of the early writers that it cannot be accepted as a trustworthy guide to the most ancient ritual.

The Aranyaka describes the ceremonies under the title of *Pitrimedha* or rites for the welfare of the manes, and gives all the mantras required for the ceremonials of the first ten days after death, leaving the *sraddha*, or the rites meet for the eleventh day, altogether unnoticed. The mantras are taken mostly from the Rig Veda, and arranged in consecutive order, but without any clue to the particular rituals for which they are intended. The two Sutrakaras supply this deficiency, and as they point out several peculiarities not to be found in Asvalayana, I propose to give here a summary of the subject. The bulk of the mantras and the rules are the same as given by Asvalayana.

Rites Immediately After Death

The first mantra given in the Aranyaka refers to the performance of a homa immediately after the death of a man who had always maintained the sacrificial fires in his house. According to Baudhayana, four offerings should be made, while touching the right hand of the dead, to the *Garhapatya* fire, with a spoon overflowing full of clarified butter. Bharadvaja prefers the *Ahavaniya* fire, and is silent as to whether the offering should be four-fold or not. Asvalayana recommends the rite to be performed at a subsequent stage of the funeral. All three take it for granted that death has happened within the house, if not near the place where the sacrificial fires are kept, and none has anything to say regarding the taking of the dying to the river-side, or of the ceremony of immersing the lower half of the body in water at the moment of death, (*antarjali*) which forms so offensive a part of the modern ceremonial in Bengal, and which has been, by a flourish of incisive rhetoric and at a considerable sacrifice of truth, called "ghat murder". Looking to this negative evidence against it, to its total absence in other parts of India, and to the oldest authorities on the subject being the most recent of the Puranas, it may be fairly concluded that it is of modern origin. None of the authorities usually quoted, enjoin it as a positive duty, and it has come into general practice probably since the date of Raghunandana and his contemporary Smritikaras of the 16th century.[1]

A New Suit of Unbleached, Uncut Cloth

After the homa, a cot made of Udumbara wood (*Ficus glomarata*) is to be provided, and, having spread on it a piece of black antelope skin with the hairy side downwards and the head pointing to the south, the corpse is to be laid thereon with the face upwards. A son, brother or other relative, or in their absence whoever takes the lead, should next address the corpse to give up its old clothing, and dress it in a new suit.[2] The body is then covered with a piece of unbleached, uncut cloth, having fringes on both sides; the operation being performed while repeating a mantra.[3] Then, wrapping it in its bedding or a mat, it is to be borne on its cot to the place of cremation. The removal, according to some authorities, should be made by aged slaves; according to others on a cart drawn by two bullocks. The mantra for the purpose, says, "I harness these two bullocks to the cart, for the conveyance of your life, whereby you may repair to the region of Yama—to the place where the virtuous resort", clearly indicating that the most ancient custom was, to employ a cart and not men. Asvalayana suggests one bullock. Anyhow, the ancient Sutrakaras evince none of the repugnance to the employment of Sudras for the removal of the corpse of a Brahman, which the modern Smarthas entertain on the subject. According to the latter, none but the kith and kin of the dead should perform this duty, and the touch of the other than men of one's own caste is pollution, which can be atoned for only by the performance of an expiatory ceremony.[4] When Sir Cecil Beadon, the late Lieutenant-Governor of Bengal, proposed the removal of the Hindu dead of Calcutta by the Mutlah Railway to Gariah, the strongest opposition was offered by the people, on the ground that it would involve a most serious pollution and loss of caste, to allow a corpse to be touched by other than its own caste men. They quoted a number of texts in support of their opinion, including those given above, and had no doubt custom—a greater authority than written laws—to plead in their favour; but the most revered and most ancient of their Sastras was opposed to them, for it recommended for the Brahman dead a bullock cart as the most fitting conveyance, and a Sudra slave as its substitute.

Three Stages of Corpse Journey

The road from the house to the burning-ground used to be divided into three stages, and at the end of each, the procession used to halt, deposit the body on its cot on the ground, and address a mantra. Asvalayana says nothing about the division of the road into stages, nor of the mantras to be repeated, but recommends the procession to be headed by the eldest member of the family. The first mantra in the Aranyaka runs as follows: "Pusha who knows the road well, has well-trained animals, to carry you, and is the protector of regions, is bearing you away hence; may he translate you hence to the region of the pitris. May Agni, who knows what is meet for you, bear you away".[5] The commentator in explaining the term *Anashtapasu* "well-trained animals", attempts to include in the text the slaves recommended by the Sutrakaras by the remark "the human bearers are two-footed animals, and the two bullocks four-footed animals:" *vahakah manushyah dvipat-pasavah anadvahau chatuspatpasu.* The second and the third mantras are, in substance, very much like the first, and call for no remark.

An Animal Sacrificed at the Funeral

A most important member of the funeral procession is an animal called *anustarani* or *rajagavi*. An old cow is recommended as the most appropriate, next a black one, next a black-eyed one, next one with black hairs, and lastly one with black hoofs. If none of these are available, a black tender-hoofed goat may be substituted. Asvalayana recommends an animal of one colour, or a black kid, and says that it should be brought with a rope tied to the near forefoot. The animal is to be brought with the mantra, "Protector of regions, this is an offering for thee". An oblation is to be poured on the fire in connexion with this offering with the *ida* or *chamasa* spoon, saying, "May this prove acceptable to wealthy Agni".

According to the Sutrakaras, the cow should be sacrificed, but should any accident happen at the time of the sacrifice, the fore left foot is to be broken, and the wound being dressed with dust, the animal is to be set free. The mantra for the sacrifice says: "Companion of the dead, we have removed the sins of the dead by thee; so that no sin or decrepitude may approach us." The address after immolation runs thus: "Companion of the dead, we have made thy life inert; thou attainest the earth by thy body, and the region of the manes by thy life. Pardon us and our children in this world". A third address to the cow follows when her body is being dusted, it is to this effect—"O dear one, say not that I am so killed, for thou art a goddess and virtuous, going to the region of the Pitris, travelling by the adorable sky: keep us well supplied with milk in this and the future world."

If it be necessary to let loose the cow, she is to be made to walk thrice round the pyre, while the leader repeats a mantra each time, then sanctified by another which simply says, "Mayest thou be a source of satisfaction by thy milk to those who are living (in my family), and those who are dead, and those who are just born, as well as those who may be born hereafter," and, lastly, let loose with the words, "This cow is the mother of the Rudras, the daughter of the Vasus, the sister of the Adityas, and the pivot of our happiness, therefore I solemnly say unto all wise men, kill not this sacred harmless cow. Let her drink water and eat grass. Om ! I let her loose."

Corpse Placed on Pyre along with the Wife

The next operations are to dig a trench, arrange fuel thereon, wash, save and pare the nails of the corpse, and place it on the pyre along with the wife. They were probably performed without the aid of any mantra, for the Aranyaka does not allude to them. The trench, according to Asvalayana, should be twelve fingers deep, five spans[6] wide, and as long as the corpse with its hands uplifted. The corpse, in the opinion of some, should be disembowelled, and the cavity filled with ghi. When placed on the pyre, it should have in its hands, if a Brahman, a bit of gold, if a Kshatriya a bow, and if a Vaisya, a jewel. The wife should lie down on the left side of the corpse according to Baudhayana and Sayana. Asvalayana recommends that she should be placed near the head on the north side. The chief mourner, or he who is to set fire to the pyre, should then address the dead saying, "O mortal, this woman, (your wife), wishing to be joined to you in a future world, (lit. to obtain the Patiloka, or the region of husbands) is lying by thy corpse; she has always observed the duties of a faithful wife; grant her your permission to abide in this world, and relinquish your wealth to your descendants." A younger brother of the dead, or a disciple, or a servant, should then proceed to the pyre, hold the left hand of the woman, and ask her to come away, saying, "Rise up, woman, thou liest by the side of the lifeless; come to the world of the living, away from thy husband, and become the wife of him who holds thy hand and is willing to marry thee." In a subsequent mantra, she is to be asked to bring away the bit of gold above alluded to, from the hand of the corpse. The words for the purpose are—"For the promotion of thy wealth, and glory as a Brahman woman, and beauty and power, take the gold from the hand of the dead, (and abide) in this (region); we (shall dwell) here well served and prospering, and overcoming all presumptuous assailants".[7] The scholiast of Asvalayana says the remover of the widow, and not the widow, herself should take the gold, and that in the event of his being a slave, this and the two preceding mantras should be repeated by the chief mourner, and Wilson and Max Muller take it in the same sense; but Sayana's comment is opposed to this interpretation. The words to be addressed to a Kshatriya or a Vaisya woman, are the same, the words *bow* and *jewel* being respectively substituted for *gold*, and *Kshatriya* and *Vaisya* respectively for *Brahmana*. Under any circumstance the removal of the widow and the articles is completed. The Aranyaka contemplates no alternative, and the Sutrakaras are silent on the subject, shewing clearly that when the Aranyaka was compiled, the inhuman practice of burning the living wife with her dead husband, had not obtained currency in the country, and as we know from the writings of Greek authors that the Sati rite had formed an important part of the Hindu funeral ceremony three centuries before Christ, and at least four centuries before that the Ramayana and the Mahabharata, alluded to it, it may be presumed that our text dates from at least eight centuries before the Christian era. The allusion in the Ramayana and the Mahabharata may, possibly, be interpolations, and if so, the Aranyaka may be a century or two later, but that it was compiled long before the advent of Alexander in India, and that Baudhayana flourished before Bharadvaja and Katyayana cannot be questioned.

Ceremonial Vessels Placed on the Dead Body

The sacrificial vessels which the defunct used to employ in his ceremonial rites, are now to be placed on the different parts of his body; the *Agni-hotra-havani*, filled with butter and curds on the mouth; the *sruva* spoon, broken into two, on the nostrils; two bits of gold or the butter spoon, (*ajyasruva*) broken into two, on the eyes; the *prasitra-harana*, broken into two, on the ears; the *kapala* pot, broken into fragments, on the head; a pot-sherd on the forehead; and, the *chamasa* spoon on the head. The mantra for the purpose consists of a prayer to Agni not to injure the *chamasa* spoon.[8] Asvalayana arranges the sacrificial vessels differently; he places the *juhu* on the right hand, the *upabhrit* on the left hand, the *sphya*, sacrificial knife, on the right side, the *Agnihotra-havani* on the left side, the *gravna* on the teeth, the *kapalas* on the head, the *dhruva* on the breast, the *sruva* on the nostrils, the *prasitra-harana* on the nostrils, the *chamasa* and the *patri* on the belly, the *sami* on the genitals, the pestle and mortar on the lower part of the thighs, the *arani* on the upper part of the thighs, the *surpa* on the feet, and other vessels on the body as convenient. He says, further, that the fat of the slaughtered cow should be placed on the head and on the eyes with the mantra "Agni etc." and her kidneys on the hands with the mantra "Ati" etc., her heart on the cardiac region, and her flesh and organs on other parts of the body; and that, in the event of the cow being let loose, imitations of her organs made with rice and barley meal, should be placed on the parts mentioned; the fat being replaced by cakes. The Aranyaka says nothing about these offerings, nor recognises any substitute. Possibly Baudhayana and Bharadvaja have provided for them. The Aranyaka, after arranging the sacrificial vessels, gives the mantra for covering the corpse with the raw hide of the cow, which should be entire with head, hair and feet, the hairy side being kept upper-most. The mantra for the purpose is addressed to the hide; "Cuirass, carefully protect this body from the light of Agni; envelope it with thy thick fat, and marrow; holding this impudent Agni, desirous of seeing and consuming it by his vigour, allow him not to go astray."

Pile Lighted with Prayer

The pile is now ready to be lighted, and a fire should be applied to it with the prayer: "Agni, consume not this body to cinders; nor give it pain; nor scatter around its skin or limbs! O Jatavedas, when the body is fairly burnt, convey the spirit to its ancestors". A second prayer to the same divinity is due when the fire is in full blaze, but its purport is not very different. It is followed by an address to the organs of the dead. It says, "May thy organ of vision proceed to the sun; may thy vital air merge in the atmosphere; mayest thou proceed, according to thy virtuous deeds, to heaven or earth or the region of water, whichever place is beneficial to thee; mayest thou there, provided with food, exist in corporeal existence."

If instead of a cow, a goat is brought with the corpse, it is to be tied with a weak string near the fire, so that it may break its bond and escape. The chief mourner should then offer twelve oblations to the fire with a spoon made of palasa wood, for which the Aranyaka supplies the necessary mantras. Nine prayers next follow, of which the first four are addressed to Agni, the fifth to Yama, the sixth to the messengers of death, and the last three for a good region for the deceased. The one addressed to Yama describes him as having two cerberi for warders at his gate. "King Yama, place this spirit under the care of thy two four-eyed dogs, which guard the roads and your mansion, and whom men avoid: keep it in ease and free from disease." The dogs are the offspring of Sarama; long-snouted, self-satisfied, and exceedingly powerful; they are the messengers of Yama and roam about in search of men. The last three prayers I shall give entire. "1. Some purify the Soma juice, others worship with clarified butter, others again follow true knowledge (*madhu vidya*) in quest of felicity; may this spirit attain the same (reward). 2. May the award of those who fight in the battle-field, and of heroes who sacrifice their lives, and of virtuous men who grant a thousand gifts, await this spirit. 3. May the award of those who in penance pass a blameless life, and of those who are gone to heaven by their penance, and of those who have performed most rigorous austerities await this spirit."

Mourners Purify themselves by Bathing

After this, leaving the funeral pyre to smoulder, the chief mourner excavates three trenches to the north of the pyre, and lining them with pebbles and sand, fills them with water brought in an odd number of jars. The people who followed the procession are then requested to purify themselves by bathing in them; which being done, a yoke is put up with three palasa branches stuck in the ground and tied at the top with a piece of weak string, and they are made to pass under it. The chief mourner passes last, and then, plucking out the yoke, offers a prayer to the sun. Thereupon, the party proceed to the nearest stream, and without looking at each other, purify themselves by bathing and a prayer to Prajapati. Asvalayana says nothing of the three trenches, but takes the people at once to the river to bathe, where "they immerse themselves, and on rising throw a handful of water into the air while they pronounce the name of the deceased, and that of his family. They then get out of the water, put on dry clothes, and after once wringing those that they had on before, they spread them out towards the north, and sit down there themselves till the stars are seen. According to others, they do not go home before sun-rise. Then the young ones walk first, and the old ones last, and when they arrive at their home, they touch, by way of purifying themselves, "the stone, the fire, cow-dung, grain, (tila seed), oil and water before they step in."[9] This part of the ceremony and mourning which follows, have been described by Manu, Yajnavalkya and others. The Aranyaka is entirely silent on the subject.

Ceremony of Burial

For the ceremony of burial, the first operation is, the collection of the half-burnt bones. This should be done according to Asvalayana on the 11th, 13th or 15th day of the wane; Baudhayana enjoins the 3rd, 5th or 7th from the day of cremation. The dates *tritiya, panchami and saptami* are, given in the feminine gender in the text, and cannot imply day, as in ordinary acceptance they indicate the age of the moon. As the ceremonies, however, of the tenth day are given in a subsequent part of the work, and the *Prayoga* noticed above names days, it is probable, that the morning of the 3rd, 5th or 7th day is meant, the ellipse in the sutra being supplied by the word *tithi* in the sense of a day. The first act is to sprinkle milk and water on the cinders, and to strike on the heap with an udumvara staff to separate the bones. This is done while repeating five mantras. The cinders are then collected and thrown towards the south side, leaving the bones behind. Three oblations are next offered to Agni with a *sruva* spoon. Thereupon the senior wife is to come forward, and, with two bits of red and blue strings to which a stone is tied, to draw out the bones with her left hand saying: "Arise hence, and assume a (new) shape.

Leave none of your members or your body behind. Repair to whichever place you wish; may Savita establish you there. This is one of your bones, be joined with the third (other bones) in glory; having joined all the bones be handsome in person; be beloved of the gods in a noble place." The bones should then be washed and deposited in an urn, or tied up in a piece of black antelope skin. The urn or bundle is then to be hung from the branch of a sami or palasa tree. Should the bones belong to a person who had performed a Soma sacrifice, they should be burnt again; otherwise they should be buried. For the latter purpose, an urn is absolutely necessary, and after placing the bones into it, it should be filled up with curds mixed with honey, and then covered over with grass. Asvalayana recommends an urn with a spout for females and one without if for males. Two mantras are given, one for pouring the mixture, and the other to be addressed to its droppings.

Subsequently, a proper place having been selected, a funeral procession should proceed to it in the morning, and the chief mourner should begin the operations of the day by sweeping the spot with a piece of leather or a broom of palasa or sami-wood. Then, yoking a pair of bullocks to a plough, he should dig six furrows running from east to west, and, saluting them with a mantra, deposit the urn in the central furrow. The bullocks should now be let loose by the south side, and water sprinkled over the place with an udumvara branch or from a jar. The covering of urn is then removed, some aromatic herbs, *sarvaushadhi*, are put into the urn, and subsequently closed with pebbles and sand; each of the operations being performed while repeating an appropriate mantra. A mantra should likewise be pronounced for every one of the operations which follow, and these include, first, the putting of bricks around the urn; 2nd, the throwing thereon some sesamum seed and fried barley; 3rd, placing some butter on an unbaked plate on the south side, 4th, spreading there some darbha grass; 5th, surrounding the tumulus with a palisade of palasa branches, and 6th, crowning the whole by sticking on the top a flowering head of the *nala* reed—*arundo karka*. The operator then anoints his body with old ghi, and, without looking at the urn, places it on the spread grass, invokes the manes, wipes the urn with a bit of old rag, sprinkles some water with an udumvara branch, or from a jar, having covered his own person with an old cloth, and then buries the urn with bricks laid over it.

Some charu rice is then cooked, sanctified by a mantra, and while the chief mourner repeats five others, is put on the five sides of the urn. Sesamum seed and barley are now scattered around, some herbs put on the mound and more bricks added. Water should subsequently be sprinkled on the place, a prayer should be addressed to the gods, a branch of the varuna tree and a lot of brick-bats, a sami branch and some barley, should be placed on the mound, and the dead be invoked to translate himself to whichever region he likes. "Go to the earth, go to the void above, go to the sky, go to the quarters, go to heaven; go to the quarters, go to the sky, go to the void above, go to the earth, or go to the waters, wherever embodied thou canst live with the good and in peace."

Double Ceremonial of Burning and Burial

A few holes being now dug round the mound, the ceremony of burial is completed. The operations, it will be seen, though oft-repeated and tedious, are of the simplest kind possible; the prayers are throughout addressed for the sensuous enjoyment and ease of the dead, and nowhere is any indication given of a desire for spiritual benefit, liberation from the wheel of transmigration, salvation or beatitude. Even sin is lightly looked upon, and the prayer for redemption from it, is slight and casual. The whole ceremony is of the most primitive type, and bespeaks an epoch of remote antiquity. It is worthy of note also that the double ceremonial of first incineration and subsequent burial, was common among the Greeks, Romans and other ancient Aryan races, and that in the fifth century before Christ, the remains of Sakya Buddha were disposed of in the same way.

Rites for the well-being of the Living

The last ceremony I have to notice is called *santikarma* or rites for the well-being of the living. It should be performed on the morning following the ninth night after death, i.e., on the tenth day. This is an addition to the shaving and paring of nails and bathing, which are enjoined by mediaeval and modern Smritikaras. Asvalayana recommends that this should be performed on the burning-ground on the 15th of the wane, i.e., on the day of the new moon. But our text fixes the day, and leaves it optional with the mourners to select any place out of a town, whether it be a burning ground or not, that may be convenient. The relatives' by blood both male and female, having assembled, a fire should be lighted, and they should be requested to sit down on a bullock-hide of a red colour spread on the ground, with its neck-side facing the east, and its hairs directed towards the north. The request should be made in the following words: "Ascend on this lifegiving (skin), as you wish to live to a decrepit old age. According to your seniority attempt carefully to abide on it. May the well-born and well-adorned fire of this ceremony bestow long life on you. Even as days follow days, and seasons are attached to seasons; even as the young forsake not their elders, may Dhata so prolong the life of these (people) according to their age." The assembly being thereupon seated, the chief mourner offers four oblations to the fire with a spoon made of varuna wood. The relatives then rise up, and placing themselves on the north of the fire, and facing the east, recite a mantra, while touching a red bull. The women are then requested to put on collyrium with these words —"Let these women, who are not widowed, who have good husbands, apply the collyrious butter to their eyes; without tears, without disease, worthy of every attention, led these wives enter the house." The collyrium should be made of a substance called *traikakuda* which is brought from the Trikakut or triple humped peak of the Himalaya, meaning evidently the sulphuret of antimony or surma of the Indian bazars. It should be applied with the three central unexpanded leaves of the kusa grass which are thin, pliant, and pointed, like a carnal hair brush, and answer the purpose better than the iron or stone style or bodkin which up-country women now use. The leaves being afterwards thrown away on a bundle of that grass, while repealing a mantra, the party proceed towards the east, leading the bull and saying: "These men, forsaking the dead, are returning. This day we invoke the gods for our good, for success over enemies, and for our merriment. We proceed eastward, having well sustained long lives".[10]

The last of the party, who is the chief mourner, should then recite another mantra, and with a sami branch efface the footmarks of the bull that precedes the party. On the departure of the last man, the Adhvaryu should place a circle of stone behind him as a Wall to prevent death overtaking those that have gone forward, praying—"I place this circle (of stones) for the living; may we and others not go beyond it in mid-life; may we all live a hundred autumns, driving death away by this heap".[11] The party then repair to the house of the chief mourner and feast on kid and barley, cooked for the purpose. Separate mantras are given for the eating of the two articles.

The Sati Controversy

The most important of all the mantras above quoted, is the one which is intended as a direction to woman to put on collyrium. It was first translated by Colebrooke, in 1795, as "the only Vaidik authority for the rite of Sati". Before him the compiler of the twenty-eight Smritis had quoted it for the same purpose, and no doubt thousands over thousands of deluded women, in the moment of their greatest grief, have been sent to the blazing pyre with this miserable passport to heaven. Dr. Wilson was the first to suspect, in 1856, in a paper published in the *Journal of the Royal Asiatic Society* (Vol. xvi, p. 201), that "it had reference to some procession, one possibly accompanying the corpse, but had nothing whatever to do with consigning live females to the fire"; and, for a guess, it was as close as it well could be. The late Sir Raja Radhakanta Deva wrote a reply to this paper, in 1858, and in 1867, in a foot-note about three times larger than the paper to which it is attached, a writer, in the same periodical, (Vol. II, N.S., pp. 184-91), entered into an elaborate verbal and punctilious criticism, but the ceremony for which the stanza was intended or to which it was applied, was left undetermined. In Raja Radhakanta's letter to Dr. Wilson, a quotation was given from the Sutras of Bharadvaja which gave the real clue to it, but none noticed it at the time. The true bearing is now made manifest, for, I believe, few will venture to question the authority of Baudhayana in such a matter. His words are—*athaitah patnayo nayane sarpisha sammrisanti*: "Now these women smear their eyes with butter." Bharadvaja says, *strinam anjalishu sampata-navanayatimanaririti:* "For placing of the sampata in the hands of the women the mantra *Ima narih*, etc." According to Asvalayana, the verse should be repeated by the chief mourner when looking at the women after they have applied the collyrium; *ima nariravidhavah supatnirityanjana iksheta.* This difference is due evidently to the authors belonging to different sakhas. Anyhow, it is abundantly clear that the verse was not intended to recommend self-immolation, but to be addressed to female mourners, wives of kinsmen, having their husbands living, not the widow, to put on collyrium, or to look at them after the operation. The *Prayogakara* says, "*tatah sampatapatramadaya sabhatrikastrinam anjalishu sampatam avanayati*, "then taking the sampata patra he places it on the hands of the women who have husbands, with the mantra *imah*, etc."

The reading of the stanza appears differently in different recensions.

According to Raghunundana, as given in the Serampur edition of his works, and in my MS. it is as follows:

इमा नारीरविधवा: सपत्नीरञ्जनेन सार्पिषा संविशन्तु।
अनस्वरोऽनमीरा सुरत्ना आरोहन्तु जलयोनिमग्ने।।

Colebrooke's version, apparently taken down from hearsay, has:

दमा नारोर् अवधिवा: सुपत्नीर् अञ्जनेन सर्पिषा संविसन्तु विभावसु
अनसरोनारिरा: सुरत्ना आरोहन्तु जलयोनिम् अग्रे।

Professor Wilson's reading, quoted from the tenth Mandala of the Rig Veda, differs materially from these; it runs thus:

इमा नारीरविधवा: सुपत्नीरांजनेन सर्पि मंविशन्तु
अतश्रवोऽनमोवा: सुरत्नारोहन्तु जनयो योनिमग्ने।

Dr. Max Muller accepts this reading correcting only *suratnarohantu* into *suratna a rohantu.* Our text, as quoted on page 262 and founded upon six manuscripts and the concurrent testimony of the Sutrakaras, differs in one important particular. It replaces the last word of the first line, *sanvisantu;* usually translated "let them enter", by *sammrisantu*, "let them smear". It changes also *surantna* "well ornamented," into *suseva* "well served" or "worthy of every attention".

With such differences in the text, it is not to be wondered at that the English renderings which have been, from time to time, published, should be markedly different. Colebrooke was the first to take the stanza in hand, and he translated it into—"Om. Let these women, not to be widowed, good wives, adorned with collyrium, holding clarified butter, consign themselves to the fire. Immortal, not childless, nor husbandless, well adorned with gems, let them pass into fire, whose original is water".[12] Ward, Macnaughten, Ramamohana Raya and others have adopted this reading, and given translations more or less different from each other. But as the reading itself has not yet been traced to any authentic MS. of the Vedas, it may be dismissed without further notice.

Wilson's translation runs thus: "May these women, who are not widows, who have good husbands, who are mothers, enter with unguents and clarified butter: without tears without sorrow, let them first go up into the dwelling".[13] Max Muller's rendering is nearly the same. He writes:

"Es treten ein die Frau'n, mit Oel und Butter,
Nicht Witwen sie, nein, stolz auf edle Manner.
Die Mutter gehn zuerst hinauf zur Statte,
In schonem Schmuck und ohne Leid und Inranen."[14]

The writer of the foot-note above alluded to, adopts Max Muller's reading but attempts to improve upon his translation by the following: "Let these women, unwidowed, having good husbands, *and* with anointing butter *on their eyes*, enter *their houses*. Let the mothers, untearful, unmiserable, possessed of excellent wealth, go up to the house first". He adds, "I have here followed Sayana, save in not rendering आ रोहन्तु by "approach", आगच्छन्तु. What is meant by योनि, Sayana's "house", is not obvious."[15]

The most material error in the above translations is due to Sayana. The great commentator, when he took up the Rig Veda, depended more upon the lexicographic meanings of words than upon the realation of the mantras to the caremonials of the Yajur Veda, and hence many discrepancies are to be met with between his interpretations and those of the ancient Sutrakaras, and sometimes in his own interpretations of the same verse in the Rig, Yajur and the sama Vedas. Nowhere is this more prominently apparent than in his commentary on the stanza under notice, in the Rig and the Yajur Vedas.

The meaning of the stanza, word for word, would be *imah* "these", *narih* irregular plural nominative of *nari*, "woman", alluding to the ladies of the kinsmen who have assembled at the ceremony; the regular form is *naryah*. The women have for predicates, *avidhavah* "not widows", or "unwidowed" and *supatni*, "having good husbands" (*supati*). Those who apply the stanza to concremation explain the first word by "not to be widowed", a meaning which it cannot be made to bear, there being neither any rule nor analogy to support it. The next word *anjanena* is an adjective qualifying *sarpisha*, both in the instrumental case, meaning "with collyrious butter". The verb necessary for these elements should be one which means "applying" or "smearing", and this is what we have in *sammrisantam*, "let smear", from the root *mris* "to smear". The Rig Vedic reading *sanvisantu*, from the root *vis* "to enter", can have no relation to the instrumental, except as entering with the butter applied to the eye, in which case the ordinary plan would be to convert the two words in the instrumental case into one epithet, serving as an adjective to the nominative, women. It is therefore probable that the root *vis* had, in ancient times, the meaning of decorating or putting on, as we have now the same root used to indicate "dressing", *vesa* whence *vesya* "a woman who lives by her dress,—a harlot." Yaska adopts this meaning when he includes *ves-ati* among the verbs for ornamentation, *kantikarma*. Sayana, not perceiving this when he commented on the Rig Veda, took the word in its ordinary signification, and so interpreted the stanza as to make the women first enter their own houses—*sagri-han privisantu*, and subsequently the house, *'joni'* of the chief mourner; in so doing he had to supply what he supposed was an elipse, and thereby entirely to mislead his readers. The new reading of the word in the Aranyaka now leaves no doubt on the subject.

The words of the second line *anasravah* "tearless", *anamivah* "diseaseless" or free from pain either of body or mind, (it has been loosely rendered in one of the above quotations by "not miserable"), *susevah* "well served", all refer to, and are epithets of, *janayah* "wives", which follows. In the Rig Veda the last epithet is changed to *suratnah* "well ornamented" without in any way altering the construction. The verb is *arohantu* "let ascend" or "proceed", and agrees with the nominative *janayah* "wives". The dative is *jonim* "to house" in the singular, the house of the chief mourner, where they are to partake of a feast, and not that of the females. The last word *agre*, "first or foremost" is an adverb qualifying the verb *arohantu*.

The words *anjanena sarpisha* have confounded all the European translators. Wilson has rendered them into "unguents and butter", and Max Muller into "oel und butter". One has dropt the word *anjanena* and used only "butter"; he is particular in reminding his readers that he has followed Sayana, but his assurance must be received with some reservation, for the scholiast neither omits the first word nor is remiss in explaining it; his words are *anjana-sadhanena sarpisha* "with butter for making collyrium" or *anjanahetuna sarpisha* "with butter the source of collyrium", that is, as I have rendered, "with collyrious butter", or collyrium made of butter, the other element of the unguent being, as stated in a subsequent mantra, a mineral of the name of *traikakuda*, which I guess to be sulphuret of antimony or *surma*. The object of the mantra is to prohibit the use of the ordinary collyrium, which is differently made. The usual practice to this day is to smear a little butter or oil in the bowl of a spoon, and to hold it over a lamp, so that a quantity of lampblack may be deposited on it, and when the two are mixed together with the fingers, they constitute the collyrium. The sulphuret is still used in the North-West Provinces.

The second mantra to which I wish to draw the attention of the reader is the one with which a brother, student, or servant of the deceased is to remove the widow from the pyre; inasmuch as it clearly shows that the widow at the time was not burnt, but taken to abide in the land of the living, and to marry if she liked. That the removal was positive and final, and not nominal, is evident from the ruler of the Sutrakaras. Baudhayana says, "He who approaches her should, holding her by the left hand, take her up", *tan pratigatah savye panavabhipadyotthapayati*. This is done after obtaining the permission of the deceased by a formal mantra, ante p. 255, and on the 3rd, 5th or 7th day after the cremation, the widow, or the eldest widow, if there should happen to be more than one, is expected to go to the burning ground and collect the bones of the dead with her left hand. Asvalayana is equally precise, and adds that, should the widow be removed by an old servant, the chief mourner should repeat the mantra, (*Kartta vrishale japet*, Sutra, 4.2. 19). The author of the *Prayoga*, it is true, takes this direction to apply to pregnant women only who should not be burnt alive, but his authority in such a case is of little value, when opposed to that of the oldest Sutrakaras, and the evident purport of the mantra. It may be also observed that the widow is to take away the gold, bow and jewel, which are put into the hands of the Brahman, Kshetriya and Vaisya dead respectively—with which, according to a subsequent mantra, she is to live in wealth, splendour and glory in the society of the remover, in this world, and this she could not do, if she were immolated.

The mantra, as given in our text, ante page 255, is slightly different from a similar stanza in the second Sukta of the second Anuvaka of the 10th Mandala of the Rig Veda, and quoted by Wilson and Max Muller in the papers above alluded to; the words *itasu* and *abhisambabhuva* of our text being replaced by *gatasu* and *abhisambabhutha*. The words, however, are synonymous, and therefore the difference is of no moment. The second word, a verb, is in the Rig Veda, in the third person, dual irregular, having for its nominative *tvan* "thou", understood, and in our text it is in the third person singular, both may therefore be taken as Vedic peculiarities.

The most important word in the mantra is *didhishu*, which Sayana, when commenting on the Rig Veda, took to imply impregnation *didhishoh garbhasya nidhatoh*. In the Aranyaka he accepts it in its ordinary well-established dictionary meaning of a man "who marries a widow" or "the second husband of a woman twice married", as

Wilson gives it. The result is a material difference in the meaning. The version given by Wilson is as follows: "Rise up, woman, come to the world of living beings, thou sleepest nigh unto the lifeless. Come: thou hast been associated with maternity through the husband by whom thy hand was formerly taken".[16] Max Muller's reading is closely similar. He writes:

"Steh auf, o Weib ! Komm zu der Welt des Lebens !
Du schlafst bei einem Todten—Komm hernieder !
Du bist genug jetzt Gattin ihm gewesen,
Ihm, der Dich wahlte und zur Mutter machte."[17]

In our verson, following Sayana's second and more recent commentary, we take the word *hastagrabhasya* "of him who holds thy hand", and the other predicates in the present tense, and the *didhishu* in its crude sense, and apply them to the party who holds the widow's hand while lying on the pyre. This appears the most consistent and in keeping with the whole ceremony, and therefore preferable to referring them to the dead. The only objection to this reading is to be found in the fact that the verb is in the past perfect tense, but seeing that Panini has laid down more than one special rule for the use of the past for the imperative (*Linarthe let* 3, 4, 7, etc.), and Sayana has accepted the same it is perfectly immaterial. In a pamphlet on the impropriety of widow marriage, lately published by some of the Professors of the Benares Sanskrit College, the word *jivalokam* "the world of living beings" has been rendered by *martyalokat anyam*, "other than the region of mortals," but such a meaning is not admissible either by any positive rule or by analogy. Sayana renders it, in one place, by—"the region of the living sons and grandsons", *jivanam putrapautradinam lokam*, and in another, by "aiming at the region of the living creatures", *jivantam pranisamuhamabhilak-shya*. Other interpretations of the Professors are equally open to question, but it is not necessary to notice them. That the remarriage of widows in Vedic times was a national custom can be easily established by a variety of proofs and arguments; the very fact of the Sanskrit language having, from ancient times, such words as *didhishu*, "a man that has married a widow", *parapurva* "a woman that has taken a second husband", *paunarbhava*, "son of a woman by her second husband", are enough to establish it; but it would be foreign to the subject of this paper to enter into it here.

Notes and References

1. The authorities usually quoted are the following:
"I shall relate to you, O handsome-faced, the merit of giving up life in the Ganges. I give him (who does so) my own rank, and pour in his ears the mantra of the Great Brahma." *Skanda Purana,* quoted in the *Suddhi tattva.*
"He who fasting dies with half his body immersed in the water of the Jahnavi (Ganges), is never born again, and attains equality with Brahma." *Agni Purana,* quoted in the *Prayaschitta tattva.*
"The embodied who dies with its body up to the navel in water attains the fruit of all the sacred waters, tirthas. There is no doubt about it." *Skanda Purana.*
"After giving up the body in the Ganges there is no second birth." *Kriyayogasara.*
"Even the crime of Brahmanicide may be expiated by giving up the body in the Ganges." *Kriyayogasara.*
2. The mantra for the purpose says:
"Give up the cloth thou hast hitherto worn; remember the ishta and purta sacrifices thou hast performed, the fees (to Brahmans thou hast given) and those (gift thou hast) bestowed on thy friends."
3. "This cloth comes to thee first."
4. This prejudice first manifested itself, though in a mitigated form, in the time of Manu, who says, "Let no kinsman, whilst any of his own class are at hand, cause a deceased Brahman to be carried out by a Sudra; since the funeral rite, polluted by the touch of a servile man, obstructs his passage to heaven". Chap. V. ver. 104. The following are the subsequent authorities:
"The Brahman (dead) should not be removed by a Sudra, or a Sudra (dead) by a Brahman. Vishnu.
"Whoever causes fire, grass, wood, and ghi to be brought by a Sudra (should perform an expiatory rite). Yama. I shall now relate to you the mode of purification as ordained by Manu, from the pollution caused by a dog, Sudra, an outcaste and the low dying in the house of a Brahman. Ten nights for a dog, month for a Sudra, twice that time for an outcaste, and twice that for the low. The house should be forsaken in the case of the lowest, says Manu. Vrihanmanu. A house becomes purified in three days after the death of a Brahman; the courtyard outside of the house is purified in one day by the touch of fire, and by smearing it with cowdung. Yama.
5. Mantra to be repeated at the end of the first stage. Mantra to be repeated at the end of the second stage.
"Pusha knows all these sides; may he bear you away hence by the safest road; may he, who is beneficent, kind to us, and mighty against all, knowing the road well, lead us without obstruction." Mantra to be repeated at the end of the third stage.
"The life, the life of the world wishes to take charge of you. May Pusha, leading, protect you in the difficult road; may the divine sun, leading you by the way of the virtuous, place you where the pious dwell."

6. Aratni extending from the thumb to the tip of the index finger,
7. This verse does not occur in the 10th Mandala of the Rig Veda, but the counterpart of it, in connexion with the bow, occurs with a different reading. Dr. Max Muller renders this as follows: "I take the bow from the hand of the dead, to be, to us, help, glory, and strength. Thou art there, we are still here, with our brave sons; may we conquer all enemies that attack us." Dr. Wilson's version is slightly different in words, but is in substance the same. "Taking his bow from the hand of the dead that it may be to us for help, for strength, for fame, (I say) here verily art thou, and here are we: accompained by our valiant descendants may we overcome all arrogant adversaries."—*Jour. R. As. Soc*, XVI. p. 202.
8. "Destroy not, Agni, this spoon; it is dear to the Devas and the performers of the Soma rites. This spoon is the drinking vessel of the Devas; may the immortal Devas therefore make us happy."
9. Journal Royal As. Soc. xvi, 213.
10. This verse, in the original, occurs a little before the one about the application of the collyrium. I have displaced it for the sake of consistency.
11. Most of the mantras quoted above occur in the loth Mandala of the Rig Veda, but their readings there are different, and they do not appear in the same order. Wilson's translations thereof do not, therefore, n many essential particulars, correspond with what I have given above. *Vide* Journal R. As. Soc. XVI, 201-2.
12. As. Researches, IV; p. 213.
13. Journal R. As. Soc. XVI, p. 202
14. Zeitschrift, Band, IX, p. XXV.
15. Journal R. As. Soc., N.S., Vol. III, p. 185.
16. Journal, R. As. Soc, XVI, p. 202.
17. Zeitschrift, IX, p. vi.

18

Widow in Ancient India

N.K. Dutt

Vidhava or widow is a woman whose husband is dead and who has not married again. It is a very old word which can be traced beyond the Vedic language to Indo-European origin, and exists with little modifications in most of the languages of the Indo-European family. Thus we get in Latin *vidita*, Italian *vedova*, Spanish *viuda*, French *veuve*, old Slavonic *vidova*, Russian *vdova*, old German *wituwa*, Gothic *widuwo*, old English *widevee* and *widuwe*, and Persian *beva*. In Latin the word *viduus* in the masculine means bereft, widowed, and in Greek the corresponding word ηιθεοζ eitheos, means an unmarried man.

Meaning of the Word Vidhava

Sanskrit grammarians derive the word *vidhava* from the base *dhava* meaning a man or a husband. According to their derivation a married woman whose husband is alive is *sadhava*. Curiously, *sadhava* is a comparatively new word, which does not occur in the whole Vedic literature. On the other hand, the word *avidhava* in the sense of a woman not widowed was commonly used in Vedic times. Again, the word *dhava* meaning a husband is not found in the Vedic literature, and its first mention is met with in the *Nirukta;* but even there the meaning given is a man and not a husband, except by implication. In the *Atharvaveda*, *Dhava* is the name of a tree mentioned together with *Plaksa, Asvattha* and *Khadira*. Thus we see that the word *vidhava* was neither in general use, nor the basic word *dhava* was known, and that instead of using a positive word like *sadhava* a double negative form like *avidhava* was current. Then again, no word similar to the Sanskrit *dhava* in the sense of a man or a husband is met with in any of the European languages.

This naturally awakens a suspicion that the etymological meaning given by Indian grammarians is not correct. Evidently the *vi* of the word *vidhava* is not a prefix but part of the main root word. It must therefore be derived from a root like Teutonic *wid*, to lack, Latin *videre*, to separate, as in *di-videre*, and Sanskrit *vidh*, to be bereft. When the true derivative meaning was lost in India, the word *dhava* in the sense of a husband came into existence in the Sanskrit language by a wrong splitting-up of the word *vidhava*. Yaska is the first writer known to make a suggestion like that, though he gives priority to the views of earlier grammarians who derived it otherwise without reference to *dhava*.[1]

Hard Life

The life of a Hindu widow is hard indeed. A widow, according to the current Smrti works, is "either to mount the funeral pyre with the dead body of her husband, or to lead the life of a brahmacarini till death.—Like a brahmacarini, she must not indulge in the luxuries of betel-chewing, piling the body and using bell-metal vessels for eating. She must take only one meal a day and never twice, and must not lie on a couch, nor use scents. She should offer daily oblations to her dead husband. She should observe some religious vow (*yrata*) in the months of *Vaisakha* and *Kartika*, and always take ceremonial baths, make gifts and recite the name of Visnu." (Raghunandana, *Suddhitattvam*). "A widow should either enter the fire with the dead body of her husband, or wear herself by asceticism with the hair shorn." (*Yama Samhita*, II. 53)

Second Husband

Such rigid rules for a widow did not exist in the Vedic period. No aversion is expressed anywhere in the *Rgveda* to the remarriage of widowed women. Indeed, the custom of a widow marrying the brother of her deceased husband seemed to be common, and hence the word *devara*, literally meaning second husband (*dvitiyo varah*), according to Yaska, came to denote a woman's brother-in-law. When the dead body was going to be burnt, the dead man's brother seized the hand of the widow lying beside and asked her to be his wife.[2] This custom is again referred to in X. 40. 2, where a widow is said "to draw her husband's brother in embrace in bed". The *Atharvaveda* (IX. 5. 27-28) declares that in case of the remarriage of a woman she would rejoin that husband in the next world who had offered the *Pancaudanam* oblation in this world. The *Taittiriya Samhita* (VI. 6.4.) regards it undesirable for a woman to have two husbands at the same time. This opinion is repeated in the *Aitareya Brahmana* (III. 12), which states that "one woman cannot have more than one husband at the same time". This passage, according to even later commentators like Mitramisra in the *Viramitrodaya, Adhivedana Prakarana*, and Nilakantha in his commentary on the *Mahabharata*, I. 195.29, indirectly recognises the marriage of a woman a second time after the death of her husband.[3]

Chaotic State of Society

Pointed reference to a chaotic state of society in the Vedic period is made in the *Mahabharata*, Adiparva, 122, where the sage Svetaketu, son of Uddalaka, is said to have for the first time laid down the law of strict womanly chastity. Another story of lax sexual morals is that of Dirghatama (Adiparva, 104), who was the first to prohibit the marriage of widows by decreeing that "a woman must remain faithful to, and dependent upon, one husband only, alive or dead, and must not marry a second time". These stories may be fanciful but they are clearly reminiscent of a period, that of the Vedic risis, when for a woman to marry a second time was not looked upon as unusual. That it was common for a woman to marry her husband's brother after his death is alluded to in the *Mahabharata*, Santiparva, ch. 72, v. 12: "As a woman marries her brother-in-law after the death of her husband, so the brahmana having failed to protect her, the earth made the ksatriya her husband." This passage finds repetition in Anusasanaparva, ch. 8, v. 22, which proves that the sentiment underlying it was quite familiar in those days.

Niyoga and Marriage of Widows during Vedic Period

One of the grounds of objection to the marrying of a widow in modern times is the feeling of repugnance to taking for wife an *anyapurva*, i.e., a woman who had been possessed by another person. Thus Yajnavalkya (I. 52) advises a man to marry a woman "that has as yet belonged to no man". Yet in the age of the Epics virginhood was not always regarded as an indispensable factor in choosing a wife. Thus Krsna appropriated the pick of the harem of the slain Naraka. Jayadratha wanted to make Draupadi "his wife". Trisanku took, the wife of a Vidarbha prince killed by him and had by her a son. King Rtuparna was eager to marry Damayanti at her second *svayamvara* knowing her to be the wife of a former husband. Satyavati was sought in marriage by king Ugrayudha shortly after the death of her husband Santanu (*Harivamsa*, XX). Arjuna accepted as wife the widowed daughter of Airavata, the Naga king, and had by her a son. It is not surprising that references to remarriage of women are meagre in the Epic literature. The wonder is that after the successive expurgations and revisions in the hands of later orthodox brahmanas so much evidence of this custom has been allowed to survive. In later times it was declared that "in the sacred texts which refer to marriage the *niyoga*, or levirate, is nowhere mentioned, nor is the marriage of widows prescribed in the rules concerning marriage." (Manu, IX. 65). Those who believe this statement as an authoritative pronouncement may be reminded of the fact that the practice of *niyoga* was quite legal and common in the period referred to, and the two, *niyoga* and marriage of widows, being bracketted together by Manu, may lead to the supposition, apart from other evidences, that one was as much in existence as the other, though brahmanical opinion represented by puritan law-makers like Apastamba and Manu was growing more and more pronounced against them.

Son of Widow Entitled to Inheritance

At the end of the Vedic period the remarriage of women was getting out of fashion and was spoken disapprovingly of even in the earlier Dharmasastras. Thus Apastamba decrees that "if a man unites with a woman who had been once married before, or belongs to a different caste, they both commit a sin". (II. 6.13.4). The putting of widow-marriage in the same category with inter-caste marriage by Apastamba shows that it was still in existence at the time, though its total abolition was a thing to be devoutly wished. Manu, too, indirectly recognises such marriage, for according to him a son born of a remarried widow, *paunarbhava*, by a brahmana father does not cease to be a brahmana, and is regarded only as much degraded as a brahmana living by trade (III. 181). Gautama (XXIX. 8) acknowledges its existence by admitting the right of the son of a widow by her second husband to inherit one-fourth of his father's property in the absence of ordinary legitimate heirs. According to Vasistha and Visnu, the son of a married widow by her second husband is fourth in order of preference in the matter of inheritance among the twelve kinds of sons, and is regarded as better than an adopted son (XVII. 18; XV. 7).

Unwidowed Wives could take Second Husbands

Vasistha, one of the liberal of the law-givers, lays down: "If a damsel has been abducted by force, and not wedded with sacred texts, she may lawfully be given to another man; she is even like a maiden. If a damsel at the death of her husband had been merely wedded by the recitation of sacred texts, and if the marriage had not been consummated, she may be married again (cf. *Baudhayana*, IV. 1.17-18). The wife a person gone abroad shall wait for five years. After five years have passed, she may go to seek a husband. In this manner (after the death of her husband) a wife of the Brahmana caste who has issue shall wait five years and one who has no issue, four years; a wife of the Ksatri a caste who has issue, five years, and one who has no issue, three years; a wife of the Vaisya caste who has issue, four years, and one who has no issue, three years; a wife of the Sudra caste who has issue, three years, and one who has no issue, one year. But while a member of her family is living, she shall certainly not go to a stranger (for marrying)" (ch. XVII). These rules show that not only widows but unwidowed wives also could take second husbands and that the marriage tie was dissoluble in certain circumstances. Divorce was recognised by law in ancient India, the equivalent expression used in Kautilya's *Arthasastra* being *moksa*. Kautilya's rules on the subject will be discussed later on.

Cf. *Narada*, XII, "When the husband is lost, or dead, or turned a recluse, or impotent or an outcast, in these five kinds of distress a woman can take a second husband. The Brahmana wife shall wait for eight years for her husband who is gone abroad; if she has no issue she shall wait for four years, after which period she may marry another. The Ksatriya woman having issue shall wait for six years, and without issue, for three years. The Vaisya woman who has issue, four years, and without issue, two years. The Sudra woman has no rule for waiting. If it be heard that the husband is alive, the waiting period should be twice as long. Such is the order of Prajapati. So in these circumstances the remarriage of a woman is not an offence".

These rules are given also in the *Devala Smrti* with little change of language.

Women-Field, Man—Giver of the Seed

It is further stated by Narada that "women have been created for the sake of propagation, woman being the field, and man the giver of the seed. The field must be given to him who has the seed. He who has no seed is not entitled to possess the field", and that "when a woman after the death of her husband rejects her brother-in-law or other kinsmen who have approached her (for marrying), and goes to a stranger through lust, she is a wanton woman". Katyayana, too, follows Vasistha and Narada and decrees that if the bridegroom be of different caste, an outcast, impotent; of vicious occupation, of the same *gotra*, a Dasa, a constant invalid, the bride, even married, should be given to another". (Quoted in *Nirnayasindhu*).

Thus it is seen that the well known verse

नष्टे मृते प्रव्रजिते क्लोवे च पतिते पतौ ।
पञ्चस्वापत्सु नारीणां पतिरन्यो विधीयते ।।

occurs not only in the law-book of Parasara (IV. 30) but also in that of Narada. It is found also in some of the Puranas, such as *Garuda* 107.28, and *Agni* 154.5. From the rules laid down by Vasistha, Narada and Devala regarding the remarriage of a woman with or without children in the case of a husband gone abroad, it is clear that this verse was not meant only for girls betrothed and not married, as is sought to be explained by more modern commentators. There are reasons to believe that this verse occurred formerly even in the law-book of Manu, as is noticed by Mitramisra in the *Viramitrodaya, Adhivedana Prakarana*, though it has dropped out from the modern editions. When we see that Manu enjoined a strict life of asceticism for widows and set his face even against the long standing practice of *niyoga* as in Ch. V. 157, 160-61, doubts may be expressed if the above-mentioned passage permitting remarriage of women could find place in his book. But such conflicting statements reflecting differences between ideals and practices, or between past and present usages, are met with in many of the law-books, including those of Manu and Parasara. Thus, Parasara in the verse immediately following the above-mentioned passage states, "that woman, who when the husband is dead, observes the vow of chastity, goes to heaven after death like a brahmacarin. "This is almost similar to the verse 160 in Manu, V. Even the waiting periods for the wives of husbands gone abroad are stated by Manu, as by Vasistha and Narada, though it is not clear what the wives are to do after the expiry of those periods (IX. 76). The commentator Nandanacarya says that the implication is that they may take second husbands. The explanation is that the law-givers of the period were trying to set-up ideals and at the same time had to acknowledge the existing usages. At a later time when the practices of the higher castes became more and more conformed to the ideals, the necessity of recording conflicting statements disappeared and many of the anachronistic passages were expurgated in the course of time.

Later Scholars Forbid Widow Marriage

Later commentators like Hemadri, Raghunandana and Kama-lakara forbid entirely the practice of widow-marriage in modern times on the strength of a passage quoted from *Adi* or *Adityapu-rana* which gives a list of practices forbidden in the Kali age. Therein also it is admitted that in ancient times the marriage of widows, like *niyoga* and inter-caste marriage, was prevalent. The supporters of the custom, on the other hand, quote a verse from the *Vyasa Samhita*, which states that in case of a difference of opinion between Sruti, Smrti and Purana, the authority is first of all Sruti and then Smrti, Purana being the last (I. 4). In this matter Vedic texts supporting the custom must be given first consideration, prohibition in the Smrtis notwithstanding. Then it is admitted that of the Smrtis the *Parasara Samhita* is meant for the people of the Kali age, Manu being of the Satya age, Gautama of Treta, and Sankha and Likhita of Dvapara. (Parasara, I. 23). The text approving of remarriage of women under certain circumstances in the *Parasara Samhita* cannot therefore be annulled for the Kali age by a different text from any other Smrti, not to speak of a text from a Purana, nay, an Upapurana. Moreover, as many of the practices banned by the *Adityapurana* are known to have currency in the present Kali age, e.g., the Asvamedha sacrifice, life-long brahmacarya, pilgrimage to distant places, ending one's life by burning in fire, acknowledgement of Putrika-putra, and sea-voyage, why should the prohibition of remarriage of women given so much sanctity? (Vidyasagara, *Marriage of Hinau Widows*).

Kautilya's Rules for Re-marriage

There are evidences other than those gleaned from the sacred literatures to show that this custom of a second marriage for women under certain circumstances existed in India even among the highest castes about two thousand years ago. Vatsyayana admits its existence and sums up the attitude of the religious teachers towards this custom when he states that "union with a woman of lower caste and a twice-married woman is neither desirable nor forbidden (*na sisto na pratisiddhah*)"—*Kamasutra*, I. 5. 3. Kautilya, however, lays down elaborate rules stating the various circumstances in which a woman can legally marry a second time at the death or during the life-time of her first husband. "On the death of her husband a woman wishing to lead a virtuous life shall at once receive not only her endowment money and jewellery but also the balance of dowry due to her. If she is desirous of a second marriage she shall be given on the occasion of her marriage whatever her father-in-law or her husband or both had given to her. If a widow marries any man other than that selected by her father-in-law, she shall forfeit whatever had been given to her by her father-in-law and her husband. . . . If a husband is of bad character, or is long gone abroad, or is guilty of high treason, or is dangerous to his wife, or has become outcast, or has lost virility, he may be abandoned by his wife. . . . If the wife of an absent husband lacks maintenance and is not taken care of by the well-to-do kinsmen of her husband, she may remarry anyone whom she likes and who is in a position to maintain her and save her from misery. . . . Childless wives belonging to Sudra, Vaisya, Ksatriya or Brahmana caste should wait for a year for their husbands who have gone abroad for a short time. Wives with children should wait in such cases for more than a year. If they are provided with maintenance they should wait for twice the length of that period. If they are not so provided, their kinsmen should maintain them for four or eight years. Then the kinsmen should leave them to marry after taking from them what had been given to them at the time of marriage". (*Arthasastra*, III 2-4).

Customary Marriages

Another evidence of the existence of this custom is supplied by references in the *Jataka* literature. From the *Asatarupa Jataka* we learn that a king of Kosala killed the king of Kasi and made the widowed queen, who was already a mother, his chief queen. A similar story is related in the *Kunala Jataka*. According to tradition as preserved in the introduction to the *Candakinnara Jataka*, many princes were desirous of marrying the wife of Gautama Buddha, who had already a son then, when he enounced his home and became an ascetic. In the *Ucchanga Jataka* a woman prays for the release of her brother, who along with her husband and son has been sentenced to death, saying that of these three she can get a new husband and a new son but never a new brother, whatever she can do.

An interesting instance of the marrying of a widow by her brother-in-law is known from the history of the Imperial Guptas. Candragupta II Vikramaditya, son of Samudragupta, murdered his elder brother Ramagupta and made the widow Dhruvadevi his chief queen (Altekar, *JBORS.*, 1928, pp. 223-253; 1929, pp. 134-141). "The conduct of Candragupta in marrying her was thus not at all opposed to the law laid down by the Smrti. If widow marriage and marrying the wife of a dead elder brother had been prohibited by the Dharmasastra, he would not have been able to perform the ceremony and, above all, his son Kumaragupta I by that queen would never have been allowed to succeed him to the throne. . . . But when we find, as we do now, that no less a personage than Vikramaditya, who made the Gupta period a Golden Age in the ancient history of India, himself marries a widow who was again the wife of his elder brother killed by himself, it cannot but shock the orthodox susceptibilities of most of us, howsoever we may like to contemplate his learning and the patronage he gave to Sanskrit literature. (Bhandarkar, 'New Light on the Early Gupta History', *Malaviya Commemoration Volume*, p. 203).

It is stated in the *Rajatarangini*, IV 35-42 that king Durlabhaka fell in love with the wife of a rich merchant, and that the latter gave her up so that the king might marry her. The issues of this marriage were Candrapida, Tarapida and Muktapida, who reigned successively in Kashmir in the 8th century A.D. and under whom the kingdom rose to the zenith of power and prosperity.

From Merutunga's *Prabandhacintamani* we learn that king Viradhavala's mother married her deceased sister's husband though her first husband was alive. Yiradhavala lived for some time in the house of his step-father before he became a ruler in Gujarat in the 13th century A.D. His famous ministers were Tejahpala and Vastupala, who were the sons of a twice-married woman by her second husband, and who achieved great fame for their administrative qualities, learning and righteousness.

Tod's *Annals and Antiquities of Rajasthan* gives an account of the marriage of Hamir, king of Mewar, with the widowed daughter of Maldeo, governor of Chitor. Though Hamir was ignorant of the fact at the time of marriage, it did not prevent the issue Khaitsi from becoming the ruler of the proudest Rajput clan on the death of his father without any diffculty in 1365 A.D.

Manu's Laws Regarding Widows

It may be remarked that the hard ascetic life prescribed for widows by later law-givers had not come into fashion before the time of Manu. There is no such regulation in the whole Vedic literature. One of the earliest Sutra-writers, Gautama, does not make any mention of it. Baudhayana and Vasistha prescribe a rigid life for widows for a short period only, and that also in the case of those who seek children by *niyoga*. A widow shall avoid during a year the use of honey, meat, spirituous liquor and salt, and sleep on the ground. Maudgalya declares that she shall do so during six months. After the expiration of that time she may, with the permission of her Gurus, bear a son to her brother-in-law, in case she has no son (Baudha., II. 2. 4. 7-9). "The widow of a deceased person shall sleep on the ground during six months, practising religious vows and abstain from pungent condiments and salt. After the completion of six months she shall bathe. . . . Then her father . . . shall appoint her to raise issue to her deceased husband" (Vas., XVII. 55-56). Manu is the first law-giver to regard life-long asceticism as a desirable practice for widows. "Let her rather emaciate her body by (living on) pure flowers, roots and fruits: but she must never even mention the name of another man after her husband has died. Till her death she should remain forbearing and restrained, and live the life of a brahmacarini. A virtuous wife, who after the death of her husband remains chaste and established in the life of brahmacarya, goes to heaven, though she may have no son, as do the brahmacarins. A woman who from a desire to have offspring proves unfaithful to her dead husband earns infamy in this world and loses her place with her husband in heaven" (V. 157-161). Manu thus condemns *niyoga*, though he could not entirely forbid it, as he states in another place, "A woman without a child can raise a son by her brother-in-law or a *Sapinda*, if duly appointed" (IX. 59). A life of rigid brahmacarya for a widow being constantly praised by the later law-givers after Manu, such as Yajnavalkya (I. 75), Parasara (IV. 31), Visnu (XXXV. 14), etc., it gradually became in the course of centuries a religious duty for her from which there was no exemption.

An alternative to such a hard life was self-immolation of a widow on the funeral pyre of the dead husband. Many scholars have expressed their disbelief in the existence of this dreadful custom during the Vedic period. There is no direct reference to it in the Vedic literature. The *Grbya Sutras*, which do not leave any important ceremony of domestic life untouched, are singularly silent about it. While minutest details are given about the cremation ceremony and the purificatory rites consequent upon bereavement, no directions are given as to how Suttee is to be performed, or what is to be done for a woman thus burnt though such direction are found in profusion in the later law-books. The authors of law books up to the time of Manu and Yajnavalkya do not refer to it.

Suttee not Mentioned in Vedic Literature

There however is one significant passage which indicates that the performance of Suttee was gone through symbolically in the Vedic period. It did not in ordinary cases have a tragic end, like the practice af human sacrifice which though actually performed at one time in some rites had, as we know, by the time of the *Yajurveda*, the *Satapatha* and *Taittirya Brahmanas*, became purely emblematic. The *Asvalayana Grhya Sutra* (IV. 2) states, "After sacrificial grass and a black antelope's skin with the hair outside have been spread out on the pile of fuel they place the dead body thereon. . . . To the north of the body they place the wife of the deceased. . . . Her brother-in-law, being a representative of her husband, or a pupil of her husband, or an aged servant, should cause her to rise from that place with the verse, "Arise, O woman, to the world of living (of the *Rgveda*)". There is no mention anywhere, either in the *Rgveda* or in the Sutras, that this verse was addressed to a pregnant woman, not entitled to immolate herself, as is explained by later commentators supporting Suttee. Originally this verse was addressed to the widowed woman only by her brother-in-law, who ordinarily married or cohabited with her. In the course of time when widow-marriage and *niyoga* had become objects of disapproval the recital of the verse became meaningless, and so a substitute for the brother-in-law might formally recite, "Arise, woman, thou art lying by one whose life is gone; come to the world of living away from thy husband, and become the wife of him who grasps thy hand and woos thee as a lover". (*Rgveda*, X. 18. 8). This verse occurs also in the *Atharvaveda* (XVIII. 3. 2), and the meaning becomes clear if the verse preceding it be studied along with it. "This woman, choosing her husband's world, lies down by thee that art departed, O mortal, continuing to keep her ancient duty; to her assign thou here progeny and property." (XVIII. 3. 1). The question is whether the woman who is described as lying by the side of the dead body of her husband was actually burnt and made to follow him to the other world. The above two verses indicate that first of all the blessing of the dead man was invoked for progeny (*prajam*) and property to her in this world (*iha*) and then she was led away from the funeral pyre by her wooing (*didhisu*) brother-in-law to fulfil the blessing of the departed husband. The supporters of the practice of Suttee, on the other hand, interpret *iha* as *asmin bhuloke janmantare* (in this world on being born again), which is no doubt a laboured explanation and is at variance with the meaning of the verse following. It is referred to as *dharmam puranam* in this verse, and was followed only to the extent of the widow lying on the pile but not being burnt at the time when these verses were composed.

Two Interpretations

Later commentators and law-givers quote a verse of the *Rgveda* (X. 18.7), which also occurs in the *Atharvaveda* (XII. 2.31) and *Taittiriya Aranyaka* (VI. 10. 2), as recommending the rite of Suttee (*vide* Raghunandan's *Suddhitattva*). Some of them seek to read *agneh* (of fire) in place of *agre* (first), while others explain *yonim* to mean 'to fire' instead of 'to house'. The verse is as follows:[4] "Let those woman, who are not widowed, who have good husbands, applying the collyrious butter to their eyes enter; without tears, without disease, and full of ornaments, let these wives first enter the house." The question is to whom the verse was addressed, is it to the recently widowed wives of the dead husband ready to accompany him by entering into fire, or to the assembled young women around ready to go back home from the cremation ground. If it were addressed to the widow, as is done in the verse following,[5] why is the plural number used without any reason? That it is not so is clearly understood from the *Asvalayana Grhya Sutra*, IV. 6. 11-12, which states, "The young woman belonging to the house should, with each hand separately, with their thumbs and fourth fingers, with young *Darbha* blades salve their eyes with butter and throw the *Darbha* blades away, turning their faces away. The priest should look at them, while they are salving themselves, with the verse 'Let these women, who are not widowed'."

Kings' and Generals' Families Performed Suttee

Yet we may believe that the custom of Suttee, inspite of the general silence of the early Sutra-writers, persisted among certain sections of the people, especially among the princely class (Zimrner, *Alt. Leb.*, 331). In many savage communities we find the existence of a custom of sacrificing wives and slaves at the time of burial of a dead chieftain with the intention of securing to him the same service and ministration in the other world as he had been used to in this. "We read in Herodotus (V. 5) that amongst the Thracians it was usual, after the death of a man, to find out who had been the most beloved of his wives, and to sacrifice her upon his tomb. Mela (II. 2) gives the same as the general custom of the Getae. Herodotus (IV. 71) asserts a similar fact of the Scythians, and Pausanius (IV. 2) of the Greeks, while our own Teutonic mythology is full of instances of the same feeling" (Max Muller, *History of Ancient Sanskrit Literature*, p. 48). From the prevalence of this custom among several branches of the Indo-Germanic race in Asia and Europe, it may be presumed that it existed in some form or other among the early Indo-Aryans. With the advancement of civilisation in the time of *Rgveda*, it was regarded with disapproval, and the Brahmana sages of the time began to treat it as a symbolical function and to discontinue the actual execution. The practice, however, persisted to a certain extent among the princely class, with whom it was sometimes a necessity in view of the miserable lot to which the wives of a slain chieftain were consigned by the victor. Almost all the cases of Suttee recorded in the Epic and Pauranic literature occurred in the families of kings and generals. The *Mahabharata* mentions two instances of Suttee, one of Madri immolating herself on the funeral pyre of her husband Pandu and another of the four wives of Vasudeva, including Devaki, mother of Krsna. But so rare was the custom even among the Ksatriyas that no Suttee took place after the carnage of Kuruksetra in which over a million combatants are said to have been killed and in which almost all the princely families of India took part. The widowed women of the Kuru family are seen duly performing the *Sraddha* ceremonies after the cremation of the dead bodies (Satriparva, 27). The fragmentary Greek accounts regarding Suttee leave an impression that it was a peculiar custom with certain military tribes of North-Western India and not a general custom throughout the country in the 4th century B.C. "A peculiar custom is mentioned as existing among the Kathaians—that the husband and wife choose each other, and that the wives burn themselves along with their deceased husbands." (Diodoros XVII. 91). A similar notice of the custom is made in connection with Taxila along with other "strange and unusual customs".

The First Sanction of Suttee to Preserve Widow Chastity

The first sanction of the custom by a Brahmana law-giver is to be found in the *Visnu Smṁrti* which states that the duty of a woman "after the death of her husband is to observe *brahmacarya* or to ascend the funeral pyre with him" (XXV. 14). Similarly, the *Brhaspatisamhita* decrees, "A wife is considered half the body of her husband, equally sharing the result of his good or wicked deeds; whether she burns herself with him, or chooses to survive him leading a virtuous life, she promotes the welfare of her husband" (XXV. 11). The reasons for Brahmana legislators gradually giving religious sanction to this horrible custom after the time of Manu and Yajnavalkya are that probably they found it more difficult to prevent moral lapses in widowed women after they had decreed the abolition of widow-marriage and *niyoga*. The introduction of Suttee is only a logical corollary to the total prohibition of widow-marriage and the maintenance of a high standard of womanly chastity. An additional factor was the great havoc and disruption caused by the barbarian invasions led by the Sakas and Hunas in the first six centuries of the Christian era. The princely families at least were sometimes compelled to resort to this dreadful practice to save the honour of their womenfolk from the hands of the victorious barbarians. Moreover, it is likely that such a practice was prevalent among the Scythians or Sakas, as has been mentioned before, and that the attempts of the Brahmana legislators to establish Suttee in the fifth and sixth centuries A.D. were helped as much by the circumstances of the time as by the continuance of this practice in the families of those barbaric chiefs who were admitted into the rank of Ksatriyas.

Custom of Suttee Criticised

Yet it must be observed that the legislation of this custom by Brahmana writers was not effected without strong protests. The poet Bana in the *Kadambari* regards it as "utterly fruitless. This is a path followed by the illiterate, is a manifestation of infatuation, a course of ignorance, an act of foolhardiness and shortsightedness, a stumbling through stupidity, that life is put to an end when a parent, brother, friend or husband is dead. Life should not be ended if it does not leave itself. If it be properly considered, this suicide has, indeed, a selfish object because it is indeed to obviate the unendurable sorrow of bereavement." Medhatithi writes, 'One shall not die before the span of one's life is run out'[6] and condemns *Suttee* as an act of suicide and not *dharma* (V. 157). It required a good deal of explanation on the part of later commentators to refute the argument of Medhatithi. Thus Madhavacarya in his commentary on *arasarasamhita* states, "The Smrti text approving of the self-immolation of a widow remains in force, otherwise it has no use. So the Sruti text relating to suicide has indeed application everywhere except in the case of women desirous of accompanying their husbands to heaven." Raghunandana, as has been mentioned before, following *Brahmapurana* misinterprets the Vedic text *ima nariravidhavah* to support the self-immolation of widows.

Widows Regarded as Inauspicious Sights on Auspicious Occasions

Widows are regarded as inauspicious sights whose presence is disliked at any auspicious ceremony like marriage. This sentiment is a very old one which can be traced to Vedic times. The repeated use of the word *avidhava* in connexion with such ceremonies, as in *Kausitaki Grhya Sutra*, I. 11-12, indicates that widows were not welcomed on such occasions. "Four or eight women who are not widowed after having been regaled with wine and food are to dance for four times on the night previous to the wedding ceremony." The association of wine and dancing with this part of the ceremony probably became disagreeable to the more puritan taste of later writers, and hence we find the substitution of unwidowed twice-born women by Sudra widows for this function in the *Sankhayana Grhya Samgraha*.[7] When the bridegroom has arrived at the house of the bride for marriage, "he is to be ushered into the hall by young women of good luck who are not 'widowed' (*avidhavah subhaga yuvatyah*)." In Bengal at the present time the young women who take part in the various rites in connexion with the marriage ceremony are called *eyo* and *suyo*, which is nothing but a corruption of the expression *avidhava subhaga*, and must not include widows, however closely related they may be to the bride or the bridegroom.

Notes and References

1. विधवनाद्वा। विधावनाद्वेति चर्मशिरा: अपि वा धव इति मनुष्यनाम। तद्वियोगाद्विधवा। (*Nirukta*, III. 15).
2. X. 18. 8. See *infra*, p. 674.
3. *Ait*. Br.,111. 12— तस्मात् एकस्य बह्वयो जाया भवन्ति नैकस्यै बहव: सहपतय:। Mitramisra—सहशब्दसामर्थ्यात् क्रमेण पत्यन्तरं भवति इति गम्यते। Nilakantha— सह इति युगपत् बहुपतित्वनिषेधो विहितो न तु समयभेदेन।
4. इमा नारीरविधवा: सुपत्नीरांजनेन सर्पिषा सं विशन्तु।
   अनश्रवोऽनमीवा: सुरत्ना आ रोहंतु जनयो योनिमग्रे।।
5. उदर्ष्व नार्य्यभि जीवलोकं गतासुमेतमुप शेष एहि।
   हस्ताग्राभस्य दिधिषोस्तवेदं पत्युर्जनित्वमभि सं बभूव।। (X. 18.8)
6. तस्मादु ह न पुरायुष: सवर्गकामी प्रेयात्।
7. That the drinking of intoxicating liquor was indulged in by Brahmana women, not to speak of women of the lower *varnas*, as late as the seventh and eighth centuries A.D. in the central region of Aryavarta, is known from Kumarila Bhatta's *Tantra-vartika*, I. III. 4, which states, "Among the people of modern days we find the Brahmana women of the countries of Ahicchatra and Mathura to be addicted to drinking". The reformer Kumarla condemns this practice in the case of Brahmanas only, but not of Ksatriya and Vaisya men and women, if the liquor was distilled from fruits or flowers (Madhvi), and molasses (Gaudi) and not from grains (Sura).

19

Wine Drinking in Ancient India

Aparna Chattopadhyay

Wine, A Forbidden Drink

The Kathasaritsagara (Kss.) of Somadeva, a work of the 11th century A.D., throws interesting light on the habit of drinking wine, which obtained among the ancient Indians since early times. The habit of drinking and also the recognition of its evil effects, and its condemnation are equally noticeable in the Rgveda. In the Rgveda it is forbidden as one of the seven sins. In the Chandogya Upanisad a dutiful king proudly declares that there is no drunkard in his kingdom. The Apastamba Dharma Sutra forbids it for all. Buddha tried to stop it; abstaining from wine is one of the five duties for a Buddhist. Kautilya, a practical politician as he was, has given rules and regulations regarding liquor and its consumption, etc., but as an ideal has explicitly advised that wine should not be drunk. It is really striking that Asoka, while he is so anxious to stop animal killing, does not say anything about drinking and its evil effects, in his edicts, excepting pointing to the evil effects of 'Samajas' which were stopped by his imperial decree. In Manu, all the 'dvijatis' are threatened with severe punishment for indulging in it. In spite of all these prohibitions we find that the practice continued since the Vedic days.

An Item of Sumptuous Meals

In the Kss., wine formed an item of sumptuous meals. Drinks followed the excellent food served to guests in a feast given by Prahlada. The same we find in other instances. Sometimes people drank first and then ate in feasts. This is what we find in the description of a banquet. Al Biruni noticed this second practice and says that 'the Hindus drink wine before having eaten anything'.

Drinking very Common Among Royalties

Apart from its use as the item of a dinner, wine was drunk independently too and excepting Brahmanas we find the three remaining classes and also women indulging in drinks. The fact that the Brahmanas in the Kss. are generally not found drinking wine, is, however, in accordance with the Dharmasastric regulations. It was strictly forbidden for Brahmanas in Manu and condemned in the Ramayana and the Mahabharata. In the Grhastharatnakara and Parasara Madhaviya written in the 13th century, wine is forbidden to the Brahmanas but permitted to the Ksatriyas and Vaisyas. In Manu, Gautama, Kautilya, Yajnavalkya, it is condemned in the case of kings too. The picture presented in the Kss. is perfectly in accordance with the regulation of the Grhastharatnakara and Parasara Madhaviya. Hsuan Tsang also had noticed that Brahmanas did not drink wine. In the Kss., we find just a few instances of Brahmanas drinking wine. Marubhuti, son of the Brahmana minister Yaugandharayana, was drunk one morning and was reproached for being drunk in improper hours. The close association of Marubhuti with the royal family especially with prince Naravahanadatta, suggests that such Brahmanas took to the habits of the Ksatriyas. Among the Ksatriyas, particularly royalties, the practice of drinking is very common. Kings like Udayana, Dharmadhvaja of Ujjayini, Virabhuja of Vardhamana, Ratnadhipati and prince Naravahanadatta are found enjoying drinks regularly. The practice is found among Vaisyas as well. Merchant Samudradatta, a virtuous and honest man, is found indulging in drinks. Among the Sudras the practice was not so common. A porter was, once, found living in luxury. A certain merchant interested to know the secret made him drunk one night and extracted the secret. Similar is the case of a woodcutter whose kinsmen extracted the secret of his wealth, one day when he was drunk. According to Al Biruni, the Sudras freely indulged in drinking, which was avoided by people of upper classes.

On festive occasions drinks were enjoyed by all. Thus, on the night of Madiravati's marriage all were drunk. In the Naisadhacarita also we find that on the occasion of marriage feasts, drinking was common especially among Ksatriyas.

Wine and Women

We find royal ladies sharing drinks along with their husbands. Thus, king Udayana used to drink along with his queen Padmavati and Vasavadatta. King Bhimabhata neglected his state duties and began to enjoy himself in his harem being engrossed in drinking, etc. Prince Naravahanadatta was enjoying drinks along with his newly-wedded wife, the princess of Stavasti. King Dharmadhvaja took inspiring wine along with his wives. The sad effect of wine-drinking on ladies, is found in the story of king Ratnadhipati who being disgusted with the faithlessness of his previous queens, married a girl named Rajadatta and kept her in a palace in a lonely island. One morning having enjoyed drinks with her he left her and went away on his regal duties. He came back, just to find the new queen in the arms of a stranger, a shipwrecked man, who had reached there by chance, and was brought in by the queen, heavily drunk, and so not in her right senses.

The ladies drank independently too. Queen Alamkaraprabha used to drink wine in her pregnancy. King Virabhuja made one of his queens drink a great quantity of wine to extract a secret.

Princesses and girls of higher rank also used to drink wine. A thief one night entered the palace of a king and got into the chamber of the princess. The princess became enamoured with the thief and spent the night in drinking and love-making with him. We find another princess, who being angry with her father, decided to leave home. She went outside the city one day and having made her followers drunk with wine, went away. Padmavati, the daughter of Samgramavardhana, a courtier of the king of Kalinga is found keeping wine about her. She entertained her old nurse with wine. When her lover entered her apartments one night, she enjoyed drinks with him. Her cheeks were flushed with wine, as we are told in the Brhatkathamanjari. In the Kss., a female ascetic is found in the habit of drinking wine. It is corroborated by the Brhatkathamanjari.

Drinking, a Grave Sin

Wine is forbidden to women in Manu, Yajnavalkya and Vasistha

Dharma Sutra. The Mitaksara on Yajnavalkya quotes a text that half of the body of him whose wife drinks 'sura' is guilty of grave sin. But the practice did not strictly conform to the ideal. According to the Sutras it was offered to women on the arrival of a bride and to women who performed a dance on marriage. In the Asvalayana Grhya Sutra it is required to be offered to the wives of forefathers when 'pindas' are offered to male forefathers. The same is found in the Paraskara Grhya-Sutra and the Kathaka Grhya Sutra. In the Ramayana we find Sita drinking Maireyaka. She promised to offer a thousand pitchers of wine to the river goddess. Kalidasa also describes ladies such as Iravati and Indumati indulging in drinking.

Wine was considered to be helpful in enhancing the charm of of ladies. We have seen that Padmavati had her cheeks flushed with wine. In the Kathasaritśagara, the princess Bhagirathayasa while drinking wine, looked more beautiful than the moon, with the intoxicated play of her eyes and eyebrows. In the Mandsore inscription, the cheeks of intoxicated women are used in a simile. In the post-Gupta period we find many references to the habit of drinking wine among women. In the Karpuramanjari, ladies are described as drinking 'varuni' a variety of wine. Hemacandra, in describing the delicate condition of Mayanalladevi, says that she had to give up drinking, due to the advanced stage of pregnancy.

The Kss. presents us with a society where motherly ladies presented wine to younger males on occasions and it was not against social etiquette to drink in the presence of motherly and elderly ladies. Thus on the occasion of the coronation of prince Naravahanadatta, Kalingasena his future mother-in-law, presented him with excellent wines. The prince of Puskalavati had a wine party one evening and then heavily drunk he went to sleep while his old nurse sat by him.

Wine and Courtesans

It is interesting and rather surprising that practice of drinking is not to be found among the courtesans of the Kss. though we get intimate details of the life of four courtesans in the work. Ksemendra also does not refer to their habit of drinking wine in his works. In the Rajatarangini, however, Kamala, the courtesan of Paundravardhana is found intoxicated with drink.

Banqueting Hall

There was a banquet with drinks and revelry on the occasion of a victory. Again there is an interesting account of a drinking party and banqueting hall (Apanabhumi). It was a splendid hall full of jewelled goblets and jugs of intoxicating liquor. It was crowded with ladies, who drank wine and thus had their faces expanded and red with contracted eyebrows and red eyes. After the drinks, people proceeded to the hall of feasting attractive with various viands. It was strewn with coverlets, abounding in dishes and hung with curtains and screens and full of all kinds of delicious enjoyments.

It is interesting to note that Caraka has given rules and details of wine parties and requires the best type of drinking hall ('Apanabhumi') to be situated either in the heart of the town or outside the town, to be adorned with flowers, and perfumed with incenses, with cushioned couches and easy chairs having soft covers.

Types of Wine in the Kathasaritsagara

The types of wine, mentioned in the Kathasaritsagara are 'sura', 'madya', or 'mada', 'asava', 'madhu' and 'sidhu'. It seems that these terms denoting wine refer to different varieties and that they have not been used indiscrimately by the author.

King Udayana is found drinking 'sura'. 'Sura' is a very old type of wine used since the Vedic days. 'Soma' and 'Sura' are the two types of intoxicating drinks in the Vedic age. But while 'Soma' was considered to be good and wholesome, 'sura' was an intoxicant, condemned for its bad effects on the drinker. Still it was a very popular drink and Ksatriyas were in the habit of drinking it. A cup of 'Sura' is placed in the hands of a king, in the Aitareya Brahmana. Thus the picture of king Udayana drinking 'sura', is in conformity with the practice of ancient Indian kings. In Sutra period it was served to women who performed a dance on marriage. 'Sura' was prepared from fermented barley or wild paddy after distillation. In Kautilya there are five varieties of 'Sura', while in the Ramayana there are two varieties.

The term 'madya' was sometimes used as a general term for wine. In works on medical science, it is used in naming the chapter on wine. But 'madya' it seems was also used to denote strong liquors. In the Kathasaritsagara its use in the cases to make one totally drunk for some purpose, suggests it has been of a very strong type. A king with a view to extract some secret from one of his queens made her totally drunk by making her drink 'madya'. The prince of Varanasi with some motive, made his wife dead-drunk by giving her 'madya'.

In both the cases the two ladies are said to have been made heavily drunk and almost senseless. We find 'madya' again used for similar purpose in connection with the elopement of Vasavadatta with Udayana. Again, queen Rajadatta became totally senseless under the influence of 'madya' and unknowingly did something disgraceful.

The term 'madhu' in the sense of wine, is used in some places. In Kautilya we find two usages of the term madhu, one as honey and the other as wine. The honey of the bee was called 'madhu' and so was the juice extracted from grapes. In the description of a banquet, in the wine party of king Udayana along with his two queens, and in the description of wine parties of kings and princes along with their wives, we find 'madhu' being drunk.

Proceedings and Judgment of a Hindu Court in Sanskrit

K.P. Jayaswal

"*Tula Rama Sarman with Co-sharers*		... *Plaintiff*"
	and	
"*Maninatha Sarman*		... *Defendant*"

The search for Sanskrit manuscripts has brought to light a unique document. This is a Sanskrit Judgment of a Hindu Law Court.

Pandit Vishnu Lal Jha Sastri who has been carrying on search in Mithila has had special instructions to keep an eye on legal literature, for the Hindu traditional law continued to be administered in Sanskrit in Mithila even in Muhammadan centuries.[1] This traditional system had remained orthodox under Brahman rule and culture of Mithila, as attested by the vast legal literature produced there in the Middle Ages and the survival of ancient Hindu offices of ministers and judges, etc. Evidence of a new type came forth in support of our expectations when Pandit Vishnu Lal Jha brought five original title deeds, written in Sanskrit, of dates from the time of Emperor Muhammad Shah to the time "of the Delhi Sultan and the White *Governor* at Calcutta" (the beginning of the nineteenth century). All these related to sales and purchases of slaves. They were written by professional scribes: in one of the documents the scribe has mentioned his fee of Re. 1.

Much more important, and certainly the most important result of our Mithila search from the point of view of the history of Hindu Law, was the discovery by Pandit Vishnu Lal Jha of the Judgment in Sanskrit which he obtained last year from the house of one Mathuranatha Jha of Darampore[2] a village near Jhanjharpur in the district of Darbhanga. When I examined it I realized for the first time how a Hindu Judgment was written, how the Sabha of the Hindu Judge endorsed that judgment and how stiff, severe and dignified, technical, methodical and scrupulously formal a Hindu Judgment used to be. We have had before this instances of examination of the accused, examination of a witness, and even arguments by advocates which the commentator Asahaya has preserved in the casual report of a case tried in the court of Pataliputra.[2a] But we have had no form of Hindu judgment. The document which we now have supplies us with that.

The judgment is called *jayapatra* or the document of success. The definition of *jayapatra* as given in Hindu law books is as follows:

> "Whatever has been transacted in a suit, the plaint, answer, and so forth, as well as the gist of the trial, should be noted completely in the document recording the success."
>
> (Brihaspati, VI, 3; Translation by Jolly)

Jayapatra recorded the gist of plaint, answer, proof (kriya), arguments (vada), and decision (nirnaya). (Brihaspati quoted by Mitra Misra, p. 192.)

It was "signed by Pradvivaka (Chief Judge) and others", sealed by the royal seal (Vriddha-Vasishtha cited by King Aparaka, Y. II. 84). According to Narada (Apararka II, 84) the decision was by the "Sabhyas" (members of the Sabha).

The present jayapatra is in the handwriting of and is signed and given by Sachala Misra who is evidently the Pradvivaka, Chief Judge or Chief Justice, referred to in the body of the judgment. The decree is addressed to other judges over whom Sachala Misra had authority. At the top-corners the judgment is signed by five men who declare their "concurrence herein".[3] These signatories are the *Parshadas*, members of the *Parshat* or *Sabha* mentioned in the body of the judgment. The Sabha according to Hindu law books was composed of 7, 5 or 3 members, the odd number having been laid down to secure, as Mitra-Misra the author of the Viramitrodaya says, a majority in cases of difference of opinion (p. 35). The function of the Sab a was, according to the law books, to determine questions of fact.[4] Here, however, we find the members giving their opinion on a point of law as well. A doubt therefore arises as to whether these men were members of the Bench presided over by Sachala Misra or a jury-Sabha.

The Chief Judge, according to Hindu law books, in addition to hearing appeals and revisions also tried original suits in the capital. The matter under the judgment was an original cause.

The judgment[5] first mentions the names of the parties *Tula Rama Sarman with his co-sharers*, Plaintiff, and, *Maninatli Sarman*, Defendant. Then it gives the case of the Plaintiff as in his plaint (bhasha). Bhasha is defined in law books as follows:

> The plaint is the first in a trial. It should be "brief in words", "rich in contents", "unambiguous", "free from confusions", "devoid of improper argument", capable of being met by the opposite party; it should not be "impossible", "unmeaning", "purposeless".
>
> [Jolly's Brihaspati, III. 2, 6, 9, etc.]

The judge after the plaintiff's case gives the substance and nature of the defendant's answer or what we call now his Written Statement.[6] Then he discusses as to on whom the burden of proof lay. After that the discussion on and determination of matters to be proved (issues) are summarized. Adjournments are dealt with next. The plaintiff having made default the fact that proceedings thereafter are in re-trial is noted. A preliminary objection on principles of the Hindu law of evidence is raised by the defendant which is allowed by the Chief Judge. The objection was that a single witness to prove a matter was inadmissible. The plaintiff then prays for leave to resort to the mode of proof extraordinary or non-secular, i.e., by ordeal. To this the defendant objects and authority in support of the objection is cited. The leave is not granted by the Chief Judge and the Parshat members. The plaintiff is held to have failed in establishing his "promised case".

The subject matter of the suit was a female domestic slave. The plaintiff could not prove his claim; the defendant on the other hand proved his possession over the slave or slave's family for three generations—the period required by law. The texts which do not recognize possession without title for any length of time to cure defects of title and which are seemingly contradictory to the texts recognizing acquirement of title by prescription, have been interpreted in the

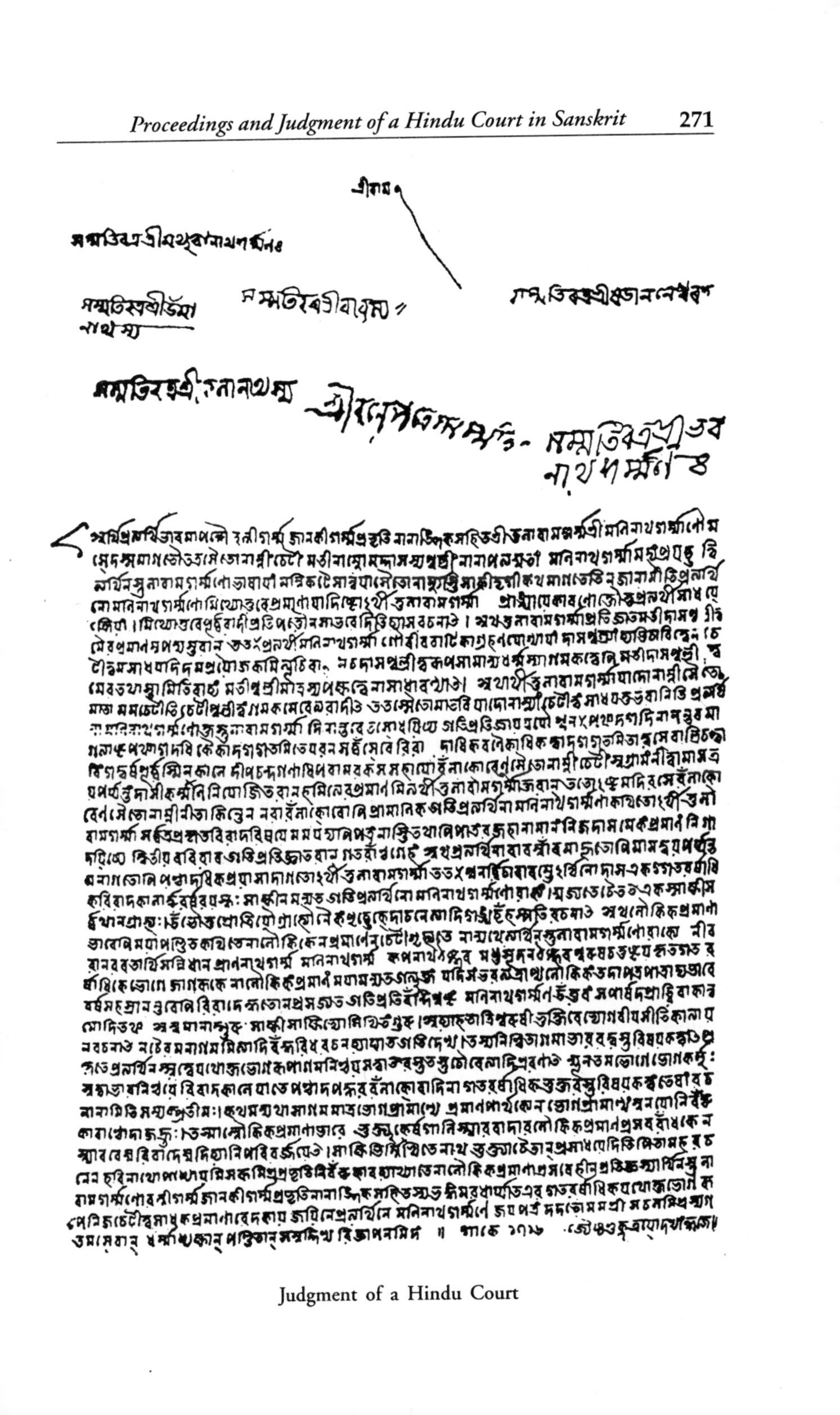

Judgment of a Hindu Court

judgment to be applicable only to such cases where title has been once decided. When there was no such decision "the certainty of right" exercised was proof of title itself. In other words, long possession would be proof presuming title. Subtle arguments on the principles of Hindu logic and law, e.g., on issues and the slave status, are advanced and discussed. Every line of the judgment is referable to Hindu law texts: I have given references to them, on the points discussed, in notes below the judgment. The judgment shows how those provisions were applied in actual administration of law.

TRANSLATION OF THE JUDGMENT IN SANSKRIT GIVEN BY SACHALA MISRA, CHIEF JUDGE

Pleadings

Having attained the condition of plaintiff and defendant, Sri Tula Rama Sarman with his several co-sharers—Balli Sarman, Janaki Sarman and others, *and* Sri Maninatha Sarman attended my court. By his plaint (bhasha) [presented] there Tula Rama Sarman, the Plaintiff (claimed) that Maninatha Sarman should restore him his domestic slave girl (Cheti) of the name of Saito, daughter of his (Plaintiff's) slave, Mati, along with her several children. The Defendant Maninatha Sarman by his answer, the same being a plea of denial (mithyottara) that Saito with children was with him but that he did not know what her status was and how she was come (descended?).

Onus of Proof

The Plaintiff Tula Rama Sarman was put on proof, for the authority of Vyasa is: "In case of a plea of former judgment (Pran-Nyaya, *Res Judicata*) or a special plea the defendant has to prove his case; in a plea of denial, the plaintiff (has to prove his case); in confession (admission) it (proof) is not required".[7]

Settlement of Issues

Now Tula-Rama Sarman proposed to prove the fact of her being the daughter of the slave (father) Mati.[8] Thereupon the Defendant Maninatha Sarman replied that it would be immaterial on account of the fallacy of not proving the slave status of a slave's daughter (...),[9] that if it were alleged that in the absence of evidence of the general factor of the status of a slave's daughter, the fact of her being the daughter of Mati Dasa should be taken to be that evidence, it would be begging the question, for the point of Mati's daughterhood was the hypothesis. Now the Plaintiff Tula Rama Sarman stated that the mother of Saito, Yado by name, was his slave,[10] that this would be evidence of the (slave) status of a female[10] slave's daughter. Hereupon Tula Rama Sarman was required by the Defendant Maninatha Sarman to prove the slave status in the mother of Saito of the name of Yado. Tula Rama Sarman undertook to prove it on the next date and departed.

Adjournments

When after a fortnight the Plaintiff Tula Rama Sarman came he said that he would adduce evidence of the fact that in the Muhammadan year 1158[11]—forty-three years before the claim in suit (i.e.,) before the year 1201,[12] he with the help of Dipachanda, Ganadhipa and Rama Baks, having forcibly brought the slave of the name of Saito to his village had employed her in slave work for three months. On the eighth day after this Defendant Maninatha Sarman said that the fact of Saito's being carried away by force established nothing: that force was no proof. The Plaintiff Tula Rama Sarman then, having no documentary evidence in this "a mere ordinary cause", offered to produce on the second Sunday one Bajaha by name, a slave of his, to depose in his favour. And he went away.

Default and Retrial

Now, even having been called by the Defendant several times for two months the Plaintiff Tula Rama Sarman did not appear.[13] Subsequently when he came after great exertions, on a retrial commencing, the Defendant Maninatha Sarman's statement (objection) was that as there was only one witness for the Plaintiff, his slave who was half the age of the period in controversy—a period over a hundred years, he would not accept the witness.[14]

Objection to Evidence

This (objection) is right, for a single witness is in every case inadmissible on the authority of Sankha and Brihaspati:

> "Two priests shall be accepted as witnesses. A single witness shall in no case be examined."

Proof by Ordeal Claimed, Objected to, and Disallowed

Now to the plea of the Plaintiff Tula Rama Sarman in the absence of secular (ordinary) proof, he would claim the slave girl by canonical (extraordinary, i.e., ordeal) proof to be directed by the Pandita[15] (spiritual Judge) and not otherwise, the reply of Maninatha Sarman was that he could not accept extraordinary proof in the face of his possession extending over hundred years and four generations—Madhusudana Thakkura, Rupanatha, Thakkura, Maninatha Sarman and Prananatha Sarman, without any voice being raised on the part of the Plaintiff and without any interruption, the Plaintiff (at the same time) being quite close;[16] and if the mode of proof extraordinary was possible in the present case, then why not be the same applicable in a case where possession had been one of thousand years, there being no oral or documentary evidence (of title)? This strong reply has the endorsement of the Chief Justice and the members of his Sabha ("Parshat") on the authority of Katyayana:

> "Witness is stronger than inference, document is stronger than witnesses. An uninterrupted possession for three generations is stronger than these."

Nor can it be pointed out that there is contradiction by the text "*without title*"[17] etc., for its applicability is to cases where there be a total want of title, and for the reason that in the present case there obtains the existence of certainty consisting in the defendant's title-by-enjoyment as required by law. We are of opinion that really the texts "thief", etc.,[17] have applicability where on an enjoyment of possession by the man in possession for only a short period his want of right is established and subsequent to the determination of it in a suit, possession is enjoyed by stealth or even force even for a hundred years.[17] And how could it be otherwise? For both code-givers (Munis) and Digest-writers lay down the "possession-evidence" as an independent kind of evidence while they treat of the evidence "possession with (not without) title".[18] Hence, in the absence of secular (ordinary) proof in the matter of immovables, etc., where superiority of possession obtains, the jurisdiction of extraordinary proof is inhabited by the text of Pitamaha[19] which has been commented upon by Harinatha Upadhyaya, Misaru Misra[20] and other Digest-authors, the text being:

> "In controversies about immovables ordeals shall be avoided. These shall be established through witneses, documents and possession;"

the extraordinary proof being outside the scope, we hold the defeat of the Plaintiff Tula Rama Sarman and his several co-sharers Balli Sarman, Janak Sarman and others, who have failed to establish their case.[21] I am giving the document of victory in favour of the successful party the Defendant Maninatha Sarman who put forward evidence proving possession over hundred years, as required by law in respect of his proprietary right over the cheti.

(Sri Sachala Misra)

This order is addressed to the impartial ones: Judges temporal and spiritual (Dharmadhyaksbas and Panditas).

In the year 1716, Jyaishtha, bright, fortnight, 13, on Tuesday.

(Signatures at top-corners)

Concurrence herein: Sri Kalanatha Sarman	Concurrence herein: Sri Mathuranatha Sarman.
Concurrence: Sri Ratnapati.	Concurrence herein: Sri Umanatha.
Concurrence herein: Bhavanatha Sarman.	Concurrence herein: Sri Bachha.
	Concurrence herein: Sri Shadananesvara.

The date of the judgment is of great interest. It corresponds to the 10th June, 1794, i.e., a date 29 year after the grant of Dewany and a year after the date of the Permanent Settlement. Now, law-courts under the grant of Dewany were being instituted during 1793—1795 (Fifth Report, p. 33) and settlement with "the Raja of Tirhut" (Fifth Report, p. 453) had not been concluded before 1800.[22] The document having been found in the village of Dharampore, district Darbhanga, and manuscripts being current there in the handwriting of Sachala Misra, it is clear, as also from the Maithili script of the judgment itself, that the judgment was given in Tirhut Schala Misra according to Maithila geneologists was an officer of the Tirhut raja and a learned man who had been honoured by the Peshwas.[23] According in the judgment of the Privy Council in the case of "Baboo Ganesh Dutt Singh and Maharaja Moheshur Singh" (6, Moore's Indian Appeal Cases, 164) "the Raj of Tirhoot", (p. 170) or "of Sircar Tirhoot" (p. 189) had been "a Principality" p. 189, "a Subordinate Sovereignty" (p. 187) having Zamindars or Talookdars under it (pp. 189-90). The holders of the Raj were the "rulers" under a grant from the Muhammadan Emperor who conferred the ancient principality of Tirhut on one Mahesh Thakur, and the descendants of this Mahesh Thakur had been the "only rulers whom" the landholders "knew" (p. 190), for their ancestors had held their lands from them and "until the East India Company assumed the dominion over this territory" the Zamindars of Tirhut paid rents "as vassals or as holders" to these Rajas of Tirhut "who were the rulers of the Country", the Zamindars "knowing nothing of the Emperor from whom the grant to this founder of the family (Mahesh Thakur) was made". In the opinion of their Lordships of the Privy Council there was "no doubt whatever" that the Tirhut Raj "before the possession of the East India Company" "was a principality indeed". About 1822 "the remnant of it" the Privy Council found to consist of some 1,500 villages, and the status of the Raj reduced to a mere impartible Zamindary (p. 190).

From the same judgment it appears that the Raja of Tirhut at the date of Sachala Misra's judgment was Madhu Singh who succeeded to the Raj in 1775 (p. 167; 178) and retired to Benares in 1807 (p. 167). Sachala Misra, thus, must have been the Prad-Vivaka, Chief Judge, of Tirhut under Raja Madhu Singh. Madhu Singh succeeded to the Tirhut principality before the effective possession of the East India Company. Madhu Singh had troubles with the East India Company and did not accept a settlement, as observed above, till 1800. At or about that date the Raj of Tirhut and its judiciary must be supposed to have come to their close. Sachala Misra's jurisdiction in 1794, when his master had been quarrelling with the East India Company about his lands and privileges,[24] must have been reduced and confined to the private lands[24] of the old raj. and within a few years when the Company's courts were firmly established that exercise of judicial privilege of doing "injustice instead of justice" must have ceased. The judgment thus is one of the very last products of the Hindu court. The tradition found in the judgment had come down from the famous Kamesvara dynasty to whose possessions and powers or the principality the Rajas of Tirhut of the house of Mahesh Thakur succeeded according to the Privy Council decision,[25] and earlier times.

It is to the peculiar culture of Mithila where since the time of Janaka kings delighted in being learned like priests and priests became kings, where kings and queens preferred to be scholars—it is to that peculiar history which "does not centre round valiant feats of arms, but round courts engrossed in the luxurious enjoyment of literature and learning",[26] that we owe this longevity of Hindu Administration of Hindu Law. It is to the fact that "when eventually the first flood of Musalman invasion, coming down the Ganges, did overspread Bihar, it subsided leaving Mithila with Hindu kings still holding courts where poetry and learning were alone honoured"[27] that legal history owes this precious gift of Hindu Judgment.

NOTES AND REFERENCES

1. Mr. O'Malley sums up the situation: "The Muhammadan conquest passed over the land without sweeping away all the ancient landmarks. In some places the Muhammadans allowed the Hindu Chiefs to remain undisturbed in their possessions, and in other they appointed new men as ruling chiefs; but in either case they did not interfere with the internal administration so long as their tribute was paid. The Hindu rulers of Tirhut were therefore practically independent, so long as they acknowledged their submission to the Muhammadans by the payment of an annual tribute." *District Gazetteer Darbhanga,* p. 17.
2. He is a descendant of Rupnatha Thakkura mentioned in the Judgment.
2a. Jolly, Narada, I. 6, Jayaswal, Calcutta Law Journal, 1913, XVII, p. 59 *n.*
3. See the text cited by Mitra-Misra (p. 144). लेखकः प्राड्विवाकञ्च सभ्याञ्चैवानपूर्वशः।।
4. "The judge (officer) does all talking (vakta); the Sabhyas are examiners of matters to be proved; the king enforces judgment." Brihaspati, Mitra-Misra, pp. 41, 42.
5. The paper on which the judgment is written has been badly worn-off in several places but fortunately the decay does not seriously interfere with the text of the document. In preparing the facsimile of the writing the Survey of India Office had to retouch the faint letters.
6. For Answer see Brihaspati, IV; Narada II on varieties of Answer and burden of proof. (S.B.E., 33, pp. 24, 235) "That Answer is not true answer which is dubious, not to the point, too narrow, too extensive, or meeting one part only of the plaint." (Jolly, Narada, p. 240.) An Answer must correspond to the plaint *(ibid.,* III. 9, 241).
7. Compare Narada, III. 8, S.B.E. 33.241 (Jolly). "In the case of a denial the burden of proof rests with the plaintiff; in the case of a special plea (it rests) with the defendant". "What the claimant has fully declared word for word in the plaint that he must substantiate by adducing evidence" *(ibid.,* 27, p. 30). "Where defendant has evaded the plaint by means of a special plea, it becomes incumbent on him to prove his assertion, and he is placed in the position of a claimant" (31, p. 31). "In a plea of former judgment, all that is required in the shape of proof is to produce the previous decree" (Joly, Narada, p. 242).
8. It should be noticed that plaintiff does not offer to prove that Mati was his slave.

9. The text of the judgment गैरीव ... योग्यायां is not clear to me.
The text seems to be corrupt. I am not sure that the reasoning which follows has been fully brought out in the above translation. The defendant means that the second proposition is vitiated by the fallacy called *asadharana anaikantika.*
10. On the subject of slavery consult Aparарka, Y.II. 182-183. The mother of a domestic slave must be a slave woman according to Apararka. A slave girl attained freedom when the master had carnal connexion with her and she had a child born. (182)
11. This was a Fasli year, as 1201F., corresponds with 1716 Saka, the year of the judgment.
12. Yajnavalkya, II. 182.
13. "One who takes to flight after having received the summons; one who remains silent; one who is convicted of untruth by the deposition of the witnesses, and one who makes a confession himself: these are the four kinds of Avasannas (losers of their suit)." Narada, 32, p. 31.
14. See below. The witness was evidently 50 years of age.
15. On the judicial officer called Pandit, see my note in the Calcutta Weekly Notes, Vol. 17, p. 234 (n.).
16. Compare Apararka, II. 22-25, 27-29, on the subject of prescription, and prohibition of ordeal proof.
17. This is the text of Narada (see Apararka, II. 25).
18. See Yajnavalkya, II. 27-29.
19. Quoted by Apararka, II. 22.
20. Misaru Misra is a famous writer of the Mithila school. Harihara is another Digest-writer of Mithila who has been quoted by Chandesvara, the Law Minister of Haradeva Simha, King of Tirhut and Nepal, who was a contemporary of Tughlak Shah.
21. On the word *Hina* see Narada, 33 (p. 31).
22. O' Malley, Darbhanga, p. 144. Possession, dispossession, and re-possession went on since 1792 (Hunter, S.A., XIII. 211), the obstinate raja declining settlement, and putting forward claims to the whole of Tirhut, etc. The charge against the raja was that "instead of doing justice he has been the instrument of injustice" (O' Malley, p. 144).
23. Sachala's descendant, Babu Kesi Misra, B.A. (Darbhanga), I am told by Dr. Ganganath Jha, still holds a property in the Central Provinces originally given to Sachala Misra by the Peshwa.
24. Cf. Fifth Report, pp. 452-53. Private lands "milkeeut of Rajah Mahdoo Sing", p. 468.
25. 6, Moore, I.A., 189: "that before the time of *Mahesh Thakoor,* above two hundred years ago, before the original founder of this family, *Mahesh Thakoor,* came into possession of it, it was a principality."
26. C.J. Stevenson Moore, Muzaffarpur Survey and Settlement Report,
27. *Ibid.*

21

The Royal Court in Hindu Period (600 to 1200 A.D.)

M.K. DHAR

(The royal court formed an integral part of the palace, and was important seat of the government where the king, along with his officials, took important decisions pertaining to the welfare of the country. As welfare of the country directly resulted in the welfare of the royal family, the function of the royal court has been described as the protection of the royal palace.[1])

In Manasara,[2] the royal court, from an architectural point of view, has been described as a type of "building, an edifice and a public hall which indicates its varied uses". "These must have been suitable structural arrangements for the transaction of judicial, commercial and political business and for the reception of the courtly, well-born wealthy persons and kings and for gambling, (indulging in) merriment, social intercourse, debates and contests".[3]

The number of courts in a palace varied between two and five. In the palaces of the Rajput kings there were usually two courts—outer court and the inner court.[4] Harsha's[5] palace contained four courts, whereas Shukla[6] has deduced from the Samarangan Sutradhara five courts in the royal palace—two in the exterior, two in the interior, together with the central one reserved for the inauspicious and unhappy occasions.

The people who used to come for an audience with the king probably waited in the first court.[7] The second court in the palace variously called *Asthana, Rajya Sabha*[8] *Sabha, Sabha-mandapa* and *Bahya Sthana mandapa*[9] was used by the king for discussing the important matters of the state with his ministers.[10] It is here that after the death of Rajyavardhana, Harsha sought the advice of his principal officers.[11] In Kadambari the court officials of Chandrapida are described to have gathered in the *Asthanamandapa* for the discussion of an important matter.[12] In King Someshvara's kingdom even the common people could come and see the king in this court. That is why this court has been called by him as *Jana-vallabha.*[13] The use of the third court is not certain as no clear reference is available about its possible use. In Rajatarangini, there is a reference to the central hall[14] where the servants were waiting for the king who was inside the palace. In Harsha Charita, Bana mentions that in the first three courts of the palace subordinate kings were waiting to have an audience with king Harsha who was sitting in the fourth court.[15] It is quite likely that the subordinate rulers waited in different courts for the Emperor, in accordance with their rank and relationship with him. Kings of higher status probably waited in the third court.[16] The fourth court was used by the kines to converse with their favourites after the meals. That is why this court has been called *Buktasthanimandapa* in the Harsha. It is here thnt Bana come to meet Harsha.[17] Thus all court officials could attend on the kins in *Bahyasthanamandapa* whereas in *Ruktasthnnamartdapa* only the ministers, favourites and samantas of the kine had the access.[18] It is on the basis of these differences that V.S. Aggrawal has compared the *Bahyasthanamandapa* and *Ruktasthnnamandapa* to *'Darbar-i-Am'* and *Darbar-i-Khas* of the M*ughals.*[19] It was in the fourth court that kings and the queens were entertained[20] with magic shows.[21] dances[22] and music.[23]

The royal court in the palaces of the Rajput kings had usually two sections, the *Mahasathana* and the *Abhyantrasthana.* Only a select number of people, enjoying the fullest confidence of the kings, had an access to the *Abhyantr asthana* the inner court. The *Mahasthana,* on the other hand, was attended by the representatives of all classes who had any part to play in the administration of the state. Matters which did not need any secrecy were discussed in this assembly.[24] It seems that these two courts were identical to the second and the fourth court of the palaces discussed above.

Separate Court of Justice

It is quite certain that there was a separate court of justice. We learn from an ancient work that the court of justice had principal deities installed in it. It had seats for advocates and for state guests and the court was either square or circular in shape.[25]

These courts, were beautifully decorated with high arches, high banners[26] and white flage.[27] Their floor was inlaid with gems,[28] crystal stones[29] and they were sprinkled with sandal water, fragrant with the perfume of musk[30] and saffron.[31] The floor was further covered with bestrewn masses of flowers and a camphor powder.[32] The shining jewels[33] and the golden necklaces were hung there in a special design.[34] There courts were draped with white silken screens[35] and made fragrant with the burning of agaru.[36]

The courts were furnished with the large thrones for the king.[37] Throne meant for the king was called the lion-throne, as the statues of eight roaring lions were carved on it.[38] The lion-throne was made of gold,[39] jewels,[40] fine stones,[41] gems[42] and of ivory.[43] The lower part of the throne was furnished with three platforms studded with jewels.[44] The upper pillars of the throne were carved with beautiful maidens, a yawning crocodile with a jewelled necklace hanging from his mouth. The fore-part of the throne was carved with deadly animals.[45] The seats were covered with extremely fine drapery[46] and cushions were spread on the throne.[47] The foot-stool,[48] placed in front of the throne, was adorned with sapphires,[49] gems[50] and girt round with a band of rubies.[51] When the court was in session the king used to sit on this throne while being fanned by the maidens with chamaras.[52] In addition to the lion throne there were couches or seats for the king. However, such couches were provided in the courts where the kings sat informally to amuse themselves or to take some rest. This could be possible in the fourth court where the kings came after meals, for rest or entertainment. Such couches were covered by counter panes, scented with floral perfume, and were furnished with silk-pillows.[53]

The courts were also furnished with numerous other thrones, covered with cushions.[54] for the ministers, army generals, priests, officials, for the princes, friends and vassals,[55] who attended the court.

An excellent description of the court proceedings has been given by king Someshvara in Manasollasa. The king after sitting on the throne used to send his chamberlain to invite people to the court. First to enter the court were the ladies of the harem beautifully, adorned with fine clothes, ornaments, flower garlands and perfumed with scents. They were carried there in litters enveloped with cotton fabrics, attended by bearers, and cane-bearers who cleared the way of the people by uttering 'get out of the way' and 'get out of the way'. Having entered the court, those ladies took their seats on the sides and in the rear of the throne. Then the princes took their seats according to their ranks in front of the king. Then the priest, dressed in white garments and wearing ear-rings sat close to the princes. Thereafter, the *Amatyas, Mantrins* and *Sachives,* with suitable dress and ornaments, took their seats allotted to them by the king on the right and left side, in front of the king. Feudal lords of different regions (mandala) and heroes, headed by the leading hero, occupied their seats. After them officers in charge of districts and of villages, *Dharmakirtis,* officers in charge of *Artha, Kama,* of treasury, of garlands, of market rate, of weights and measures, of passports, of messengers, of islands, of criminal tribes, of sacred places, of roads, of gates, of body-guards; of infantry, of harems, of prostitutes, of sudras, etc., all dressed in the cotton coats with long arms and with auspicious head-dresses and golden ornaments, occupied their respective seats with their heads bent in royal devotion and with open hands held together and looking at the king.

Lastly, the chamberlain, under king's orders, let in such kings of other countries as had come seeking the king's protection. On entering the court, they had to prostrate before the king and get-up only when asked by the king who, thereafter, offered them seats according to their ranks. When seated, the king pleased them with kind looks and suitable words and also with suitable presents and lodged them in quarters befitting their position. Next, the king dispersed the princes, *mantrins, amatyas, sachives,* lords of mandalas, soldiers and expert courtiers with suitable greetings. The rest, present in the court were similarly sent away and thereafter the king himself left the court.[56]

It was daily business of the king in the court to please everybody gathered there, by smiling at the some, talking with some, offering seats to some, giving charity to some and by honouring some.[57] For, by honouring people in the court, king, it was presumed, attained progress, fame and glory.[58]

An analysis of the royal court described by king Someshvara throws a good deal of light on the contemporary society. Though the queens wore veils, yet they had a right to attend the court.[59] In addition to the queens, women of other countries also attended the royal court on invitation. These women were considered to be the ornaments of the court.[60] The priest's seat which was near the king shows that during this period the kings had come to rely heavily on them in regard to the religious matters and the interpretation of scriptures.

Court Etiquettes

The admission into the court was highly restricted. There were hosts of chamberlains who regulated the entry into the court.[61] Only those who had the permission of the king were let in by the chamberlains.[62] The chamberlain announced humbly, with folded hands touching his fore-hand[63] or by kneeling down in front of the king,[64] the arrival of a person who wanted to have an audience with the king. In the Rajput states the chamberlain held a very high position. He was charged with the duties of silencing the people who made noise, making all the officials do their prescribed duties, turning out the people who had no right to be at the court, showing respect with folded hands to those who deserved it, and many other duties. He taught newcomers to the court the right way to salute. Very often he had to be won over by offering rich presents, for it was through him that a person could have an easy access to the king.[65]

When coming into the court, the person had to be well-dressed and fully decorated with the ornaments.[66] On entering the court he had to prostrate before the king and then, at the king's command, had to take the seat allotted to him.[67] Nobody could leave when the court was in session, and those present in the court had to look constantly at the king.[68] When the king got up to disperse the *darbar,* every body had to stand and prostrate before him till he left the hall. Thereafter, they were also to disperse.[69]

The real object of these court etiquettes was to impress upon the feudatory kings and the royal officials the magnitude of the royal prestige and authority. It was necessitated by the fact that the king was the social symbol of the nation. He had a divine legend behind him, and that legend, throughout, continued to be entrenched in society, in thought as well as in expression. He was far above the masses and the status he enjoyed demanded of him a gorgeous life in its many facets. One of that aspect was the magnificence of the palace he lived in. Grandeur of the palace represented both the status and prestige of the king, and it was the function of the royal court to protect the royal palace,[70] and thus ensure the stability of the kingdom.

Notes and References

1. Samrangana Sutradhara, XV. 49.
2. Manasara, Eng. tr. Oxford Univ. Press, 1933, III 7-8, XVIII 200, XXXIV 552-63.
3. Acharya, P.K., Encyclopaedia of Hindu Architecture, p. 515.
4. *Loc. cit.*, 4.
5. Harsha Charita, (English tr.) E.B. Cowoll and F.W. Thomas, 1961, p. 56.
6. Vastusutra, Shukla, D.N., p. 363.
7. Harsha Charita, Cowell and Thomas, p. 56.
8. Harsha Charita Ka Ek Sanskritik Adhyayana, V.S. Aggrawal, Patna, 1964, p. 205.
   Prabandha Chintamani, Merutungacharya, (Hindi tr.), p. 78.
9. Harsha Charita Ka Ek Sanskritik Adhyayana, p. 205.
10. Nalachatnpu, Trivikrama Bhatta (1967), p. 50.
    Yashastilaka Champu, Somadeva Suri (Hindi tr.) Banaras, 1960, p. 225.
11. Harsha Charita Ka Ek Sanskritik Adhyayana, p. 205.
12. *Ibid.*, p. 205.
13. Abhilashatirtha Chintamani, Someshvara, Mysore, 1926, III. 11. 1216.
14. Rajaratangini, Stein, 1900 VIII. 307.
15. Harsha Charita, Cowell and Thomas, p. 56.
16. Vastu Shasira, D.N. Shukla, Chandigarh (1960), p. 363.
17. Harsha Charita, Cowell and Thomas, p. 56.
18. *Ibid.*, pp. 56-57; Kadambari, (Eng. tr.) by P.L. Vaidya, Poona, 1951, p. 26.
    Nalachampu, p. 202.
19. Harsha Charita Ka Ek Sanskritik Adhyayana, pp. 205-06.
20. Harsha Charita, Cowell and Thomas, p. 61.
21. Karpuramanjari (Suru's tr.), Poona, 1960, pp. 87-88.
    Shishupala Vadha, Magha, Bombay, 1917, p. III. 56.
    Maha Purana, XVII. 4.
    Rajatarangini, VII. 944.
22. Rajatarangini, V. 420.
    Shishupala Vadha, XIII. 56.
23. Nalachampu, p. 202.
    Mahapurana, 74, 528.
24. Sharma, Dashratha, Lectures on Rajput History and Culture, p. 110.
25. Vishwakarma, Introduction, p. XLIV.
26. Trisistisalakaputusacaritra, Hema Chandra, Vol. II, p. 160.
27. Yashastilaka Champu (Hindi tr.), p. 210.
28. Kadambari, (Eng. tr.) by P.L. Vaidya, p. 25.
29. Yashastilaka Champu, p. 213.
30. Kadambari (Eng. tr.), P.L. Vaidya, p. 25.
31. Yashastilaka Champu, p. 213.
32. Kadambari, (Eng. tr.), P.L. Vaidya, p. 25.
33. Yashastilaka Champu, p. 213.
34. *Ibid.*

35. Kadambari (Eng. tr.), P.L. Vaidya, p. 25.
36. *Ibid.*
37. Si-yu-ki, Beal's translation, 1906, Vol. II, p. 133.
38. *Ibid.*, Abhilashatirtha Chintamani; III. 9-1201-129. Satnrangana Sutradhara, XII. 24.
39. Nalachampu, p. 399; Navasahansaka Charita, Parimala Padma-Gupta (Hindi tr.), Varanasi, 1963, XVIII. 29.
40. Kiratarjuniyam, I. 38; Janakiharanam, Kumara Dass, Allahabad, 1966, VII. 59; Navasahansaka Charita, XVII. 29.
41. Harsha Charita, Cowell and Thomas, p. 56.
42. Chanda Caushikam, V. 25; Dasha Kumaracarita, Dandin, (Eng. tr.) Bambay, 1956, p. 151.
43. Prasanrraraghave, Jayadeva (Hindi tr.), Benaras, 1956, p. 40.
44. Abhilashatirtha Chintamani, III. 9, 1202.
45. Nalachampu, p. 399.
46. Si-yu-ki, Vol. II, p. 133.
47. Harivamsha Purana, 49.3; Agnipurana, Cal. 1901 (Eng. tr.), p. 783.
48. Kadambari, P.L. Vaidya, pp. 12, 25.
49. Harsha Charita, Cowell and Thomas, p. 58.
50. Si-yu-ki, Vol. II, p. 133; Kadambari, P.L. Vaidya, p. 25.
51. Harsha Charita, Cowell and Thomas, pp. 58-59.
52. Yashastilaka Champu, p. 213; Kadambari, P.L. Vaidya, p. 12. Mahapurana, 63.1.
53. Kadambari, P.L. Vaidya, p. 25.
54. Harivamsha Purana 49.3.
55. Mahapurana, Vol. 7; Trisistfsalakapurusacaritra (Eng. to.), Vol. III., p. 261.
56. Abhilashatirtha Chintamani, III.11. 1216-1300.
57. Mabapurana, V. 8.
58. Abhilashatirtha Chintamani, III. 11. 1301.
59. Rajatarangini, VIII. 928, 931.
60. Abhilashatirtha Chintanaani, III. 11. 1254-55.
61. Harsha Charita, Cowell and Thomas, p. 49.
62. Abhilashatirtha Chintamani, III. 11. 1216-1300. Harshacharita, Cowell and Thomas, p. 49.
63. (a) Kadambari, P.L. Vaidya, pp. 11-12.
    Karpuramanjari (Sum's tr.), p. 87.
    (b) Dashakumara Charita (Kale's tr.), p. 4.
64. Kadambari, P.L. Vakiya, p. 11.
65. Sharma, Dashratha, Lectures on Rajput History and Culture, pp. 111-17.
66. Abhilashatirtha Chintamani, V. III. 11, 1216-1300.
67. Harsha Charita, Cowell and Thomas, p. 121; Kadarabari, P.L. Vaidya, p. 18; Shastri Nilakantha: A History of South India, p. 193.
68. Kadambari, P.L. Vaidya, p. 14.
69. *Ibid.*, p. 20.
70. Samrangana Sutradhara, XV. 49.

22

The Angel and Devil in Indian Scriptures

Rev. H. Heras

INTRODUCTION

A treatise on Angelology, much less one on Demonology, does not exist in ancient Indian scriptures. Information about angels and demons must be patiently culled from innumerable passages spread throughout the vast range of Indian *sruti* (revelation) and *smrti* (tradition). Such has been the work of the present writer on this occasion. It is, as far as he knows, the first attempt at gathering all this information and piecing all these traditional fragments systematically in a scientific shape.

The Angels in Indian Scriptures

Since the demons are angels by nature, not different in their origin from the angels who people heaven, the first question that naturally arises is this: Are there real angels mentioned in Indian scriptures ?

To this question we emphatically reply in the affirmative: Angels are definitely mentioned in the ancient scriptures of India. They are called *devas*. This word is often being translated as "gods". But putting aside a few passages of the *Rgveda,* which may doubtfully be interpreted as polytheistic, later Indian scriptures are clearly monotheistic. Consequently the word *devas* cannot be interpreted as "gods" in a polytheistic sense.

The word *devas* etymologically means "bright being".[1] It comes from the same root as the Latin words *Deus, divus, dies,* which all bear the connotation of light and brightness, either spiritual or moral or material. In the case of the Latin word *Deus* it has finally come to signify not any "bright being", but "the Bright Being" par excellence, the Supreme Lord, the Creator God. But the fact that the *devas* in Sanskrit literature are very often mentioned in the plural, does not allow us to interpret this word thus. In point of fact there is a clear distinction established between the *devas* and God, when the latter is mentioned as "the Supreme *Deva* among all the *devas*".[2] "The word *deva*", says Berridale Keith, "undoubtedly denotes a being connected with the heaven. . . . What is clear is that in the use of the *Rgveda* the word has essentially this sense: the *devas* stand out against the demons".[3] Hence a numbers of authors have already translated the word *devas* as angels.[4] Among them there are a few Indian writers who, knowing the meaning of the word "angels" in the Bible and in Christian usage, do not hesitate to give this interpretation to the word *devas:* Dr. Ananda K. Coomaraswamy, for example, whose vast erudition in the field of Christian theology and asceticism is acknowledged by all,[5] and Swami Vivekananda, who studied Christian asceticism and lived long among Christians.[6] We may also mention Prof. Harischandra Sircar, of the University of Calcutta, an author of repute on mystical subjects,[7] and finally the great Mahatma Gandhi, who made a deep study of the Gospels.[8] Among Christian writers one is Prof. Rawson,[9] while the late Prof. Rhys Davids had already accepted this translation, at least for some time.[10]

That this translation of the word *deva* is correct may also be proved by the meaning of its contradictory *adeva,* by which negative name the demon *Vrtra* is called twice.[11] If *adeva* therefore means "a demon", *deva* cannot but mean "an angel".

Such a translation was contemplated as possible by that great eclectic spirit, Fr. Roberto de Nobili, S.J., in the beginning of the 17th century, when he wrote: "The noun *deva* may in a sense be used when speaking of the angels".[12] This interpretation is a visualisation of the problem in the same spirit as St. Augustin who also styles some so-called "gods" of the Platonists as "angels".[13]

The nature of these *devas* will confirm the correctness of our interpretation.

The Nature of the Angels

The first essential difference between God and the *devas,* is that the former is Self-subsisting, and the latter are created. It is acknowledged that God is the Creator of heaven and earth,[14] heaven being precisely understood not as the heavenly palace (which the Upanisads do not acknowledge as necessary), but "the heavenly ones" as the ascetic Manikkavasagar puts it.[15] In fact God speaks to Markandeya thus: "By my own *maya* (omnipotence) I create the celestials, the man...and all the mobile and immobile things".[16] The *devas* in fact are often described as created[17] and indeed out of nothing *(asat).*[18]

This creation was only done by the mind of God,[19] who besides supports them.[20] A few *devas* in particular are mentioned as created, for instance Agni, Indra and Soma,[21] the first two being of the highest rank. To another *deva* the following words are being addressed: "Thou art a *deva* coming into existence... Thou art becoming".[22] Hence the first period of creation is styled "the first age of the *devas*", for during it they passed "from *asat* (non-existence) into *sat* (existence)".[23] In other works the *devas* are mentioned as the first-produced of the creation.[24] The *devas,* therefore, being created, received their names from the Creator Visvakarman: "By whom alone their names were given to the *devas.*"[25]

What is the nature of these *devas 1* In one of the texts referred to above Indra, Agni and Soma are equated with Paramesthin Prajapatya under the common denomination of *devas*[26] Now Paramesthin Prajapatya is the first man created by Prajapati, "the Lord of creatures".[27] Could this text mean that the three mentioned *devas,* and all the rest by mere association, were like men ? There is an older text which explains the former one in no doubtful way. It refers to the Adityas, who, as we shall see later, are a kind of *devas.* It is there said that of the eight Adityas "the eighth angelic being (the last Aditya) is in human guise (*manusvat daivyam astamam*)".[28] Now these Adityas are called so, because they are sons of Aditi, the Absolute One, in whose spiritual nature they must naturally participate. They are therefore spirits, and so is also the soul of man, but the latter remains on the earth "in human guise". Hence the spiritual nature of the *devas* is clearly suggested in these texts, in such a way as to call the soul of man *daivyam* "angelic", because it is spiritual. This must be the reason why the creation of the *devas* is called in Vedic literature "the super-creation",[29] in opposition to the material-creation which is called creation pure and simple.

After studying all the Vedic texts concerning the *devas* Dr. Ananda Coomaraswamy describes further this spiritual nature of the angels, emphasizing their intellectual leanings. "The Angels (he says) [are] conscious intellectual substances, partaking of eternity as to their immutable nature and understanding, but of time as regards their accidental awareness of before and after, the changeability of their affections (liability to fall from grace, etc.) and inasmuch as the angelic independence of local motion, whereby they can be anywhere".[30] The clearness of their understanding is also admitted by Prof. Dasgupta, while studying the *Visnu Purana*. He says that God "created the *devas* who are always happy and can know both their inner feelings and ideas and also external objects, and communicate with one another".[31] Moreover, it is the opinion of the prince of Indian philosophers, Sankaracarya, that the angelic nature consists precisely in this that the daily food, as it were, of the *devas,* is the understanding of high metaphysical concepts. He says: "In that the angels are wonted to the use of *(grahana-priyah)* metaphysical notions *(paroksa-namani),* thereby it is that they are angels *(yasmad devah)*"; that is to say, in that theirs is the habit of first principles.[32]

As regards their habitat it is understood that the angels dwell in God's palace above the sky. "The *devas* dwell above".[33] They are certainly subordinated to the Supreme Being, whether He be called Brahma, Varuna or simply Isvara,[34] who, on the other hand, is described as "source and origin",[35] "Father"[36] or "Lord" of the *devas.*[37] Accordingly Varuna is said to be seated "among his people",[38] i.e., the *devas.* Another text introduces the *devas* in the presence of "Prajapati (being his) dear sons".[39] At a later period God is styled "Lord of hosts",[40] or "Lord of Heaven's host".[41] Moreover God is mentioned as united with the *devas,*[42] which union, both parties being spiritual, cannot but be spiritual also, i.e., a union of intellects and wills.

Beside, the *devas* are mentioned together with men as "co-sharers of gracious gifts".[43] What were these gifts which are called 'gracious', i.e., graciously given, as a grace from God? One seems to be immortality. So says a very ancient text: "After Aditi (the Absolute) were the blessed *devas* born, sharers of immortal life".[44] Besides they were endowed with brilliance, power and beauty.[45]

Some accidental differences among the *devas,* seem to be admitted, for certain groups of *devas* are mentioned as having different characteristics. These differences specially appear in the Upanisadic period, during which three hierarchies of angels are referred to, of whom the highest are simply called *devah* or "angels"; next to them come the "angels with respect to works", *karma-devah,* who are called *karmatmanah devah* or "angels whose self is works", by Manu,[46] and finally *ajanajah devah* or "begotten angels".[47] Another text puts two categories, the *Ksatras* or "potestates", such as Indra, Varuna, Soma, Rudra, Parjanya, Yama, Mrtyu and Isana; and the *Visas* or common ones, i.e., the Vasus, the Rudras, the Adityas, the Visvedevas and the Maruts.[48] Other kinds of *devas* are the Gandharvas, the Apsarasas, the Sadhyas, the Maharajukas, etc.[49]

The Function of the Angels—Rulers and Administrators

The first function which the *devas* seem to perform is that of helping God in the government of the world. In a text already referred to we read:

> Varuna, true to holy law, sits down among his people;
> Most wise sits there to govern this all.[50]

Evidently in these verses the Rgvedic poet depicts God as in his council of state; the *devas* cannot be called his counsellors but certainly those by whom God's decrees are immediately obeyed and put into practice for the government of the universe: "Whose commandment all the *devas* acknowledge".[51] In fact He is worshipped by them all.[52] After the study of the Rgvedic hymns Fr. Thomas Siqueira, S.J., acknowledges that the *devas* are "the guardians of the universal order (*rta*)",[53] and Prof. Lefever calls them "rulers and administrators".[54]

In order to fulfil God's decrees among men, the *devas* are God's messengers. "His messengers are seated around Him".[55] They come down to the earth by order of the Almighty. "His messengers hastily descend from heaven hither, surveying the whole world with their thousand eyes".[56] The *devas,* says a *rsi* of the Rgvedic age, "have arrived hither by the sending of this One".[57] Their main aim in this function as messengers is to make God known to all men, so that through this knowledge He might abide in their souls. Thus Vac, "the Word" of God, "first of those who deserve worship", says in a famous hymn: "Thus the *devas* have established me in many places with many homes to enter and abide in".[58]

As regards the material world the *devas* are supposed to preside over all the forces of the universe. Thus Varuna presides over the sky,

Agni over the fire, Vayu over the wind, Indra over the rain, Surya over the sun, etc.[59]

Modern Indian scholarship acknowledges this important function of the *devas*. Prof. Sircar, for instance, admits that the *devas* preside over the forces of nature.[60] The same is the opinion of the orthodox Hindus. "They (the *devas)*", says a sort of orthodox Hindu catechetical handbook, "are concerned with the material side of nature, and the guidance of its evolution; and all the constructive energies studied by science are the energies of the *devas*. On their work depend the fruits of all human activities concerned with production in all its branches".[61]

Equality of Nature between Angels and Demons

The equality of nature between the angels and the demons is one of the clearest points in Indian angelology. The demons, at least from the period of the *Brahmanas,* are generally called *asuras.*[62] "The asuras", says Keith, "also are more probably to be taken as the powers of darkness than as men".[63] Thus we read in one of the *Samhitas:* "Prajapati created the *devas* and the *asuras.*"[64] That this mention of both together meant equality of nature, and not only equality of origin, is explained by a *Brahmana* and indeed of another school: "At first the *devas* were all alike, all good."[65] The first two w.ords of this text, "at first" clearly suggest that this equality among all the *devas* did not last long; and consequently that some of these *devas* who "were all alike", *afterwards* became *different,* i.e., were turned into *asuras,* as the full text clearly shows. Hence when the former text avers that the *devas* and the *asuras* were all created by Prajapati, it means that all were created alike, having no difference among themselves, all endowed with the same high nature.

It is furthermore stated that both the *devas* and the *asuras* received from God a certain grace, which is not qualified: "The *devas* and the *asuras* both of them sprung from Prajapati, entered upon their father Prajapati's inheritance".[66] It is therefore evident that the *devas* and the *asuras,* both being equal by nature were likewise equally treated by God in the very beginning, without establishing any difference among themselves.

What was the cause of the difference that arose at a later period?

A Period of Trial for All the Angels

During the period that preceded the great upheaval about which we shall speak presently, the *devas* seem to have undergone a trial, the end of which was not the same for all. We read to this effect: "They say that the *devas* and the *asuras* (i.e., those who had to become *asuras)* strove together. Truly, the *devas* and the *asuras* did not thus strive together".[67] This striving is evidently the subjective effort to reach a success in the trial. The text says that they strove together, i.e., all strove at the same time, in the same trial, unitedly as it were; but suddenly the writer, as if checking himself, says: No, this is not correct; they did not strive together, for their efforts were different, they strove in opposite directions and consequently their success was not the same either. We have here clearly outlined the period of trial and the contradictory result at the end of that period.

More explicit still is a somewhat earlier text, in the midst of a protracted symbolism.

> "The *devas* and the *asuras,* both of them sprung from Prajapati, entered upon their father Prajapti's inheritance, to wit, speech—truth and untruth, both truth and untruth: they, both of them, spoke the truth, and they both spake untruth: and, indeed, speaking alike, they were alike. The *devas* relinquished untruth, and held fast to truth, and the *asuras* relinquished truth, and held fast to untruth. The truth which was in the *asuras* beheld this, and said, 'Verily, the *devas* have relinquished untruth, and held fast to truth: well, then, I will go thither'. 'Thus it went over to the *devas*. And the untruth which was in the *devas* beheld this, and said, 'Verily, the *asuras* have relinquished truth, and held fast to untruth: well, then I will go thither'. 'Thus it went over to the *asuras*. The *devas* spake nothing but truth, and the *asuras* nothing but untruth'.[68] In this text the period of trial is definitely marked in a symbolical manner. While it lasted, all *devas,* both those who were going to remain faithful *(devas)* and those who were going to fail *(asuras)* could speak truth or falsehood, i.e. adhere to virtue or commit a sin. Some of them did the former, others the latter. Here the text introduces truth and falsehood personified, following their respective votaries and remaining with them for good. The result of it was that the *devas* could not in future speak but truth, and the *asuras* but falsehood.[69] This final result evidently puts an end to the period of trial, for in future the *devas,* always speaking truth, could not commit any sin.

The *Avesta* of Persia also seems to suggest the same period of trial. In Zoroastrian literature the word *daivas* or *devas* is applied to the demons. Now it is said of them, that they "chose" the wrong side "for infatuation came upon them as they took counsel together so that they chose worst thoughts".[70] The verb ''choosing" seems to suppose a time where they could choose that way or another. Rightly therefore says Moulton that this verb "suggests distinctly that they 'kept not their first state'."[71] Hence they had undergone a trial, in which they had not been successful.

The Rebellion of the Angels

The end of that period of trial, during which there was no difference between *devas* and *devas* is always marked by a wrong deed committed by some of them. The general enunciation that the *asuars* spoke only falsehood is realised concretely in other texts. One says: "Originally the devas were all alike all pure. Of them, being all alike, all pure, three of them desired: May we become superior".[72] We have here a generic sin of pride mentioned as the cause of their rebellion.[73] This is the only text that refers to three *devas* as committing this sin; other texts are more general.

In the following one the generic sin of pride is mentioned more specifically. "The devas (once upon a time) did not acknowledge that Indra had the right of primogeniture and leadership".[74] The sin of the *devas* as a whole apparently directed against the first-born of the Almighty; but this was not Indra, who was only one of the *devas*. Yet the fact that he took the leadership against the rebels, as we shall see presently, may have been the cause of this confusion.[75] Consequently the *devas* did not want to acknowledge the authority of the first-born of God. Who was this? He is indifferently called Vac, "the Word" and Hiranyagarbha, the "Golden Seed", generated "the first of all",[76] "who was engendered in the beginning",[77] "a second to Him",[78] "before the *devas*".[79] Accordingly the authority of Vac seems to have been defied by the rebellioui *devas*.

Some other texts speak symbolically of this rebellion, though mentioning an outstanding evil *deva* by name: "The *asura* Svarbhanu struck the Sun with darkness. The *devas* desired an atonement for him".[80] The fact that the *devas* wished an atonement for Svarbhanu shows that he had actually committed a sin. The effect of this sin is expressed by the symbol of striking the Sun with darkness, a most appropriate symbol, for any sin is a spreading of darkness in the universe, and a sin committed in heaven may be properly described as an attempt to darken the face of the Sun itself.

There is still a third series of texts which refer to another rivalry among the *devas,* a text which may reflect a new aspect of this great conflict. It is narrated that there existed among men three brothers named Rbhus who were excellent artisans. Impressed by their reputation and skill, the *devas* deputed Agni to order them to fashion out of the cup of the *devas,* four others like it. They immediately accomplished their work. The *devas* were so pleased that they searched for the Rbhus in the world of men, and having finally succeeded they introduced them to the company of the *devai* themselves, where they found the reward of their industry. But not all the *devas* were satisfied. There was one called Tvastar who was deeply overcome by jealousy. Tvastar was, undoubtedly, one of the highest *devas.* since he is called *Bhuvanasya saksani* which means "Companion of the creation". But Tvastar had also been the workman of the *devas* and the cup out of which the Rbhus made four cups had been his own masterpiece. He was therefore infuriated against them.[81] Moreover it is recorded that some *devas* abhorred the Rbhus "on acconnt of their human smell".[82] We have here therefore the cause of a conflict between, on the one side, the *devas* who hated the Rbhus owing to their being men originally, all led by Tvastar, (also moved by personal jealousy); and, on the other side, the *devas* who invited the Rbhus to their company, at whose head was Indra, who is described as their greatest friend.[83]

We have in this mythological story all the elements that produced the outbreak: a division of opinion between two bands of *devas* caused by the fact that some did not want the company of the men who had been received among them. The modern Hindu interpretation acknowledges the existence of the element "man" in the original story, though interpreted to a rationalistic way. "The devil", says a modern author, "was the highest of the gods; he wanted to assert himself, to augment himself all at once, but God wanted him to wait and achieve his object through Time—Space—Causation. God ordered him to bow to Man=Time—Space—Causation. He would not; he rebelled; hence he was banished to the Nether Regions, from where he issues out in conflict".[84]

The Fight between the Good and the Evil Angels

The battle between the *devas* and the *asuras* is in a very ancient text briefly but unmistakably described. "The devas and the asuras were in conflict .... The *devas* having defeated (the *asuras)* . . .;"[85] or "The *devas* and the *asuras* were in conflict. . . . That was the highest victory that the *devas* won over the *asuras*".[86]

In the Brahmanic period the description of the battle is enlarged and becomes, as it were, an intellectual battle, i.e. in a spiritual sphere: "The *devas* and the *asuras* contended. The *devas* sang the *udgitha* with the mind. The *asuras,* running against this (mind) of them mixed with evil. . . . The *devas* sang the *udgitha* with breath. Then the *asuras* ran against it thinking: We will treat it in the same manner. As a clod of earth colliding with a stone would break to pieces, even so the *asuras* broke to pieces".[87] In another *Brahmana* the battle is more spectacular: "The *devas* went to war with the *asuras* in order to defeat them. . . . Having taken the shape of three rows, (they) attacked the *asuras* in three battle lines in order to defeat them......They defeated them beyond expectation. Then the *devas* put down the *asuras.* The enemy, the incarnate sin *(papman),* the adversary of him who has such a knowledge, perishes by himself".[88]

In this text a new element has ceen introduced which is of great importance. One *asura* has been singled out, and is called "the enemy, the incarnate sin". He seems to be the leader of the *asuras,* perhaps he who was named Svarbhanu in a text quoted before. Another later text says of him: "The enemy, the evil one, who hates him (Brahman) is defeated".[89]

In the same way another leader of the *devas* appears in the opposite camp. He is Indra, "the Lord of hundreds",[90] "mighty conqueror of hostile armaments",[91] "who hates the high and haughty",[92] "chief deva of lofty spirit by power and might became God's protector",[93] often spoken of as "the favourite son of Prajapati".[94] Even later non-Vedic works praise him above the skies: "The wise Deva, who immediately on his birth became foremost and who surpassed other *devas* in strength, at whose breath heaven and earth tremble on account of the greatness of his might".[95] "By earnestness did Maghavan (Indra) rise to the lordship of the *devas.*"[96]

All these texts not only emphasize the great strength and power of Indra, but also the magnificent effort he made in favour of God's authority, with an evident allusion to his fight against the *asuras.* Thus Indra in the *Rgveda* has some characteristics similar to Varuna which is there the name of the Supreme Being. "These two personalities", says Barth, "coincide in many respects. There is however this difference between them, that Indra has, above all, appropriated the active and, so to speak, militant life of heaven, while Varuna represents rather its serene, immutable majesty".[97]

This Varuna of the *Rgveda* becomes Prajapati at a later period. Indra on the contrary is depicted as a humble, submissive subject of Prajapati, by whose power, he defeats the enemy. "Indra had recourse to Prajapati, to him he gave these victories; he offered them; then indeed were the *devas* victorious over the *asuras*."[98] "Prajapati bestowed victories on Indra the strong, he who is dread in battle and contest".[99] This power given by Prajapati to Indra has been symbolised twice in an individual weapon, in the *Rgveda*. On one occasion it is said that Tvastar has wrought "a celestial thunderbolt for him".[100] When Indra realised the might of his enemy, the leader of the rebellious *asuras*, he is said to have feared him. "He ran up to Prajapati (saying) 'A foe has sprung up for me'. He (Prajapati) dipped his bolt and gave it to him (saying): 'Slay with it'. He went against him with it."[101] In another text it is Vac himself, the Word of God, who gives him a bow, "that his arrow may strike the hater of Brahma".[102]

The fight of Indra against the *asuras*[103] culminates in the slaying of their leader Vrtra, which is Indra's most heroic deed, mentioned a thousand times in all Vedic works. Thus Vrtra becomes the leader of the opposition, he who was called Svarbhanu in other texts. In this gigantic enterprise Indra, at one time, fights alone, at another, he is helped by the Maruts, Visnu and other *devas*. Vrtra, who is generally depicted as, and called, a serpent, Ahi, lies in the deep darkness of mountains keeping in with his coils the streams of waters. According to different versions Indra strikes Vrtra on his back, or smites his face, or pierces his vital parts by his hurling a thunderbolt at him. Vrtra, who is also named Ahi and Susna, is surrounded by a crowed of other monsters. The final result is the slaying of the monster.[104] On account of this Indra is always honoured with the title of 'Slayer of Vrtra'.[105]

It may be objected that Lucifer was not actually slain by St. Michael, as the Angels are naturally immortal. But the slaying of Vrtra is only symbolical: it refers to Vrtra's spiritual death. In the same strain it is said in the Prophecy of Daniel with reference to Lucifer or Satan: "And I saw that the beast was slain, and the body thereof was destroyed, and given to the fire to be burnt".[106]

This successful end of the fight for the defenders of the cause of God is reflected in a statement of the *Rgveda*, concerning the security of Varuna's power and kingdom. He is styled "the god whom enemies threaten not".[107] That is the reason why Barton states that "in India the struggle between the God and the demon is and will always remain an unqual one",[108] for God is triumphant *a priori*.

Some texts speaks of the feelings of the other *devas* during Indra's combat with Vrtra. It is first of all recorded that "the *devas* were afraid lest the Sun should fall down from the world of heaven."[109] This feeling of fear is especially recorded during the struggle when the snorting of Vrtra especially frightened them and they ran away leaving Indra alone, "When with terror all the *devas* shrank from the Dragon's furious might, fear of the monster fell on them".[110] This is also said in the case of the fight against Tiamat in Babylon.[111] Yet in the case of India this is expressly denied in the *Rgveda* when it is said that "the *devas* stood firm *(atistha),* each enlinked with the other *(susamrabhda),* during that calamity, when the pungent dust *(tivra renu)* arose as it were from the feet of dancers *(nrtyatam).*"[112] In point of fact it is even said in early Vedic literature that all "the *devas* had slain Vrtra".[113]

Yet in Indian *smrti* (tradition) another parallel story of this fight appears, which in some way is linked with that of Vrtra. It is narrated that when the rebellion of the *asuras* took place, let their leader be named Taraka, Mahisasura or any other name, Siva (God)[114] was in need of a son to oppose the evil one. It was then that Kartikeya was born.[115] When Indra heard that Siva's son was born to defeat Tarakasura "he was troubled thinking that his kingdom was taken away from him"; but, he recovered his peace of mind when he heard Siva saying to his son Kartikeya: "Thou wast born in order that thou mightest slay Taraka and protect the realm of Indra. Therefore, do your own duty". Skanda received from Agni a weapon of extraordinary efficiency in his combat with the *asuras.* It is called *sakti.* It possessed great lustre and seemed to blaze with light; when during the conflict Skanda repeatedly hurled this blazing missile, meteors and thunderbolts dropped upon the earth and millions of darts came out of it. Thus Skanda reduced millions of *asuras* to ashes and finally killed Tarakasura, their leader.[116]

There seems therefore to be some connection between the Son of God and the rebelion of the *asuras.* What this real connection was it is difficult to say. In preceding texts it is the Word of God who holds the weapon to Indra to destroy the *asuras.* Here it is the Son of God Himself who is deputed to fight the *asuras* and to uphold the kingdom of Indra. There is an evident confusion of terms from the original tradition.

This confusion grows round the person of Indra in other texts.

The Corruption of the Original Tradition

It is indeed strange that Indra, the great Deva who becomes the leader of those who defend the honour and sanctity of God, in later traditions takes on a doubtful character, one who looks after his own glory. That is finally the reason why he is depicted as jealous of the authority of the Son of God and is not satisfied till he hears from God Himself that the Son of God will make his realm safer and steadier. That text quoted above makes Dr. Ananda K. Coomaraswamy state that "Indra is an angel jealous of his throne",[117] without considering the earlier texts.

Proceeding further in this direction, in other texts he is described as fighting against the heavenly powers, and it is only by theft or bribery that he gets possession of the heavenly *soma* (ambrosia), which was originally Varuna's own property and was watched over by the Gandharva Visvavasu, otherwise named Krsanu.[118] In particular, he is shown fighting with Skanda himself, Siva's son. He is said to have hurled a thunderbolt on the Son of God, with which he pierced his right side; but out of the wound a golden youth named Visaka issued. At the sight of this phenomenon Indra realizes the superiority of Skanda garlands him and proclaims him generalissimo of the heavenly army for the destruction of the Danavas or *asuras*.[119] This tradition, which evidently flowed through the wrong channel, comes back again to the original source confessing the unity of action between Indra and Skanda.

More distorted still is another myth according to which Indra, after having slain Vrtra and won the victory in various battles, said to Prajapati: "I will have thy rank, that of the supreme deity; I will be great !" Prajapati, consequently said: "Who am I".[120] Thus, Indra is depicted as a second Svarbhanu, in open rebellion against God. Totally different from this, but for practical purpose as far as this from the original tradition, is the legend narrated in the same *Taittiriya Samhita,* according to which Indra does not kill Vrtra, but concludes a compact with him[121] co-operating as it were, with his evil intentions.

On the other hand some more ancient Vedic texts depict Indra as being sorry for having defeated the *asuras* and doing penance for that action, as if it were a sinful deed. It is related of Indra that, after having slain Vrtra, "like a scared falcon, he fled to the depths of space across and beyond the nine and ninety rivers". The *devas* sought him to bring him back. Prajapati told them: "He who first finds him will have the first share." The Pitrs (ancient ancestors gone to heaven) actually found him. The *devas* met him saying: "Our treasure dwells at home today", "for Indra is supposed to be the treasure of the *devas*".[122]

It is not strange therefore that Coomaraswamy after the study of all these spurious and contradictory traditions, and without considering the original one recorded in so many ancient texts, would have written this final opinion of Indra: "He must be regarded as a personification of the ego-principle, *aham, abhimana.* That ego-principle in Deity, set up as an independent person and usurping many of the divine functions, could have developed only as: (1) the king of an inferior heaven, or (2) as a demon deliberately laying claim to the supreme throne. The latter development seems to have taken place in Christianity, in the case of Lucifer-Satan, and likewise in the *Avesta,* where Indra and *daeva* are demoniac powers."[123] All this only emphasises the importance of starting the study of these ancient traditions from the correct viewpoint.

Final Punishment of the Asuras

We have already said that Vrtra is also called Ahi in the Veda.[124] Ahi means "dragon" or "serpent". "This is the first manifestation of a substantial change in Vrtra. The leader of the *asuras* is named Svarbhanu, before his fall, which, as we said before, means "Bright as the Sun" meaning that on account of his spiritual nature's close similarity to that of God, he shone as the Sun itself. Now he has become a serpent or dragon. So is Apep depicted in Egypt. He also rebelled against God and is fastened to the earth by the "hidden hand".[125] Again the enemy of God who fights against him, among the Hittites, is named the serpent Illujanka.[126] Maximus Tyrius narrates a fearful conflict between Cronos and the dragon Ophioneus for the lordship of nature, in the beginning of creation. Only when Cronos wins and the dragon is cast into the sea can Zeus set about his creative task.[127] Tiamat who fights against God in the Babylonian cosmogony is again depicted as a dragon in the stone monuments.[128] Our Vrtra must similar to Tiamat, for in a Vedic text he receives a similar name, "the black serpent, the Taimata, the brown serpent, the poison that is not fluid."[129] In these epithets the quality of darkness is emphasized to establish the contrast with his primitive brightness.

Now this dragon that was Vrtra is said to be "the Dragon of the Deep" *Ahi Budhnya.*[130] His dwelling therefore is not "above", with the *devas;* he is not "a heavenly one" any more. His dwelling is in the deep, consequently the furthest spot from heaven. What the nature of this deep be may be gathered from the very text we mentioned just now concerning Taimata. The latter is said to be "the daughter of Urugula, the evil one born with the black of all those who have run to their hiding-place".[131] The deep therefore is a hiding place where the *asuras* have run to cover their shame from the sight of the whole universe. In the Accadian language this place is called Urugala, which means "the great city" and denotes the great Nether World.[132] This is, so we understand, to be taken in a moral sense rather than in a physical one. It refers more to the worsening of their nature than to the place itself where they ordinarily live.

This idea of inferiority, of lowering their natural state, of degradation among all other creatures is also clearly implied in the Gospel phrase: "I saw Satan as a lightning fall from heaven;"[133] or when the author of the *Imitation of Christ* says: "The stars of heaven fell down."[134]

This lowering of the status of the *asuras* and in particular of their leader after their sin was well understood and vividly expressed by Fr. Nicholas Pimenta, a Jesuit Visitor of India towards the end of the 16th century, though he mistook the name and condition of the leader: "It was said", he writes, "that Hanuman was a god *(deva),* but owing to some sin committed by him, he was converted into a monkey with many other thousands of *devas.*"[135]

The Reward of the Devas

The rebellion of the *asuras* occurred during the period of trial of all the *devas*. According to Indian tradition the triumph of the faithful *devas* over the *asuras* ended this period of trial, for after the asuric defeat the *devas* are spoken of as receiving their reward. "O Indra, thou hast filled mid-air's wide region, and given the *devas* by battle room and freedom."[136] The victory of Indra therefore won room in "mid-air's wide region" for the *devas,* that is heaven; and that for good, as they were already in heaven before, and they will not be disturbed by fear of losing it at any time, which is the meaning of that freedom. The victory therefore placed them in the possession of their eternal reward.

This immunity from change with assurance of ever being associated with God in life everlasting is recorded beyond doubt: "Verily that God having struck-off the evil, (i.e.) death, of those *devas,* carried them beyond death."[137] Just as Vrtia is said to have been slain, for the life of grace was lost to him for good, in the same way the *devas* were carried beyond death, for they could not lose that spiritual life any more.

This full attachment of the *devas* to God is explained in contrast with the godless life of the *asuras*. (In Sanskrit the word *satya* means both existence and truth, and is rightly applied to God himself who is *satyasya satyam,* "the truth of truths, the Supreme Truth," "the Reality of realities"). It is therefore said of the period of probation that both the *devas* and *asuras* spoke truth and falsehood, *satya* and *asatya*. "Speaking alike, they were alike. Then the *devas* abandoning falsehood, adopted truth; while the *asuras* abandoning truth adopted falsehood... The *devas* then spoke entirely truth and the *asuras* entirely falsehood".[138] On this account it is also said of the *devas* that "they keep one law, namely, *satya*";[139] and even that "they are *satya*".[140] Elsewhere also the devas are styled "Lords of truth and *rta* knowing."[141] *(Rta* is the eternal uncreated Law, which in the *Rgveda* is identified with God himself).

This knowledge of *rta,* that is, of God, was to be their eternal reward in heaven; this is perhaps the reason why it is said that "the *devas* in going to the world of heaven were afraid of ignorance"[142] i.e., were afraid lest they should not understand fully the subject of their knowledge, i.e. God. In fact another text depicts the *devas* saying to one another: "Come ! Let us search out that Self (Atman=God), the Self by searching out whom one obtains all world and all desires!"[143] This knowledge did the *devas* fully obtain; hence it is said: "Verily the *devas* who are in the Brahma world reverence the Atman".[144]

Part of this reward of the *devas* is the exaltation of Indra as the Supreme Prince of the heavenly host. His *mahabhiseka* (anointing ceremony) is described at length with an extraordinary richness of details. It is as follows:

> "The *devas,* headed by Prajapati, said to one another (pointing with their hands to Indra): "This one is among the *devas* the most vigorous, most strong, most valiant, most perfect, who carries best out any work (to be done). Let us instal him (to the kingship over us)." They all consented to perform this ceremony *(mahabhiseka)* on Indra. They brought for him that throne-seat, which is called Rg-formed .... They made Glory its covering, and Fortune its pillow, Savitar and Brahspati were holding its two fore-legs, Vayu and

Pusan the two hind-legs, Mitra and Varuna the two top-boards, the Asvins the two side-boards.

"Indra then ascended the throne-seat, addressing it thus: "May the Vasus ascend thee with the Gayatri metre, with the Trivrit Stoma, with the Rathantara Sama. After them I then ascend for obtaining universal sovereignty. May the Rudras ascend thee with the Tristubh metre, the fifteen-fold Stoma, and the Brhat Sama. After them then I ascend for obtaining increase of enjoyment. May the Adityas ascend thee with the Jagati metre, the seventeen-fold Stoma, and the Vairupa Sama. After them I ascend for obtaining independent rule. May the Visvedevah ascend thee with the Anustubh metre, the twenty-one-fold Stoma, and the Vairaja Sama. After them I ascend for obtaining distinguished rule. May the divine Sadhyas and Aptyas ascend thee with the Pankti metre, the Trinava (twenty-seven-fold) Stoma, and the Sakvara Sama. After them I ascend for obtaining royal power. May the divine Maruts and Angiras ascend thee with the Atichandas metre, the thirty-threefold Soma, and the Raivata Sama. After them then I ascend for obtaining the fulfilment of the highest desires for becoming a great king, for supreme mastership, independence, and a long residence." By these words one should ascend the throne-seat.

"After Indra had seated himself on this throne-seat, the Visvedevah said to him: "Indra cannot achieve any feat if he is not everywhere publicly proclaimed (as hero); but if he be thus proclaimed, he can do so." They then consented to do so, and consequently turning towards Indra, cried aloud (calling hin by all his titles).

"The *devas* bestowed on him (Indra), by proclaiming him as "universal ruler", universal rule; by proclaiming him as "enjoyer (of pleasures)", they made him father (of pleasures); by proclaiming him as "independent ruler", they granted him independence of rule; proclaiming him as "distinguished king", they conferred on him royal distinction; by proclaiming him '"king", they made him father of kings; by calling him "one who has attained the highest desires", they granted him fulfilment of the highest desires.

"The *devas* then continued proclaiming his heroic virtues in the following manner: "The Ksattra is born; the Ksattriya is born the supreme master of the whole creation is born; the devourer of the (hostile) tribes is born; the destroyer of the hostile castles is born; the slayer of the *asuras* is born; the protector of the Brahma is born; the protector of the religion is born."

"After his royal dignity was thus proclaimed, Prajapati, when just about to perform the inauguration ceremony, recited over him (consecrated him with) the following *mantra:*

> "Varuna, the faithful, sat down in his premises—for obtaining universal rule, enjoyment (of pleasures), independence, distinction as sovereign fulfilment of the highest desires—he, the wise, etc." (1,25,10). Prajapati, standing in front of Indra who was sitting on the throne-seat, turned his face to the west, and after having put on his head a gold leaf, sprinkled him with the moist branch of an Udumbara, together with that of a Palasa tree, reciting the three Rk verses, *ima apah sivatama,* i.e. these most happy waters, etc. {*Ait. Br.,* 8, 7); and the Yajus verse, *devasya tva (Vajasan. Samh.,* 1, 10, *Ait. Br.,* 8, 1); and the great words ....

"Indra thus became by means of this great inauguration ceremony, possessed of the power of obtaining anything wished for, as had been only the prerogative of Prajapati. He conquered in all the various ways of possible conquest and won all people. He obtained the leadership, precedence, and supremacy over all *devas.* After having conquered the position of a *samraj* (universal ruler), etc., he became in this world self-existing *(svayambhuh)* an independent ruler, immortal, and in the heaven-world, after having attained all desired wishes for, he became immortal".[145]

As a result of this enthronement Indra is often described in the epic as surrounded with three hundred and thirty-three millions of *devas.*

The Fight Between the Devas and the Asuras in Myth and Iconography

The gigantic struggle described above between the *devas* and the *asuras* has found an echo in Epic and Puranic literature a thousand times,[146] and has consequently been represented plastically very often in the vast field of Hindu iconography. We shall study a few cases only just to show the effect produced by the tradition in the national folk-lore and in the field of sculpture.

Fights of the *asuras* against the *devas* are very often mentioned in later Sanskrit literature. The war of the demon Taraka against the *devas,* is the cause why Kamadeva wounds the widower Siva with his arrows of love, to turn his mind towards Parvati, (a new form of his previous wife Sati) who could beget him a son who will defeat

Taraka.[147] Two more *asuras* Sumbha and Nisumbha are also mentioned as having waged war against all the assembly of the *devas,* who having sent Mahamaya (Durga) against them obtained through her not an easy victory.[148] Another asura Jalamdhara helped by an army of *asuras* who had heads of horses, elephants, camels, cats, tigers and lions, rebelled against the *devas* and for some time he succeeded expelling them from heaven. But the *devas* under the leadership of Siva attacked the army of the *asuras* and after a number of episodes a single combat between Siva and Jalandhara ensued, at which the latter is slain, this being the end of the rebellion.[149]

Fights between *asuras* and Siva, as in the last battle of the preceding rebellion, are very numerous. "He", as Sir William Jones noted long ago, "is represented in human form . . . some times in the act of trampling on or destroying demons".[150] One of such representations is the well known image of Siva as *Nataraju* ("the King of Dance"), whose left foot stamps a pigmy demon. Another is a statue very often found in South Indian temples called *Gajasamharamurti.* They say that a demon in the shape of an elephant once attacked Siva who killed him, and having removed its skin he danced with it in his hands. Siva in fact in these images is shown having one of his feet upon the head of the elephant whose skin is fully spread as the background of the image by his own hands.[150a]

Another myth relates how from one of his own hairs Siva produced a gigantic demon named Virabhadra, who had to punish Daksa, one of Siva's enemies who had slain his wife Sati.[151] Virabhadra is often represented in iconography as a furious form of Siva himself.[152] Perhaps on account of this and similar cases Siva is given the title of Bhutesvara or "Lord of Bhutas", who are ugly malicious spirits not different from demons.[153]

Visnu also is spoken of as fighting with demons on different occasions. Such was for instance the occasion of some of his *avataras* or incarnations. Thus it is said that the strong demon Hayagrva approached Brahma when he was sleeping at the close of the last *kalpa* (age of the world) and stole from him the Vedas which had flowed from his lips. This caused the flood of the world wherein the Vedas were going to perish. Visnu took the form of a fish *(Matsya avatara),* slew the demon and thus recovered the sacred books.[154] In another flood, so it is said, the whole earth was in the bottom of that sea. Again Visnu took the form of a boar *(Varaha avatara),* plunged into the waters and soon after arose with the earth upon his tusk. But he was seen by the demon Hiranyaksa, who claimed the earth as his property and defied Visnu. They fought upon it and the demon was finally slain.[155]

There is still another incarnation of Visnu engaged in exterminating demons, and that is Krsna, the most popular *avatara* of Visnu in modern times. From his very boyhood he is described doing this task faithfully. A great demon named Kansa successively sent against him three demons, two of them in the shape of a colossal crane and an immense snake. But the three were slain not without a fight by the young hero.[156] Iconography represents the young boy fighting and subduing another serpent named Kaliya, but this does not seem to be an *asura* in the spiritual sense of the term, but one of the ancient Naga chiefs dwelling on the banks of the Yamuna.[157] Nevertheless Krsna is very often represented in iconography killing Kaliya as a serpent, as if the latter were a demon: Krsna as a little boy is shown dancing upon the serpent's head while he holds the tail of the serpent with his left hand.

On another occasion Krsna is said to have been attacked by another demon called Kesin, who appeared in the shape of a horse. Krsna also slew him, whence one of his titles is Kesava, "the slayer of Kesin."[158] Finally another demon called Arista, in the shape of a fierce bull, met with the same fate at the hands of the courageous youth.[159]

Another of Visnu's incarnations, Balarama is also described as having squeezed another demon called Pralamba while the latter carried him away by deception and magic.[160]

Another story renews the original fight between the *devas* and the *asuras*, when a mighty demon named Durga waged war against heaven and succeeded in dethroning Indra; but on this occasion Siva deputed his wife Parvati to defeat the monster and his army. The battle is described at length. Durga even took the form first of an elephant and then of a buffalo, but at the end he reappeared as a great giant, the original form. After Parvati slew him, she took the feminine form of the demon's name, by which she is known as Durga.[161] Iconography very often reproduces this story in a statue styled "Mahisasuramardhini". Parvati is shown with her foot upon a buffalo. The buffalo's head is cut off and from the beast's neck the giant issues. Parvati is going to pierce him with her trident. In a famous stone relief panel at Mahabalipuram, there is another iconographical expression of the fight. The two opposing armies are very well represented. Parvati flies to encounter her enemy mounted on her usual vehicle, the lion. Durga appears as a colossal giant with the head of a buffalo. This is one of the greatest specimens of Indian sculpture dating from the 5th century A.D.

In another myth Indra himself is shown righting successfully with a demon called Kesin.[162] But the most interesting demoniacal myth concerning Indra is the life long feud between him and Jalamdhara, because the myth is an echo of the wrong tradition of Indra's fight, which we have commemorated above. On a certain occasion Indra accompanied with the other *devas* betook themselves to Siva's abode on Mount Kailasa to entertain him with music and dance. Siva delighted with their music, tells Indra to ask a boon. Indra in a defiant tone, asks that he might be in battle a warrior like Siva himself. Accordingly Siva granted the boon, but no sooner had the *devas* left than Siva asks his attendants if they had not noticed Indra's haughty tone. As a result of this Jalamdhara was born to combat Indra; but he, having finally succeeded in his enterprise and having expelled the *devas* from heaven, turns against Siva himself by whom he is slain, as we have described above.[163]

In any case the idea of the kingdom of Indra and his superiority over all the *devas* as the result of his victory over the *asuras* has deep roots throughout the vast field of Indian mythology. In one of the Jaina caves at Ellora there is a colossal statue of Indra crowned as a king seated on an elephant his ordinary vehicle. And since a king must also have his Queen, the latter, Indrani, is also represented in a similar way at the other side of the cave.

It may easily be noticed that it is a general practice to describe the demons in the shape of animals or as having animal heads at least. It is a practical admission that the attitude of the demon in creation, as the constant rebel, is unreasonable, or perhaps that by their suggestion and temptation man is led to yield to the lower animal passions and feeling which assimilate him with the animals.

The Intervention of the Demon in the Original Fall of Man

Ancient Indian scriptures and tradition leave no doubt as regards this point: The devil invited man to break God's law. First of all they speak of the reason why the devil acted thus: "The *devas* saw that in man were divine things (*devata),* which would enable him to succeed them in heaven after he had lived well on earth."[164] These *devas* had evidently been expelled from heaven, for they realized that man living well on earth would *succeed to them in heaven*. They were therefore *asuras*. These divine things they saw in man, by which he could obtain the possession of heaven, if they were really divine, cannot but be God's grace. The general tone of the text is of envy though this passion is not expressly mentioned. The *devas* were not pleased at seeing that men could succeed them in heaven by making good use of these *devatas* during their life-time. It is therefore implicitly understood that these *devas* would try their best to hinder this future happiness of man by tempting him to break God's laws.

This temptation is clearly described in the religious traditions of the Khasis of Assam. It is said that in the beginning, when man was happy, he "met a stranger, who was eating some food out of a net in his hand. The stranger, who was a demon in disguise, tempted man with the strange food." First man resisted the temptation, but finally he yielded to the invitation of the demon, and from that time, he and the entire human race had become subject to the power of the demon."[165] The temptation therefore came from outside man, and the devil was the mover. Owing to this sin, so says the tradition, the whole human race became subject to the devil.

The Devil in Man's Daily Life

The envy of the devil before the prospect of man's occupying the seat from which he was expelled from heaven (as revealed in the text of the *Jaiminiva Brahmana),* which caused him to tempt man to commit the original sin, is quite enough to urge him likewise to tempt men during their life time. Yet, in ancient Sanskrit ascetical books one does not come across any information about the temptations of the devil, perhaps because those books are concerned with the positive practice of ascetism, as acquisition of knowledge *(gnana)* and attainment of renunciation *(sannyasa),* rather than with the negative side of the same that is destroying evil and resisting temptations.

Nevertheless the idea that the devil was much interested in the evil doing of men and busy to make them fall from the path of virtue existed among the ancient Hindus, as Buddhist literature clearly shows.[166] The idea of the devil's temptations of a man is clearly disclosed while studying the life of the Buddha himself. The early writers who narrated the history of their master intertwined a number of temptations in the historical process of his meditation and ascetical life, not perhaps as they actually occurred, but as they themselves considered as likely to hava occurred. This is still much more interesting for studying the psychological process of the temptations, according to the Hindu mind.

So, for instance, narrates Asvaghosa Bodhisatva after having described Gautama doing his protracted meditation under the Budh-Gaya tree: "The spirits, Nagas and the heavenly multitude all were filled with joy (when they saw the Buddha in that fervent attitude) ; but Mara Devaraja (such is the devil's name in Pali literature), enemy of Religion, alone was grieved and rejoiced not; lord of the five desires, skilled in all the arts of warfare, the foe of those who seek deliverance, therefore his name is rightly given Pisuna".[167]

This is only the introduction to explain the future intentions of man's enemy. These intentions are revealed in a speech the devil is supposed to have made to his daughters *(sic)*. This speech is as follows: "His (Buddha's) object is to get the mastery in the world, to ruin and destroy my territory; I am myself unequal to him, for all men will believe in him, and all find refuge in the way of his salvation; then will my land be desert and unoccupied. But as when a man transgresses the laws of morality, his body is then empty, so now, the eye of wisdom not yet open in this man, whilst my empire still has peace, I will go and overturn his purpose, and break down and divide the ridge-pole of his house".[168]

Accordingly Mara addresses Gautama very diplomatically, not advising him to do anything wrong lest his advice should not be heard. He ever leads him to the practise of charity, his only wish is that he should give up the meditation he had begun. But if the Sakyamuni continues the same way, Mara threatens him with his poisonous darts. It is of interest to study the logic displayed in this made up speech of the devil. Here it is:

> "Ksatriya! rise up quitely ! for you may well fear ! your death is at hand; you may practice your own religious system, but let go this effort after the law of deliverance for others; wage war in the field of charity as a cause of merit, appease the tumultuous world, and so in the end reach your reward in heaven. This is a way renowned and well established, in which former saints have walked, *tin's* (sages) and kings and men of eminence; but this system of penury and alms-begging is unworthy of you. Now, then, if you rise not, you had best consider with yourself, that if you give not up your vow, and tempt me to let fly an arrow, how that Aila, grandchild of Soma, by one of these arrows first touched, as by a fanning of the

wind, lost his reason and became a madman. And how the *rsi* Vimala, practising austerities, hearing the sound of one of these darts, his heart possessed by great fear, bewildered and darkened, he lost his true nature; how much less can you—a late born one—hope to escape this dart of mine. Quickly arise then ! if hardly you may get away ! This arrow full of rankling poison, fearfully insidious when it strikes a foe ! See now ! with all my force, I point it! and are you resting in the face of such calamity ! How is it that you fear not this dread arrow? Say ! Why do you not tremble?"

Mara finally discharged his arrow and at once the three daughters of Mara came in front of the Bodhisatva. Yet the latter did not look at the arrow nor regarded the women, but he with shut eyes, montionless continued his meditation.[169]

This defeat did not discourage Mara in his evil intentions. He forthwith assembled his army of devils round the Bodhisatva to shake his undisturbed constancy. These devils are described minutely: "Each assumed his own peculiar form; some were holding spears, others grasping swords, others snatching up trees, others wielding diamond maces; armed with every sort of weapon. Some had heads like hogs, others like fishes, others like asses, others like horses; some with forms like snakes or like the ox or savage tiger; lionheaded, dragon-headed and like every other kind of beast. Some had many heads on one body-trunk with faces having but a single eye and then again with many eyes; some with great-bellied mighty bodies. And others thin and skinny, bellyless; others long-legged, mighty-kneed; others big-shanked and fat-calved; some with long and claw-like nails. Some were headless, breastless, faceless; some with two feet and many bodies; Some with big faces looking every way; some pale and ashy-coloured; others coloured like the bright star rising, others steaming fiery vapour, some with ears like elephants, with humps like mountains, some with snaky forms covered with hair. Some with leather skins for clothing, their faces partly-coloured, crimson and white; some with tiger skins as robes, some with snake skins over them, some with twinkling bells around their waists; others with twisted screw-like hair, others with hair dishevelled covering the body, some breath-suckers, others body-snatchers, some dancing and shrieking awhile, some jumping onwards with their feet together, some striking one another as they went. Others waving in the air, others flying and leaping between the trees, others howling, or hooting or creaning, or whining, with their evil noises shaking the great earth".[170]

The purpose of Mara was to disturb the Bodhisatva in his pious enterprise and to make him interrupt it. But he did not succeed; Gautama remained calm and unshaken "surrounded with an uncounted host of devils, shaking the heaven and earth with sounds ill-omened".[171] These numberless hirelings of Mara could not stand that unexpected rout. "Like as when some cruel chieftain slain, the hateful band is all dispersed and scattered, so the host of Mara disconcerted fled away".[172]

Nevertheless Mara did not consider himself finally defeated. Even when Gautama had already finished his meditation and become a Buddha, Mara tempted him with feelings of desperation. "Thou art bound by fetters, and canst not escape me", he told the Buddha. But he received the following uncompromising reply: "I am delivered from all fetters, from all desires: thou art defeated".[173]

After this, it is said that Mara did not leave the Buddha alone. The Nikayas very often commemorate these temptations which are always rejected by him while saying: "I know you, evil one" or "wicked one". They say that when he was already an old man, this thought was still inspired by the devil: "Now all your mission has been accomplished: disciples, monks and nuns, laymen and laywomen have been trained, who can teach and explain the doctrine to others. Let the Blessed one enter on his final extinction." The Buddha still replied that he would die at the prescribed time, not at the time, selected by Mara.[174]

Such is thb daily intervention of the devil in the life of man, according to Hindu ideas. The evil spirit is the ill-adviser of man on all occasions. This interference of the devil in procuring the evil of man, both in the physical and in the moral realm, is undoubtedly the foundation of the so-called "demon worship".

It is not correct to say, as has been unfortunately stated that "demon worship" is "so closely combined with Hinduism that it is now impossible to discriminate the rival elements". This worship first of all is not worship at all, but only propitiation not to be persecuted by the devils. It is an act born out of fear, not caused by devotion.[175] Nothing is said about it in Indian scriptures; it is only a popular practice, very common in South India not among the Dravidians, but among the aboriginal population only.

Conclusion

The story of the devil, as has been studied from ancient Indian scriptures, is a striking confirmation of what we know of the nature, rebellion and intervention of the devil in the life of man, from the time of our first parents' fall in the earthly paradise, from the biblical text. Has there been any influence from either side? We cannot trace it at all, nor do we consider it probable.

The modern study of the religions of the ancient civilized nations, as well as of the myths of primitive tribes and peoples, have revealed many such extraordinary similarities between those faiths and those legends and some biblical dogmas. A fortuitous coincidence cannot explain them nor is it a sound principle of criticism to suppose a general influence from one to another in all the cases. Independent anthropologists have explained these parallelisms by invoking the first original revelation of God to man. Relics of this revelation are found in all the nations. The faith of the Indian nation in the nature, sin and punishment of the devils, as well as in their intervention in the Fall of mankind is only one of those relics, which Indian *sruti* has preserved, by a wonderful Providence of God, for the enlightenment of the people of India in the high tenets of the true religion.

Notes and References

1. Cf. Griswold, *The Religion of the Rigveda,* pp. 106-107; Macdonell, *Vedic Mythology,* pp. 156-58.
2. *Svetasvatara Upanisad,* VI, 7.
3. Keith, *The Religion and Philosophy of the Veda and Upanishads,* I, p. 75.
4. John Bunyan, when describing Beulah "upon the borders of heaven" calls the Angels "the Shining Ones". *The Pilgrims' Progress,* p. 153.
5. Coomaraswamy, *A New Approach to the Vedas,* pp. 8, 11, 104, n. 116; Coomaraswamy, "The Growth of Indian Philosophy" in Radhakrishnan—Muirhead, *Indian Philosophy,* p. 132 and *passim;* Coomaraswamy in *Isis* No. 55 (April 1933).
6. Vivekananda, *The Science and Philosophy of Religion,* pp. 124, 343.
7. Sircar, *Mysticism in Bhagavat Gita,* p. 156.
8. Gandhi, *Christian Missions,* p. 33.
9. Rowson, *The Katha Upanisad,* p. 188.
10. Cf. (Mrs.) Rhys Davids, *Indian Religion and Survival,* p. 31.
11. *Rgveda,* III, 32, 6; VI, 22, 11.
12. de Nobili, *Catechism,* II Khanda, ch. II *(Nobiliana,* II, p. 178: Archives of the Madura Vice-Province S.J., Shembaganur, S. India).
13. St. Augustin, *De Civitate Dei,* X, 1: Migne, P.L., XVI, col. 277.
14. *Svetasvatara Upanisad,* III, 3.

15. *Tiruvasagam*, III, v. 18 (Pope's ed., p. 19).
16. *Mahabharata,* Vana Parva, CLXXXIX, v. 30.
17. *Taittiriya Samhita,* 37; *Satapatha Brahmana,* X, 4, 2, 2; XI, 2,3,1; *Jaiminiya Upanisad Brahmana,* 2,4,1; *Taittiriya Brahmana,* II, 8, 8, 9; *Brhadaranyaka Upanisad,* I, 4. 11; *Aitareya Upanisad,* I, 2, 1.
18. *Atharvaveda,* X, 7, 25. Plato also speaks of "created gods" in the *Timaeus.* Cf. Caird, *The Evolution of Theology in the Greek Philosophers,* p. 191.
19. *Taittiriya Samhita,* 1, 2, 3.
20. *Svetasvatara Upanisad,* III, 4; IV, 12.
21. *Satapatha Brahmana,* XI, 1, 6, 14. As regards Indra cf. *Rgveda,* IV, 18, 1-2.
22. *Jaiminiya Upamisad,* III, 20, 3.
23. *Rgveda,* X, 72, 2.
24. Cf. *Satapatha Brahmana.* XI, 2. 3, 1. Yet in *Rgveda,* X, 129, 6, the *devas* are said to be "later than this world's production". This passage is wrongly understood by Dr. Betty Heimann, *Indian and Western Philosophy,* p. 43. This otherwise very erudite authoress here confuses "God" with "the gods"; they are in fact very different.
25. *Rgveda,* X, 82, 3.
26. *Satapatha Brahmana,* XI, 1,6, 14.
27. *Satapatha Brahmana,* XI, 1, 6, 17. Cf. *Brhadaranyaka Upanisad,* II, 6, 3; IV, 6, 3.
28. *Rgveda,* II, 5, 2.
29. *Brhadaranyaka Upanisad,* I, 4, 6.
30. Coomaraswamy, "The Growth of Indian Philosophy", *op. cit.,* pp. 126-27.
31. Dasgupta, *A History of Indian Philosophy,* III, p. 501.
32. Sankara in his commentary on the *Aitareya Upanisad,* III, 14.
33. *Rgveda,* I, 25, 9.
34. Cf. Macdonell, *Vedic Mythology,* pp. 11-14.
35. *Svetasvatara Upanisad,* III, 4.
36. *Rgveda,* I, 69, 1.
37. *Atharvaveda,* IX, 10, 24; *Svetasvatara Upanisad,* IV. 7 and 13; *Bhagavad Gita,* XI. 20.
38. *Rgveda,* I, 25, 10.
39. *Jaiminiya Upanisad Brahmana,* II, 4, 1.
40. *Srimad Bhagavatam,* II, 3; *Tiruvasagam,* XXI (Pope's ed.).
41. *Triuvasagam,* XXIX, v. 5, p. 255; XXXVII, v. 5, p. 292. Cf. *Ibid.,* II, 121; V, 117; XXVIII, 34; XLII, 1, etc.
42. *Rgveda,* II, 1, 15. In the early Rgvedic period the name of the Supreme Being was not yet fixedly adopted. At limes he is called Varuna, at times Agni, as in this case, but he is evidently the supreme, as He is said to surpass the *devas* in majesty.
43. *Vajasaneyi Samhita,* XXXIII, 94.
44. *Rgveda,* X. 172, 5.
45. Cf. Griswold, *op. cit.,* pp. 106-07.
46. *Manava Dharmasastra,* I, 22.

47. *Taittiriya Upanisad,* It, 8.
48. *Brhadaranyaka Upanisad,* I, 4, 11-12. Winternitz translates Visvedevas as "five angels", *A History of Indian Literature,* I, p. 561.
49. Cf. Griswold, *The Religion of the Rigveda,* p. 103.
50. *Rgveda,* I, 25, 10.
51. *Vajasaneyi Samhita,* XXV, 13.
52. *Atharvaveda,* XI, 4, 11.
53. Siqueira, "Sin and Salvation in the Early Rig-Veda", *Anthropos,* 1933, p. 184.
54. Lefever, *The Vedic Idea of Sin,* p. 29. "Other gods and deities (viz. the *devas)* are under the control and guidance of the Supreme Lord" (according to Madhvacarya). Sharma, *The Reign of Realism in Indian Philosophy,* p. 669.
55. *Rgveda,* I. 25, 13.
56. *Atharvaveda,* IV, 16, 4.
57. *Rgveda,* X, 129, 6.
58. *Rgveda,* X, 125, 3 (Griffith's trans., II, p. 571). A full discussion about the nature of Vac would carry us too far. We shall perhaps do that on another occasion. He is high above the *devas* as He is generated before them. *Vajasaneyi Samhita,* XXXI, 20. Cf. *Jaiminiya Upanisad,* III, 38, 1; and *Mahabharata,* Vana Parva, 12602. Cf. Weber, "Vak und logos", *Indischen Studien,* IX, pp. 473-480.
59. Cf. Macdonell, *Vedic Mythology,* pp. 17-18, 22-30. At times these *devas* are confused with the very natural forces over which they preside, but this was not the original idea. The same happened among other nations. Cf. Cohen, *The Teachings of Maimonides,* p. 70. Even David calls the elements angels. "Who makest thy angels winds; and thy ministers a burning fire", Ps. CIII, 5.
60. Sircar, *Mysticism in Bhagavat Gita,* pp. 146-157.
61. *Sanatana Dharma,* pp. 74-75. Even the *Apocalypse* speaks of the angel "*qui habebat potestatem supra ignem*" (XIV. 18). That all the visible things have always an angel who presides over them is opinion of St. Augustin *(Liber quaestionum* LXVIII, 71, 1: Migne, *P.L.,* XL, col. 90); Andreas Caesariensis *(In Apoealypsim,* c. 43); St. Thomas Aq., *(Summa Theologica,* I, q. 110, a. 1, in Corp.); Eckhart *(Super Oratione Dominica,* in *Opera Latina,* I, p. 56); El Tostado, *(In Matheum,* XVIII, p. 57). About this opinion St. Thomas says: "This opinion is common not only among the saintly Doctors, but even among all authors who acknowledge the existence of incorporeal substances" *(Loc. cit.)* Cf. Aristotle, *Metaphysics,* XXII, 44.
62. Keith, *op. cit.,* I, p. 75. Cf. Macdonell, *Vedic Mythology,* p. 156 ff.
63. *Ibid.,* I, p. 131. The word *asura* has had several meanings in Sanskrit literature. In early *Rgveda* it meant "powerful", "strong". Thus Indra and other *devas* are called *asuras.* When it was adopted to mean the evil angels, the word had the general meaning of' enemy. Thus in some cases *asura* was synonimous for Dravidian when the Aryas were styled *dtvas,* as in the myth of the Kurmavatara. In this later period the *devas* were also named *suras,* in opposition to *asuras.*

64. *Taittiriya Samhita,* III, 3, 7.
65. *Satapatha Brahmana,* IV, 5, 41. This Brahmana belongs to the White School of the *Yajurxeda* while the *Taittiriya Samhita,* quoted above, is of the Black School.
66. *Ibid.*, IX, 5, 1, 16.
67. *Jaiminiya Upanisad Brahmana,* II, 4, 1; *Jaiminiya Upanishad,* II, 10, 1.
68. *Satapatha Brahmana,* IX, 5,1, 12-16.
69. According to ancient Indian Philosophy any sin is a lie in practice, for it places the sinner in a false plane of independence from God. In the same way Our Lord Jesus Christ describes the devil in almost the same lines as the above Indian text: "*We homicida erat ab initio et in veritate non stetit, quia non est veritas in eo; cum loquitur mendacium, ex propriis loquitur quia mendax est et pater ejus*". *Joann.*, VIII, 44. Though he was created in the sphere of truth, as St. Isidore says: "*(Diabolus) in veritate conditus, sed non stando, confestim a veritate est lapsus*". *Sententiarum,* I, 10, 7. Prophyrius says of the demons: "*Mendacium ipsis proprium est. Cupiunt enim dei haberi: et quae praesidet ipsispotestas, videri deus esse maximus vult*". *De abstinentia,* II, 42, (ed. Didot).
70. *Gathas,* Yasna XXX, 5.
71. Moulton, *Early Zoroastrianism,* p. 307.
72. *Satapatha Brahmana,* IV, 5, 4, 1.
73. "*Ipse est rex super omens filios superbiae*". *Job,* XLI, 25. "I will ascend above the height of the clouds; I will be like the Most High". *Is.*, XIV, 14. "The proud angel who turned from God to himself, not wishing to be a subject, but to rejoice like a tyrant in having subjects to his own". St. Augustine, *De Civitate Dei,* XIV, 11, 1, "*Lucifer in via per superbiam peccavit*". Suarez, *De Angelis,* VII, c. YIII, p. 843 (Vives ed.). "*Angelus absque omni dubio peccavit appetendo esse ut Deus.*" St. Thomas Aquinas, *Summa Theologica,* I, q. 63, a 3.
74. *Aitareya Brahmana,* IV, 4, 25.
75. The confusion concerning Indra is also found in other texts, which will be studied later.
76. *Satapatha Brahmana,* VI, 1, 1, 8.
77. *Svetasvatara Upanisad,* V, 2.
78. *Pancavimsa Brahmana,* XX, 14, 2.
79. *Vajasaneyi Samhita,* XXXI, 20.
80. *Taittiriya Samhita,* II, 1,1.; *Pancavimsa Brahmana,* IV, 5, 2; IV, 6,13; VI, 6, 8: XIV, 11,14. The name Svarbhanu means "the Bright Sun". There seems to exist a striking similarity between the meaning of this name and of the name of Lucifer.
81. *Rgveda,* I, 110, 2-4; 161, 1-5; II, 31, 4; III, 60, 2; IV, 33, 5-6: 36, 4. Cf. Neve *Essai sur le Mythe des Ribhavas.*
82. *Aitareya Brahmana,* III, 3, 30.
83. *Pancavimsa Brahmana,* XIV, 2, 5.
84. Singh, *Secrets of Spiritual Life,* p. 25.

85. *Taittiriya Samhita,* I, 5, 1. Fr. Fenicio, S. J., an old missionary of Malabar, saw the battle between the good and evil angels in the fight between the *devas* and *asuras. Livro da seita dos Indios, Orientals,* pp. 153-54. The same has in modern times been realised by Mgr. de Broglie, *Problemes et Conclusions de l' Histoire des Religions,* p. 55.
86. *Ibid.,* II, 42 or II, 4, 2.
87. *Jaiminiya Brahmana,* I, 63, 1-7. In the Upanisadic period this description is much enlarged without adding any new element. Cf. *Brhadaranyaka Upanisad,* I, 3, 1-7; *Chandogya Upanisad,* I, 2, 1-8.
88. *Aitareya Brahmana,* III, 4, 39.
89. *Aitareya Aranyaka,* II, 1, 7.
90. *Rgveda,* VI, 47, 9.
91. *Ibid.,* VIII, 37, 2.
92. *Ibid.,* VI, 47, 16.
93. *Ibid.,* II, 12, 1. He is styled *satakratu,* "of a hundred powers". Cf. Keith *The Religion and Philosophy of the Veda and Upanishads,* I, p. 126.
94. *Nirukta,* X, 10. Cf. *Atharvaveda,* XX, 34, I.
95. *Dhammapada,* II, 30.
96. *Satapatha Brahmana,* II, 2, 10, 1; *Pancavimsa Brahmana,* XVI, 4 ff; *Taittiriya Brahmana,* II, 2, 10, 1.
97. Barth, *The Religions of India,* p. 16.
98. *Taittiriya Samhita,* III, 4, 4.
99. *Ibid.*
100. *Rgveda,* I, 32, 3.
101. *Taittiriya Samhita,* II, 5, 2.
102. *Ibid.,* X, 125, 6. In this text nevertheless instead of Indra, Rudra's name appears. This is the only time that Rudra is introduced in this story of the Fall of the Angels. I take it, nevertheless, that this is a mistake for Indra: First, because of the evidence of the passage itself: "the hater of Brahma" cannot but be the leader of the *asuras,* who must be struck by order of Vac. Secondly, because of the natural confusion between Indra and Rudra, the former being in charge of rain and the latter of the storm. In the same way Vrtra, who is in the Veda the leader of the *asuras,* the hater of Brahma, and who is defeated and slain by Indra, is in other places said to be slain by other *devas,* for instance Agni or Soma. Such phenomena of syncretism are not uncommon in the Veda. Cf. Keith, *op. cit.,* I, p. 127.
103. "Indra est le plus terrible ennemi des demons. II est en guerre perpetuelle avec eux. Sans repit il les chasse et les poursuit; sans pitie il les aneantit". Guerinot, *Recherches surV origine de Vide de Dieu,* p. 250.
104. *Rgveda,* I, 32, 8, 10; 61, 8, 10; II, 12, 3; 13, 5; III, 30, 5; 33, 6; VI, 30, 4; *Pancavimsa Brahmana,* VIII, 8, 9; XIV, 4, 5; XVIII, 5, 2; 9, 6; 11, 1, etc.
105. *Rgveda,* I, 16, 8; 32, 11; 84, 3; 100, 18; 186, 3,11,1, 11; 3, 1; 13, 5; 19, 3; III, 20, 4; 30, 5; 52, 7; IV, 30, I; VI, 16, 48; 30, 4; 45, 5; 47, 6; VIII, 67, 7; 82, 15-16; *Vajasaneyi Samhita,* VIII, 33; *Pancavimsa Brahmana,* IX, 10, 1; *Mahabharata,* Vana Parva, 1511, etc. Cf. Bergaigne, *La Religion Vedique,* It,

pp, 196ff. Vrtra seems to be the Verethraghna of the *Avesta*. This victory of Indra over Vrtra is the cause of his being invoked by the Vedic *rsis* to obtain his help in their battles against the Dasas. All the theories deviced to explain the story of Indra and Vrtra as a natural phenomenon have proved unsatisfactory. Cf. Keith, *op. cit.,* I, pp. 126-27. There cannot be any doubt about the nature of Vrtra. In the epic he is styled "the excellent Deva". He was therefore a *deva* who had become an *asura*. Cf. *Mahabharata,* Santi Parva, CCLCXXXI—CCXXXt. In the *Pancavimsa Brahmana* the enemy of Indra is called Namuci, whose head he cut off "at dawn", i.e., in the beginning of time (XII, 6, 8). Fr. Fenicio calls him Chupaga or Chirpaga. *Livro da Seita dos Indios Orientals,* pp. 152-53.

106. *Dm.,* VII, 11.
107. *Rgveda,* I, 25, 14.
108. Barton, *The Religions of India,* p. 13.
109. *Pancavimsa Brahmana,* IV, 5, 9.
110. *Rgveda,* VIII, 82, 14.
111. Cf. Sayce, *Lectures on the Origin and Growth of Religion,* pp. 102-03.
112. *Rgveda,* X, 72,6.
113. *Taittiriya Samhita,* II, 5, 2.
114. In the philosophical works of India God is always named as Brahma, Isa or Isvara; but in the *Mahabharate* and the Puranas, when the philosophical religion of India is becoming mythological, God is generally styled Siva, at times also Visnu. In the former case, the Vac of the Vedic period, also becomes Kumara, Skanda, Sakra, Subramanya, Sanatkumara or Kartikeya, which are all different names of Siva's son.
115. Kalidasa, the great Sanskrit poet of the 5th century A.D., composed one of his *mahakavyas, the Kumarasambhava* based on this tradition.
116. *Mahabharata,* Vana Parva, 14311-15; 14402; 14368-86; 14423-28; 14520-14627; Salya Parva, 2455-61; 2498; 2523; 690-94; Santi Parva CCLXXXI— CCLXXXII; Anusasana Parva, 4212-14; *Matsya Purana,* CLIII-CLX; *Skanda Purana,* XX-XXIX; *Katha Sarit Sagara* (Tawney's trans.). I, p. 5; II, p. 102.
117. Coomaraswamy, *A New Approach to the Vedas,* p. 107.
118. *Rgveda,* IV, 27. 3; 30, 3-5.
119. *Mahabharata,* Vana Parva, CCXXVI, 15-16; CCXXVIII, 22-23.
120. *Aitareya Brahmana,* III, 2, 21.
121. *Taittiriya Samhita,* II, 4, 12.
122. *Rgveda,* I, 32, 14; *Taittiriya Samhita,* II, 5, 3 and 11. Cf. VI, 5, 5, 2.
123. Coomaraswamy, *op. cit.,* p. 74.
124. Cf. de la Vallee Poussin, *Le Vedisme,* p. 92, note 2.
125. See paintings in the sarcophagus of Seti I. Cf. Wallis Budge, *The Teachings of Amen,* pp. 111-12.
126. Delaporte, *Les Hittites,* p. 251.
127. Maximus Tyrius, *Dissertations,* XXIX, p. 304 (Davies ed.). Cf. Origen, *Contra Celsum,* VI, 42-43: MG, XI, col. 1360-1, 1364. Philo of Byblos

suggests that this story is borrowed from the Phoenicians. Cf. Euscbius Caesariensis, *Praeparatio Evangilica,* I, 10, 33.

128. Cf. Jastrow, *Civilization of Babylonia and Assyria,* pl. XXX; Barton, "*Tiamat*", *J.A.O.S.,* XV, p. 1 ff. This author identifies Tiamat with the Dragon of the *Apocalypse* XII, 13; XVII, 8, etc., which is finally said to be Satan. *Ibid.,* pp. 26-27.
129. *Atharvaveda,* V, 13, 6. Taimata was long ago identified with Tiamat by Lokamanya Tilak in *Bhandarkar Commemoration Volume,* pp. 34ff.
130. *Rgveda,* X, 92, 12; *Taittiriya Samhita,* I, 3, 3.
131. *Atharvaveda, loc. cit.*
132. Jensen, *Kosmologie der Babylonier,* pp. 217-22.
133. *Luke,* X, 18.
134. *Imitation of Christ,* III, 14. "(The devil) being a most noble angel and prince of the first order and the most excellent of God's creatures was notwithstanding presently cast down from heaven." St. Gregory the Great, *Moralium,* XXXIII, 24.
135. Letter of Fr. Nicholas Pimenta to Fr. Claude Aquaviva, Goa, 21 December 1599; *Lettres du P. Nicolas Pimente,* pp. 36-37, Hanuman, a well known figure in the story of the *Ramayana,* has nothing to do with the sin of the angels.
136. *Rgveda,* VII, 98, 3.
137. *Brhadaranyaka Upanishad,* I, 3, 11.
138. *Satapatha Brahmana,* IX, 5, 1, 12-13 and 16.
139. *Ibid.,* I, 1, 1,5; III, 4, 2, 8.
140. *Ibid.,* III, 9, 4, 1.
141. *Atharvaveda,* XIX, 11,5.
142. *Pancavimsa Brahmana,* V, 7, 11.
143. *Chandogya Upanisad,* VIII, 7, 2.
144. *Ibid.,* VIII, 12, 6.
145. *Aitareya Brahmana,* VIII, 3. (Haug's translation, pp. 514-19).
146. "In India the struggle between the gods *(devas)* and the demons . . . will give rise to an infinite number of myths". Barton, *The Religions of India,* p. 13.
147. *Vamana Purana.*
148. *Markandeya Purana.*
149. *Mahabharata.*
150. *Indian Wisdom,* p. 325.

150a. Kalidasa, *Meghadutam,* Purvamegha, stanza 36.

151. *Bhagavata Purana.*
152. For instance in one of the large panels of the Elephanta Caves, Bombay Bay.
153. This denomination nevertheless seems to be sectarian as it is found in sectarian passages, for instance the account of the Sacrifice of Daksa where even Siva himself is being cursed by Bhrgu.
154. *Bhagavata Purana.*
155. Some authors mention Hiranyakasipu, brother of *Hiranyaksa* are connected with the *Navasimha avatara* as another demon. Putting aside this

relationship we sincerely believe that Hiranyakasipu is not a demon. He is called by the Vaisnavites an *asura* in the sense of being a Dravidian who defended the cult of Siva against the intromissions of the cult of Visnu. The same is to be said of the *asura* Sambara in relation with Pradyumna, and of another *asura* named Dhenuka who fought with Balarama and was slain by the latter.

156. *Bhagavata Purana.*
157. *Visnu Purana.*
158. *Ibid.*
159. *Ibid.* The numerous adventures of Krsna fighting with monsters of various shapes were the cause why some old writers identified Hercules with Krsna. The identification was too candid. The real Indian protoype of Hercules is Bhima.
160. *Visnu Purana,* V.
161. *Skanda Purana; Vamana Purana.*
162. *Mahabharata.*
163. *Ibid.*
164. *Jaiminiya Brahmana,* I, 98.
165. Narayan, "Khasi Folk-Lore", *The New Review,* XVI, p. 454.
166. It is well known that the Buddha did not preach a new religion or ascetism, but followed the ancient path of the sages of other times. His aim was only to found a monastic order, the *sangha.*
167. Asvaghosa Bodhisatva, *Life of the Buddha,* Ch. III: Sacred Books of the East (New York), p. 369.
168. *Ibid.,* pp. 369-70.
169. *Ibid.,* p. 370.
170. *Ibid.,* p. 171. This scene has been represented many times by Indian and Tibetan painters from the days of Ajanta up to now. The modern Spanish artist Eduarado Chicharro has once more reproduced this scene in vivid colours. The French artist Collot in his painting of the temptations of St. Anthony the Abbot seems to have been inspired by reading the above description of the devils by Asvaghosa.
171. *Ibid.,* p. 372.
172. *Ibid.,* p. 374.
173. *Maha Vagga* (S.B.E).
174. *Parinibbana Sultana,* 39.
175. Cf. Macnicol, *The Living Religions of the Indian People,* p. 55.

23

Ancient Military India

I
KING AND HIS ARMY

C.S. SANGAMESWARAN

Every student of Indian History would have heard of the famous treatise, the Kautilya Arthasastra. Few however would have had the opportunity to read it in detail, even in translations. The Arthasastra is ascribed to the famous Brahmin Kautilya also named Vishnugupta, and the patronymic Chanakya, who overthrew the last King of the Nanda dynasty and installed Chandra Gupta Maurya on the throne. Kautilya was not only a King-maker but was the greatest exponent of the art of government, the duties of Kings, ministers and officials and the methods of diplomacy. He codified well known principles then in vogue. (Ed.)

Duties of Kings

The King was expected to lead a well regulated life, to be active, to devote a portion of his time daily for the inspection of his fighting forces and consideration of military operations, and to discharge his duties efficiently. When in court he was not to cause his petitioners to be ever detained at his door, for when a King makes himself inaccessible, and entrusts his work to his immediate officers, he may be sure to engender confusion in business and to cause public disaffection thereby. He was to hear all urgent matters at once and never to put them off for, when postponed these would prove intractable or impossible to accomplish. The maxim was that in the happiness of his subjects lay his happiness; in their welfare, was his welfare. The root of wealth was supposed to be action and the root of evil its reverse.

Council Deliberations

All administrative measures were preceded by confidential deliberations in a well-formed council. Whoever disclosed official secrets was visited with condign punishment. Carelessness, intoxication, talking in sleep, love affairs and other evil habits were the causes of betrayal. The council deliberations included consideration of the following:

(a) Capacity to carry out the task,
(b) Allotment of manpower and finance,
(c) Allotment of time and place,
(d) Remedies against failure, and
(e) Achievement of final aim.

National Prosperity—Causes

The causes contributing to national prosperity were as follows:

(a) Public prosperity,
(b) Reward for meritorious conduct,
(c) Eradication of corruption,
(d) Economy in government expenditure,
(e) Abundance of harvest,
(f) Prosperity of commerce,
(g) Diminution of taxes and levies,
(h) Peace and tranquillity, and
(i) Investment in gold and so on.

Subsistence to Government Servants

(a) The King was to look to the bodily comforts of his servants by providing such emoluments as could infuse in them the spirit of enthusiasm to work. The following were the annual emoluments:

Emoluments category	*Emoluments in panas*
Commander-in-Chief of the Army	48,000 With this amount of subsistance, he would scarcely yield to temptation and hardly be discontented.
Army Commander	24,000 With this amount he would remain useful.
Superintendent of Factories	12,000 With this he would be loyal and a powerful supporter of the King.
Chief of military Corporations	8,000 With this they could have a good following in their own communities. Chief of Elephants.
Chief of Cavalry	"
Chief of Chariots	"
Chief of Infantry	"
Chariot Driver	2,000
Physician of the Army	"
Trainer of Horses	"
Carpenter Foreman	"
Animal Rearer	"
All Superintendents of Departments	1,000
Trained Soldiers	500
Clerks	"
Fresh recruits	60

(b) The sons and wives of those who died while on duty got subsistence and wages. Infants or aged persons related to the deceased servants were also shown favour. On occasions of funerals, sickness or child birth, the King gave presentation to the servants concerned. The King increased their subsistence and wages in consideration of their learning and work. When wanting in money the King gave forest-produce, cattle or fields along with a small amount of money.

Control of Departments

(a) Each department was officered by several temporary heads as they would then be under the fear of betrayal by one another and would scarcely by liable to act in concert in a disloyal manner. This also applied to boundary guards and repairers of fortifications. The Chief Officer of each department was required to thoroughly scrutinise the real amount of the work done in detail and in the aggregate and he carried on his duties assisted by accountants, treasurers, coin examiners and military officers. Hour glasses were maintained to measure time.

(b) Any officer who was slack in the performance of his duties was punished in proportion to the wages paid and the deficiency in output. When a man engaged by Government for any work absented himself, his sureties who conjointly received money from government, or his legal heirs were liable to recoup the loss caused to the government. Just as it was impossible not to taste the honey or the poison that found itself at the tip of the tongue, so it was impossible for a government servant not to eat up, at least a bit. of the King's revenue. Not only was ill-gotten wealth confiscated from Government servants but they were also transferred from one work to another so that they could not misappropriate government money.

(c) A government officer might occasion loss of revenue to the government by the following:

- (i) Not being vigilant and not obtaining secret intelligence regarding his department,
- (ii) Neglecting to supervise the output,
- (iii) Ignorance of regulations,
- (iv) Indolence,
- (v) Timidity and being afraid of taking bold decisions,
- (vi) Corruption, that is, selfish desire when he was favourably disposed towards those who were desirous of achieving their selfish ends,
- (vii) Absence of equanimity of temper and taking hasty and incorrect action in a passion,
- (viii) Lack of dignity when he was surrounded by self-seeking sycophants,
- (ix) False calculation due to greed, and
- (x) Use of false weights and measures and so on.

In all such cases, the punishment was proportional to the guilt. At the same time, government servants were protected against malicious accusers who were fined for making false accusations.

Security

(a) When any one seized from arsenals commodities such as raw materials, manufactured articles and so on he was punished with punitive fines which might extend to over 100 times the value of the goods. When a Superintendent or independent officer issued or made use of unauthorised orders or seals, he was fined, punished in any other way or even condemned to death, according to the gravity of the crime.

(b) A nightly curfew was announced by blow of trumpet between about 8.30 p.m. and 3.30 a.m. and transgressors were fined depending on the time and the circumstances. Whoever was found moving suspiciously outside the fort during curfew period was fined at four times the maximum amount. Heavy fines were also prescribed for people who ascended the fortifications of the capital. The spies (Police) were empowered to search suspicious persons found inside arsenals and factories. The City Magistrate was required to make a daily inspection of water reservoirs, all hidden escape routes of forts, fortifications and other defensive work. The magistrate was punished for failing to report untoward incidents and not reporting arrival and departure of strangers. Sentries were liable for a fine for negligence of duty or for exceeding their authority. Those among them found guilty of dereliction of duty and molestation of women were severely -punished or even put of death.

Fire Prevention

(a) Destruction due to fire being irremediable, the kindling of fire was therefore regulated even in households to specified times. A small fine was levied for any transgression. Whoever carelessly set fire to a building was fined, but the incendiary who intentionally started a conflagration was liable to be bodily thrown into the fire.

(b) The following fire fighting equipments were to be maintained in each house:

(i) Five water pots,
(ii) One large water container,
(iii) One large wooden water trough,
(iv) A ladder for fire-fighting,
(v) An axe to cut-off beams,
(vi) A hook to pull down burning wooden panels,
(vii) Pincers to remove burning hay bundles, and
(viii) A leather bag for fire protection.

(c) In main thoroughfares and major road junctions, pots filled with water were to be kept in thousands in orderly manner. The same arrangement applied to government building. Everybody was expected to rush to render aid in fighting fires and any person who failed in this was fined according to his status as a house owner or tenant.

Weapons and Armour

(a) The Superintendent of the Armoury was to employ experienced workmen of tried ability to manufacture in a given time and for fixed wages, wheels, weapons, mail, armour and other accessory instruments for use in battles, in the construction or defence of forts, or in destroying the cities or strongholds of the enemies. All these weapons and instruments were to be kept in places suitably prepared for them. They were not only to be frequently dusted and transferred from one place to another, but also to be exposed to the sun. Such weapons as were likely to be affected by heat and vapour and to be eaten by insects or worms were to be kept in safe localities. They were to be frequently examined with reference to the class to which they belonged, namely, their forms, characteristics, size, source, value and total quantity. Any other new invention of expert workmen was also to be kept in stock. The Superintendent of Armoury was expected to precisely ascertain the demand and supply of weapons, their application, their wear and tear as well as their decay and loss.

(b) The Superintendent of Chariots attended to the construction of chariots. He attended to the accounts of provision and of wages paid to permanent and temporary employees, working in manufacturing establishments. These employees were kept contended by adequate rewards. Those who increased the King's revenue, instead of eating it up and were loyal to the King were made permanent in service.

(c) Weapons and armour were to be entered into the armoury only after they had been marked with the King's seal. When weapons were either spoilt or lost, the Superintendent had to pay double their value. An account of the weapons that were destroyed was maintained. Persons with weapons were not allowed to move anywhere unless they had a passport on them. Musical instruments, ornaments of horses, chariots and elephants were invariably kept inside the palace. There were seven models of chariots for various purposes. When both receipts and expenditure were properly cared for, the King would never find himself in financial or military difficulties.

Weapons

The type of weapons commonly used were as follows:

(a) Static Weapons

Sarvotobhadra — A cart with wheels and capable of fast revolution. This when rotated threw stones in all directions.

Jamadagnya — A large machine to shoot arrows.

Yanaka — A pole or rod mounted on a wheel so as to be thrown against the enemies.

Bahumukha — A tower on the top of a fort provided with a leather cover (as armour) and facing all sides. From this, archers could shower arrows in all directions.

Visvaasaghati — A cross beam above the moat at the entrance of a fort designed to crush approaching enemies.

Samghaati — A long pole to set fire to towers.

Parjanyaka — A water machine to put out the fire.

Ardha Bahau — Collapsible pillars designed to crush the enemy.

Ourdhava Bahau — A large pillar on high pedestal and thrown against enemies.

(b) Mobile Weapons

Panchaalika — A big wooden platform with sharp spikes floated in the moat as an obstacle to the advancing enemy.

Devadanda — A long scimitar located on the top of a fort wall.

Sookarika — A mat of bamboo bark covered with leather to protect towers against stones propelled by the enemy.

Musala and Yashti — Javelins.

Hastivaaraka — A trident to fight elephants.

Taala Vrinta — A fan like discus.

Mudgara — A staff.

Gaada — A crowbar.

Spriktala — A spiked staff.

Kuddaala — A spade.

Aasphaatima — A noise producer to imitate explosions.

Audhghaatima	—	A weapon to demolish towers.
Sataghni	—	A spiked pillar.
Trisula	—	A trident.
Chakra	—	A disc.

(c) Edged Weapons

Sakti	—	A metallic weapon 4 hands long.
Prasa	—	A double edged two-foot weapon.
Kunta	—	A distaff.
Hastaka	—	A rod triangular or quadrangular in section with sharp edges.
Bhindivaala	—	A mace. Soola — A spear.
Tomara	—	A spear with arrow like edge.
Varaahakarna	—	A rod with edges like the ears of a bear.
Kanaya	—	A rod held in the middle with triangular edges on both sides.
Karpana	—	An arrow thrown by hand.

(d) Razor Sharp Weapons

Parasu	—	A scimitar 24" long and semi-circular in shape.
Kuthara	—	An axe.
Pattasa	—	Scimitar shaped like a trident at both ends.
Krakacha	—	A saw.
Kanda Chheda	—	A battle axe.

(e) Rock Missiles

Yantra pashan	—	Stone propelled by machine.
Gosh pana pashana	—	Stone propelled by stick.
Mushti pashan	—	Stone hurled by hand.

(f) Archery (Bow and Arrows)

Karmuka	—	Bow made of palmyra timber.
Kodanda	—	Bow made of bamboo.
Dhanvana	—	Bow made of Daru wood.
Dhanus	—	Bow made of bone or horn.
Bow strings	—	These were made of various materials like sinew or bamboo bark, hemp and other vegetable fibres.
Arrows	—	These were variously made of materials like iron, bone or wood and were intended to cut, rend or pierce.

(g) Swords

Swords were of three types, namely, with crooked handle, disc topped or very sharp and long. The handles were fashioned out of rhinoceros horn, buffalo horn, ivory, hardwood or root of bamboo.

(h) Armour

These were made of tough material like iron, skin with hoof, and horns of cow, bison, rhinoceros or elephants.

(i) Battle Dress

There were various varieties of personal armour as follows:

Helmet, visor, cover for neck, cover for the trunk, long mail coat covering neck to heel, armless waist coats, and gloves.

(j) Personnel Defence Gear

A duffle coat made of vegetable creeper, a leather jerkin, a wooden board to cover the body, a wooden shield, bamboo bark shield, an elephant staff and trumpet.

Miscellaneous Weapons

(a) The Ordnance also stocked incendiary equipment. It could spread flames over waters or extinguish raging fires. Fire protection salves were held.

(b) Chemical warfare was practised by the extensive use of poisons. These were administered internally, applied externally, inflicted by weapons or propagated by gas warfare (smoke). These vitiated water courses, cook houses and the commissariat. The poisons were many and varied and were of vegetable, animal, mineral and magical origin. Some were virulent and some slow insidious poisons and were capable of causing blindness, deformity, disease or even death.

(c) Antidotes to poisons were kept in readiness and the Army marched with the medical corps in close support. Camouflage was widely practised and chemicals were stocked which could alter the appearance radically by changing the colour of the hair or the pigment of the skin. Special magical remedies were held which could help in endurance trials. Magical and psychological warfare was extensively practised.

Conclusion

The above excerpts throw a vivid light on the society in Ancient India over two thousand years ago. It will be seen that social polity even then was in a very advanced state of development. It is also evident that time has altered, but little, the fundamental characteristics of human nature.

II
FIRE-ARMS IN ANCIENT INDIA

G.N. VAIDYA

High Achievements of Ancient India

At the beginning of the last century, very little attention and less respect was paid to the achievements of the ancient Indians in the domain of science. Political needs, however, necessitated a more thorough understanding of the civilization of the conquered race, and the victors discovered that the ancestors of their subjects had made very marked advances in many departments, e.g., medicine, astronomy, mathematics. Some scholars thought that they saw the germs of some discoveries which had been made very recently in the western world. Some went yet futher and declared that a few departments of science had been developed on a much greater scale by the ancient *Rsis*. It was claimed that these great sages had perfected the arts of painting and music, architecture and polity; that they knew and used aeroplanes and gunpowder!

No scholar is now prepared to deny the high achievemets of the ancient sages. But every such alleged discovery must be carefully examined before we come to any conclusion about it. We are here concerned with the contention that gunpowder and fire-arms were used in warfare in ancient India.

Pros and Cons of the Question

Many learned scholars have given their opinions on this interesting topic, but I think that the arguments on both sides have not been subjected to a critical and exhaustive inspection. It is, therefore, the aim of this article to state the pros and cons of the question and examine them in detail.

Halhead started this discussion in his introduction to the *Code of Gentoo Laws*.[1] He relied mainly on the words *agnyastra* and *Sataghni:* "The word fire-arms is literally Sanskrit agniastra, i.e., a weapon of fire." These fire-arms were condemned in the 'Code', and as the Code was based on authoritative Smrtis, Halhead argued that the Smrtis knew of the fire-arms, but looked on them with disfavour. Elliot[2] comes to the same conclusion but maintains that somehow these weapons had fallen into disuse at the time of the Mahommedan invasion. Bohlen,[3] who gives a number of quotations from various commentaries, contributes to the same opinion. Wilson,[4] in his studies, has argued on nearly the same lines as above. He has specially emphasized the thundrous impact of the *Vajra* and concludes that this could have been only due to some sort of explosive substance. He, moreover, points out that all the principal ingredients of gunpowder were found in abundance in North India and so a discovery of the compound could be easily explained.

Mostly Puranic Evidence

The evidence used by all these authors is mostly Puranic, describing wonderful weapons and their miraculous effects. Other scholars could say that poets and mythologists use their imagination rather freely and that conclusions drawn from their statements would not be sound. But Oppert[5] now came forward and was able to give convincing descriptions of real guns in works on polity. The Sukranitisara and the Nitiprakasika, indeed, offer us an account of a weapon, which is, in every respect, like the cannons of the seventeenth century. On the description of Nalika in the Nitiprakasika, Rajendralal Mitra[6] observes, "It is difficult to read the above, without a feeling of suspicion about its authenticity; the flint-lock of the last three centuries comes so vividly to mind that it is difficult to set it aside; but the arguments urged by Dr. Oppert are strong and I must leave them to speak for themselves." Oppert maintained that the Sukranitisara was composed by the same Sukra, who is quoted in the Mahabharata and that the author of the Nitiprakasika is the same Vaisampayana, who is supposed to narrate a greater portion of the epic. Har Bilas Sarda[7] has reiterated the same conclusion, without adding any new argument. But it must be noted that this work is absolutely uncritical and hence unreliable. The author, in his zeal to prove that the ancient Indians had perfected the most modern inventions, has relied on passages, wrenched violently from their context, and has quoted from the works of European scholars, out of date and exploded theories, without any comments or justification. He is thus able to prove that the old sages and kings possessed a highly developed artillery as also a large flotilla of aeroplanes. This work has been rendered into Marathi; but the translator[8] has taken no pains to improve upon the original.

Oppert's Arguments

The arguments of Oppert did not convince some scholars, who regarded the Sukranitisara and the Nitiprakasika either as later works, or as fuli of interpolations. Quite a new colouring is, however, given to the problem by the discovery of the Kautiliya Arthasastra. Prof. Banerjee[9] has thus analysed the composition of the "fire-powders" in the Arthasastra,[10] and shown that one of them agrees very closely with the 'gun-powder' in the Sukranitisara and that the ingredients given are even today used for the same purpose. The authenticity of the passage has not been questioned and the problem, therefore, presents quite a new appearance.

The other Side

This is only one side of the problem; as against it a number of scholars have all along contended that the invention is too complex to be known in very ancient times. They also point to numerous descriptions of ancient battles, in all of which fire-arms are conspicuously absent. Hopkins,[11] has thoroughly sifted and examined the passages from the great epic, which are alleged to refer to the fire-arms. Maclagen[12] has also come to the conclusion that fire-arms in the sense of a modern gun or cannon were unknown in ancient India. Many other scholars have similarly expressed themselves against the view of Oppert and others, but a detailed examination was not attempted. Especially in view of the fresh data supplied by the Arthasastra, the problem must be thoroughly investigated. Dr. Banerjee[13] rightly says *(op. cit.,* p. 206), "The question is yet unsettled and open for further discussion."

But before we launch into a detailed examination of the various arguments, some issues of great importance must be settled. Thus let us be clear about the exact scope of the word 'fire-arms'.

Meaning of Fire-arms

'Fire-arms' do not include any weapons which are in some way connected with fire. The term is used with reference to those weapons which are discharged by the force of fire. A modern gun, which propels large shells by means of an explosion of burning gunpowder, is one of the 'fire-arms' in the fullest sense of the word. But a torch in flames, flung at an opponent and used like a weapon, cannot lay claim to the title. It *does* carry fire and it is destructive, but it is not discharged or propelled by fire. Similarly, arrows, which are tipped with burning rags, do not fall under the category of 'fire-arms'. The distinction between combustibles and explosives has to be carefully borne in mind. The essential characteristics of fire-arms is not that they burn, but that they are discharged by an explosion.

We have also to remember that the use of gunpowder and fire-arms cannot have obtained at a single stride. It presupposed several other things. Thus, the three principal ingredients of gunpowder, *viz.*, saltpetre, charcoal and sulphur must be known. Then again their cumulative effect in a compound must also be discovered and finally such a property must be exploited for use in war, in order to discharge volleys of bullets and shells, etc. With this distinction in mind we can now turn to the discussion proper.

Missiles Discharged Accompanied by 'Mantras'

The argument most emphasised is the presence of the miraculous astras in the epic war and elsewhere. The agnyastra, which burnt up whole armies, is thus believed to be nothing less than a mighty cannon. Now with regard to this it must be noted that the power of these missiles was not inherent, but wholly due to the incantations which accompanied them. Their appearance and the mode of discharging them are generally not different from the ordinary weapons. An ordinary quoit or an arrow or even a blade of grass, when discharged to the accompaniment of the mysterious mantra, would obtain miraculous powers. Now fire-arms are discharged in a conspicuously peculiar way, and cannot therefore be the same as these astras. Moreover, the effect of these astras can very well be doubted and the instruments are perhaps not to be taken literally. In any case the astras did not materially affect the conclusion of the great war.[14] Miraculous spells and incantations are a regular feature in Indian civilization ever since the age of the Atharvaveda, and whatever actual effect these weapons may have had, was certainly not due to any explosive material, but to the mantras. In the minute description of the epic war, we have not a shred of evidence for assuming the presence of a weapon like the modern cannon.

Leaving then these miraculous weapons, which certainly do not correspond to 'fire-arms' in our sense of the word, we turn towards some other words which are supposed to denote some kinds of fire-arms.

Sataghni—A Hundred-killer

The Sataghni.—This weapon is mentioned very frequently in the epics and in the later literature. Much emphasis has been laid on the literal meaning of the word, "a hundred-killer"; apparently, this can be nothing less than a cannon. Then again, it is very often mentioned as stationed on the walls of fortresses.[15] The references can be roughly divided into two sets. One seems to refer to a handy weapon. Such a Sataghni is often mentioned as being thrown by the hand,[16] and as stored in the chariot by the side of other weapons like the sword and the mace.[17] Among a mass of weapons flung at Bhima is the Sataghni, which he splits with an arrow.[18] Yudhisthira also casts a Sataghni at Salya, who deals with it in a similar manner.[19] Other references in the war are of a similar nature. The apparent implications of the title Sataghni do not lead to any conclusion, as, even an ordinary ankusa is sometimes called a Sahasraghatin.[20] It will thus be clear, that in epic usage Sataghni did not mean a species of firearms, but only a sort of mace. Even as late as Kalidasa, a Sataahni; covered with iron knobs, is mentioned. It is then cut down with an arrow.[21] As to the other kind of the Sataghni, which is stationed on the walls of a fortress, we must remember that ammunition is nowhere mentioned. The Sataghni must have been some machine in the nature of a catapult, which would suit the general picture of warfare in ancient India. This conclusion is convincingly established by a reference to the old lexicons. In their copious lists, fire-arms are conspicuous by their absence. On the other hand, the 'Sataghni' is expressly defined in the Vaijayanti as

> *'sataghni tu catustala laha-kantaka-sancita |*
> *ayahkantaka-sanchinna sataghnyeva mahasila ||*[22]

Thus the Sataghni is a long weapon, covered with iron knobs; it is also a large slab of stone, bristling with iron spikes. Obviously, the two species are here explained, and they have nothing to do with fire-arms.

Nalika—The Gun

Nalika is supposed to mean a 'gun' in all cases. This is supposed to be the same as the Nalika, which, according to the Nitiprakasika, is a kind of flint-lock. But this latter word never occurs in the older works. Nalika, which is often mentioned there, is only a particular kind of arrow. It is frequently grouped with the Naraca and the

Karnin. The lexicons again come to our help. The Vaijayanti says '*nalikamabje bane va*'. In the works on the Dhanurveda, the Nalika is described as a small dart, propelled by means of a hollow tube and particularly serviceable for the purpose of a seige:

> *nalika laghavo bana nala-yantrena noditah* |
> *atyucca-dirgha-patesu durgayuddhesu te matah* ||[23]

These references are clear enough.

A similar claim has been made about the Bhusundi or the Bhusunthi. Monier Williams in his dictionary is half inclined to accept this meaning. But looking up the passages in the epic, where this weapon is mentioned, we discover that it occurs by the side of clubs and spits.[24] Many times it is also used along with the Sula and Pattisa and probably meant a longer spear; that it cannot mean a gun is, however, quite obvious. The Vaijayanti again defines Bhusunthi as a wooden club with iron knobs.[25]

Oppert[26] contends that the surmi was also a sort of gun. The word occurs in the Vedas,[27] and if the meaning given were acceptable, it would prove a very high antiquity, for the use of gunpowder, in ancient India. But the interpretation does not stand a critical scrutiny; and it is quite obvious that the surmi is only the bright flame of agni.

Oppert has brandished the Rgvedic verse as a triumphant stroke which would completely settle the much-debated problem. But we have to note that the surmi here is a divine weapon and in the interests of sober history, it is dangerous to jump to any conclusions. Then again, even the commentators do not necessarily understand a gun by this word. The word Karnakavati is not sufficient to lead us to such a drastic conclusion. It is better to construe it to mean 'with a handle' or 'with a hole' as the PW has done. Surmi then would mean a blazing weapon with a handle or a hole. It was moreover used by the gods only. Similarly as regards the thundrous impact of the Vajra,[28] it is clear that the terrific sound ensues when the Vajra dashes against its objective. In the case of the fire-arms, the sound of the explosion occurs when the weapon is discharged.

Fire-arms Unknown in Vedic Age

All these arguments, I think, prove conclusively that 'fire-arms' were not known in the Vedic and the epic periods. At the same time, the possibility that they were known in the classical age has also to be considered. Emphasis is, in this case, laid on the Sukranitisara and the Nitiprakasika, which are supposed to be very old. There is no doubt, that both these words make unmistakable references[29] to fire-arms. The only question is about their dates. The doctrines propounded in them are generally on the same lines as those in the Arthasastra and the Kamandakiya Nitisara but in many respects very peculiar differences can be noted. The budget system,[30] the proportions of elephants and chariots in the army,[31] the posts of some high officials, etc. all mark out a much later age for the Nitisara. The same remarks hold good about the Nitiprakasika. Oppert[32] has attempted to place these works at a high age, because they are ascribed to Sukra and Vaisampayana respectively. But such a conclusion is obviously as absurd as the attempt to put the Yajnayavalkya Smrti in the Vedic age, merely because he is referred to in the Brahmanas and the Upanisads. The Nitisara and the Nitiprakasika do not, therefore, entitle us to detect fire-arms in the warfare of ancient India.

No Mention of Fire-arms in the Smrtis

In the *Code of Gentoo Laws* we read, "The Magistrate shall not make war with any deceitful machine or with cannons and guns or with any kind of fire-arms." This code was compiled in the 18th century by learned Pandits, who drew mainly on the most authoritative Smrtis. But we must note that the Smrtis are not quoted verbatim and that changes have been made according to the times. The original passage in view, seems to be from the Manusmrti,[33] which speaks only of barbed and poisoned arrows, etc. Now just as the Pandits in their code substituted the 'Magistrate' for the 'King' so did they substitute 'cannons and guns' for the out-of-date arrows. We cannot, therefore, infer the presence of old Smrtis, which forbade fire-arms.

Similarly, Nilakantha has also read later inventions in the original epic verses.

But, as no such weapon is in conclusive evidence, in the actual descriptions of the fighting, we may again assume that the commentator is trying to give an up-to-date picture of the old terms; for gunpowder is rarely mentioned in the epic, the only powder, which is referred to, being asma-curna. This again is classed, surprisingly, among the number of unimportant weapons used by the fighting class of trained soldiers. Had fire-arms been widely known, they would surely have commanded a better position.

Notes and References

1. Halhead, *op. cit.,* Introduction, p. 52f.
2. Elliot, *History of India,* Vol. VI, pp. 455-82.
3. Bohlen, *Alt-Indien,* pp. 64-68.
4. H.H. Wilson, *Works*, Vol. IV, p. 303.
5. Oppert, Nitiprakasika (1882) pp. 10-131, Sukranitisara, pp. 194 ff.; *On Weapons etc.,* p. 32.
6. R. Mitra, *Indo-Aryans,* Vol. I, p. 311.
7. Har Bilas Sarda, *Hindu Superiority,* pp. 300-309.
8. *Bharatiya Sresthatva* (Chitrasala Press, Poona).
9. Pramathanatha Banerjee, "International Law and Customs in Ancient India", *Journal of the Department of Letters,* University of Calcutta, Vol. I, pp. 343-48.
10. Arthasastra, XIII, 4.
11. Hopkins, "The Ruling Caste in Ancient India" *JAOS*, XIII, pp. 297-304; also CXV ff.
12. R. Maclagen, "On early fire-weapons" *JASB.* 1876. pp. 40-56.
13. Dr. Banerjee, *Public Administration in Ancient India.*
14. C.V. Vaidya, *Mahabharataci Upasamhara,* p. 515.
15. Mahabharata, XII, 69. Ramayana, I. 5. 9; V. 3,18; V. 4, 17-20.
16. Mahabharata, XI, 12-21.
17. *Ibid.,* VIII. 16-17; VIII. 11.8.
18. *Ibid.,* VI. 113.39 ff.; VI. 96-57.
19. *Ibid,* IX. 12.21.
20. *Ibid.,* VII. 29-17. *Cf. JAOS.* XIII, CXCVI.
21. Raghuvamsa, XII. 95.96.
22. Vaijayanti, Bhumi-Kanda; Ksatriyadhyaya, 169.
23. Sarngadhar-padhati, Dhanurveda (1788).
24. Mahabharata III, 170.3; *JAOS.* XIII, CXCVI.
25. Vaijayanti, Bhumikanda, Ksatriyadhyaya, 171.
26. Nitiprakasika, pp. 11-13.
27. Rgveda VII, 1-3; Yajurveda (Vajasaneyi), I. 5-7-6.
28. Wilson, *Works,* Vol. IV, p. 302.
29. Nitiprakasika, II. 17, Nitisara IV, 7, 195-211; Oppert, *Weapons, etc.,* pp. 12-14.
30. Nitisara, IV, 7, 26-29.
31. *Ibid.,* IV, 7, 20-26.
32. Oppert, *op. cit.*
33. Manu, VII, 90.

24

Strategy of Alexander the Great and his Campaign Against Porus

SHARU S. RANGNEKAR

Introduction

In the drama of History, the role for a conqueror is that of a 'hero' or a 'villain'. Many of the controversial figures amongst the conquerors have the doubtful distinction of playing the roles of heroes as well as villains in different depictions of their careers. One of the foremost amongst them is Alexander, The Great.

The task accomplished by Alexander has dazzled historians through ages. Considering his young age, short span of career, limited resources, and the vast area he covered in the days of almost primitive communications, his achievements are simply stupendous.

Attempts have been made to attribute the achievements to various reasons—ranging from 'divinity' of Alexander to chance and luck.[1] Except in extreme cases, the explanations emphasize the 'strategy' of Alexander.

In this paper, it is proposed to study the strategy of Alexander in the main encounters of his career—the campaigns against Tyre, Darious, Spitamenes, and Porus. The approach has been comparative: by comparison with the strategy of his direct adversaries as well as with that of comparable conquerors through history.

Discussion

Definition of 'Strategy'

Although man has been fighting wars since times known, the science of war—the military science—has been developed systematically only in the last two centuries.[2] The technical terms of this science have not yet attained universality and are found to have been used to different connotations in different treatments. Consequently, it is necessary to define as clearly as possible the principal terms used in this paper.

The term strategy is used to cover all the moves made in a campaign. Strategy is considered in two broad grounps: moves on the battlefield are termed 'field-strategy', while the moves 'off' the battlefield, i.e. the moves relating to the overall conduct of the campaign (as different from that of particular battles) are said to comprise 'grand strategy'. The distinction between field-strategy and grand strategy is by no means a sharp one. In aspects like communications, there is a considerable overlap. Furthermore, since results of battles have important implications on the grand strategy, and *vice versa,* the *interaction* between the field-strategy and the grand strategy is an important aspect of the study of strategy.

However, operationally, it is advantageous to distinguish between field strategy and grand strategy, even though, in some aspects the distinction may be subjective to a certain extent. Generally, the field-strategy in a campaign changes appreciably from battle to battle; changes in the grand strategy are relatively slower. Furthermore, a grand strategy is operative in a wider field and may have, relatively, far-reaching effects—not only on the course of the campaign, but also on the course of subsequent history. A failure of the grand strategy ultimately leads to failure of the campaign—in spite of successes in battles. In fact, it is possible to win every battle and yet to lose the war; this was nearly the experience of the Mughal Emperor Aurangzeb, whose campaign in Deccan from 1681 to 1707 A.D. ended disastrously in the death of the Emperor and ruin of his empire—although he was never defeated on the battlefield.[2a]

Field-strategy

Field-strategy may be analaysed in three major aspects: first, the army—the principle tool of field-strategy; second, the nature of command over the army; and third, the field-craft—actual movement of the army in the field of battle.

The main points of comparison with respect to army are: its (numerical) strength, composition, equipment, and quality. Flexibility and co-ordination are the main features of army command. Use of terrain, order and differential intensity of attack, and use of 'surprise' are the most significant components of field-craft.

Grand Strategy

Morale of the army is the most important factor in the grand strategy. In the words of Napolean: "the morale is to the physical as three to one".[3] The arithmetic proportion is a subjective evaluation; yet, the emphasis on morale is most appropriate. The remarkable difference in the resistance offered by the German and the Italian troops at the final stage of the Second World War underlines the importance of morale. The recent Israel-Arab war has also demonstrated the importance of morale. Prestige and status of the leader have strong influence on the morale. Especially, at the time of Alexander this was a vital aspect, since the organization was centred on the leader. The leader-centred organization emphasises the importance of the personal safety of the leader. In the battle of Gunaxa (400 B.C.), the army of Cyrus defeated the army of Artaxerxes; but Cyrus was killed in the battle and the campaign was doomed.[4]

In ancient times, when the leader was expected to lead the army in person on the battlefield, the prestige and safety of the leader could be conflicting.

Control on communications is another important factor in grand strategy. Communication and supply break-down has converted many a triumphant armies into a dismal rout—the fate of Nepolean in Russia is an outstanding example.

In this context, attaining and maintaining congenial relations with the people in territories traversed becomes more significant as the scope of the campaign increases. Satisfactory 'public relations' facilitate supply and communications, reduce resistance to consolidation, and enhance the morale of the army. Even a passive resistance by the conquered people can multiply the difficulties of supply and communication and can wreck the nerves of the conquering army. To advance in spite of active resistance in the conquered people has proved disasterous time and again, the latest example being that the German army in Russia in the Second World War. The significance of the ultimate goal of a campaign to the various levels in the army is also a determinant of the morale. Morale of the U.S. army in the

Korean and Vietnam Wars suffered appreciably due to a feeling of irrelevance of the War, i.e. a feeling of fighting 'somebody else's war'.

Interaction

The interaction between the field-strategy and the grand strategy has been noted before. The preceding discussion of the field-strategy and grand strategy also shows the interaction and feedback with respect to the various factors of the strategies. In fact, there is no completely independent variable in the field of strategy.

This interaction makes the learning ability highly significant. The leader with a greater learning ability will make suitable modifications in his strategies earlier than his adversary and thus may gain a significant advantage over the adversary. Even 'not making the same mistake' can be a valuable attribute, since in the case of war, history has often repeated itself.

Factors of Comparison

The important factors brought out in the discussion of strategies, form the basis of the comparative analysis in the subsequent sections. Attempt has been made to quantify the relative strength in each of these factors by using a three unit ordinal scale: good (xxx), fair (xx), and poor (x). There is essentially an element of subjective evaluation in this approach. However, such an evaluation—or interpretation—can be held in the understanding of the military science (or for that matter, any social science) and has a definite place by the side of the objective data.

Campaign Against Tyre

Importance

The siege of Tyre (332 B.C.) occupies a prominent position in the campaigns of Alexander in various aspects. It has strategic importance for the subsequent campaigns; as Alexander addressed his army officers:[5] ". . . an expedition to Egypt will not be safe for us, so long as Persians retain the sovereignty of the sea; nor is it a safe course, both for other reasons, and especially looking at the state of matters in Greece, for us to pursue Darius, leaving in our rear the city of Tyre itself in doubtful allegiance.... If Tyre were captured, the whole of Phoenicia would be in our possession, and the fleet of the Phoenicians, which is the most numerous and the best in the Persian navy, would in all probability come over to us..."[6]

Conduct of the siege stresses the imagination and learning ability of Alexander. It was indeed a battle of wits with an adversary well versed in siege-defence tactics and Alexander came out the winner. To cite an example: the Tyrians made near approach to the island impossible by dropping rocks into the sea. Alexander brought up merchant ships to sweep-off the obstacles; the Tyrian warships attacked them and cut their anchor-cables. He covered the sweepers with warships; Tyrian divers cut the cables under water. Then he anchored the sweepers by chains; the Tyrians had no reply, and Alexander got the rocks out.[7] Capturing of Tyre in seven months—a city considered impregnable since it stood a siege by Nebuchadrezzar for thirteen years[8]—enhanced the prestige of Alexander and boosted the morale of his army. Strategically, an importance risk in the subsequent campaigns against Egypt and Darius was removed.

Comparison of Strategies

Comparison between Alexander and the garrison of Tyre regarding the more significant strategy factors is given in Chart 1. The overall position shows distinct advantage in favour of Alexander. In the ultimate analysis, the comparison shows that the advantage of terrain to the Tyrians was neutralized by superior plan of attack and that the more favourable position of Alexander with respect to the strength of army, communications, and learning ability were the deciding factors.[9]

Campaign Against Darius

Importance

Campaign against Darius was an inheritance for Alexander. The campaign was a Panhellenic war of revenge—which Isocrates had preached.[10] Conquering the empire of Darius was the greatest feat of Alexander's career. The campaign had far reaching effects not only on the political history, but also on the course of culture—economic and social structures, science, and philosophy.

Comparison of Strategies

Strategy is a dynamic concept; consequently, comparison over an appreciable period (the campaign against Darius lasted over 3 years) should take into consideration the changes during the period. This is particularly important for the field-strategy, which may change considerably from battle to battle.

CHART 1

Alexander vs. Tyre

Strategy Factor	*Alexander*	*Tyre*
A. Field-strategy		
(a) Army—		
(i) Strength	xxx	xx
(ii) Composition	xxx	xxx
(iii) Equipment	xxx	xxx
(iv) Quality	xxx	xxx
(b) Army Command Co-ordination	xxx	xxx
(c) Field-craft—		
(i) Use of terrain	XX	xxx
(ii) Plan of attack	xxx	xx
B. Grand Strategy		
(a) Morale of Army	xxx	xxx
(b) Leader—		
(i) Prestige and status	xxx	xxx
(ii) Personal safety	x	XX
(c) Communications—		
(i) Necessity*	—xx	—xxx
(ii) Control	xxx	x
(d) 'Public Relations'	xxx	xx
(e) Significance of 'Ultimate Goal'	xxx	xxx
C. Interaction and Feedback		
Learning ability	xxx	xx
Total Points	37	32

*The points for 'Necessity of Communications' are considered negative, since higher necessity is an adverse factor.

The campaign against Darius, therefore, has been analysed in two ways. The grand strategies and interactions—in which changes had been relatively minor—have been compared on overall campaign basis (Chart 2). The field-strategies have been compared separately for the Battle of Issus and the Battle of Gaugamela (Chart 3) which mark the opening and closing stages of the campaign.

CHART 2
Alexander *vs.* Darius
COMPARISON WITH RESPECT TO GRAND STRATEGY AND INTERACTION

Strategy Factor	*Alexander*	*Darius*
A. *Grand Strategy*		
(a) Morale of Army	xxx	xx
(b) Leader—		
(i) Prestige and status	xxx	x
(ii) Personal safety	x	xxx
(c) Communications—		
(i) Necessity	—xxx	—x
(ii) Control	xx	xx
(d) 'Public Relations'	xxx	x
(e) Significance of Ultimate Goal	xxx	xxx
B. *Interaction and Feedback*		
Learning ability	xxx	xx
Total points	15	13

CHART 3
Alexander *vs.* Darius
COMPARISON WITH RESPECT TO FIELD-STRATEGY

Strategy factor	*Battle of Issues*		*Battle of Gaugamela*	
	Alexander	*Darius*	*Alexander*	*Darius*
(a) *Army* —				
(i) Numerical strength	xxx	xxx	xx	xxx
(ii) Composition				
Balance	xxx	x	xxx	x
Special arm	xx	—	xx	x
(iii) Equipment	xxx	xxx	xxx	xxx
(iv) Quality—				
Infantry	xxx	xx	xxx	x
Cavalry	xxx	xxx	xxx	xxx
(b) *Army Command*—				
(i) Flexibility	xxx	xxx	xxx	xxx
(ii) Co-ordination	xxx	x	xxx	x
(c) *Field-craft*—				
(i) Use of terrain	x	xxx	xxx	xx
(ii) Plan of attack	xxx	xx	xxx	xx
Total Points	27	21	28	20

In each of the comparisons, Alexander has an appreciable overall advantage. His personal prestige and his policy of establishing cordial 'public relations' were his strongest points against Darius. In the latter respect, his policy excells in comparison with most of the other conquerors of history. Like Alexander, Napolean and Hitler were received as liberators at the opening stages of their campaigns. However, unlike Alexander, they soon alienated the conquered people and eventually were vanquished as tyrants. A similar example is found in the Indian history; Bajirao I (1720-40) extended the rule of Marathas from Western India up to Delhi by preaching the ideal of a Hindu Empire. His successors, however, lost the sympathy of other Hindus by callous behaviour and soon lost their empire.[11]

The habit of Alexander to lead his army personally and to take part in active combat contributed considerably to his prestige. However, considering the campaign would have been totally lost at the death of Alexander, this policy has to be taken as a weak point in his strategy. On the other hand, Darius carried his concern for personal safety too far and withdrew from the field in both the battles when they were at the critical stage, thus precipitating his own defeat.

Alexander's army was well-balanced between infantry and cavalry. Persian cavalry was comparable, but their infantry was weak. This weakness was accentuated after the battle of Issus in which the Persian infantry was largely destroyed and the main body of Greek mercenaries under Amyntas left the Persians being disgusted with the cowardice of Darius. This proved an irreverside change for the Persians and they were left without adequate 'defensive base' that is provided by a strong infantry. Consequently, a reverse at any wing of the army quickly deteriorated into a route—in spite of a favourable position of the other wing.

The special arm of Alexander's army was the Hypaspists— light armed infantry—which acted as a link between the faster moving cavalry and the slower moving phalanx. This 'hinge' maintained an unbroken front and protected the flanks.[12] The action of the Hypaspists protected the phalanx in both the battles. Persians had no special arm at Issus. They tried to use elephants and scythed chariots at Gaugamela; however, their own horses were not accustomed by elephants and the chariot-drivers were poorly trained. Consequently, the use of these special arm did little damage to Alexander.

Alexander's army command was balanced in flexibility and co-ordination. Each commander was free to take decisions within the general plan of action. Persian army command showed poor co-ordination and could not take advantage of partial successes of some of the commanders at various stages of battle.

Thus, better balance in army and army command, superior infantry, effective special arm, and better plan of attack proved decisive in favour of Alexander in both the battles. From Issus to Gaugamela, the Persians deteriorated—rather than improved—in field-strategy in comparison to Alexander.

Campaign Against Spitamenes

Importance

The campaign against Spitamenes marks the last stage of conquest of the Persian Empire and is generally regarded as an extension of the campaign against Darius. However, from the viewpoint of studying strategy, the campaign against Spitamenes forms a class by itself. In this campaign Alexander had to face a national war and national leader who used the most appropriate strategy and proved himself the best opponent Alexander ever met.[14]

Comparison of Strategies

Chart 4 shows the comparison at two stages of the campaign: beginning and the end.

At the beginning of the campaign, Spitamenes neutralized the advantage of Alexander's army in strength, equipment and overall quality by using superior field-craft—full use of the terrain, desert or 'Parthian' tactics of combat—and use of light cavalry. Alexander's commanders had no adequate answer to these strategies and were repeatedly defeated.

However, Alexander had an excellent learning ability. He countered the strategies of Spitamenes by covering the country with a network of fortified posts and garrisons and thus severely reduced the destructive power and the field of influence of Spitamenes. Furthermore, he developed a fairly strong light cavalry to match that of Spitamenes.

On the other hand, the army of Spitamenes deteriorated in morale, strength, and equipment by the end of the campaign. At last, Coenus—one of Alexander's commanders—who had mastered the tactics of Spitamenes, defeated him so decisively that his demoralized followers murdered him and thus ended the campaign which had lasted for almost three years (300-328 B.C.).

CHART 4

Alexander *vs.* Spitamenes

Strategy Factor	*Beginning of the Campaign*		*End of the Campaign*	
	A.	*S.*	*A.*	*S.*
A. *Field-strategy—*				
(a) Army—				
(i) Strength	xxx	xx	xxx	x
(ii) Equipment	xxx	xx	xxx	x
(iii) Quality—				
Overall	xxx	x	xxx	x
Light Cavalry	x	xx	xx	x
(b) Army Command	xx	xxx	xxx	xxx
(c) Field-craft—				
(i) Use of terrain	xx	xxx	xxx	xxx
(ii) Plan of attack	xx	xxx	xxx	xxx
B. *Grand Strategy—*				
(a) Morale of Army	xxx	xx	xxx	x
(b) Prestige and Status of Leader	xxx	xxx	xxx	xxx
(c) Communications—				
(i) Necessity	—xxx	—xx	—xxx	—xx
(ii) Control	x	x	xx	x
(d) 'Public Relations'	xx	xxx	xxx	xxx
(e) Significance of Ultimate Goal	xxxxx	xxx	xxx	
C. *Interaction and Feedback—*				
Learning process	xxx	xx	xxx	xx
Total Points	28	28	34	24

The effective use of desert war tactics against Alexander shows that if such tactics were used earlier, the progress of Alexander would have been considerably hampered—if not altogether stopped. In fact, at the very beginning of Alexander's campaigns such a plan was proposed. In 334 B.C. one of the commanders of Darius, Memoon, proposed to retire before Alexander and waste the country—the 'scorch-earth' policy. However, the local satrap Arsites refused to allow his satrapy to be laid waste and consequently the plan was never tried.[15]

Alexander's excellent public relations in Eastern Persia and his liberal policy towards Persian commanders helped Alexander in localizing the uprising of Spitamenes; if the fire had swept over the entire Persia, that might have been the funeral of Alexander.

Campaign Against Porus[16]

Importance

Campaign against Porus is the last major campaign of Alexander. The campaign is remarkable in three aspects. Firstly, for the first time in Alexander's career, the morale of his army was deteriorating. Secondly, he was faced with an efficient use of elephants, so that he could not use his cavalry to break the enemy-lines—a tactics which was mainly responsible for 15 out of his total 22 victories in battles. Lastly, this was the only campaign in which he won the battle, but lost the war.

Comparison of Strategies

Chart 5 compares the more significant strategy factors. Alexander had an advantage in having more balanced army with better equipment and more flexible command. With his superior plan of attack and use of muddy battlefield—unfavourable to the archers of Porus—he more than neutralized the advantage of special arm—elephants—that Porus had. This superiority in the field-strategy won him the battle.

However, he had serious deficiencies in his grand strategy. Up to the conquest of Persia, his army could spmpathise with his goal. But when the campaign in India got into a full swing, 'they did not know what they were doing or where they were going; they wanted to go home'.[17] The army had lost significance of his goals. This had a serious effect on the morale of his army, and contributed to the overall deficiency of his grand strategy. Ultimately, he had to abandon the campaign in spite of victory in battles.

Highlights

The analysis in the preceding sections brings out some of the most significant aspects of Alexander's strategy—which probably form the 'key' to his success. Regarding field-strategy, his army in its quality, equipment, and balance at least equalled—and often surpassed—the army of his adversaries. His army command had an excellent balance between flexibility and co-ordination. It is by no means a chance occurrence that most of Alexander's deputies proved themselves to be able generals and administrators after his death. This contrasts

CHART 5

Alexander *vs.* Porus

Strategy Factors	*Alexander*	*Porus*
A. *Field-strategy—*		
(a) Army—		
(i) Strength	xxx	xxx
(ii) Composition		
Balance	xxx	xx
Special arm	—	xxx
(iii) Equipment	xxx	xx
(iv) Quality—		
Cavalry	xxx	xxx
Infantry	xxx	x
(b) Army Command—		
(i) Flexibility	xxx	x
(ii) Co-ordination	xxx	xxx
(c) Field-craft—		
(i) Use of terrain	xxx	xx
(ii) Plan of attack	xxx	xx
B. Grand Strategy—		
(a) Morale of army	xx	xxx
(b) Leader —		
(i) Prestige and status	xxx	xxx
(ii) Personal safety	x	x
(c) Communications—		
6 (i) Necessary	— xxx	—x
(ii) Control	xx	xxx
(d) Public Relations	xxx	xx
(e) Significance of Ultimate Goal	x	xxx
C. Interaction and Feedback		
Learning ability	xxx	xx
Total Points	39	

favourably with the deputies of Napolean. A substantial part of Alexander's success is due to his unusually able army command.

However, it is in the grand strategy and learning ability that Alexander proves his personal excellence. A special mention is appropriate to his 'public relations' policy. Instead of treating the conquered people—the Persians in particular—as 'barbarians', he treated them as almost equals and tried to achieve an integration of the Greek and the Oriental cultures. This policy won him rich dividends in the form of public co-operation and facilitated the extension of his campaign to that vast an area. Similarly, his personality had a great influence in maintaining the high morale of his army.

Conclusion

This paper has been an experiment in comparative analysis of strategies *vis-a-vis* Alexander's campaign against Porus—with an attempt to quantify some of the most significant factors. Work in this direction can lead to a better evaluation of the strategies used in the various ages and may contribute to the understanding of 'Progress' in this field through the course of history.

Notes and References

I. The word 'Sikandar' (Indian version of 'Alexander') is synonymous with 'Lucky' in many Indian languages.

2. Q. Wright, *Study of War,* Vol. I, pp. 29-31; Vol. II, pp. 707-8.

2a. R. C. Majumdar and others, *An Advanced History of India,* pp. 504-7; 523-6.

3. B.H.L. Hart, *Strategy: The Indirect Approach,* p. 24.

4. J.F.C. Fuller, *A Military History of the Western-World,* Vol. I, p. 81.

5. Comparison in this section is based on Arrian, Anabasis, II, xv-xxiv and W.W. Tarn, *Alexander The Great,* I, pp. 37-40; II, pp. 286-7.

6. Arrian, II, xvii.

7. *Ibid.*, II, xxi and Tarn, I, p. 39.

8. Tarn, I, p. 37.

9. Comparison in this section are based on Arrian, II, vi-xi; III, viii-xvi; Tarn, I, pp. 24-28 and 45-51; II, pp. 135-69, 171-9, and 182-90; and Fuller, I, pp. 87-107.

10. Tarn, I, p. 8.

11. Majumdar, *op. cit.,* pp. 545-7.

12. Fuller, I, p. 98; and Wright, 1, p. 581.

13. Comparison in this section is based on Arrian, IV, iii-vi and xvi-xvii; and Tarn, I, pp. 68-73.

14. Tarn, I, p. 67.

15. *Ibid.,* I, p. 16.

16. Comparison in this section is based on Arrian, V, viii-xix; Tarn, I, pp. 92-6 and II, pp. 190-8; Hart, *op. cit.,* 6. 41; and Majumdar, pp. 66-7.

17. Tarn, I, pp. 98-9.

Select Bibliography

All India Oriental Conference.
Ancient India As Described by Megasthenes and Arrian (McCrindle).
Ancient Indian Political Thought and Institutions (Saletore).
A View of the History, Literature and Religion of the Hindoos (W. Ward).
Buddhism of 2500 Years (P.V. Bapat).
Bulletin of the Dcccan College Research Institute.
Calcutta Review.
Civil & Military Law Journal.
Civil & Military Review.
Classical Law of India (R. Lirjgat).
Early History of India (Vincent Smith).
History of Ancient India (R.S. Tripathi).
India and the Indian Ocean (K.M. Pannikar).
India: Past and Present (Pannikar).
Indian Historical Review.
Indian Historical Studies.
Indian History Congress.
India's Past (Macdonnel).
International Law & Practice in Ancient India (H.S. Bhatia).
Journal of Asiatic Society.
Journal of Bihar & Orissa Research Society.
Journal of (the) Indian History.
Journal of (the) Rajasthan Institute of Historical Research.
Journal of University of Bombay.
Ordnance.
Religious Thought and Life in India (Monier Williams).
The Indian Historical Quarterly.
The Indian Review.
The Punjab: Past and Present.
The Wonder that Was India (A.L. Basham).
Women in the Sacred Laws (Shakuntala Rao Shastri).
Yajnavalkya Smriti.

Index

Acharya Dharmapala, 67
Afghanistan and N.W. Frontier, 61
Aitareya Brahmana, 248
Ajanta Caves:
  Authors, 103
Ajanta Paintings:
  First to Note Foreigners, 98
Ajanta Pass, 92
Alexander, J.E., 92
Ancient Hindu Geography, 150
Ancient Hindus:
  Funeral Ceremonies, 227
Ancient India:
  Greek Influence, 117
  Widow, 246
  Village Headman, 48
  Foreign Influence, 110
  Law of Nations, 31
  Mathematical Achievements, 209
  Disposal of the Dead, 219
  Period of Renaissance, 117
  Wine Drinking, 262
  Fire-Arms, 328
  High Achievements, 328
Ancient Law:
  Modern Light, 178
Ancient Military India, 319
  Security, 322
Angels and Demons:
  Equality of Nature, 291
Angels:
  Function, 290
  Nature, 288
Rebellion, 293
Animal Sacrificed at the Funeral, 229
Anirudha, 72
Apastamba Dharma Sutra, 262
Arab Countries, 156
Archaeologist's Testimony, 145
Arithmetic:
  Mathematical Notations, 211
Art Education, 97
Arthasastra:
  Earliest Codification of Laws, 56
Aryabhata, 210
Aryas, 30
Asatarupa Jataka, 253
Asia:
  Nine Principal Divisions, 153
  Jambu Dvipa, 152
Asuras:
  Final Punishment, 299
Atharvaveda, 165, 248
Avani-Narana, 75
Ayurvedic Literature:
  General Treatment, 172
  Ethics, 172
  Woman, 171

Bactrian Conquest and Influence, 120
Bactrian Greeks, 103
Bactrian:
  Irrigation Schemes and GT Road Built, 119
Banqueting Hall, 265
Battle Dress, 327
Belli, De Jure, 39
Bhan Daji, 95, 103

Bodh-gaya, 67
Brahmacarya, 259
Brhaspatisamhita, 259
Buddha:
  Cremation, 223
Buddhism at Variance with Hinduism, 114
Buddhist India, 60
Buddhist Literature, 223
Burial Ceremony, 234
Burning:
  The Most Accepted Mode, 222

Campaign Against Spitamenes, 344
Campaign Against Porus, 346
Candakinnara Jataka, 253
Ceremonial Vessels Placed on the Dead Body, 232
Chakravartin:
  Concept, 37
Champa, 77
Chaotic State of Society, 248
Chinese Visits to India, 66
Chaotic State of Society, 248
Charya Dharmapala, 72
Chattopadhyay, Aparna, 262
Chwang, Yuan, 67
Council of Deliberations, 320
Corpse Journey:
  Stages, 229
Court Etiquettes, 283
Customary Marriages, 253
Custom of Suttee Criticised, 259

Dalai Lama, 80
Darius Occupied Panjab, 115
Das, Sarat Chandra, 80
Devil in Man's Daily Life, 307
Dharmagupta, 66
Dharmakirti, 72
Dhammapada, 63
Dhar, M.K., 279
Diseases of Woman, 174
Disposal of Dead and Funeral Ceremonies, 219
Disposal of the Dead:
  Various Modes, 220
Double Ceremonial of Burning and Burial, 236
Dramas:
  Indian and Greek, 128
Drinking:
  A Grave Sin, 264
Dust Abacas, 214
Dutt, N.K., 246
Dvaravati, 74

Early Foreign Influence, 115
East and West Interaction, 129
Eastern India:
  Celebrated Ancient Countries, 1
Edged Weapons, 326
Ekholm, Gardon F., 136
Embalming the Dead Body, 221
Eminent Mathematicians, 210
End Justifies the Means, 196
Exchange of Empasses, 41

Fa Hien, 67
Field Strategy, 337
Fight Between Devas and the Asuras, 303
Fire-arms:
  Meaning, 330
Fire Prevention, 323
First Sanction of Suttee, 259
Foreigners in Ajanta Paintings, 92
Foreigners in India, 42
Foreign Invasions, 40
Foreign Trade, 42

Ganguli, D.K., 48
Ghosal, B.M., 178
Glorious End and Liberation, 208
Good and the Evil Angels:
  Right, 294
Government Servants:
  Subsistence, 320
Gramika, 52
Grand Strategy, 338
Greek Artists, 125
Guilds:
  Composition, 157
  in Ancient India, 157

Origin, 158
Functions, 160
Constitution, 161
Gramabhiojaka, 49

Headman:
Functions, 48
Heras, H., 288
Hindu Geography:
Kinds, 151
History of Art, 97

Ibn Batuta, 65
India and the West:
Overland Route, 113
India:
Family of Nations, 32
Indian Scriptures:
Angel and Devil, 288
India's Extensive Sea-Borne Trade, 144
Indo-Greek Culture, 121
Indo-Roman Trade, 144
Indus Valley, 111
Intercourse between:
India and Soloman's Judaea, 112
Interesting Jail Regulations, 57

Jain Period, 222
Jatakas, 49
Jayaswal, K.P., 268
Jetavanarama, 73
Judgement of a Hindu Court in Sanskrit:
Proceedings, 268
Just and Unjust Wars, 38
Justice:
Separate Court, 281

Kaiuvaka Jataka, 49
Kalinga, 14
Kamasutra, 253
Kambuja, 74
Kathaka Grhya Sutra, 265
Kathasaritsagara:
Types of Wine, 266
Kausitaki Grhya Surta, 260
Kautilya:
Jails and Jail Administration, 56
Kautilya Refers to Cremation, 224
Kautilya's Arthasastra, 33
Khan, Gushi, 87
Kharasara Jataka, 49
King and His Army, 319
King and Women, 176
Kingdom of Vaicali, 5
Kings' and Generals' Families Performed Suttee, 258
Kings:
Duties, 319
Kiratas, 26
Knowledge of Asia, 152
Kopano Kanepki, 124
Krishnamurthy, K., 219
Kunala Jataka, 253

Lal, Chaman, 135
Life Paintings, 96

Magadha, 2
Mahabharata, 248
Mahabhiseka, 301
Mahaprajnaparamita, 67
Mahathupa, 73
Mahosada Jataka, 112
Majumdar, B.K., 56
Man of Central Asiatic Race, 101
Manu's Dharmasastra, 33
Maritime Jurisdiction, 42
Marriage Market, 116
Master of Law, 66
Mazumdar, Akshoy Kumar, 150
Migration in Third Century, 136
Ming Dynasty, 68
Misra, Sachala, 272
Mitra, Jyotir, 162
Mitra, Rajendra, 92
Mobile Weapons, 325
Mongolian Tablelands, 29
Mookerjee, Chaman, 135
Moral Judgement:
Characteristics, 184
Postulates, 184

Object, 185
Necessity, 185
Regulative, 186
Highest Good, 188
Implies Freedom, 189
Virtue, 190
Wealth, 190
Pleasure, 191
Personality, 192
Motive, 195
Intention, 200
Agent, 201
Hindu Conception, 184
Moral Standards, 190
Mourners Purify themselves by Bathing, 233
Muir, John, 95

Nalanda, 67
Nalika, 332
Narapati, Bhoja, 137
Narasimhavarman, 67
Natesan, V., 157
National Prosperity, 320
Nawaz, M.K., 31
Negro Looking Servants, 102
Nehru, Jawaharlal, 40
No-War Doctrine, 39

Objection to Evidence, 273
Odra, 20
Original Tradition:
Corruption, 298

Panjab:
Meeting Place of Nations, 119
Parasara Samhita, 252
Pargiter, F.E., 1
Peace and Hostages:
Treatise, 40
Peculiar to Hinduism, 204
Persian Embassy in Indian Court, 101
Physiological Peculiarities, 172
Pile Lighted with Prayer, 233
Pillai, K. Rahavan, 204
Prabandhacintamani, 254
Prag-jyotisa, 21
Prechistoric Trade Ties, 110
Prisoners of War:
Status, 39
Prisoners Set Free on Auspicious Occasions, 58
Proceedings and Judgment of a Hindu Court in Sanskrit, 268
Pleadings, 272
Onus of Proof, 272
Settlement of Issues, 272
Adjourments, 273
Default, 273
Pundra and Paundra, 16

Queen Alamkaraprabha, 264

Raising a Manual over the Grave, 221
Rajatarangini, 254
Ramachandran, T.N., 60
Ranade, H.G., 171
Rangnekar, Sharu S., 336
Rawlinson, 110
Razor Sharp Weapons, 326
Re-marriage:
Kautilya's Rules, 252
Revival of:
Brahmanism, 127
Hindu Art, 127
Reward of the Devas, 300
Rgveda, 164, 288
Rites for the Well-being of the Living, 236
Rites Immediately After Death, 227
Rock Missiles, 326
Royal Asiatic Society, 94
Royal Court in Hindu Period, 279
Royalties:
Drinking very Common, 263

Sailors of Sixty Centuries:
When Indians went to America, 136
Evidence from Sanskrit Literature, 137
Ships, 138

Carried 1000 Passengers, 139
Early History, 139
Literary Evidence, 140
In Ramayana, 140
In Mahabharata, 141
Evidence from Sculpture, 142
Temples give Proof, 142
Sculptures at Boro Budur, 143
What Historians Say, 143
In Old Paintings, 147
Sakals Arrival and Influence, 123
Saka Tribes, 115
Sakti Sangama Tantra, 153
Samadhi, 90
Samrambhayoga in Hindu Thought:
Concept, 204
Essentials, 206
Sangameswaran, C.S., 319
Sanghamitra, 71
Sanskrit Literature, 137
Santikarma, 236
Sarma, R.S., 49
Sataghni, 332
Sati Controversy, 238
Second Group of Five Nations, 6
Self-determination, 189
Ships:
Classes, 138
Siha, Charu Chandra, 184
Smrtis:
No Mention of Fire-arms, 334
Son of Widow Entitled to Inheritance, 249
Spiritual Life:
Passion, 207
Sron tsan-Gampo, 80
Static Weapons, 325
Strategy:
Definition, 337
Strategy of Alexander the Great, 336
Suhma and Tama-lipta, 19

Taittiriya Brahmana, 248
Taittiriya Samhita, 48
Tale Lama, 88
Takua-pa Inscriptions, 75
Tantrik Cult, 82
Tantrik Priest, 82
Temperamental Belli, 38
Thera Buddhadatta, 71
Thera, Dipanka, 72
Two Thousand Years Old Ajanta Paintings, 105

Udyoga Parvan, 184
Unwidowed Wives, 250
Ursekar, H.S., 209
Utkala, 27

Vaidya, G.N., 328
Vajrabodhi, 67
Vajradhara, 84
Vanga, 14
Varahamihira, 210
Vedic Age:
Five-arms Unknown, 333
Vedic India:
Medical Sciences and Industries, 162
Vedic Literature:
Suttee not Mentioned, 256
Vedic Period:
Niyoga and Marriage of Widows, 248
Videha, 2
Vidhava:
Meaning, 246
Village Headman in Ancient India:
Status in Maurya Period, 50
Office Becomes Hereditary, 50
Gupta Period, 52
Powers and Positions, 53
Under Royal Control, 49
Under System of Manu, 51
Vinaya Pitaka, 49
Visnu Smrti, 259
Vyasa Samhita, 252

War and Peace, 36
Weapons and Armour, 324
When India Ruled Waves, 149
Widow Marriage, 252

Widow:
    Hard Life, 247
    Second Husband, 247
    Manu's Laws, 255
Wine and Courtesans, 265
Wine:
    A Forbidden Drink, 262
    An Item of Sumptuous Meals, 263
Women:
    Relationship of a Patient, 173
    as a Wife, 175
    as Mother, 174
    and the Bhisaj, 173
    and Wine, 264
Women's Role as Dhatri, 175

Yajnavalkya, 248
Yakshini, 112
Yi Tsing, 67

Zero, 211
Zodiac Cave, 103